RELIGION AND NATIONAL IDENTITY

RELIGION AND NATIONAL IDENTITY

Wales and Scotland c.1700–2000

edited by

ROBERT POPE

UNIVERSITY OF WALES PRESS
CARDIFF
2001

© The Contributors, 2001

First published 2001
Reprinted 2005

British Library Cataloguing-in-Publication Data.
A catalogue record for this book is available from the British Library.

ISBN 0-7083-1662-X

All rights reserved. No part of this book may be reproduced, stored in a retrieval system, or transmitted, in any form or by any means, electronic, mechanical, photocopying, recording or otherwise, without clearance from the University of Wales Press, 10 Columbus Walk, Brigantine Place, Cardiff, CF10 4UP.
www.wales.ac.uk/press

The publishers wish to acknowledge the financial support of the Higher Education Funding Council for Wales in the publication of this book.

Printed in Great Britain by Cambridge Printing, Cambridge

Contents

Editor's Foreword	vii
Preface	viii
Notes on Contributors	x
Introduction ROBERT POPE	1
1 'The New Birth of a People': Welsh Language and Identity and the Welsh Methodists, c.1740–1820 E. WYN JAMES	14
2 'Thou Bold Champion, Where art Thou?': Howell Harris and the Issue of Welsh Identity GERAINT TUDUR	43
3 'Preaching Second to No Other under the Sun': Edward Matthews, the Nonconformist Pulpit and Welsh Identity during the Mid-Nineteenth Century W. P. GRIFFITH	61
4 In Pursuit of a Welsh Episcopate ROGER L. BROWN	84
5 Welsh Nationalism and Anglo-Catholicism: The Politics and Religion of J. Arthur Price (1861–1942) FRANCES KNIGHT	103
6 Continuity and Conversion: The Concept of a National Church in Twentieth-Century Wales and its Relation to 'the Celtic Church' TRYSTAN OWAIN HUGHES	123
7 'The Essence of Welshness'?: Some Aspects of Christian Faith and National Identity in Wales, c.1900–2000 D. DENSIL MORGAN	139

CONTENTS

8   Civic Religious Identities and Responses to Prominent
    Deaths in Cardiff and Edinburgh, 1847–1910   163
    JOHN WOLFFE

9   The Fluctuating Fortunes of 'Old Mortality':
    Identity, Religion and Scottish Society   186
    DOUGLAS ANSDELL

10 Revival: An Aspect of Scottish Religious Identity   200
    KENNETH B. E. ROXBURGH

11 Unity and Disunity: The Scotch Baptists, 1765–1842   221
    BRIAN TALBOT

12 'Our Mother and our Country': The Integration of
    Religious and National Identity in the Thought of
    Edward Irving (1792–1834)   242
    LIAM UPTON

13 The Formation of a British Identity within Scottish
    Catholicism, 1830–1914   268
    BERNARD ASPINWALL

14 The Language of Heaven?: The Highland Churches,
    Culture Shift and the Erosion of Gaelic Identity in the
    Twentieth Century   307
    DONALD E. MEEK

Select Bibliography   338

Index   341

Editor's Foreword

For several generations, and certainly since the middle of the nineteenth century, Scotland and Wales have maintained a strong link through the interaction of their ministers of religion and academics. An opportunity arose during 1999 for the Centre for the Advanced Study of Religion in Wales to enhance this relationship further by helping to arrange a conference and enable a dialogue to occur between representatives of the two nations. The invitation to participate and to contribute was accepted without hesitation.

The main topic of conversation in both countries at that time was the question of devolution, and it was seen that discussion of the issue, more often than not, led to a need within each of the constituent nations of the United Kingdom to rethink the nature and manifold expressions of national identity. It was therefore decided that this theme should be investigated in its historical context, and the conference held at New College, Edinburgh, enabled the participants to engage not only in individual studies but also in comparative assessments of the subject.

This collection of papers is therefore considered a valuable addition to the *Bangor History of Religion* series as it contributes to our understanding of the past and thereby of the present. In looking over our national boundaries we are enriched by the experiences of others, while at the same time enabled to share our understanding of ourselves and of the world in which we live.

Geraint Tudur
Centre for the Advanced Study of Religion in Wales
University of Wales, Bangor

Preface

The chapters in this book were originally read as papers during a conference on Religion and National Identity in Scotland and Wales, c.1730 to c.1930, held at New College, Edinburgh, in September 1999. At the conference, the running order was chronological with papers on Welsh subjects following those on Scottish themes. For publication, it was thought that grouping the Welsh and Scottish papers together would help the reader to get a slightly broader picture of the two nations and their religious histories. Inevitably there are gaps, but what is presented here may encourage readers to further research into what is a fascinating, if occasionally perplexing, subject.

Each chapter conveys the thoughts of the author, and there may be points over which each one disagrees profoundly. This is unavoidable when dealing with historical interpretation, particularly over something as multifaceted as national identity (or, for that matter, religion). However, each author was given the freedom to express his or her own opinion in order that readers be presented with different views and make their own minds up about the subject as a whole.

Many people have helped to bring the book to publication. Professor Stewart J. Brown of New College, University of Edinburgh, should be thanked for his organization of the conference: he did much to ensure its success while also providing the best hospitality for those who attended. The conference was held under the joint auspices of New College, the Centre for the Advanced Study of Religion in Wales, the Scottish Church History Society and the Welsh Religious History Society. Gratitude should be expressed to the officers of these respective bodies for their support of the project. The contributors responded positively to the idea of publication and I am grateful to them for their work. Dr Matthew Cragoe of the University of Hertfordshire, Professor David Bebbington of the University of Stirling, and Dr Geraint Tudur, Director of the Centre for the Advanced Study of Religion in Wales, have all

PREFACE

helped considerably in the behind-the-scenes work to prepare the book for publication. Preparing an index is a complex and tiresome task and I am grateful to Llinos Williams for her help in completing the job. Finding an appropriate illustration for the jacket was no easy task and so it was decided to commission one which would in some way reflect the subject matter of the book. Margery Stephenson's jacket illustration uses the Welsh dragon and the Scottish lion to reflect the strength of national identity and its potential to become rampant. Through imposing the Cross on to both, she hints that, through the Christian faith, national identity can find its true vocation and be protected from the excesses into which it can too easily fall. I am grateful to her for her work and for realizing in pen and ink a representative vision from which we can all learn. Finally, I am grateful to the staff of the University of Wales Press, particularly its director Susan Jenkins and editorial manager Ceinwen Jones, for their support of the project and their production of a further fine volume in the series.

Notes on Contributors

DOUGLAS ANSDELL gained a Ph.D. from the University of Edinburgh and has taught in a number of universities. He is the author of *The People of the Great Faith: The Highland Church, 1690–1900* (1998). He currently works for the Scottish Executive.

BERNARD ASPINWALL is Senior Research Fellow in Scottish History at the University of Strathclyde. Formerly Senior Lecturer in Modern History at the University of Glasgow, he was educated at the University of Manchester and the University of Indiana. He has taught at the Universities of Notre Dame, Miami, and Eastern Kentucky as well as at universities in Poland and Algeria. He has published extensively in American and Catholic history particularly on the Scottish and Irish emigrant experience.

ROGER L. BROWN is the Vicar of Welshpool and Rector of Castle Caereinion. An Honorary Research Fellow in the Centre for the Advanced Study of Religion in Wales, University of Wales, Bangor, he is the author of *The Welsh Evangelicals* (1986), *David Howell* (1998) and numerous articles on aspects of Welsh religious history.

W. P. GRIFFITH is Senior Lecturer in the Department of History and Welsh History, University of Wales, Bangor. His publications include *Learning, Law and Religion: Higher Education and Welsh Society, c.1540–1640* published in the Studies in Welsh History Series by the University of Wales Press (1996).

TRYSTAN OWAIN HUGHES is the Head of the School of Theology and Religious Studies, Trinity College, Carmarthen. His publications include *Winds of Change: The Roman Catholic Church and Society in Wales, 1916–1962* published by the University of Wales Press (1999).

E. WYN JAMES is Senior Lecturer in the Department of Welsh at Cardiff University. He has published extensively on Welsh

NOTES ON CONTRIBUTORS

literature and culture in the modern period and has been editor of the Bulletin of the Welsh Hymn Society since 1978. He is a leading authority on Welsh hymnology and executive committee member of the Welsh Folk Song Society and a member of the International Ballad Commission. In 1998 the prestigious Gregynog Press published his highly acclaimed edition of the work of the Welsh hymn writer, Ann Griffiths (1776–1805).

FRANCES KNIGHT is Senior Lecturer in the Department of Theology and Religious Studies, University of Wales, Lampeter. A graduate of the University of London and the University of Cambridge, she has published work on the history of the Anglican Church, including *The Nineteenth Century Church and English Society*, published by Cambridge University Press in 1995.

DONALD E. MEEK, a native of the Inner Hebridean island of Tiree, has been Professor of Celtic at the University of Aberdeen since 1993. Educated at the Universities of Glasgow and Cambridge, he has previously taught at Glasgow and Edinburgh. The author of several books including *The Scottish Highlands: The Churches and Gaelic Culture* (1996) and *The Quest for Celtic Christianity* (2000), he writes extensively on the interaction of the Christian faith and Gaelic culture in the Scottish Highlands and Islands.

D. DENSIL MORGAN is Senior Lecturer in the Department of Theology and Religious Studies, University of Wales, Bangor. Educated at the University of Wales and the University of Oxford, his study of Christianity in Wales during the twentieth century, *The Span of the Cross: Religion and Society in Wales, 1914–2000*, was published by the University of Wales Press in 1999.

ROBERT POPE is Lecturer in Contemporary and Applied Theology in the Department of Theology and Religious Studies, University of Wales, Bangor. His published work includes *Building Jerusalem: Nonconformity, Labour and the Social Question in Wales 1906–1939* (1998) and *Seeking God's Kingdom: The Nonconformist Social Gospel in Wales 1906–1939* (1999), both published by the University of Wales Press.

KENNETH B. E. ROXBURGH is the Principal of the Scottish Baptist College. A graduate of the University of Aberdeen and the

University of Edinburgh, he has published on aspects of Scottish religious history. His book, *Thomas Gillespie and the Origins of the Relief Church in Eighteenth Century Scotland* was published in 1999. He is the editor of the *Scottish Bulletin of Evangelical Theology*.

BRIAN TALBOT is the minister of Cumbernauld Baptist Church. He was recently awarded the degree of Ph.D. from the University of Stirling for a thesis on the subject of 'The Origins of the Baptist Union of Scotland, 1800–1870'.

GERAINT TUDUR is Lecturer in Church History and Director of the Centre for the Advanced Study of Religion in Wales in the University of Wales, Bangor. Educated at the University of Wales and the University of Oxford, he has researched the diaries of the eighteenth-century revivalist Howell Harris and the fruit of his research was published in 2000 by the University of Wales Press as *Howell Harris: From Conversion to Separation 1735–1750*.

LIAM UPTON is a graduate of University College, Dublin, and the University of Edinburgh. He is currently engaged in doctoral research at the University of Edinburgh on 'The life and works of Edward Irving.'

JOHN WOLFFE is Senior Lecturer and Head of the Department of Religious Studies at the Open University. His publications include *God and Greater Britain: Religion and National Life in Britain and Ireland 1843–1945* (1994) and *Great Deaths: Mourning, Religion and Nationhood in Victorian and Edwardian Britain* (2000).

Introduction

ROBERT POPE

Nations are the wealth of mankind, they are its generalised personalities; the smallest of them has its own particular colours, and embodies a particular facet of God's design.
(Alexander Solzhenitsyn)

On 11 September 1997, the Scottish people voted to establish their own Parliament. A week later, on 18 September, the Welsh people voted by the narrowest of margins to establish a National Assembly for Wales. The Scots already had in place many of the legal and educational structures and institutions, not to mention a distinct system of local government, which made the establishment of a Parliament relatively straightforward. Such an infrastructure was not present in Wales, which made the establishment of the Welsh Assembly all the more significant, despite the fact that its legislative powers are more restricted than those of the Scots. Both events reflect the sense in which Scotland and Wales are seen to form distinct national, rather than regional, entities which consequently have the right to more localized bureaucracy and to control it democratically. It seems clearer than for centuries that Scotland and Wales are nations, and yet the definition of Scottish or Welsh identity is far from straightforward.

For a number of reasons, the reality is that Scottish and Welsh life is, and to some degree always has been, diverse and pluralistic. It is true in both nations that there is no one ethnic group, no real binding principle and no common outlook which would provide distinct, uniform national identities. Geography,

INTRODUCTION

language, ethnicity and a common history all play a part, but these are often interpreted in different ways and influenced by different factors in different parts of the two countries. Finding the significance of these, and showing to what degree they exist in tension, is not an easy task partly because unhelpful stereotypes are difficult to get out of the mind. The Scots are associated with golf, whisky, haggis, thriftiness, caber-tossing, the kilt and the bagpipes, as well as to heroic struggles in the past captured Hollywood-style in Mel Gibson's portrayal of William Wallace. Even today, Wales is portrayed as the rugby-loving land of song, of male-voice choirs and hymn-singing coal-miners, living in a strangely paradoxical world scarred by the wounds of industrialization but reminded of its agrarian past by ubiquitous sheep, images that were endorsed by such romanticized versions of history as Richard Llewelyn's *How Green Was My Valley?* Important as some of these things have been in forging Scottish and Welsh history and helping to shape characteristics which the Scots or the Welsh respectively have claimed as their own, there are also countless other factors that have played on the formation of the two 'nations' that have made them the diversity they are today. And yet there is even within this diversity a sense of belonging to a distinct nation, a definite group; of being Scottish or of being Welsh rather than being anything else.

Identity, especially as a nation, concerns self-recognition and the recognition of the self by others, both of which are influenced by remembering, and adopting, a common past. The essays in this volume are historical more than sociological or ideological, and they concern the way in which religion has been invoked to encourage the common recollection of past events by particular groups, in order to give those groups a sense of uniqueness, purpose, relationship and belonging. Religion, or more specifically Christianity, provides a common core in each nation's history, but simultaneously demonstrates the diversities prevalent in both societies. The Scots had (and still have) an Established Church, though its presbyterian polity has, on occasion, brought it into conflict with the English and their episcopal version of a religious establishment, and has contributed much to a sense of identity not least through the commitment, and martyrdom, of the Covenanters. Despite the

INTRODUCTION

existence of an Established Church, or perhaps because of it, Scottish church history is redolent with division and secession from the Church of Scotland (outlined briefly by Donald Meek in his chapter), while significant numbers of Catholics and Episcopalians together with the sporadic presence of smaller denominations make up a patchwork of Christian witness and organization.

Wales lost its Established Church in 1920 after a long and bitter campaign for disestablishment. Prior to that, the Anglican Church could hardly have been considered to be a national institution, both because of its claim to be nothing but part of the province of Canterbury and because the vast majority of religious Welsh people attended one or other of the Nonconformist chapels. Religion as a whole in Wales declined during the twentieth century, with Welsh Nonconformists apparently coming off worst. Conversely, the sense of serving a nation has increased within the Church in Wales while the Roman Catholic Church, for various reasons, has an alternative story of expansion and consolidation. It is the way in which all this affects questions of identity and how it helps to identify a nation (or use the nation's boundaries in mission strategy) that concerns us in the following chapters.

Even if Wales emerged from a religious awakening in the fifth century (as Densil Morgan asserts at the beginning of his chapter), Wales's history as a nation since then has been ambiguous to say the least, a fact which caused Gwyn A. Williams to ask provocatively *When Was Wales?*[1] Wales was rarely, if ever, united as a national entity in pre-Tudor times but existed as a collection of small kingdoms and fiefdoms, each having its own chieftain or prince. The attempts to subsume Wales into England, which gained a tremendous boost with the Act of Union in 1536, continued unabated and reached an all-time low point with the infamous entry in the *Encyclopaedia Britannica* that 'for Wales, see England'.[2]

The tension which existed between a gradually emerging Welsh identity and its association with Christian faith is explored by E. Wyn James. He insists that, so long as the Welsh existed, they had been forged in part by Christian belief and practice. The evangelical revival of the eighteenth century is often seen as a watershed when the leading revivalists concentrated on the task of saving souls to the detriment of Welsh language and culture. Wyn James argues that there remained a continuity with traditional claims through the revivalists' emphasis on and support for the Welsh language as the means to evangelize and to instruct the monoglot population in the faith. Myth and reconstruction can here be seen to combine with historical fact to produce a sense of Welshness in which the Welsh are identified as descendants of the ancient Britons and the language is defined as classical, along with Latin, Greek and Hebrew. As a result, Welsh would emerge as the language of religion and a literate *gwerin* (common folk) emerged through the remarkable success of circulating schools inaugurated by Griffith Jones, the energetic vicar of Llanddowror, Carmarthenshire.

Ambiguity remained, of course, but the seeds of a national identity were planted during the eighteenth century, revealed by Geraint Tudur's analysis of one of the revival's primary leaders, Howell Harris. Harris's attitude towards the Established Church, the monarchy and the land of Wales suggests that there was no real, developed sense of a specifically Welsh identity in the eighteenth century, though Harris identified Wales as a unit and saw himself as belonging to it. The situation was complicated by the association of Wales with England, yet Harris held a commitment both to the Welsh language as the medium to reach the unconverted masses and to Wales as an entity to which he had been called by God.

Welsh identity became more marked during the nineteenth century, fuelled partly by the religious developments which had seen the Methodists finally secede from the Anglican Church and secure a specifically Welsh denomination, the Calvinistic Methodists (later the Presbyterian Church of Wales), in 1811. By mid-century, Welsh language and culture were coming under fire from external, establishment forces, the low point being reached in 1847 with *Brad y Llyfrau Gleision* (The Treachery of the Blue Books) in which English government inspectors accused the Welsh of poor morals and standards and found the cause in chapel religion and the Welsh language. W. P. Griffith shows that, building on the inroads made by Griffith Jones, Welsh was

INTRODUCTION

the lingua franca for religious instruction throughout the nineteenth century when Welsh preaching developed into a particular style which, though paralleled to an extent in other countries, was virtually a unique expression and one that came to be important in national identity. Lacking a state structure, it was this sense that its religion was unique which marked the Welsh out as special and different from their neighbours. Nonconformist religion and the Welsh language were sufficiently close during the nineteenth century for establishment figures to attack the Welsh for immoral standards: this in turn added to the sense of identity and geared the Welsh against the establishment and its larger neighbour. Yet through a belief in their divine election the Welsh held that they existed under God's grace and were marked out as special, even if that very reason meant that there was no room for exclusiveness: other nations, too, existed under God's grace.

It was not Nonconformity alone that was concerned with issues of language. The Anglican Church, also, came increasingly to recognize that it required officers who could speak to the people in their own language, particularly if it was going to be a truly national church, disestablished or otherwise. Roger L. Brown guides us through the latter half of the nineteenth century, an interesting period in Welsh church history when arguments were made concerning the responsibility of a national church regarding the language of Wales. The argument was largely won, but only in the context of a wider discussion concerning the role of the bishop. As it was concluded that scholarship and breeding were less important than pastoral suitability, so the issue of language came to the fore. A pastoral bishop needed to communicate with his flock in their own language. So identity was being forged as the church became more Welsh. It was the creation of a 'semi-indigenous church' which perhaps stood the Anglican Church in Wales in better stead than many realized for disestablishment when it came in 1920.

The image of a Welsh-speaking, Nonconformist nationalist is questioned in Frances Knight's chapter on Arthur Price (1861–1942). She gives us an insight into the political and religious motivation and ideas of one who played a significant role behind the scenes of the Anglican Church in Wales prior to and following its disestablishment in 1920, and in the Nationalist Party, founded in 1925. Price argued for nationalism on historical grounds: the Welsh were, after all, an ancient nation. He personifies the questions concerning the relationship between religion and national identity. How is a church to relate to the nation, especially if it is disestablished? The future of Wales was wrapped up in a Welsh church, but Price saw the church as Anglican and ritualistic, not Nonconformist, and this despite the apparent success of Nonconformity which, collectively, enjoyed the allegiance of more Welshmen than did the Church. Furthermore, Price was a non-Welsh speaker, indicating the complexities of an identity and a nationalist movement which has been united around a common concern for the language, yet finds many in sympathy who have no working knowledge of Welsh.

Personal interpretations are vitally important in identifying ourselves, as shown by Trystan Owain Hughes who also demonstrates effectively the way in which construction takes the upper hand in order to achieve a sense of 'one-upmanship'. The Anglican Church had struggled against Nonconformity and against a growing awareness of nationhood to lay claim to continuity with the ancient and original church in Britain and in the Celtic lands. By the 1920s, a further threat to its homogeneity emerged in the shape of a rejuvenated and expanding Roman Catholicism. Trystan Hughes shows that both communions sought a reappropriation of the ancient, Celtic, Christian tradition in order to support claims of legitimacy as national churches. Then, as now, there was much romanticized reconstruction as hagiographic methods were employed in drawing out the significance of the ancient past. History itself played second fiddle to the needs of the present as both churches struggled to assert a Christian identity that could appeal to the Welsh as their own while belonging to communions which ostensibly found their greatest strength well beyond Offa's Dyke.

D. Densil Morgan offers an overview of Welsh religious history during the twentieth century. He places Wales into a historical context in which the association of Christian faith and Welshness was extremely close. His assessment of the situation serves to show the complexities and fluctuating fortunes of denominational history, the Welsh language and culture, and social, economic and political movements, all of which demonstrate the fact that Welshness had, by the end of the twentieth century, been divorced from its religious past. He ends on a positive note, finding little to be optimistic about regarding the future of Christian observance but recognizing that hope is central to its doctrinal content.

Civic ritual needs religious ritual in order to express the strength and solidarity of a community, to achieve a sense of group consciousness, argues John Wolffe in his chapter. Through analysing responses in Cardiff and Edinburgh to the death of prominent national characters, he concludes that, as the nineteenth century passed, so civic dignitaries in the two places adopted more 'English' approaches to the commemoration after death of notable individuals. What is clear is that social changes in the two places resulted in a sharper sense of identity and significance, which in turn led to changes in civic practice. Commemoration and collective memorial are once again emphasized as central to questions of identity.

Collective remembering is what binds together a cohesive and distinct group of people. Identity is forged through historical events, recorded, passed on and partly reconstructed in the form of myths around which people can unite. Douglas Ansdell shows that national identity is forged by a collective memory, and an active propagation (reminding) of a formative, possibly even heroic, event in the past. The Scottish memory, he says, revolves around both the Covenanting period of the seventeenth century, when Presbyterians risked all in defiance of coercive moves towards episcopal rule, and the Disruption of the mid-nineteenth century, when Thomas Chalmers and company broke away from the Established Church. Scottish identity, when linked to the dominant Presbyterian tradition, looks back to the Covenanters and to the Disruption as formative events; they let people know who they are and in what tradition they stand. Yet this is not a homogeneous tradition, for the Lowland Scot is reminded of a different past from that idealized by his Highland cousin and both look to different cultural influences. One was an identity that was willing to hold recent history at arm's length in order to associate itself with a wider British identity, while the

INTRODUCTION

other was Gaelic-speaking and evangelical in religion. However, 'reminding' and 'remembering', argues Douglas Ansdell, are insufficiently strong to overcome social factors and, he claims, the situation is no longer the same for either Lowland or Highland Scot. Where they have come from, and in what tradition they stand, have been overcome by the all-pervading and all-powerful strength and exigencies of the present.

Kenneth B. E. Roxburgh's chapter takes us through eighteenth-century Scotland where the two conflicting forces of evangelical thought conveyed through religious revival and Enlightenment philosophy were both, to some extent, forging a religious and cultural context for the Scottish people. It was the perception of religious decline that led some to a collective, partial remembering and partial reconstruction about a glorious spiritual past associated with the Reformation and Covenanting periods. Revival, when it came, gave added force to this remembering and, alongside evangelical zeal and commitment, offered 'ordinary people' an identity as Scots, Presbyterians and Evangelicals. Christianity's appeal was, in part, to be seen in its association with a golden era in the past which, through renewed commitment to Christ and to the nation, could become true again.

Brian Talbot opens up the whole question of religious identity as something corresponding to national identity, though different from it. In looking at the Scotch Baptist movement, he shows that denominational structures may work in such a way as to provide a distinct identity, jealously guarded by strict entrance procedures both for individual members and for whole congregations. Ecclesiology rather than ethnicity was the differentiating factor within the Baptist communion and Scotch Baptists were to be found in Wales and in England. However, they finally found it difficult to maintain the connection across the national boundaries and went their separate ways.

The correspondence of national and religious identity can be seen in the work of Edward Irving (1792–1834). Liam Upton demonstrates that, for Irving, to be English was coterminous with membership of the Church of England, while to be Scottish meant, of necessity, membership of the Church of Scotland: an ironic position, maybe, for one who was to find himself ejected from the Kirk for heresy. Irving's reappropriation of the past was

INTRODUCTION

more than a simple remembering and reminding but included that most creative of elements, construction. The Scottish nation was, for Irving, synonymous with Lowland Presbyterianism, a claim which tended to exclude the Highland and Catholic Scots. Indeed, the nation had been forged through Presbyterian heroism against Romanism and Episcopalianism. Irving's use of the Covenanting tradition owed as much to myth and reconstruction as it did to historical fact, as did his reclamation of ancient history which saw the Celts as proto-Presbyterians. But he saw in the 'killing times' down to the Glorious Revolution a forging of nationhood in which the civil liberty of the common people, which was central to the Reformation, took hold in the national psyche. Even when church order was subject to the authority of presbytery and synod, Calvinistic Christianity's recognition of God's relationship with the individual with no need of a priestly mediator imbued the human race with incontrovertible rights which could be extended to groups and nations. For Irving, the identity of a Christian individual led directly to forging the identity of a nation.

One of the paradoxes of Welsh and Scottish identity is that Wales and Scotland have existed within the context of Britain, in the shadow of their larger English neighbour. National identity for both nations has occasionally descended into claims of difference from England while at other times English customs and characteristics have been adopted under the guise of Britishness. The concept of a homogeneous 'British' identity is, perhaps, more questionable and more elusive than that of the Welsh and Scottish, and all too often is identified with the characteristics of English nationalism. Bernard Aspinwall suggests that Catholics in Scotland abandoned their Irish or Highlander past and adopted a 'British' identity under the influence of a long succession of convert priests, often from across the border and usually Oxbridge-educated from landed or 'new-wealth' families. For economic as much as cultural and spiritual reasons, Scottish Catholics drew strength from the status quo and were good 'Britishers', content to be united under the Union Jack. Ultramontanism and social concern may have prevailed over nationalism, but Bernard Aspinwall draws out the pressures placed on Scottish Catholics to succeed and, consequently, has to

INTRODUCTION

affirm that part of the Catholic mission was the production of 'quintessential Englishmen' motivated by the ideals of service and duty.

A danger which arises in discussing Scottish identity is to restrict observation to the Lowland districts and to ignore the contribution and distinctive culture of the Highlands and Islands. Even at this basic level it becomes clear that Scottish culture is diverse. Donald E. Meek gives a fascinating account of religion in the Highlands, showing effectively that, while affected by developments in the Lowlands, Highlands and Islands culture developed in a distinctive way, enhanced by, and simultaneously affecting, religious observance. Presbyterianism certainly exiled Roman Catholicism to the periphery even in the Highlands and an evangelicalism was later adopted which became a distinctive feature of Highland Christianity. The church was a civilizing but also controlling factor in society as Lowland and ultimately British (English) rule was exercised. Worship in Gaelic had arguably resulted in the development of distinct preaching, praying and singing styles but its initial association with barbarism and the more recent difficulties experienced in maintaining a Gaelic-speaking ministry (alongside the not insignificant ambivalence shown by some church leaders towards the language) has resulted in a great deal of negativity within all denominations bar the Established Church. The trend in the Highlands, however, is similar to that in other parts of Scotland. A pluralist culture has developed with the consequent displacing of the Gaelic language. Professor Meek's conclusion is that Gaelic is no longer the medium for propagating the gospel in the Highlands, not simply due to a paucity of Gaelic speakers but also because of a lack of will and of a strategy to provide Gaelic ministry and to use modern technology effectively. Consequently, an element of Highland identity, Gaelic-speaking and evangelical Christian, is in mortal danger.

The chapters in this book offer denominational and biographical evidence alongside general and particular approaches to the subject, all of which serve to show that the issue of national identity concerns union in diversity rather than monotonous ubiquity. Like other nationalities, the Welsh and the Scottish are what they are because they maintain a difference within their national and cultural boundaries that reflects a life and dynamism which in itself is a central characteristic of humankind in general. There are, of course, some common elements which can be discerned in these essays, particularly in the way in which an identity is forged. The past is always important, even when it is reappropriated through myth. The relationship with the English has a part to play, whether in order to assert difference or in adopting what might be called 'British values'. Revival has been important in the religious history of the two nations, particularly the evangelical awakening of the eighteenth century which is seen to be an indigenous phenomenon rather than an import from England. Both nations have been dominated by forms of Calvinistic Protestantism which proved to be hostile towards Catholicism, and this developed in the nineteenth century into a pervading evangelicalism in Scottish and Welsh religious life. Both nations suffered pangs of disappointment concerning certain national institutions such as the universities, as seen in the work of Edward Irving and Arthur Price. And there was a more direct connection in the nineteenth century as Welsh Nonconformists, denied the right of access to Oxford and Cambridge, entered the Scottish universities to study in preparation for their vocation as ministers. Scottish influence on Wales is not obvious prima facie, but it is significant for Welsh theological and ministerial education that Lewis Edwards studied in Edinburgh and came under the influence of Thomas Chalmers. Though Chalmers was possibly too intellectual, both he and Edward Irving are identified as Scotsmen admired in Wales for their learning and their preaching style (see W. P. Griffith's chapter).

There are, of course, many differences and the two nations go separate ways in the detail. Perhaps the issue of language demonstrates this more clearly than any other. Language is far more significant an element in Welsh identity, as demonstrated in the chapters in this volume, even if there has been a concerted effort in Scotland to ignore the rights of Gaelic. Welsh was the language of the *gwerin*, the ordinary folk, making it the natural medium for religious instruction. In turn, a sense developed of its existence under the providential hand of God, thus making its survival and its propagation a matter of specifically religious concern. Perhaps Gaelic was never spread sufficiently throughout Scotland for similar developments to have occurred there on a national scale. Nevertheless, in those areas where Gaelic predominated it also was the natural language for religious expression and became associated with specific forms of worship and preaching, identifying it as 'the language of heaven' (see Donald Meek's chapter). Indigenous languages were considered differently in the two nations. Their importance, both in a practical and in a theological sense, can be seen in the way in which Christian denominations in Wales sought to associate themselves with Welsh and the ancient Welsh Church (see Trystan Owain Hughes's chapter). In Scotland, the approach was very different, with Scottish Catholics in the nineteenth century developing a sense of British rather than Scottish (or Irish) identity (see Bernard Aspinwall's chapter) while many of the Presbyterian denominations during the twentieth century saw the propagation of the gospel as more important than securing the future of unique social and cultural factors and making provision for the continuation of a Gaelic ministry (see Donald Meek's chapter). Despite the zeal with which Welsh Nonconformists established 'English causes' during the nineteenth century, the medium and the message were more closely associated with each other within mainstream Welsh Protestantism than seems to have been the case within Scottish Presbyterianism.

The adoption and assertion of a *national* identity serves to unite an otherwise disparate group of people in mutual relationship. It can, of course, have dangerous effects as people may identify 'the other' as an enemy to be destroyed. Religion can exacerbate this danger, and it can mitigate it. The recognition of a national identity can result in a fruitful exchange and closer appreciation of other nations, something which can only bode well for the future. It is this kind of national identity, catholic, humane and unmistakably Christian, that is historically present in the two nations and which needs to be asserted above partisan approaches to race and ethnicity. It is captured as well as anywhere in the words of Robert Ambrose Jones, a nineteenth-century Calvinistic Methodist minister known by his bardic name of Emrys ap Iwan and prominent among forgers of nationalist sentiment in Wales, who told the youth of his homeland:

> Remember first of all that you are *men*, of the same blood as the English, the Boers, the Kaffirs and the Chinese; therefore, be prepared to grant them the privileges that you wish for yourselves. Remember in the second place, that you are a nation by God's ordinance; therefore do what you can to keep the nation inviolate, by nurturing its language and every other valuable thing that belongs to it. If you are unfaithful to your country and language, how can you expect to be faithful to God and to humanity?[3]

Notions of 'identity' and 'nation' have been raised at various times in history for a variety of reasons, and the search for their misuse does not take long to discover their dreadful potential. This book is offered in the belief that this is a point in history where these notions need to be scrutinized once again. For the Scots and the Welsh in particular, national identity is something that has to be worked out again over the next few years as the two nations take more responsibility for their government. The hope is that, in understanding the respective histories, identities can be forged that are not blinkered but are respectful of the identities and nations in which others are located. Anything less will be a failure of our collective memories, our religion and our basic humanity.

Notes

[1] See Gwyn A. Williams, *When Was Wales?* (London, 1985).
[2] Quoted in Kenneth O. Morgan, *Rebirth of a Nation: Wales 1880–1980* (Oxford and Cardiff, 1981), p. 3.
[3] R. Ambrose Jones, *Homiliau* (Denbigh, 1907), pp. 52–3, quoted in R. Tudur Jones, *The Desire of Nations* (Llandybïe, 1974), pp. 181–2.

~ 1 ~
'The New Birth of a People':
Welsh Language and Identity and the Welsh Methodists, c.1740–1820

E. WYN JAMES

From the earliest dawning of the Welsh nation, Christianity has played an integral part in its life and culture. Saunders Lewis, the founding father and prophetic voice of twentieth-century Welsh nationalism – himself a committed Christian – could write thus in June 1926 in Y *Ddraig Goch* (The Red Dragon), the monthly organ of the newly formed Welsh Nationalist Party:

> We are Christians in a Christian country. When Wales was formed, when the name and language were fashioned, we were already Christians. The ideals of Christianity determined our mind. It taught us that a special dignity has been bestowed on man, on every man, and a Christian cannot think politically at all without believing that it is right for men to live in bliss and with dignity and to achieve the purpose for which they were created.[1]

The centuries which followed the demise of the Roman Empire witnessed the gradual emergence of Wales as a distinct and conscious entity, as the relentless westward advance of Anglo-Saxon conquerors eventually isolated the Welsh territorially from their compatriots – or 'Cymry' – in the north and south-west of the island of Britain, creating a 'Romano-British' (or 'Welsh') enclave on the western peninsula we now call 'Cymru' or 'Wales'.[2] In European history, the centuries that followed the fall of Rome are often termed (rightly or wrongly) the 'Dark Ages'. From a Welsh perspective, however, these not dark ages but rather the 'Age of the Saints' – a period of marked cultural and spiritual vitality, the age of Dewi Sant and Taliesin Ben Beirdd.[3]

Indeed Professor John Davies, in his monumental *A History of Wales*, goes so far as to describe south-east Wales in that nascent period of Welsh history as 'the axis of the Christianity of the Celtic-speaking peoples' and 'the starting point of a [Christian] movement which was to revitalize Europe'.[4]

From the very beginning, then, Christianity surfaces as a key element in Welsh national identity, in contrast to the paganism of the Germanic invaders, with Wales in this early period forming not only a 'Romano-British' but also a 'Christian' enclave on the western peninsula of Britain. A tangible expression of this symbiotic relationship between Christianity and Welsh identity is embodied on a memorial stone dating from around AD 550, from Cynwyl Gaeo in present-day Carmarthenshire in south Wales. The stone commemorates one Peulin, or Paulinus, who is described in the inscription as 'preserver of the Faith, constant lover of his country . . . [and] the devoted champion of righteousness'.[5] Interestingly in the present context, this stone was erected only a few miles from the home, in the eighteenth century, of the great Methodist hymn writer, William Williams of Pantycelyn.[6]

An anecdote from that same county of Carmarthenshire illustrates how this interweaving of Christianity and national identity continued in Wales throughout the Middle Ages and into the early modern period. Gerald de Barri (*c*.1146–1223), called 'Giraldus Cambrensis' (or Gerald of Wales), was part Norman and part Welsh. In his *Descriptio Kambriae* (Description of Wales), written *c*.1193, he tries to keep an even-handed approach by concluding with a section giving the Normans advice on 'how the Welsh can be conquered [and] how Wales should be governed once it has been conquered', followed immediately by a final chapter on 'how the Welsh can best fight back and keep up their resistance'![7] The concluding sentences of this final chapter relate an anecdote that has come to be regarded as 'one of the classic statements of Welsh nationhood'.[8] It tells of a conversation between Henry II of England and an old man of Pencader in Carmarthenshire during a military expedition in those parts by Henry in 1163. This old man who, according to Gerald, 'had joined the King's forces against his own people, because of their evil way of life', was asked by King Henry what he thought would be the outcome of the war with the Welsh. The old man's reply was as follows:

> My lord King, this nation may now be harassed, weakened and decimated by your soldiery, as it has so often been by others in former times; but it will never be totally destroyed by the wrath of man, unless at the same time it is punished by the wrath of God. Whatever else may come to pass, I do not think that on the Day of Direst Judgement any race other than the Welsh, or any other language, will give answer to the Supreme Judge of all for this small corner of the earth.[9]

Significantly, the Welsh Protestant humanist, Dr John Davies (c.1567–1644) of Mallwyd, saw fit not only to quote the answer of 'that excellent old British man' (as he calls the 'Old Man of Pencader') in a prefatory letter to his great grammar of the Welsh language, *Antiquae Linguae Britannicae . . . Rudimenta*, published in 1621, but also to follow it immediately with a stanza from a popular prophetic medieval Welsh poem, spuriously attributed to the sixth-century poet, Taliesin:

> Eu Nêr a folant,
> Eu hiaith a gadwant,
> Eu tir a gollant
>   ond gwyllt Walia.

> Their God they will praise,
> Their language they will keep,
> Their land they will lose
>   except wild Wales.[10]

That anecdote and stanza have been recited frequently down through the centuries – George Borrow, for example, took the closing words of the stanza as the title of his well-known travelogue, *Wild Wales* (1862). Their regular repetition is indicative of a continuing sense of Welsh national consciousness, despite ever-increasing Anglicization. They also emphasize the interweaving of Christianity and Welsh culture and identity, an interweaving that continued from the Catholic Middle Ages into modern

Protestant Wales. They underline the paramount role of the Welsh language over the centuries in forming and preserving Welsh national identity. Furthermore, they reflect the main thrust of traditional Welsh historiography, namely an awareness of lost glories, a gritting of teeth in the face of present difficulties and a quiet confidence in the future – to quote the influential contemporary political activist and ballad singer, Dafydd Iwan, in the chorus of perhaps his most popular song: 'Er gwaetha pawb a phopeth/Ry'n ni yma o hyd' (Despite everyone and everything/We're still here).[11]

Where do the Welsh Methodists of the eighteenth century feature in this continuing awareness of Welsh national identity? Indeed, do they feature at all? Christianity over the centuries has, on the whole, bolstered and strengthened Welsh national identity. Is this the case with the powerful religious revival of the eighteenth century, or is the converse true? In other words, would it be appropriate to inscribe on the tombstone of William Williams of Pantycelyn those words found on the memorial stone of the sixth-century Paulinus in nearby Cynwyl Gaeo: 'preserver of the Faith, constant lover of his country'?

Traditionally, Welsh Methodist historiography has portrayed the Methodist Revival of the eighteenth century as a great turning-point in modern Welsh history, as a period of 'light' and 'heat' as compared to the spiritual darkness and frigidity which had characterized Wales prior to the beginnings of the revival in the 1730s. In this, Methodist denominational historians have followed in the footsteps of the early Welsh Methodist leaders themselves – one needs only to quote a frequently-repeated verse from Williams Pantycelyn's elegy to that fiery leader of the early Welsh Methodists, Howell Harris (1714–73) of Trevecka, which refers to Harris's role in the earliest beginnings of the revival:

> Pan 'r oedd Cymru gynt yn gorwedd
> Mewn rhyw dywyll farwol hun,
> Heb na phresbyter na 'ffeiriad,
> Nac un esgob yn ddi-hun;
> Yn y cyfnod tywyll, pygddu
> Fe ddaeth dyn fel mewn twym ias,
> Yn llawn gwreichion golau tanllyd
> O Drefeca-fach i ma's.

> When Wales lay
> in a dark deathly sleep,
> with neither presbyter nor priest
> nor bishop awake;
> in that dark, pitch-black time,
> a man [Howell Harris] as if in fever,
> full of bright and fiery sparks,
> came out from Trevecka.[12]

There is an element of poetic licence in that statement, of course, and Williams would have been the first to acknowledge that there were among the evangelical Anglicans and Nonconformists of pre-Methodist Wales those who had worked hard in preparing the ground for such a revival; but it does also reflect both Williams's belief, and that of his fellow Methodists, that revival was 'a sovereign, spontaneous, and saving activity of the Holy Spirit'[13] and the main means of the promotion of 'true religion'.[14]

In recent years, 'secular' historians – and Professor Geraint H. Jenkins most notable among them – have followed in the footsteps of the older Nonconformist historians in criticizing this Methodist historiography and emphasizing that 'the Methodist revival was not a creation *ex nihilo*, but that it grew from roots laid in [the previous] period'.[15] While I accept this view wholeheartedly, the danger by now, I feel, is that the pendulum has swung too far in the direction of emphasizing a continuum at the expense of recognizing that there was a new, powerful and transforming spirit abroad in Wales from the advent of the Methodist Revival in the mid-1730s – whether that 'spirit' be designated a capital 'S' or otherwise!

As regards the early Methodists' attitude to Welsh language, culture and history, the tendency of historians and commentators, both 'Methodist' and otherwise, has been to emphasize a break with the past, new beginnings and a relative disregard for and apathy towards traditional Welsh culture. Some, such as Gareth Miles, in his review of Professor Bobi Jones's *Ysbryd y Cwlwm* (1998), have gone as far as describing the eighteenth-century Welsh Methodist revivalists and their successors as 'blatant Britishers all. It was in English that they kept their diaries and corresponded with each other, only preaching and composing hymns in Welsh because the common people were monoglot.'[16] Significantly, the book being reviewed by Gareth Miles, which is a detailed survey of the portrayal of nation and nationhood in Welsh literature from the earliest times to the present day, does not actually discuss the eighteenth-century Methodist revivalists in any detail, not even such prominent authors as Williams Pantycelyn and Thomas Charles of Bala. Bobi Jones's silence in these matters would seem, on the surface at least, to concur with the views of scholars such as the late Professor A. O. H. Jarman, who stated that the Methodist movement was not 'interested in Welsh nationality or in the Welsh language as such, [although its] ultimate influence on the fate of both was profound',[17] or Dr Eryn M. White, who has argued that, while 'the [Methodist] Revival – unwittingly – had a positive influence on the Welsh language', yet

> neither the leaders nor the members were aware that Methodism was an intrinsically Welsh or Welsh-speaking movement. Unlike writers like Griffith Jones and Theophilus Evans, Methodists did not appeal to the past or refer to the traditional links between the Christian faith and the Welsh language. They preferred to celebrate their connections with other evangelical movements across the world.[18]

The tendency, then, has been to present the Welsh Methodist leaders of the eighteenth century as being, if not actively antagonistic to things Welsh, at the very least rather unconcerned about and ignorant of such matters.

While not wishing to portray the likes of Howell Harris, Williams Pantycelyn or Thomas Charles as rabid twentieth-century Welsh nationalists, and while accepting that they were not on the whole as well-grounded in Welsh literature, history and culture as others of their period, it is my contention that these early generations of Welsh Methodist leaders were actually far more positive towards the Welsh language and Welsh culture, history and identity than has generally been portrayed; and that (as in the case of the Methodist Revival itself) one needs to redress the balance – in this case, by emphasizing a continuity with the past as well as new beginnings.[19]

In true Methodist fashion, I should like to discuss these matters under three headings; and the first point I should like to emphasize is that the eighteenth-century Welsh Methodist leaders were *the heirs of traditional Welsh historiography,* especially as expounded by the Welsh Protestant humanists of the sixteenth century and their successors.

It is important to realize that the efforts and activities of the small band of Welsh Protestant humanist leaders were driven not only by their paramount concern for the salvation of souls and the furtherance of the Protestant faith, but also by their Welsh patriotism. William Salesbury (c.1520–84?) – perhaps the greatest of all the Welsh humanists and the main instigator and executor of the Welsh translation of the New Testament and Book of Common Prayer in 1567 – could say, for example, in an appeal in 1547 for the Welsh to secure both the Bible and Renaissance learning in their own tongue:

> Unless you wish to become worse than animals . . . seek learning in your language. Unless you wish to be more unnatural than any nation under the sun, honour your language and those who honour it. Unless you wish to abandon Christ's faith altogether . . . get the holy scripture in your language, as it was in the time of your happy ancestors, the ancient Britons.[20]

This was a decade *after* the Act of Union of 1536 had outlawed Welsh as the language of governance in Wales.[21] Furthermore, the success of William Salesbury and his fellow Welsh Protestant leaders in convincing the Elizabethan government that the Bible and the Book of Common Prayer should be published in Welsh for use in the churches, established Welsh as an official language of public worship, if not of government. Indeed, the significance of the translation of the Bible into Welsh, not only for the promotion of the Protestant Reformation and the Renaissance in Wales, but also for the preservation of the Welsh language and Welsh identity in modern Wales, can hardly be overemphasized.[22]

Keen patriots as they were, the Welsh humanists were prepared, in the main, to accept traditional Welsh historiography and to defend it against the attacks of other Renaissance scholars. Indeed, this was true of Welsh historians in general down to around the middle of the nineteenth century. There were adaptations, of course, with some elements gradually being dropped and others added – such as the new emphasis on Celtic origins which came into Welsh historical writings in the eighteenth century as a result of the (very different) work of Edward Lhuyd and Abbé Pezron[23] – but Welsh Protestant historiographers down to the nineteenth century are, to a large degree, heirs of the myths and traditions which abounded in medieval and early modern Wales, and heirs in particular of Geoffrey of Monmouth's twelfth-century *Historia Regum Britanniae* (History of the Kings of Britain), 'the most famous work of nationalistic historiography in the Middle Ages'.[24]

Ancient and exalted origins were the keystone of traditional Welsh historiography (which drew upon 'monkish fables' and Renaissance forgeries as well as Geoffrey of Monmouth). The descendants of Samothes, a grandson of Noah, who occupied the Celtic parts of Europe, were said to have established the learned orders of Druids and Bards; Brutus of Troy was said to have founded the line of kings that ruled the Island of Britain until the Romans came and again after they left; and Joseph of Arimathea was said to have brought the gospel of Christ to Britain within thirty years of the Crucifixion.[25] This latter myth was exploited by the Welsh Protestants of the sixteenth century to refute the accusation that Protestantism was a new and foreign faith foisted on the Welsh by the English; it was, rather, a re-establishing of the original pure Protestant faith of the ancient Welsh Church which had been corrupted through contact with the English Roman Catholic Church of the Middle Ages.[26] A further strand was the belief that the Welsh were descended from another of the grandsons of Noah – Gomer, the son of Japheth – and that Welsh was one of the oldest languages in the world, one of the languages that emerged from the confusion of tongues at Babel, and closely related to Hebrew.[27]

In origin, then, the Welsh language and culture were venerable, on a par with the great classical languages of Hebrew, Greek and Latin. Welsh had also been a great repository of high learning, but had fallen on hard times, with much of this wealth of learning having been lost to posterity through wars, neglect and the malice of enemies; and the Welsh humanists saw it as their responsibility to make Welsh once more a language of high learning, to attempt to make it once again a classical language in the fullest sense.[28]

The other key element in Welsh traditional historiography is a deep awareness that the Welsh at one time had ruled over the whole of the Island of Britain: they were the 'ancient Britons' and the Welsh language the 'ancient British tongue'. That is why the learned Welsh society founded in London in the mid-eighteenth century is called the Honourable Society of Cymmrodorion ('Cymmrodorion' meaning 'the first inhabitants'). The Welsh, then, in their own eyes at least, were the 'aborigines' of the Island of Britain. They had lost the high crown of the Island – 'the crown of London' – either through their own sins or through the duplicity of their enemies. However, according to prophecy, they would eventually regain that crown; and the later Middle Ages abound with Welsh prophetic poetry, proclaiming that a messianic figure, 'y Mab Darogan' (the Son of Prophecy), would come and retake the crown of London for the ancient British. This was generally regarded by the Welsh to have been accomplished when the Tudor monarch, Henry VII, took the throne of England in 1485, and finally completed when James VI of Scotland ascended the throne of England in 1603 as James I, thus uniting the whole of the Island of Britain under one monarch.[29] To the Welsh, James was a descendant of the 'Brittish line' and '*Brutus* right heire', as Robert Holland described him in 1604.[30] All this explains, in part, why the Welsh have remained so loyal to the throne of England since Tudor times. This Welsh fixation with the 'Island of Britain' is also a timely warning when one comes across the word 'British' in Welsh writings, for – until Victorian times, at least – that word was not normally used to emphasize the unity of the peoples of Britain, but rather as a synonym for 'Welsh' – which is why we can find Welsh historians of the nineteenth century, for example, who (not unlike many a Protestant in twentieth-century Ulster) wholeheartedly supported the crown and union, and rejoiced in being 'British', while being at the same time 'bashers of the English'.[31]

While the eighteenth-century Welsh Methodists did not dwell on these matters, and were on the whole more concerned with making history rather than writing about it, there is every indication that they too embraced traditional Welsh historiography. Howell Harris (1714–73), for example, refers in his diaries to the Welsh as 'ye old Britons',[32] as does Robert Jones (1745–1829), Rhos-lan, in his history of the Methodist Revival in Wales, *Drych yr Amseroedd* (A Mirror of the Times; 1820).[33] Again, Thomas Charles (1755–1814) of Bala, in his extremely influential scriptural dictionary, *Geiriadur Ysgrythurol*, which began appearing in parts in 1802, shows familiarity with the work of Abbé Pezron, and in the entry on 'Iaith' (Language), argues that Welsh is closely related to Hebrew, that it is the oldest and purest language in the West, and only one step removed from the original language of the world.[34] While this traditional Welsh historiography would have come down to the Methodists in part through oral tradition,[35] through the extremely popular religious verse of the Vicar Prichard of Llandovery,[36] through the writings of the Protestant humanists[37] and through the work of the Puritans Morgan Llwyd and Charles Edwards, whose *Y Ffydd Ddi-ffuant* (The Unfeigned Faith; 1677) includes a whole chapter comparing Welsh and Hebrew,[38] the main source is likely to have been Theophilus Evans's *Drych y Prif Oesoedd* (A Mirror of the Earliest Ages; 1716, 1740), 'the most widely read history book in Welsh in the eighteenth and nineteenth centuries', with at least twenty editions having appeared by 1900.[39]

Theophilus Evans was an Anglican clergyman from south-west Wales who was, among other things, chaplain to a close friend of Howell Harris, the Methodist squire Marmaduke Gwynne (1694?–1769). A further Methodist connection is that William Williams of Pantycelyn became Evans's curate shortly after the publication of the second, enlarged edition of *Drych y Prif Oesoedd* in early 1740;[40] and it is significant that Marmaduke Gwynne, Williams Pantycelyn and the great Methodist preacher, Daniel Rowland of Llangeitho,[41] appear in the list of subscribers to that edition. Theophilus Evans was far from being sympathetic to the Methodist cause. Pantycelyn did not last long as his curate, and perhaps it is not surprising, given the clashes between them, that 'Chaplain' Evans was not present at the wedding of Marmaduke Gwynne's daughter to Charles Wesley in 1749. In 1752, Theophilus Evans wrote a book in English, *A History of Modern Enthusiasm*, attacking all forms of Nonconformity – Puritan, Congregational, English Methodist, Quaker – but tantalizingly he made no mention of the Welsh Methodists, although he was surrounded by them![42] Yet despite their differences, there is no reason to believe that the Methodists did not read and digest his volume on Welsh history.

The second point to emphasize with regard to the Welsh Methodists' attitude to Welsh language and culture is that they were *the heirs of Griffith Jones of Llanddowror*. Although he also came from south-west Wales, Griffith Jones (1684–1761) was a very different Anglican clergyman from Theophilus Evans (1693–1767). A powerful evangelical preacher, he devoted much of his time and energies from around 1731 onward to establishing Welsh-medium circulating charity schools aimed at teaching people of all ages to read the Bible and to learn the Church Catechism. This was the first major effort through the medium of Welsh to educate the common people of Wales, and it proved extremely successful. It is estimated that almost half the population of Wales during those years learned to read through his schools and, as a result, Wales in the middle years of the eighteenth century became one of the first countries in the modern world to become literate on any large scale, with observers coming from as far afield as Russia to study Griffith Jones's achievements.[43]

If anything prepared the soil for the Methodist Revival, it was Griffith Jones and his circulating schools.[44] Although he had an ambivalent, and sometimes stormy, relationship with the Methodists, he was at the same time a father figure to the movement. He had direct personal links with the main leaders of the first generation of Methodists; and from among the second generation, Thomas Charles of Bala, who was born in a parish adjacent to Llanddowror during Griffith Jones's time as rector there, regarded his own educational efforts, which ultimately developed into a powerful Sunday-school movement, as a continuation of Griffith Jones's pioneer work.

Griffith Jones depended heavily for support for his charity schools on benefactors from outside Wales, and published a series of annual reports in English, entitled *Welch Piety*, for distribution among his supporters. In them we find him having to justify using 'the British tongue' (that is, Welsh) rather than English as the medium of instruction in his schools. Significantly in the present context, his arguments are not confined to the purely practical and are strongly under the influence of traditional Welsh historiography. The main thrust of his arguments may be summarized as follows:[45]

(a) Monoglot Welsh speakers (i.e. the vast majority in Wales in his day) could be taught to read much quicker by being taught to read in their mother tongue. The main priority should therefore be for people to obtain the means of spiritual instruction as quickly as possible. Eternal salvation was the paramount concern.

(b) Having first learnt to read Welsh, it was easier to proceed to learn to read English.

(c) There was no truth in the suggestion that the Welsh were any less loyal to the crown because they did not speak English. Indeed, the contrary had been true ever since the days of Henry VII, 'who descended from the ancient Britons'.

(d) Some had argued that it would be feasible to use English-language charity schools to replace Welsh by English, in the same way as such means were being used to undermine Irish, Gaelic and Manx. Griffith Jones argues that the situations of those languages were totally different from that of Welsh. Unlike Welsh speakers, the speakers of those languages were 'almost destitute of all the necessary means of knowledge, and worship of God in their own language', while the Irish tongue had 'been the foster-mother of the Romish religion'. In contrast, Welsh was 'perhaps the chastest [language] in all Europe', whose literature was free from 'Atheism, Deism, Infidelity, Arianism, Popery, lewd plays, immodest romances, and love intrigues'.

(e) The Welsh language acted as a bulwark against materialism and 'the growing corruption of the times in the English tongue'. If 'the common and labouring people' of Wales spoke English, says Griffith Jones, there would be a 'great and speedy impoverishing of the whole principality', since 'they would soon desert their callings in low life here, and seek abroad for better preferments in English countries'.

(f) It was impractical to consider extirpating the Welsh language. It had survived for thousands of years, 'through so many revolutions and conquests', and was likely, says Griffith Jones, to remain until the day of judgement, as prophesied by the 'Old Man of Pencader'.

(g) The Welsh language was worth preserving in its own right. It was one of the earliest of all languages – it was one of the languages 'which sprung out of the Hebrew at the tower of Babel; [and] consequently may be said to have God himself for the immediate Author of it'; it was the language of Gomer and the ancient Celts, as Edward Lhuyd and Abbé Pezron had shown – and that, together with its excellence and purity, made Welsh deserving of preservation: 'Although now greatly reduced in estate', said Griffith Jones,

> . . . she has not lost her charms, nor chasteness, remains unalterably the same, is now perhaps the same she was four thousand years ago; still retains the beauties of her youth, grown old in years, but not decayed . . . Let it suffice, that so great a part of her dominions have been usurped from her; but let no violence be offered to her life. Let her stay the appointed time, to expire a peaceful and natural death, which we trust will not be till the consummation of all things, when all the languages of the world will be reduced into one again.

(h) God had acted for good in the confusion of tongues at Babel. Wickedness would have grown apace if people had continued to be of one language. 'Thus, Sir,' he says,

> appears the loving-kindness of God, in his confounding the languages, and dispersing the people, by giving them different tongues . . . May we not therefore justly fear, when we attempt to abolish a language . . . that we fight against the decrees of Heaven, and seek to undermine the disposals of divine providence?

Given their close connections with Griffith Jones and his circulating schools, it is inconceivable that the Welsh Methodist leadership would not have been familiar with the above arguments; and it is indicative that, when they themselves set up schools, there was no question but that they used the vernacular. Thomas Charles, for example, argued strongly that charity schools in Ireland and Scotland should use the vernacular rather than English;

and significantly, when advising the Edinburgh Baptist minister, Christopher Anderson, in 1811 regarding the formation of a society to encourage establishing circulating schools in the Highlands and Islands to teach the people to read in their native Gaelic, he not only warmly applauded the venture, but also sent him on loan his own bound set of Griffith Jones's *Welch Piety*.[46]

My final point is in part *an argument from silence*. The Welsh Methodist leaders of the eighteenth century certainly did not expound at length on matters regarding the Welsh language and Welsh identity. At one level they were too preoccupied with other things. However, it must also be remembered that they had no need to elaborate on traditional Welsh historiography since there were ample materials available in print. Similarly, they did not need to justify the use of Welsh as a medium of instruction since Griffith Jones had fought that battle for them. Nor was the language under any great threat during their lifetimes, with most community life in Wales in the period being through the medium of Welsh. However, when the need arose, they could be vociferous regarding the use of Welsh. Howell Harris was more than ready to scold his listeners for turning to English. For example:[47]

Carmarthen, 10 November 1769
Declared myself ye servant of ye Welsh, & was cutting to such as are ashamed of their Language & Country.

Dolyswydd, near Pen-y-bont, Radnor, 21 June 1770
Discoursed ag[ains]t ye. Pride of England com[in]g like a flood, mak[in]g them despise their old Language.

Trevecka, 31 August 1771
Discoursed, how Pride, Luxury &c is coming in among us to Wales like a flood – even depising att last our own Language & learn English to our children before that ancient Language which God has given us, & in this shew[in]g a folly & madness that no other Nation in ye. world but ourselves do shew.

There is a significant difference here between the Welsh Methodists and the English Methodist leader, John Wesley. When faced with his inability to understand Welsh, he could speak of the curse of Babel. 'O what a heavy curse was the Confusion of Tongues!' Wesley exclaimed in Llangefni, Anglesey, in 1748.[48] In contrast, it is difficult to think of one example of a Welsh Methodist leader of the eighteenth century using the word 'curse' in connection with Babel. Most references point to the contrary position. Listen to Thomas Charles extolling the praises of the Welsh language:

> The Welsh language is of exceptional worth; pure; remarkably complete as regards the variety of words and phrases; melodious and adorned; it is exceptionally suited to discuss spiritual matters . . . It is simple, but not common; bold, but not barefaced; ornate, but not affected . . . tender, without being effeminate; strong, but not coarse.[49]

These are hardly the words of someone who only used the language grudgingly, because most of the people were monoglot Welsh. And although noting their opposition to their members partaking in the cultural competitive festivals called *eisteddfodau*, it is significant that a Welsh Methodist Association meeting in 1840 went out of its way to emphasize that this was because of the corruption usually associated with such meetings, and that they were in no way opposed to the Welsh language, learning or poetry.[50]

It is also worth emphasizing that, whatever their contacts with the wider Methodist and evangelical world – and they were numerous and wide-ranging – Welsh Methodist leaders were very consciously Welsh: 'When *Wales* lay in a dark, deathly sleep . . .', said Williams Pantycelyn; Robert Jones, Rhos-lan, wrote a history of *Welsh* Methodism; Daniel Rowland was prepared to defend the jumping of the Welsh Methodist worshippers against the criticism of their English brethren;[51] and in what was to prove a crucial factor in the preservation of the language and national identity, the Welsh Methodists of the eighteenth and early nineteenth centuries created and sustained, through their itinerant preaching and association meetings, a denominational structure that was consciously Welsh and a body of believers that were networking regularly through the medium of Welsh at a national as well as a local level.

While the main aim of the Welsh Methodists was, of course, the salvation of souls and the edification of believers, all things considered, it is difficult to argue with the authors of *The Welsh People* (1900) when they describe the Methodist Revival thus:

> It was no doubt a religious revival, but . . . it was a good deal more than that. It was, in fact, the new birth of a people . . . It was the chief agent in the preservation of the Welsh language. It is probable that but for the immense impetus given to the study and use of the Welsh language by reading the Welsh Bible and by listening to pulpit oratory [the language] would have more and more tended to die out.[52]

These words are echoed by R. T. Jenkins as he eulogized the Methodist Revival in his classic history of eighteenth-century Wales: 'It took hold of a silent nation and gave her a voice, putting on her lips the refined language of the noble Tudor Bible that Griffith Jones and his followers had taught the people to read.'[53] Fuelled by revival success, the Welsh Methodist leadership in the second half of the eighteenth century, and Williams Pantycelyn in particular, were full of hope that the millennial dawn was about to break.[54] And I have no doubt that Williams, like the 'Old Man of Pencader', fully expected that the Welsh language would hold sway in Wales over that millennial period and give answer on the day of final judgement for that small corner of the earth.

However, what was finally ushered in was not a millennial dawn, but rather the Victorian era – a very different era from that of the Methodist Revival of the eighteenth and early nineteenth centuries, not least as regards Methodist attitudes to the language. It was an age of rapid Anglicization; a more materialistic, 'Thatcherite' age; an age in which theories of evolution and the survival of the fittest were to the fore. This was the era when the Welsh in general embraced the belief – as articulated by the authors of the notorious report on Welsh education of 1847 – that the Welsh language kept the populace 'under the hatches' and that the only way to advance in the world was to learn English.[55] This attitude was embraced widely by Christian leaders in Wales, including the Methodists, as the century progressed. Would that Howell Harris had been there to scold them for forsaking their ancient language in the cause of pride and materialism!

Yet even in such an atmosphere, very few Methodist leaders were willing to make such extreme statements as, 'I consider the Welsh language a serious evil' or 'I shall be delighted to see the Welsh people Anglicised'.[56] The more common response was that English was the language of business and the market-place; and Welsh the language of poetry and hymns, sermons and theology. Both should be retained and utilized in their respective spheres.[57]

The twentieth century witnessed the dire results of confining Welsh to certain domains. During that century the Welsh language and Christianity declined hand in hand in Wales. Ironically, in the same period, a disproportionately high number of committed Christians were active in trying to help the language break out of the confines of religious life and become again the language of all aspects of Welsh life – a battle that seems very gradually to be being won.

We are at the beginning of a new millennium, but at the end of the 'modern Wales' that was to a significant degree the creation of the Methodist Revival. While it is true that a remarkably high percentage of those active in Welsh cultural and academic life still hold strong Christian convictions,[58] we are now facing a new, 'cool' and very secular Wales and Welsh culture, together with (perhaps) the final demise of the Welsh adherence to the old myth of the Island of Britain, as Wales becomes increasingly regarded as a defined geographical area rather than an 'experience', linguistic or otherwise. The first two millennia of the Christian era witnessed Christianity and the Welsh language and culture walking very much hand in hand. What, one wonders, does this millennium hold in store for this long-standing partnership?[59]

Notes

I am grateful to Professor R. Geraint Gruffydd for reading the final draft of this chapter and for his valuable comments.

[1] Reprinted in Saunders Lewis, *Canlyn Arthur* (1938; 2nd edn.,

Llandysul, 1985), p. 20: 'Yr ydym yn Gristnogion mewn gwlad Gristnogol. Pan ffurfiwyd Cymru, pan luniwyd yr enw a llunio'r iaith, yr oeddym eisoes yn Gristnogion. Delfrydau Cristnogaeth a bennodd ein meddwl. Dysgodd inni fod urddas arbennig ar ddyn, ar bob dyn, ac ni all Cristion feddwl yn wleidyddol o gwbl heb gredu bod yn iawn i ddynion fyw yn ddedwydd ac yn urddasol a chyflawni amcan eu creu.' The Welsh Nationalist Party, originally called Plaid Genedlaethol Cymru, and now known as Plaid Cymru: The Party of Wales, was formed in 1925. On Saunders Lewis, a Roman Catholic convert from a prominent Welsh Methodist family, see Alun R. Jones and Gwyn Thomas, *Presenting Saunders Lewis* (2nd edn., Cardiff, 1983).

2 On the terms 'Cymry' (a Celtic word meaning 'fellow countrymen', cf. 'Cumbria') and 'Welsh' (a word used by Germanic-speaking peoples to denote Romanized foreigners), see Meic Stephens (ed.), *The New Companion to the Literature of Wales* (Cardiff, 1998), under 'Britain', 'Cymru' and 'Wales'. On the belief that the Welsh were 'in some way the last representatives of *Romanitas* in Britain', see Ceri Davies, *Welsh Literature and the Classical Tradition* (Cardiff, 1995), p. 3.

3 Cf. Gwynfor Evans, *Magnus Maximus and the Birth of Wales the Nation* (Swansea, [1983]), p. 31. On Dewi Sant (St David, the patron saint of Wales) and Taliesin Ben Beirdd (Taliesin Chief of Bards), see Stephens (ed.), *The New Companion to the Literature of Wales*. Some of Taliesin's poems have been translated into English by Tony Conran in his *Welsh Verse* (3rd edn., Bridgend, 1992).

4 John Davies, *A History of Wales* (London, 1994), pp. 74, 72.

5 See G. H. Doble, *Lives of the Welsh Saints*, ed. D. Simon Evans (Cardiff, 1984), pp. 155, 33. Cynwyl Gaeo, the parish in which the stone was originally located – it is now in a museum in Carmarthen – is also the location of the important Roman gold mines of Dolau Cothi and was an early centre of Methodist activity in the eighteenth century. Some 12 miles north along the Roman road, at Llanio in south Cardiganshire – the site of a key Roman fort, and again, interestingly, near centres of major significance for both early and medieval Christianity in Wales and the beginnings of Welsh Methodism – is to be found a striking recent reminder of this centuries-long symbiotic relationship between Christianity and Welsh culture. A plaque was unveiled at Llanio in June 2000 to commemorate a local boy who grew to become one of the most influential figures in Welsh cultural life in the second half of the twentieth century, Alun R. Edwards (1919–86) – on him, see

Stephens (ed.), *The New Companion to the Literature of Wales*. The stark description of Alun Edwards on that plaque at the close of the twentieth century, 'Y Cymro a'r Cristion' (The Welshman and the Christian), begs comparison with that of Paulinus in the sixth!

6 William Williams (1717–91) of Pantycelyn was a key Welsh Methodist leader of the first generation, an influential author and 'father of the Welsh hymn'. The English version of one of his hymns, 'Guide me, O Thou great Jehovah', is one of the most popular hymns in the English language. Glyn Tegai Hughes's *Williams Pantycelyn*, 'Writers of Wales' Series (Cardiff, 1983), provides a good English introduction to his life and work. I attempt a brief, popular overview in my article, 'William Williams: The sweet singer of Wales', *Evangelical Times* (April 1991), 7.

7 Gerald of Wales, *The Journey through Wales and The Description of Wales*, tr. Lewis Thorpe (Harmondsworth, 1978), pp. 267, 271, 273.

8 Stephens (ed.), *The New Companion to the Literature of Wales*, under 'Old Man of Pencader'.

9 Gerald of Wales, *The Journey through Wales and The Description*, p. 274.

10 A Welsh translation of Dr John Davies's Latin prefatory letter is to be found in Ceri Davies, *Rhagymadroddion a Chyflwyniadau Lladin 1551–1632* (Cardiff, 1980); see also his *Latin Writers of the Renaissance*, 'Writers of Wales' Series (Cardiff, 1981), section 3.

11 The song was written in 1983 to commemorate the 1600th anniversary of the withdrawal by the Roman commander, Magnus Maximus (Macsen Wledig in Welsh tradition), of Roman troops from Wales in AD 383, which 'has been romantically viewed as the act which symbolized the entrusting of the control of Wales to Cunedda, the legendary founder of the Welsh princely dynasties'. See Ceri Davies, *Welsh Literature and the Classical Tradition*, pp. 2–3; cf. Gwyn A. Williams, *When Was Wales?* (London, 1985), p. 20. The words and music of the song may be found in the comprehensive collection of Dafydd Iwan's songs, *Holl Ganeuon Dafydd Iwan* (Tal-y-bont, 1992).

12 Quoted from the edn. of the elegy in Gomer Morgan Roberts (ed.), *Gwaith Pantycelyn* (Llandysul, 1960), p. 138.

13 Eifion Evans, *Fire in the Thatch: The True Nature of Religious Revival* (Bridgend, 1996), p. 13; see also *Pursued by God* (Bridgend, 1996), Eifion Evans's translation of Williams Pantycelyn's poem, *Theomemphus*.

14 See Emyr Roberts and R. Geraint Gruffydd, *Revival and its Fruit* (Bridgend, 1981), p. 36.

15 Geraint H. Jenkins, *Literature, Religion and Society in Wales, 1660–1730* (Cardiff, 1978), p. 307; cf. idem, *The Foundations of Modern Wales 1642–1780* (Oxford, 1993), pp. 183, 347–8.
16 Gareth Miles, 'Pa beth yw cenedl?', *Barn*, 426/7 (July/August 1998), 68: '. . . Prydeinwyr rhonc bob un. Yn Saesneg y dyddiadurent ac y gohebent â'i gilydd, gan bregethu ac emynydda yn Gymraeg oherwydd unieithrwydd y werin.'
17 'Wales a part of England 1485–1800', in D. Myrddin Lloyd (ed.), *The Historical Basis of Welsh Nationalism* (Cardiff, 1950), p. 95.
18 'The Established Church, Dissent and the Welsh language, c.1660–1811', in Geraint H. Jenkins (ed.), *The Welsh Language Before the Industrial Revolution* (Cardiff, 1997), p. 265.
19 In this context, it is interesting to see Saunders Lewis in 1950 retracting statements he had made about Williams Pantycelyn and Welsh culture in his influential volume on the hymn writer in 1927: 'Erbyn heddiw barnaf mai amrwd a ffôl oedd dweud, "Nid oedd ganddo ddiwylliant Cymraeg". Bu dylanwad llenyddiaeth Gymraeg a dylanwad diwylliant a thraddodiadau ei fro yn lletach a dyfnach ar ei waith nag a ddëellais i'r pryd hynny' (By today I consider it to have been crude and foolish to say, 'He had no Welsh culture'. The influence of Welsh literature and the influence of the culture and traditions of his locality were wider and deeper on his work than I understood at that time), *Y Fflam*, 9 (August 1950), 63.
20 Dafydd Johnston, *A Pocket Guide: The Literature of Wales* (Cardiff, 1994), p. 47. For the Welsh-language original, see Garfield H. Hughes (ed.), *Rhagymadroddion 1547–1659* (Cardiff, 1951), p. 11; William Salesbury, *Oll Synnwyr pen Kembero ygyd*, ed. J. Gwenogvryn Evans (Bangor and London, 1902).
21 In his earlier writings especially, William Salesbury actively encouraged his fellow-Welshmen to learn English, 'as a language moste expediente, and most worthiest to be learned, studied and enhaunced . . . even for the attaynement of knowledge in Gods word, and other liberall sciences' (1550), and in a dedication addressed to Henry VIII in 1547, he applauds the king for having established English as the overall language of the realm, for the sake of its unity; see R. Brinley Jones, *The Old British Tongue* (Cardiff, 1970), pp. 36–7. This did not mean, however, that Salesbury desired the demise of the Welsh language, for while English might have been to him a language of humanist and Protestant learning, and of political expediency, it is obvious from both his words and deeds that to Salesbury, despite his acknowledged ability in more than seven languages, Welsh remained for him the 'language of the heart'; see W. Alun Mathias,

'William Salesbury a'r Testament Newydd', in *Llên Cymru*, XVI/1–2 (1989), 40–68; idem, 'William Salesbury', in Geraint Bowen (ed.), Y *Traddodiad Rhyddiaith* (Llandysul, 1970), chs. 2 and 3; R. Brinley Jones, *William Salesbury*, 'Writers of Wales' Series (Cardiff, 1994).

22 See Glanmor Williams, *Wales and the Reformation* (Cardiff, 1997), ch. 13; Prys Morgan, *A Bible for Wales* (Aberystwyth, 1988).

23 See P. T. J. Morgan, 'The Abbé Pezron and the Celts', *Transactions of the Honourable Society of Cymmrodorion* (1965), 286–95; Prys Morgan, *The Eighteenth Century Renaissance* (Llandybïe, 1981), pp. 85–100; Jenkins, *The Foundations of Modern Wales 1642–1780*, pp. 223–5; Caryl Davies, *Adfeilion Babel* (Cardiff, 2000).

24 Halvdan Koht's description of the work, quoted by R. M. Jones, 'Macsen Wledig a'i berthynas â'r genedl', in Geraint H. Jenkins (ed.), *Cof Cenedl XV* (Llandysul, 2000), p. 19. An English translation of Geoffrey of Monmouth's work by Sebastian Evans and revised by Charles W. Dunn was published in the Everyman's Library series in 1963. Another English translation, by Lewis Thorpe, was published in the Penguin Classics series in 1966. On the almost unanimous Welsh loyalty, down at least until the late eighteenth century, to Geoffrey of Monmouth's version of Welsh history, see Brynley F. Roberts, *Brut y Brenhinedd* (Dublin, 1971), appendix; idem, 'Ymagweddau at *Brut y Brenhinedd* hyd 1890', *Bulletin of the Board of Celtic Studies*, XXIV/2 (May 1971), 122–38; idem, 'Sieffre o Fynwy a Myth Hanes Cenedl y Cymry', in Geraint H. Jenkins (ed.), *Cof Cenedl VI* (Llandysul, 1991), pp. 1–32.

25 On these myths, see R. Geraint Gruffydd, 'The Renaissance and Welsh literature', in Glanmor Williams and Robert Owen Jones (eds.), *The Celts and the Renaissance* (Cardiff, 1990), pp. 19–20; Glanmor Williams, *Renewal and Reformation: Wales c.1415–1642* (Oxford, 1993), ch. 19; Prys Morgan, 'Keeping the legends alive', in Tony Curtis (ed.), *Wales: The Imagined Nation* (Bridgend, 1986), pp. 19–41; Glenda Carr, *William Owen Pughe* (Cardiff, 1983), pp. 182–3; Ceri Davies, 'Dyneiddwyr Cymru ac Ewrop', in Geraint H. Jenkins (ed.), *Cof Cenedl VII* (Llandysul, 1992), pp. 44–5.

26 See Saunders Lewis, 'Damcaniaeth Eglwysig Brotestannaidd', in R. Geraint Gruffydd (ed.), *Meistri'r Canrifoedd* (Cardiff, 1973), ch. 13; Glanmor Williams, *Welsh Reformation Essays* (Cardiff, 1967), ch. 9. In his article, 'The tradition of St David in Wales', Glanmor Williams suggests that this belief in the evangelical purity of the early British church was crucial to the survival of the reputation of St David and the celebration of his feast day of 1 March into the

early modern period, see his *Religion, Language and Nationality in Wales* (Cardiff, 1979), pp. 118–20.

27 Although this myth was promoted by some historians from the late sixteenth century onward, it seems not to have gained widespread popularity in Welsh-speaking circles until the eighteenth century; see Geraint H. Jenkins, 'The cultural uses of the Welsh language 1660–1800', in idem (ed.), *The Welsh Language Before the Industrial Revolution*, pp. 369–79; Bedwyr L. Jones, 'Drych y Prif Oesoedd', *Y Traethodydd* (1963), 35–6; Ceri Davies, *Rhagymadroddion a Chyflwyniadau Lladin*, pp. 107–8, 170; Carr, *William Owen Pughe*, pp. 77, 183; Caryl Davies, *Adfeilion Babel*. As the name 'Britain' had been seen to have derived from 'Brutus', so the word 'Cymro' (Welshman) was seen as having derived from 'Gomer', and the Welsh language, 'Cymraeg', as having come from 'Gomeraeg', the language of Gomer (see the national dictionary of the Welsh language, *Geiriadur Prifysgol Cymru*, p. 1458). It is significant that one of the first Welsh-language periodicals, established in 1818, was called *Seren Gomer* (The Star of Gomer): Huw Walters, *A Bibliography of Welsh Periodicals, 1735–1850* (Aberystwyth, 1993), pp. 51–3; idem, 'The Welsh language and the periodical press', in Geraint H. Jenkins (ed.), *The Welsh Language and its Social Domains, 1801–1911* (Cardiff, 2000), pp. 353–4, 357. A letter pressing for the establishment of a 'Celtic Missionary Society', which appeared in a Methodist publication in 1838, opens 'Gwyddoch, ein bod ni, Cenedl y Cymry, wedi disgyn o Gomer fab Japheth, fab Noah' (You know, that we, the Welsh nation, are descended from Gomer the son of Japheth, the son of Noah): *Y Drysorfa* (May 1838), 149.

28 See R. Geraint Gruffydd, 'The Renaissance and Welsh literature'; idem, 'Wales and the Renaissance', in A. J. Roderick (ed.), *Wales through the Ages*, II (Llandybïe, 1960), pp. 45–53; Branwen Jarvis, 'Welsh humanist learning', in R. Geraint Gruffydd (ed.), *A Guide to Welsh Literature c.1530–1700* (Cardiff, 1997), ch. 5.

29 See Roberts, *Brut y Brenhinedd*, pp. 55–63; Peter Roberts, 'Tudor Wales, national identity and the British inheritance', in Brendan Bradshaw and Peter Roberts (eds.), *British Consciousness and Identity: The Making of Britain, 1533–1707* (Cambridge, 1998), pp. 37–42.

30 In the preface to his Welsh translation of King James's book, *Basilikon Doron*, published by Thomas Salisbury in 1604 (and reproduced in facsimile by the University of Wales Press in 1931). Robert Holland (*c*.1556/57–1622?) was at the time rector of Llanddowror in Carmarthenshire and a key figure in an important

literary circle in south-west Wales; see Glanmor Williams, *Wales and the Reformation* (Cardiff, 1997), pp. 392, 395; J. Gwynfor Jones, 'Robert Holland a *Basilikon Doron y Brenin Iago*', in J. E. Caerwyn Williams (ed.), *Ysgrifau Beirniadol XXII* (Denbigh, 1997), pp. 161–88. Thomas Salisbury (c.1564–1623), a London stationer who was related to the Bible translator, William Salesbury, seems to be have been the focal figure of a circle of Welsh Protestants with strong Puritan leanings, including Robert Holland and Edward Kyffin, who had an ambitious publishing programme in Welsh which was thwarted by the London plague of 1603. Of significance in the present context is that the fragments of their publications that have survived, while naturally showing a deep concern for the spiritual welfare of the Welsh people, also show a keen desire to preserve and promote the 'ancient British' identity and the Welsh language, and not for reasons of evangelistic expediency alone. For example, Thomas Salisbury in a preface to Wiliam Midleton's versification of the Psalms, published in 1603, entreates 'all that are zealous of Gods honour, and louers of their natiue countrey, and the ancient Brytish tongue (so miraculously preserued of God, these seuen and twenty hundred yeeres and upwards . . . since *Brutes* time)'; while the preface to Edward Kyffin's versification of the Psalms, published in the same year, is addressed to 'fyngharedigion wlâd-wyr y Sawl a gârant Ogoniant yr Arglwydd, ag ymgeledd ei gwlad-iaith' (my beloved countrymen, those who love the glory of the Lord and the succour of their native tongue). On this publishing venture, see especially R. Geraint Gruffydd, *Thomas Salisbury o Lundain a Chlocaenog: Ysgolhaig-Argraffydd y Dadeni Cymreig* (Aberystwyth, 1991); cf. idem, *'In that Gentile Country': The Beginnings of Puritan Nonconformity in Wales* (Bridgend, 1975), where he outlines the emergence of a consciously Welsh Puritan movement in the 1630s, which could perhaps in some ways be considered heirs of the Salisbury/Holland circle.

[31] Dafydd Glyn Jones, *The Secret of the Island of Britain* (Cardiff, 1992), p. 10. It is worth quoting here A. H. Dodd on the word 'British' in his 'The pattern of politics in Stuart Wales', *Transactions of the Honourable Society of Cymmrodorion* (1948), 16: 'The word "British" was still [at the time of the ascent of James I] for most people synonymous with "Welsh," a term as objectionable to patriotic Welshmen (since it made them strangers in their own land) as was "British" (the badge of a conquered people) to Englishmen. To distinguish the "old and true inhabiters" from the "mere possessors" the epithet "ancient" or the prefix

"Cambro-" was often added to "British" when applied to the former.' Interestingly, Linda Colley, in her important and influential book, *Britons: Forging the Nation 1707–1837* (London, 1994), notes that, following the Act of Union with Scotland in 1707, 'many eighteenth-century Englishmen . . . bitterly disapproved of "English" and "England" giving way to "British" and "Great Britain", as they were in both official and everyday vocabulary by the 1750s' (p. 13). Unfortunately, Linda Colley's discussion of the growth of a new 'British national' identity during the eighteenth and nineteenth centuries is flawed in respect to Wales to the extent that it does not take into consideration the older 'ancient British' identity that coexisted with and predated it. It is worth noting, perhaps, that the terms 'Great Britain' and 'the British Empire' both have their origins in this older 'ancient Britishness' – see Peter Roberts, 'Tudor Wales, national identity and the British inheritance', in Bradshaw and Roberts (eds.), *British Consciousness and Identity*, pp. 29–33, 39–40. As Jenny Wormald has pointed out, part of the appeal of adopting the title 'King of Great Britain' for James I arose from 'the misunderstanding that "Great" was equated with power, when in fact it was a purely geographical term, to distinguish this Britain from Lesser Britain, which was Brittany'; see her 'James VI, James I and the identity of Britain', in Brendan Bradshaw and John Morrill (eds.), *The British Problem, c.1534–1707* (London, 1996), p. 159. Dafydd Glyn Jones has discussed various aspects of this Welsh fixation with the 'Island of Britain' in a series of important monographs and articles; see the bibliography in his *Un o Wŷr y Medra: Bywyd a Gwaith William Williams, Llandygái 1738–1817* (Denbigh, 1999), p. 334; see also R. R. Davies's lecture, *Beth yw'r ots gennyf i am – Brydain?* (Aberystwyth, 1999).

32 Richard Bennett, 'Odfeuon dwyieithog Howell Harris', *Journal of the Historical Society of the Presbyterian Church of Wales*, XV/3 (September 1930), 110.

33 *Drych yr Amseroedd*, ed. G. M. Ashton (Cardiff, 1958), p. 127. Such references do not mean of course that the newer 'one-nation' Britishness did not coexist increasingly with the awareness of 'ancient Britishness', especially as a result of the warring between Britain and France in the eighteenth century; see, for example, J. Gwynfor Jones, 'Methodistiaeth Gynnar, y gyfraith a'r drefn gymdeithasol yng Nghymru', *Cylchgrawn Hanes: Historical Society of the Presbyterian Church of Wales*, XVI–XVII (1992–3), 49–99; R. Watcyn James, 'Ymateb y Methodistiaid Calfinaidd Cymraeg i'r Chwyldro Ffrengig', *Cylchgrawn Hanes: Historical*

Society of the Presbyterian Church of Wales, XII–XIII (1988–9), 35–60; cf. the use of 'Britain' in the hymns and poems of the Methodist hymn writer, Edward Jones (1761–1836) of Maes-y-plwm, *Caniadau Maes y Plwm* (Holywell, 1857), pp. 21, 97, 234, 243; in the hymn book edited by the Congregationalist, David Jones (1770–1831) of Holywell, *Casgliad o dros Saith Cant a Thri Ugain o Hymnau* (2nd edn., Holywell, 1821), nos. 228, 455–7, 495; and in the political pamphlet by the influential Methodist leader, Thomas Jones (1756–1820) of Denbigh, *Gair yn ei Amser* (1798), reprinted in Frank Price Jones, *Radicaliaeth a'r Werin Gymreig yn y Bedwaredd Ganrif ar Bymtheg* (Cardiff, 1977).

[34] Thomas Charles was in contact with a number of prominent Welsh scholars of the day, including William Owen Pughe, Walter Davies ('Gwallter Mechain') and Edward Williams ('Iolo Morganwg'), mainly through his editorial work on the British and Foreign Bible Society's Welsh New Testament (1806) and Bible (1807). Charles was greatly attracted to William Owen Pughe's linguistic theories and unconventional orthography; see the index to D. E. Jenkins's 3-volume *The Life of the Rev. Thomas Charles* (Denbigh, 1908); R. Tudur Jones, *Thomas Charles o'r Bala: Gwas y Gair a Chyfaill Cenedl* (Cardiff, 1979), pp. 29–33; Carr, *William Owen Pughe*, pp. 76, 136, 158–9.

[35] See, for example, the instances of popular poetry, noted in J. Beverley Smith, *Llywelyn ap Gruffudd: Tywysog Cymru* (Cardiff, 1986), p. 402, which include references to the Welsh descent from Brutus.

[36] For example, Rhys Prichard (1579?–1644) opens one of his poems by addressing his Welsh audience as Britons, the race of Brutus: 'Hil Frutus fab Silfus, Brutaniaid brwd, hoenus . . .'; see Nesta Lloyd (ed.), *Cerddi'r Ficer* (Cyhoeddiadau Barddas, 1994), p. 33. On the popularity and influence of Prichard's homely verse, see Jenkins, *Literature, Religion and Society in Wales, 1660–1730*, pp. 150–4. Ironically in the present context, Thomas Charles translated a description of Prichard wearing his beard long, 'after the manner of the Puritans', as allowing his beard to grow 'yn ôl dull yr hen Frutaniaid' (according to the custom of the ancient Britons)! See Gruffydd, '*In that Gentile Country*', p. 7.

[37] For example, Bishop Richard Davies's influential 'Epistle to the Welsh', which prefaced the Welsh New Testament of 1567 and which expounds the belief in an early British 'Protestant' church, was reprinted in 1671, 1744, 1819 and 1850; see Garfield H. Hughes, 'Cefndir meddwl yr ail ganrif ar bymtheg: rhai ystyriaethau', in W. J. Rees (ed.), *Y Meddwl Cymreig* (Cardiff,

1995), p. 110; Glanmor Williams, *Welsh Reformation Essays*, ch. 9. Thomas Charles quoted from the Epistle in the article on the Bible in his scriptural dictionary, and the dictionary shows a thorough familiarity with the 1567 text of the Welsh New Testament; see R. Tudur Jones, 'Diwylliant Thomas Charles o'r Bala', in J. E. Caerwyn Williams (ed.), *Ysgrifau Beirniadol IV* (Denbigh, 1969), p. 106. English translations of the Epistle are to be found in T. Walters, *The Introductory Letters to the Welsh New Testament* (Bangor, n.d.) and in A. O. Evans, *A Memorandum on the Legality of the Welsh Bible and the Welsh Version of the Book of Common Prayer* (Cardiff, 1925), pp. 83–124.

38 See Derec Llwyd Morgan, *Rhai Agweddau ar y Beibl a Llenyddiaeth Gymraeg* (Llandysul, 1998); Charles Edwards, *Hanes y Ffydd yng Nghymru*, ed. Hugh Bevan (Cardiff, 1948).

39 Prys Morgan, 'The clouds of witnesses: the Welsh historical tradition', in R. Brinley Jones (ed.), *Anatomy of Wales* (Peterson-super-Ely, 1972), p. 32; Geraint H. Jenkins, 'Historical writing in the eighteenth century', in Branwen Jarvis (ed.), *A Guide to Welsh Literature c.1700–1800* (Cardiff, 2000), p. 29.

40 Gomer M. Roberts, *Y Per Ganiedydd*, I (Llandysul, 1949), pp. 44–7, 67.

41 On Rowland, see Eifion Evans, *Daniel Rowland and the Great Evangelical Awakening in Wales* (Edinburgh, 1985). In light of the rather extreme statement that Williams Pantycelyn 'was the only Methodist leader of his generation with a genuine love of learning and literature' (Jenkins, 'The cultural uses of the Welsh language 1660–1800', pp. 383–4), it is worth noting that Daniel Rowland's library contained works by the likes of Homer, Virgil and Juvenal, in addition to the more staple Methodist diet of Puritan divines; see Derec Llwyd Morgan, *The Great Awakening in Wales*, tr. Dyfnallt Morgan (London, 1988), pp. 111, 67; Evans, *Daniel Rowland and the Great Evangelical Awakening in Wales*, p. 30; idem, 'The sources and scope of Daniel Rowland's sermons', *Cylchgrawn Hanes: Historical Society of the Presbyterian Church of Wales*, XVIII (1994), 46–8; cf. idem, 'Howell Harris and the printed page', *Cylchgrawn Hanes: Historical Society of the Presbyterian Church of Wales*, XXIII (1999), 33–62. The *halsing* was a type of popular religious verse which flourished in the Teifi valley in the second half of the seventeenth century and the first half of the eighteenth. As can be seen from a manuscript collection of such poems (National Library of Wales, Cwrt Mawr MS 189A), some of these poems refer specifically to the Welsh descent from Brutus of Troy, while one poem in the collection has a number of classical references,

including Venus, Cassandra, Minerva, Virgil and Juvenal; it is significant in the present context that another of the poems in that collection is by Daniel Rowland, composed by him in 1737. See Jenkins, *Literature, Religion and Society in Wales 1660–1730*, pp. 158–61.

42 R. T. Jenkins, *Yr Apêl at Hanes* (Wrexham, 1930), pp. 35–46. On Evans, see Gwyn Thomas, 'Two prose writers: Ellis Wynne and Theophilus Evans', in Jarvis (ed.), *A Guide to Welsh Literature c.1700–1800*, pp. 54–63.

43 Glanmor Williams, 'Griffith Jones, Llanddowror', in Charles E. Gittins (ed.), *Pioneers of Welsh Education* (Swansea, [1964]), pp. 11–30; Gwyn Davies, *Griffith Jones, Llanddowror: Athro Cenedl* (Bridgend, 1984); David Salmon, 'A Russian report on Griffith Jones's schools', *Transactions of the Carmarthenshire Antiquarian Society*, XIX (1925–6), 76–8.

44 Cf. Robert Jones, Rhos-lan, *Drych yr Amseroedd*, ed. G. M. Ashton (Cardiff, 1958), p. 29, where he states that the beginning of the Methodist Revival in Wales may be attributed to the charity schools of Griffith Jones, which were like the crowing of a cock, signifying the approach of dawn.

45 The arguments and quotations which follow come from Griffith Jones's letter in *Welch Piety* dated 11 October 1739; see W. Moses Williams, *Selections from the Welch Piety* (Cardiff, 1938), pp. 37–59. See also R. Tudur Jones, *The Desire of Nations* (Landybïe, 1974), pp. 131–3; R. M. Jones and Gwyn Davies, *The Christian Heritage of Welsh Education* (Bridgend, 1986), pp. 49–51.

46 D. E. Jenkins, *The Life of the Rev. Thomas Charles*, III (Denbigh, 1908), chs. 53 and 61.

47 Richard Bennett, 'Odfeuon dwyieithog Howell Harris', pp. 110–11; cf. Tom Beynon, *Howell Harris's Visits to London* (Aberystwyth, 1960), pp. 2–4; Gomer M. Roberts, *Portread o Ddiwygiwr* (Caernarfon, 1969), pp. 31–2; idem, 'Howell Harris, Lladdwr y Gymraeg?', *Y Goleuad* (11 May 1966), p. 5.

48 A. H. Williams (ed.), *John Wesley in Wales 1739–1790* (Cardiff, 1971), p. 36; idem, *John Wesley a Chymru* (Tre'r-ddôl, 1969), p. 7.

49 In his scriptural dictionary under 'Iaith' (Language): 'Y mae yr iaith Gymraeg yn odidog, yn bur, yn gyflawn hynod o amrywiaeth geiriau ac ymadroddion; yn bêrsain ac yn addurnedig; yn neillduol addas i ymadroddi am bethau ysbrydol . . . Y mae yn syml, heb fod yn isel; yn hyf, heb fod yn ddigywilydd; yn addurnwych, heb gymhendod . . . tyner, heb fod yn fursenaidd; yn gryf, heb erwinder.' Cf. the pamphlet by the prominent Methodist musician, Richard Mills (1809–44), on

the 'duty of the Welsh to care for their language', *Traethawd ar Ddyledswydd y Cymry i Goleddu eu Hiaith* (Llanidloes, 1838), where he not only quotes on more than one occasion from this section of Charles's scriptural dictionary, but also states categorically regarding the Welsh language: 'Gellir profi yn anwrthwynebawl, ei bod mor hyned a *Gomer* ab *Japheth*' (It can be proved irrefutable, that it is as old as Gomer the son of Japheth), p. 7!

50 Ann Rosser, *Telyn a Thelynor* (National Museum of Wales, 1981), pp. 45–6; cf. R. Tudur Jones, 'Agweddau ar ddiwylliant Ymneilltuwyr (1800–1850)', *Transactions of the Honourable Society of Cymmrodorion* (1963), 184–8.

51 Roberts and Gruffydd, *Revival and its Fruits*, p. 35.

52 John Rhys and D. Brynmor-Jones, *The Welsh People* (4th edn., London, 1906), pp. 474–5; cf. J. E. Caerwyn Williams, 'Y Beibl a'r ymwybod cenedlaethol', in R. Geraint Gruffydd (ed.), *Y Gair ar Waith* (Cardiff, 1988), pp. 156–8. The choice of the title *Drych yr Amseroedd* (A Mirror of the Times; 1820) for Robert Jones's story of the birth and growth of Methodism in Wales, echoing as it does the title of Theophilus Evans's story of the supposed early formative years of the Welsh nation, *Drych y Prif Oesoedd* (A Mirror of the Earliest Ages; 1716, 1740), emphasizes the fact that the eighteenth-century Welsh Methodists saw their times as 'the new birth of a people'; cf. Dafydd Glyn Jones's comment that according to *Drych y Prif Oesoedd* the golden age of the Welsh was over by 1700, whereas according to *Drych yr Amseroedd* it did not start until after 1700; see his *Yn Nrych yr Amseroedd* (Eisteddfod Genedlaethol Cymru, Bro Madog, 1987), p. 6.

53 R. T. Jenkins, *Hanes Cymru yn y Ddeunawfed Ganrif* (Cardiff, 1931), p. 103, 'Gafaelodd mewn cenedl fud – gwnaeth hi'n llafar; rhoes ar ei gwefusau iaith goeth y Beibl Tuduraidd hardd y dysgodd Gruffydd Jones a'i ganlynwyr y bobl i'w ddarllen.'

54 See, for example, Dewi Arwel Hughes, 'William Williams Pantycelyn's eschatology as seen especially in his *Aurora Borealis* of 1774', *Scottish Bulletin of Evangelical Theology*, IV/1 (Spring 1986), 49–63.

55 See Saunders Lewis's influential lecture, 'Tynged yr iaith' (The fate of the language), (1962), tr. Gruffydd Aled Williams in Jones and Thomas, *Presenting Saunders Lewis*.

56 The quotations come from addresses by two barristers, H. A. Bruce (1815–95), later Lord Aberdare, and E. R. G. Salisbury (1819–90), in 1851 and 1858 respectively; quoted in A. H. Williams, *Cymru Oes Victoria* (Cardiff, 1973), p. 30.

57 On attitudes to Welsh language and identity in the Victorian era, including the often schizophrenic attitude of Welsh religious leaders towards the Welsh language and the strong movement in Victorian times among the Methodists and other denominations to plant English-medium causes which were intended eventually to supersede the older Welsh-medium causes as the language declined, see Jenkins (ed.), *The Welsh Language and its Social Domains 1801–1911*; Prys Morgan (ed.), *Brad y Llyfrau Gleision* (Llandysul, 1991); R. Tudur Jones, 'The Welsh language and religion', in Meic Stephens (ed.), *The Welsh Language Today* (Llandysul, 1973), pp. 71–3; idem, 'Religion, nationality and state in Wales, 1840–1890', in Donal A. Kerr (ed.), *Religion, State and Ethnic Groups* (Aldershot, 1992), pp. 261–76; idem, 'Agweddau ar ddiwylliant ymneilltuwyr (1800–1850)', 181–4; idem, 'Yr eglwysi a'r iaith yn Oes Victoria', *Llên Cymru*, XIX (1996), 146–67; Emyr Humphreys, *The Taliesin Tradition* (Bridgend, 1989), ch. 22; Williams, *Cymru Oes Victoria*, pp. 29–36; Ieuan Gwynedd Jones, 'Language and community in nineteenth century Wales', in Paul H. Ballard and D. Huw Jones (eds.), *This Land and People* (Cardiff, 1979), pp. 22–39; idem, 'The religious frontier in nineteenth century Wales', *Cylchgrawn Hanes: Historical Society of the Presbyterian Church of Wales*, V (1981), 3–24; Frank Price Jones, 'Yr Achosion Saesneg', in *Radicaliaeth a'r Werin Gymreig yn y Bedwaredd Ganrif ar Bymtheg*, pp. 108–31; R. M. Jones, *Ysbryd y Cwlwm* (Cardiff, 1998), ch. 7; Hywel Teifi Edwards, 'Y Gymraeg yn y bedwaredd ganrif ar bymtheg', in Geraint H. Jenkins (ed.), *Cof Cenedl II* (Llandysul, 1987), pp. 119–51; E. G. Millward, 'Kilsby Jones, Darwin a Rhagluniaeth', in *Cenedl o Bobl Ddewrion* (Llandysul, 1991), pp. 158–65.
58 See, for example, Stephens (ed.), *The New Companion to the Literature of Wales*, under 'Calvinism'; cf. Bobi Jones, *Crist a Chenedlaetholdeb* (Bridgend, 1994), p. 93.
59 See Welsh Churches Survey, *Challenge to Change: Results of the 1995 Welsh Churches Survey* ([Swindon: Bible Society, 1997]); Glanmor Williams, *The Welsh and their Religion* (Cardiff, 1991), pp. 68–72; cf. E. Wyn James 'Restoring faith', *Third Way*, XXII/5 (June 1999), 9.

~ 2 ~
'Thou Bold Champion, Where art Thou?': Howell Harris and the Issue of Welsh Identity

GERAINT TUDUR

On 20 October 1742, Daniel Rowland of Llangeitho, Cardiganshire, sat down to write a letter to Howell Harris.[1] Being involved in the work of the revival, and having the additional burden of parochial responsibilities, he was frustrated that Harris was spending so much time in London. Harris had first been taken there by George Whitefield during April 1739, and, once introduced to the bubbling cauldron that was the evangelical revival in the capital, he returned there regularly every year. In 1740 his visit lasted for six weeks, in 1741 for three and a half months, and in 1742 for a further three months. By this time Rowland was of the opinion that Harris was neglecting his duties as a revival leader in Wales. He therefore wrote his letter and asked,

> Don't you hear all the brethren in Wales crying out loudly, Help, help! help! help! Brother Harris, thou bold champion, where art thou? What, in London now in the day of battle! . . . [H]as not London champions enough to fight for her? Where are the great Wesleys, and Cennick? Must poor Wales afford assistance to England?[2]

Here, a brief glimpse can be seen of how a Methodist viewed Wales during the first half of the eighteenth century. While there is no developed sense of national identity, what may be described as a 'cross border' tension is clearly discernible, even though the letter was penned over two hundred years after the 1536 Act of Union[3] which united Wales to England. Whatever Wales's legal status, Rowland's words clearly demonstrate that he did not regard his country as one that had been totally assimilated by another. On the contrary, there is in his words the unexpected suggestion of an independence of spirit which reveals itself through his allocation of specific spheres of activity based on each worker's nationality; while the Wesleys and Cennick were intended for England, Harris and Rowland were to labour in Wales. What troubled Rowland was that Harris seemed to be ignoring the national boundaries, and thereby the needs of his own people. Since he was spending so much time over the border, apparently unconcerned about developments back home, did this not suggest that Harris preferred to be in England? Where did his commitment lie, and on which side of Offa's Dyke would his contribution be made? There was no doubt in Rowland's mind that he was a 'bold champion', but the question 'where art thou?' needed to be answered concerning not only Harris's physical location but also his cultural orientation.

Evidence of Harris's apparent lack of enthusiasm for 'things Welsh' is not difficult to find. The fact that he kept his diary in English, and that he was not only profoundly loyal to the Church of England and to the crown, but also served for a time in the militia, have all been offered as proof that he lacked passion for the nation and the culture to which he belonged. However, these things must be viewed in context.

When Harris first began to keep a diary as a result of his conversion in 1735, it was mainly in Latin that he recorded his thoughts,[4] possibly to safeguard the contents from prying eyes, but also to practise as it was intended that he should soon go to Oxford to prepare himself either for holy orders or for a career in teaching.[5] When he went up to matriculate in November 1735, he found himself unable to stay there because of 'the irregularities, and immoralities' which surrounded him.[6] He arrived on Saturday, 22 November, matriculated on Tuesday the 25th, and by Friday the 28th was back at Trevecka. Such was the extent of his education at Oxford.

The brevity of his stay did not prevent him from using the name of the university to impress others from time to time. In January 1741, on being questioned about his education by a persecuting clergyman outside Bala in north Wales, Harris boasted that he had been 'entered at Oxford'.[7] Five years later, at Frogmill in Oxfordshire, he used the same phrase while being taunted by some men on account of his Methodist activities.[8] What he forgot to mention to these gentlemen, and others whom he met on other occasions,[9] was that he had only been there for four days.

His elder brother, Joseph, was eager for him to return to Oxford during 1736, but it soon become apparent that Howell, because of his involvement in the work of the revival, had other ideas. He therefore ceased using Latin to record his thoughts and activities, and turned to English, a choice that can hardly be considered surprising as the ability to use and express oneself in English was regarded among the Welsh of the eighteenth century as a characteristic of sophistication. That said, it could still be argued that Harris could have used Welsh had he so wished. If William Williams of Pantycelyn[10] could write his hymns, poetry and books in Welsh, then Howell Harris could certainly have used the language to keep his diary. It is a sad reflection of the man, and of the period, that he chose not to do so.

Harris's loyalty to the Established Church is another aspect of his work which some have found difficult to understand. It was rooted in a number of factors: his strong Anglican upbringing; his dramatic conversion; his later belief that the Articles of the Church were theologically sound; and the fact that the Church of England was the church of the overwhelming majority of the people; all contributed towards making Harris staunchly loyal to it. As early as 1737, he wrote, 'I am persuaded 'tis from God – be true to [the] Church of England. I find that I am called there.'[11]

By 1740 he was recommending to the Methodists that they should read Thomas Rogers, *On the Thirty-nine Articles*, and insisting 'That our Church is pure'. 'I stay not in it because I was brought up in it,' he told them, 'but because I see it according to God's Word.'[12] As the years went by, he saw no reason to change his mind. In 1744 he claimed that he had 'been again and again satisfyd' that he was to stay in it.[13] It was, after all, 'ye Church of Christ', and he could see no justification for a Methodist withdrawal from it.[14]

The depth of his commitment is illustrated by an entry in the diary of Thomas Morgan,[15] who, after this incident, became the

Independent minister of Henllan Amgoed in Carmarthenshire. He wrote in 1744,

> My friend Tho: Wm [Thomas William of Eglwysilan in Glamorganshire[16]] called at our house & I had a long conversation with him, & he told me among other things yt ye Methodists had once all of 'em agreed to depart from ye Church of England, excepting Mr Howell Harris, who opposed their design with all his might.[17]

However, though Harris was a staunch defender of the Church, it cannot be claimed that he was in any way blind to its failings. On the contrary, he could at times be severely critical of it, as can be seen in one of his diary entries during May 1745: 'I see much legality and Judaism left in the constitution of our Church – holy days, holy places, holy persons, priest, vestments, tythes, hour and forms of prayers, and all performances, and faith lost.'[18]

The difference between Harris and some of the other Welsh Methodists was that he would not allow the condition of the Church to drive him to despair; he pinned his faith on continuous reformation by which God would restore the Church and purge it of all 'human Invention and popish Ceremonies'.[19] When other Methodists argued for leaving, because of the failure of the clergy to satisfy their spiritual needs, Harris stood against them saying, 'though [it is] Corrupt, 'tis our Mother'.[20] Notwithstanding its faults, he always declared himself 'much for the Church'[21] and, though offended by sights such as the people 'babbling through God's service',[22] he maintained that the conduct of carnal professors should not be allowed to mar the beauty of Christ's bride. He regarded himself as a loyal churchman, and when Griffith Jones of Llanddowror suggested in October 1745 that the Methodists had established for themselves a sect, he 'said no; we waited either to be engrafted fully to the Established Church, or to be turned out'.[23] It was as simple as that. As Buick Knox has stated,

> He saw his work as an attempt to awaken the Established Church to its high calling and to encourage within it the development of 'powerful heart-searching ministers'. He regarded his organisation not as a rival to the Church of England but as a ginger-group within it.[24]

In looking at Harris's loyalty to the Church, especially after 1740, his response to his own early radicalism must be considered to be part of the equation. In 1736, Pryce Davies, his vicar, had written to him claiming that he was interfering with the work of the ministry and demanding that he should cease immediately from itinerant preaching and delivering 'public lectures from house to house'.[25] Harris, because of his Anglican upbringing and his hopes for ordination, was fearful of being accused of undermining the Church, but at the same time he insisted that, as he believed his actions were motivated by God, he could not obey the vicar, nor, for that matter, the bishop.[26] When it was suggested that he was not authorized to preach, he argued that divine commission was sufficient authority, and though he recognized that a human commission was necessary for the administration of the sacraments, he held that it was not *absolutely* necessary for proclaiming the gospel. John Wesley adopted a similar position when he emphasized the difference between the office of priest and that of the roaming evangelist.[27] It was Harris's work as a lay evangelist that had first led to a number of conversions among his hearers, and then, in time, to the establishment of societies. These religious groups, meeting as they did in various parts of the country, were in a unique position; though claiming to be Anglican in spirit, they were not governed by the hierarchy of the Church. They made their own rules and sometimes seemed perilously close to Dissenting.

By the early 1740s, as the organization of Welsh Methodism was nearing completion, Harris could see that he and his movement were walking the edge of a precipice. On the one hand, because of the rumours that were circulating at the time that the Methodists were soon to be ejected from the Church, there was need for a solid, well-founded organizational structure to cater for the needs of the converts when they were turned out. On the other hand, Harris could see that his work in organizing the Methodist movement to ensure its survival following any ejection from the Church made it easier for those who were dissatisfied with the Church to leave it. He therefore found it necessary, while organizing the movement and setting up the structure, to argue vehemently against what was the inevitable consequence of his own radicalism. It was for that reason that he appeared 'more loyal to the Church'[28] than the other revival leaders; he wanted to avoid the accusation that it was he who had been primarily responsible for any damage that might have been done to the Church.

What Harris considered a virtue is now regarded as a weakness, and he stands accused of being primarily responsible for persuading Welsh Methodism to remain within the Church of England during the eighteenth century. It is suggested that if he had led the Methodists out, the course of Welsh history would have been very different.[29] As it was, because of his failure to grasp the nettle and act, Wales had to wait another 180 years for the grip of the Anglican Church to be broken through its disestablishment in 1920.

Closely connected with his intense loyalty to the Church was Harris's allegiance to the crown. The 1740s were years of great tension in Britain as rumours circulated about the intentions of Charles Edward Stuart, and as war with France raised the hopes of disheartened Jacobites that here, at last, was a real possibility of recapturing the throne of England.[30]

In much the same way as Whitefield and Wesley responded to the increasing social tension, Harris also emphasized his attachment to the throne and government of the day through what Luke Tyerman called 'language stronger than they merited'.[31] Because of this, while he appears to some a faithful and obedient subject of the king, to others he seems no more than a grovelling royalist overwhelmed by a desire to improve his lot through obsequious association with the English. However, behind his verbal extravagance there existed a social reason for his frequent displays of loyalty; they were part of the effort to undermine the popular belief that the Methodists were in some way connected to the young pretender and party to the political intrigues of the day.[32] Harris's declarations must not therefore be taken at face value or regarded as a form of denial of his own nationality. He may indeed have harboured a measure of true affection towards the king (as we shall see), but there was also a need to prove publicly that neither he nor any of the other Methodist leaders were revolutionaries who were involved, through their network of Methodist societies, in some form of subversive activity.

Nevertheless, it is surprising to find that his protestations of loyalty invaded his dreams. In a letter to George Whitefield in 1744 he said that he dreamt that the king

> gave me a Handfull of Gold in my Hand, & that I staid with Him 'till 2 in the evening, & that He mentioned His feeling the Love of God in His heart at a certain time, & that then I Mentioned the Particular affection I had felt wrought in my Soul to Him . . .[33]

Though we can say with Geoffrey Nuttall that 'to dream of the Wesleys was natural, but one may wonder why he should dream of the King',[34] it is possible that the dreams and nightmares were stimulated by his awareness of the prevailing social and political tension and by the widespread public fear of invasion by a foreign power. Harris dreamt about many strange things; in 1746 he saw himself preaching in Westminster Hall before the Lord Chief Justice,[35] and at another time he saw himself being prepared for execution by Joseph Saunders, the blacksmith at Trevecka, who also happened to be one of his converts. In other dreams he saw himself being imprisoned, preaching on his father's grave, accepting communion from the Dissenters,[36] and fleeing Trevecka because a war had erupted there.[37] Opinions about the significance of such dreams may vary, but it seems probable that they arose directly from Harris's circumstances and experiences. It is therefore only fair to assume that the same is true of his dreams about the king. His experiences manifest no more than the spirit of the age in which he lived, when even the slightest suggestion of disloyalty was looked upon with deep suspicion. As people were already suspicious of the Methodists, it was essential that Harris and the other leaders were seen to be loyal, and not only in public, but also in their private writings, their letters and diaries, items which could at any time be intercepted or impounded by agents of the state.

Thus, in the diary for May 1741, Harris claims that he had his heart 'drawn out for ye King & for Liberty';[38] four days later, it was 'set in' him, he claimed, 'to plead for ye King & ye Royal Family'.[39] In 1744 he prayed with 'great earnestness for ye Nation & for ye King, & my Soul,' he says, 'was drawn out for ye Church against ye Papists – crying, O! Lord, stand for us . . . be on our side'.[40] He was not alone; through his diary we catch a glimpse of Daniel Rowland also praying 'for ye King & ye Nation',[41] while, at the height of the 1745 crisis, we find Harris recording at a quarterly association that 'all ye Brethren were loyal to ye King'.[42] During the same period he also reminded his congregations that 'King George is our Lawfull King'.[43]

With such an attitude, it is hardly surprising that Harris was saddened when he heard, on 21 March 1751, of the death of Frederick, the prince of Wales. As the king was also unwell, Harris wisely committed 'ye Management of ye Nation in general and particular' to God,[44] and when the king died nine years later, in 1760, Harris admits that he was distraught. At that time he was at Yarmouth serving with the militia, and at dinner on 26 October he heard 'of the death of our good old King George'. He wrote,

> I was so affected I could hardly hide it, the same as if my own Father had died indeed. Crying that He would crown and anoint the new King George 3rd with the oil of his blessed spirit, having heard of his seriousness [or graciousness] and good disposition and love to truth.[45]

On the last day of the month he went to hear the proclamation of the new king at the town hall,[46] and on 2 November prayed that God would make him 'a Josiah and Solomon indeed', that is, a good and wise king.[47] On the eleventh of the month, he recorded that George II was being buried, and that the guns at Yarmouth were fired as a mark of respect. 'I had my soul affected suitable to the occasion,' he wrote, 'he having been a most public blessing to the nation in keeping the door open to the pure Gospel, so that I saw that every soul that was converted was instrumentally owing to him.'[48] Such was his love for the king.

His decision to offer his services to the militia was, to Harris, an act of faith. In 1759, Britain was again at war with France, and the struggle between the two countries was seen by Harris and many others as a struggle between Protestantism and Catholicism. In 1756, as the Seven Years War began, such was the fear felt even in rural Wales that five young men from

Harris's Christian community at Trevecka joined the army. They were later to see active service with the 58th regiment in Canada and the West Indies.[49]

Harris himself did not enlist until 1759, when he and over twenty other men from Trevecka joined the Breconshire Militia. Militias had existed in England since Tudor times, but their importance had been gradually undermined from the late seventeenth century by the development of a standing army. In 1757, due to the demands of expansionist foreign policy, they were reorganized and a national force of 32,000 men was established, to be raised in quotas in each county. This would release regular soldiers from their duties at home so that they could be sent overseas.[50] So important to Harris was the defence of Protestant Britain that he declared himself willing to enlist, provided that he would be allowed to preach and to care for the spiritual needs of those who enlisted with him. In November 1759 he was given the rank of ensign, and in January 1760 joined his fellow-officers at Brecon. It was not until August that he was posted to Yarmouth, and two months later, in October, he was promoted to the rank of captain lieutenant. The regiment was disbanded three days before Christmas in 1762, Harris having served king and country, as an officer and a gentleman, for a little over three years.

These facts seem to suggest that Howell Harris was an unmitigated anglophile who felt little zeal for his own culture. Though born in Wales of Welsh stock, and fluent in the language of his forefathers, he not only wrote extensively in English, but was also inflexible in his loyalty to the Church of England and an ardent royalist who felt no misgivings about wearing the uniform of an English military officer. To this can be added that he also adopted a 'one-nation' view of the population of Britain despite its ethnic diversity. It seems that in much that he wrote, he saw no significant difference between the English and the Welsh, or the Welsh and the Scots. When he considered the population *in toto*, they were to him one and the same people.

Consequently, his use of the word 'nation' is interesting. It has already been noted that in 1744 he prayed with 'great earnestness for ye Nation & for ye King',[51] and that he claimed in 1745 that Daniel Rowland used similar words, praying 'for ye King & ye

Nation'.[52] In 1751, conscious that many Protestants were fleeing from the continent to Britain because of persecution, he felt a cry within him 'that this nation shd be a refuge indeed to sincere Pilgrim believers'.[53] It is clear that he was not referring to his own people, the Welsh, but rather to the general population of Britain, and his use of the word 'nation' seems to have no ethnic significance whatsoever. It is used not so much in the traditional sense, to denote a community of persons bound by common descent, language and history, but in the more modern sense of an aggregation of peoples from different cultures and races who have been organized into a single state. It is a term that he uses loosely in order to suggest unity; with only one king and one parliament, he believed there could only be one nation.

Equally interesting is Harris's apparent infatuation with the phrase 'Great Britain', which became common currency following the union of Scotland and England in 1707. Harris seems to have discovered the phrase late in 1750, for on 4 November he claimed that he 'had vast faith and cries for Great Brittain [sic]' as he prayed to God.[54] During January 1751, he was again experiencing 'great freedom to cry for Great Brittain',[55] but by the middle of June he was making strange claims, saying that he felt as if he were 'married' to it. Though feeling the burden of the cares and concerns of the nation upon his spirit,[56] he was enabled eleven days later, while again at prayer, to rejoice that God had guided him over the years. 'Lord,' he said, 'Thou has marryd me to Great Brittain & especially to the Church of England, & particularly to Wales.' He then added as a postscript, 'O! how I loved it indeed'.[57] Whether he was referring to Wales or to Great Britain is a matter of conjecture.

Uncritical acceptance of the above as proof of some form of betrayal by Harris would not only be to oversimplify the situation, it would also lead to a distorted view of Harris himself. In many of the statements that express his understanding of his own nationality, there lurks another dimension to his character, and behind the broad canvas of all that made him 'British' there exists a strange affection and a profound loyalty to that tract of land which is known as 'Wales'. Moreover, throughout his career Harris felt a deep sense of responsibility towards the people of that land.

Strange as it may seem, it was as a Welshman that Harris saw himself. Despite Daniel Rowlands's misgivings, it was Harris's belief in 1742 that he was 'not called to labour among the rich and the great', but that he was 'sent among the Hills of Wales to [his] poor Ignorant despised Country men'.[58] While in London during February 1744, he felt

> a strong drawing of affection to Wales, and vast liberty to cry that I might be sent there, and if it be God's will that I should go, then He should send me some money, then my way would be clear. They [the Welsh] were made more dear and precious to me than ever.[59]

Later on, in June, he claimed that he had been 'satisfy'd . . . to what part of ye Vineyard [he] was called',[60] and explained that this had been revealed to him during an association meeting at Watford near Caerphilly in south Wales in 1743, when he had been appointed 'Superintendent over Wales' and given responsibility for supervising the work throughout the country.[61] Shouldering such a burden was no easy feat, and it is indicative of the way in which he viewed his work that he often prayed to God, 'hear me for poor Wales'.[62]

In 1749, he again claimed that he saw 'Wales given as my Labours'[63] and, believing death to be near, he noted that when he died, it would be Wales that would experience the greatest loss.[64] Twenty years later, while preaching at Carmarthen he declared that he still saw himself as the servant of the Welsh, and, interestingly, claimed that he was cutting to those who were ashamed of their language and country.[65] In Pembrokeshire in 1770, he said that he encouraged 'the old Britons' [that is, the Welsh], 'not to swallow the English pride and language, and despise their own, [I said] that God is a Welshman and can talk Welsh, and has said to many in Welsh, "Maddeuwyd dy bechodau" [Your sins are forgiven]'.[66] These are not the words of a man who has severed the links with his roots. On the contrary, they are the words of one who was admittedly a child of his age, but who felt a burden of responsibility for his countrymen. In 1737 when the revival was still very much in its embryonic stage, he had lamented at the condition of his country,[67] and as he neared his early retirement from the work fourteen years later in

1751, a tired and broken man, he still felt 'ye country, Wales, exceeding dear to [him] indeed. O! how I loved it', he wrote, 'and cared for it'.[68]

In June 1752, looking back over the years, and aware of his own prominent position in the now long history of the revival, Harris declared that he saw that he had been made 'a father to poor Wales'.[69] A month later he repeated the claim as he spoke to some workmen at Trevecka. 'I declared God had made me a father to Wales,' he wrote, 'I have not spared myself but have laboured more than any man – night and day thro cold, rain & snow ... & [God] has & does & will reward me for ever'.

Though this proud view of his own national identity seems in stark contrast to his admiration and affection for 'things English', it is not impossible to reconcile the two. Harris's attitude and conduct must be viewed solely in the light of the period in which he lived. For example, the basic education that he received as a young man at various local schools was delivered mostly through the medium of English, while at the Llwyn-llwyd Academy[70] he was taught the rudiments of Latin. It is not surprising, therefore, that it was in these two languages that he decided to record the day-to-day account of his labours when he began keeping his diary during May 1735. The use of English should not be interpreted as a rejection of Welsh, especially when there are other factors which should be taken into consideration.

His attitude to the work of Griffith Jones of Llanddowror serves as a case in point. Though Harris himself had been educated through the medium of English, when he saw that Griffith Jones was involved in teaching basic literacy skills to the poor through circulating schools conducted in Welsh, he not only supported the project but also contributed towards its success. Before the end of 1736, during a bout of uncertainty concerning his future, he agreed to act as an organizer and supervisor over several of the schools. His contribution was not insignificant; Mary Clement claimed that it was both 'useful' and 'important'.[71]

Harris's attachment to the Church of England also needs to be brought into sharper focus, and in order that his thinking process may be properly understood it must be remembered that, during the eighteenth century, the Church of England in Wales was a bilingual church by Act of Parliament.[72] In what must be one of the great paradoxes of British history, the state institutions which so keenly attempted to undermine the Welsh language in the sixteenth century by denying it legal and administrative status were later to decree that the Church, within the boundaries of Wales, was to use the Welsh language where the majority of parishioners were Welsh speakers. Anglican services were therefore held in Welsh in all parts of the country, as visitation returns show.[73]

Harris opposed the suggestion that Methodists should leave the Church not only because he was himself loyal to it, but also because he was fearful of anything that could undermine the Church. The mid-eighteenth century was, as has been noted, a period of political instability, as Jacobites stubbornly refused to abandon their hope of seeing a Catholic monarch on the British throne. Harris, and others, realized that this would have its consequences; the dismantling of the Church of England would be followed by the restoration of the Catholic Church. Not only would Welsh be replaced by Latin as the language of worship, but the use of Welsh Bibles, distributed as they were in their thousands by Griffith Jones through his circulating schools,[74] would also be banned. The Welsh would then be denied the Word of God in their own language. In supporting the Church, therefore, it could be argued that Harris was asserting the right of the Welsh to worship in their own language. He believed that a strong, stable Church was essential if it was to withstand the powers that sought to undermine it and, from a Welsh Methodist perspective, leaving the Church of England would not have served any useful purpose. On the contrary, it would simply have meant deserting the only establishment in the country in which the status of the language was assured and Welsh national identity was recognized.

The same line of argument can be applied to the claims concerning Harris's loyalty to the crown and to his period of service in the militia. In the eighteenth century, the king was still the subject of much devotion, and as a symbol of government was regarded as a bulwark against popish tyranny and coercion.[75] According to Harris's understanding of divine providence, the monarch possessed not only military power but also divine authority through which he would be able to defend both the realm and the faith. Harris's allegiance to the crown, and his decision to join the militia, did not spring from any wish to deny his national identity, but from his willingness to stand, suffer and die for a way of life which he believed to be threatened by Catholic invasion. It was not the standing army that he joined, but the Breconshire militia, a local motley collection of men eager to do what they believed to be their duty as good Protestant citizens.

Had Harris wished to deny his identity as a Welshman, it would have been easy for him to have left his native land and abandon his Welsh heritage. Joseph, his eldest brother, was employed at the Tower of London as the Assay Master of the Royal Mint, while Thomas, his other brother, had made his fortune, again in London, manufacturing uniforms for the army. Despite the fact that it would have been natural for Howell, ambitious as he was, to follow his brothers to the capital and turn his back on his home, his country, his culture and his language, he chose to remain in Breconshire to serve not only God but the people that he believed had been given to him as his own special responsibility.

Early in the 1740s, Harris considered the possibility of accompanying George Whitefield across the Atlantic to work as a missionary in the newly established colony of Georgia. The idea of becoming a missionary had occurred to him before the two men had met,[76] but it appears to have been at Whitefield's instigation in 1741 that the possibility became the subject of serious consideration.[77] By the autumn of 1742, Harris believed that he would soon be leaving for the New World,[78] but by mid-November, it was to Pennsylvania rather than Georgia that he saw himself going.[79] Whitefield then suggested that they should sail during January 1743,[80] but Harris was by then aware of a strong desire within him to remain in Wales. 'I felt great tenderness set in me to Wales & to my spiritual children,' he wrote, 'so that a cry was in me deep – O! if it be Thy will, let me stay here in poor Wales to feed & lead ye Lambs.'[81]

Two days later, as the ministers and exhorters met for the first Anglo-Welsh Association, he prayed that God would show him

His will 'abt going, or not going, beyond sea'.[82] The following day, the prayer was repeated yet again.

> Then, I had a Cry in me again – Lord, if Thou wilt have me stay in Wales, then let me feel Union with them – ... then He did so unite my Soul to Wales & so answer my Soul that it is His will [that] I should stay here ... O! dear, dear, dear Wales, how can I leave thee?[83]

Harris's affection for his country was such that he abandoned his plans to leave; so utterly overwhelmed was he by his sense of belonging that it was impossible for him to escape. The work of grace upon his soul had not obliterated what he was by nature, but added to it a keen edge, an awareness of his responsibility, and a longing for the salvation of his fellow countrymen. It was this, entwined with a deep desire to fulfil God's will, that spurred him on and enabled him to have such a profound influence upon his people.

Notes

[1] For brief biographies of Howell Harris (1714–73) and Daniel Rowland (1713–90), see J. E. Lloyd and R. T. Jenkins, *The Dictionary of Welsh Biography* (London, 1953) (hereafter *DWB*), pp. 339–40 and 891 respectively.

[2] Trevecka Letter 705; *Account of the Progress of the Gospel* (1742), II, Issue 1.

[3] For the Acts of Union (1536 and 1543), see Meic Stephens (ed.), *A New Companion to the Literature of Wales* (Cardiff, 1998), p. 6.

[4] See M. H. Jones, *The Trevecka Letters* (Caernarfon, 1932), p. 8.

[5] See *A Brief Account of the Life of Howell Harris, Esq.* (Trevecka, 1791), p. 22.

[6] Ibid.

[7] Howell Harris Diary 68b: 29 January 1741. The diaries are kept as part of the Calvinistic Methodist (Presbyterian Church of Wales) Archive in the National Library of Wales, Aberystwyth.

[8] T. Beynon, *Howell Harris's Visits to London* (Aberystwyth, 1960), p. 105.

[9] For example, ibid., p. 259.

[10] William Williams, Pantycelyn (1717–91), was a Methodist cleric, author and hymn writer who was converted under the preaching of Howell Harris. See *DWB*, pp. 1077–8.

11 Howell Harris Diary 23a: 2 April 1737.
12 T. Beynon, *Howell Harris's Visits to Pembrokeshire* (Aberystwyth, 1966), pp. 31–2.
13 Howell Harris Diary 110: 6 June 1744.
14 Ibid., 116: 6 May 1745.
15 For Thomas Morgan (1720–99), see *DWB*, pp. 653–4.
16 For Thomas William (1717–65), see *DWB*, p. 1022.
17 NLW MS 5456A, quoted in R. T. Jenkins, *Yng Nghysgod Trefeca* (Caernarfon, 1968), pp. 44–5.
18 Beynon, *Howell Harris's Visits to London*, p. 68.
19 Trevecka Letter 2799.
20 Howell Harris Diary 116: 6 May 1745.
21 Ibid., 23a: 1 April 1737.
22 Ibid., 25: 9 October 1737.
23 Idem, *Howell Harris's Visits to Pembrokeshire*, p. 115.
24 R. Buick Knox, 'Howell Harris and his doctrine of the Church', *Journal of the Historical Society of the Presbyterian Church of Wales (JHSPCW)*, XLIX/3 (1964), 73.
25 Trevecka Letter 65: 27 February 1736.
26 Harris applied for ordination four times but was rejected by Nicholas Claggett, the bishop of St Davids on account of his itinerating. See Howell Harris Diary 152b: 7 September 1751, 'to ye Bishop 4 times to be ordained but was refused' because he 'had gone abt'.
27 John Wesley, *Works*, VII, pp. 273–7.
28 G. F. Nuttall, *Howell Harris: The Last Enthusiast* (Cardiff, 1965), p. 42.
29 See, for example, Gareth Miles, 'Pa beth yw Cenedl', *Barn* 176–7 (July/August 1998), 65–9.
30 See Trevecka Letter 2811, in G. M. Roberts, 'Gleanings from the Trevecka letters', *Brycheiniog*, II, p. 80.
31 L. Tyerman, *The Life of the Rev. George Whitefield*, II (London, 1877), p. 498.
32 J. Wesley, *Journal*, III, 129, 132; cf. Colin Podmore, *The Moravian Church in England, 1728–1760* (Oxford, 1998), p. 175.
33 Trevecka Letter 1138, 5 March 1744, quoted in Nuttall, *Howell Harris*, p. 9.
34 Ibid., p. 8.
35 Howell Harris Diary 123: 6 [5] July 1746.
36 See G. M. Roberts, *Portread o Ddiwygiwr* (Caernarfon, 1969), pp. 45–9.
37 D. E. Jenkins, 'An outline of Howell Harris' journeys in north Wales: extracts from his journal', in *JHSPCW Trevecka MSS Supplement* (June 1940), 422.

[38] Howell Harris Diary 72: 13 May 1741.
[39] Ibid., 17 May 1741.
[40] Ibid., 109: 3 April 1744.
[41] Ibid., 115b: 3 January 1745.
[42] Ibid., 118: 3 October 1745.
[43] Ibid., 1 October 1745.
[44] Ibid., 150: 21 March 1751.
[45] T. Beynon, *Howell Harris: Reformer and Soldier* (Caernarfon, 1958), p. 93.
[46] Ibid.
[47] Ibid., p. 94.
[48] Ibid., p. 95.
[49] Jones, *The Trevecka Letters*, pp. 13–14.
[50] W. A. Speck, *Stability and Strife: England 1714–1760* (London, 1977), p. 28.
[51] Howell Harris Diary 109: 3 April 1744.
[52] Ibid., 115b: 3 January 1745.
[53] Ibid., 150: 15 March 1751.
[54] Ibid., 146a: 4 November 1750.
[55] Ibid., 147: 17 January 1751.
[56] Ibid., 151b: 13 June 1751.
[57] Ibid., 24 June 1751.
[58] Trevecka Letter 2800, quoted in G. M. Roberts, *Selected Trevecka Letters* (Caernarfon, 1956), p. 63, fn. Also in G. F. Nuttall, 'Howel Harris a "Bwrdd y Byddigion"', in E. Stanley John (ed.), *Y Gair a'r Genedl: Cyfrol Deyrnged i R. Tudur Jones* (Swansea, 1986), p. 156.
[59] Beynon, *Howell Harris's Visits to London*, p. 51.
[60] Howell Harris Diary 110: 6 June 1744.
[61] See 'Early association records', *JHSPCW* XLVIII/2 (1963), 38–9.
[62] Beynon, *Howell Harris: Reformer and Soldier*, p. 12; Howell Harris Diary 122: 28 April 1746.
[63] Howell Harris Diary 133: 17 January 1749.
[64] Ibid., 138: 22 November 1749, quoted in E. M. White, *Praidd Bach y Bugail Mawr* (Llandysul, 1995), p. 66.
[65] Beynon, *Howell Harris's Visits to London*, p. 3; idem, *Howell Harris: Reformer and Soldier*, p. 233.
[66] Idem, *Howell Harris's Visits to London*, p. 3.
[67] Howell Harris Diary 22: 19 February 1737.
[68] Ibid., 153: 11 December 1751.
[69] Ibid., 159: 1 June 1752. He had expressed a similar belief in the 1740s; ibid., 122: 28 April, 1 May 1746.
[70] See H. P. Roberts, 'Nonconformist academies in Wales, 1662–1862', *Transactions of the Honourable Society of Cymmrodorion* (1928–9), 19–20.

[71] See Mary Clement, 'Perthynas mudiad Gruffydd Jones a chyfodiad Methodistiaeth', in G. M. Roberts (ed.), *Hanes Methodistiaeth Galfinaidd Cymru*, I (Caernarfon, 1973), p. 87.
[72] E. M. White, 'The Established Church, Dissent and the Welsh language', in Geraint H. Jenkins (ed.), *The Welsh Language Before the Industrial Revolution* (Cardiff, 1997), p. 236.
[73] Ibid., pp. 270ff.
[74] Clement, 'Perthynas mudiad Gruffydd Jones a chyfodiad Methodistiaeth', p. 86.
[75] See, for example, Trevecka Letter 2811, in Roberts, 'Gleanings', p. 80.
[76] Howell Harris Diary 34: 17 October 1738.
[77] Ibid., 73: 13 June 1741, '... had a letter from Mr Whitefield calling me away'.
[78] Beynon, *Howell Harris: Reformer and Soldier*, p. 28.
[79] Ibid., p. 41; Howell Harris Diary 96: 23 November 1742.
[80] Richard Bennett, *Methodistiaeth Trefaldwyn Uchaf* (Bala, 1929), p. 57.
[81] Howell Harris Diary 97: 3 January 1743.
[82] Ibid., 5 January 1743.
[83] Ibid., 6 January 1743.

~ 3 ~
'Preaching Second to No Other under the Sun': Edward Matthews, the Nonconformist Pulpit and Welsh Identity during the Mid-Nineteenth Century

W. P. GRIFFITH

This chapter seeks to outline some features of the Welsh religious experience between c.1830 and c.1870 and to discuss especially the social significance of the Welsh pulpit and its oratory. This was a period when Welsh evangelicalism and the Welsh Nonconformist denominations were becoming predominant, and when a sizeable community of worshippers responded to popular evangelical proselytizing.

The quotation in the title is drawn from an account of Welsh preachers and preaching published in 1863 by the Revd Edward Matthews of Ewenni, Glamorgan, a prominent minister among the Calvinistic Methodists. The passage as a whole represented a hiatus in Matthews's account which he employed to emphasize, or rather re-emphasize, how blessed was Wales in its provision of ministers of the Word:

> Yes, yes, our Lord saw fit to bless Wales with preaching second to that of no other nation under the sun. Their dust [those past preachers] is sacred to the memory of the nation and she is proud of her sons today who blow the trumpet, calling together the armies of the living God.[1]

This was, moreover, a preaching tradition which was intimately associated with Welsh Nonconformity and marked out those associated denominations from the Anglican Established Church in Wales. Preaching was depicted as being an insignificant trait in the Anglican priesthood. When Lewis Edwards speculated in

1830 whether he might not do more good by leaving the Calvinistic Methodist Connexion and taking holy orders in the Church of England, he was speedily chided by his father:

> I do not believe it would be advantageous to be useful; because the circle in which you would turn would be too narrow; because the thing which has least importance among them is preaching, and that is the great ordinance by which the Lord down the ages has best succeeded in saving souls; as for being useful, I do not know where you would be more so than among the poor Methodists. I see no grounds for deserting your godly friends and brothers, thousands of them, save for worldly position and creature comforts.[2]

Edwards stayed with the Methodists. In time, he became a part of the preaching ministry and a contributor to that image, portrayed in many accounts besides that by Matthews, of a nation proud of having forged a tradition of preaching. Such was the elevated place of the preacher in Welsh society, so natural and accepted, that children even played at being preachers, thereby becoming, like the great John Elias, socialized into religion and into fulfilling the duty of piety and evangelism.[3]

Wales, if not exactly a preacher-ridden society, was certainly well supplied with them. The Independent or Congregationalist minister, Evan Jones (Ieuan Gwynedd), estimated that Wales in 1847 had 1,975 Nonconformist preachers (including, presumably, lay preachers), over double the number of Anglican clergymen and representing about one Nonconformist preacher to 700 people.[4] By the early 1860s, according to Thomas Rees, the four main Welsh Nonconformist denominations (the Calvinistic Methodists, the Independents, the Baptists and the Wesleyans), had together 2,415 ministers and lay preachers, approximately one for every 530 people.[5] Indeed, probably some 55 per cent of the population had links of some sort with the Nonconformist denominations, about one-third as full members or communicants and the rest as adherents.[6]

Of course, the 1851 Religious Census had already confirmed to the Nonconformists how far they and their evangelical style of religion predominated in Wales. The returns for places of worship and seating provision certainly emphasized this and, imperfect as they were, they gave a clear indication of the power of Nonconformity to attract people. The best guess would suggest that some 57 per cent of the Welsh population had attended a place of worship on that Census Sunday in 1851, about 89 per cent of them at a Nonconformist chapel or meeting-house. Moreover, what gave great satisfaction was that a higher proportion of the Welsh had attended a place of worship (57 per cent) compared with the English (39 per cent).[7]

Religion, therefore, became a badge of patriotic, if not indeed nationalistic, sentiment among the Welsh, which Edward Matthews's account well expressed. In this, it reflected the sort of historical sense and popular memory of the mid-century. The Welsh were depicted as a conquered nation, the victim of the innate oppressive and rapacious tendencies of the English, but morally and spiritually superior because of the people's piety which had been nurtured by unique preaching.

The exploitative nature of the English, according to Matthews, had seen Wales being deprived of her natural resources and condemned to serve the interests of the English state. This echoed what Ieuan Gwynedd had written c.1850, when he depicted the Welsh, the Scots and the natives of the overseas colonies, in their different ways, as exploited peoples.[8] The Welsh were fated to become a nation of miners, the Scots a nation of managers and the natives cheap and expendable labour. England, through its materialism, but also through its genuine civic advances, conceded Matthews, had become superior to Wales in all ways except the most fundamental one of all, religious commitment. Here, the peculiar and special religiosity of the Welsh people shone through.[9]

This was a theme that was played out quite regularly in the Welsh denominational press and the seemingly intense religiosity found among the Welsh drew the attention of opinion-formers in England, but not by any means favourably. The reports of health inspectors around 1840, Thomas Campbell Foster's articles in *The Times* in 1843, the Commission Report into the Disturbances in south Wales in 1844, and of course, the reports of the Commission of Inquiry into Education in Wales in 1847 supplemented earlier travellers' accounts in depicting a society limited in its culture and values. The world-view of the Welsh was, it was asserted, confined by language, the population being largely monoglot. Religion, including the Sunday schools and also chapel worship, had, it was conceded, given the Welsh some standards of civilization but ones that were not wholly attuned with the new age of commercial and material advancement.

> The language cultivated in the Sunday-schools is Welsh; the subjects of instruction are exclusively religious: consequently the religious vocabulary of the Welsh language has been enlarged, strengthened, and rendered capable of expressing every shade of idea, and the great mass of the poorer classes have been trained from their childhood to its use. On the other hand, the Sunday-schools, being religious instruments, have never professed a wider range. They have enriched the theological vocabulary, and made the peasantry expert in handling that branch of the Welsh language, but its resources in every other branch remain obsolete and meagre, and even of these the people are left in ignorance.[10]

Chapel education, indeed, defined the career horizons of the Welsh lower orders:

> The position of teacher is coveted as a distinction, and is multiplied accordingly. It is not unfrequently the first prize to which the most proficient pupils in the parochial schools look. For them it is a step towards the office of preacher and minister.[11]

It is fair to add that these sorts of conclusions and observations were much influenced by evidence from Welshmen, including many Anglican clergy *and by some Nonconformist ministers* who did not entirely subscribe to the view portrayed by colleagues such as Ieuan Gwynedd and, later, by Edward Matthews. Some English Nonconformist views of the Welsh were more sympathetic, inasmuch as they recognized the achievement of the Welsh pulpit in conveying, with conviction, difficult soteriological concepts to a wide cross-section of Welsh society in accessible and evocative language. The religious devotion and scriptural learning of the Welsh lower orders were qualities to be emulated by their English counterparts.[12]

Indeed Matthews, and earlier Ieuan Gwynedd, attempted to convey the idea that the religiosity of the common man in Wales (there was no distinct reference to the Welsh woman) was a positive feature of modern life and in turn they conveyed a stereotypical view of the lower-class Englishman as worldly, ignorant, complacent: happy enough with his state so long as he got plentiful supplies of beer and beef![13] The Welsh, by contrast, set their minds on higher things. Moreover, it was argued, they were more moral since they suffered less from social problems and other evils than their English (particularly urban) counterparts. This was a particularly important assertion to make, given that the social investigators and commentators (as in 1847) had alluded to the darker side of lower class Welsh life. Welsh writers did not deny that there was this dark side, but it was no worse than that of the English working classes. In fact, the English were deemed to be more deficient since, unlike the Welsh, they had received better opportunities for social and moral advancement and had not seized them. Significantly, the Nonconformist denominations in England had not made the evangelical and missionary effort of their Welsh counterparts.[14]

How had this happy state of affairs come about, that the Welsh lower classes were so much more committed to religion?[15] It had emerged by virtue of a distinctive 'style' of Welsh preaching that declared the gospel of salvation and embraced scriptural truth by deploying techniques which were empathic to the people and, crucially, employing the Welsh language itself. Though there might have been differences of approach between individual preachers, this is essentially what defined a Welsh 'style' and was claimed as such not only by Matthews but by others such as Christmas Evans in the previous generation, Owen Thomas, a contemporary of Matthews, and John Puleston Jones, who belonged to the generation after Matthews.[16] Even some English contemporaries acclaimed (or followed) this distinctive style.[17]

There was an innate and expressive euphony about the Welsh language that made it a conduit for conversion that was superior to English, which, in comparison, sounded harsh and angular when spoken.[18] This was, of course, a riposte to those who saw Wales's future progress as dependent exclusively on the English language ('the commercial language of Wales', as the 1847 Education Report put it),[19] and it elevated the Welsh language into becoming practically 'the language of heaven'.[20] The poetry of the language was such that even sympathetic outsiders could undergo a spiritual experience although they might not have fathomed the content and thrust of a sermon.[21]

But it was more than a matter of language *per se*. It was, according to Matthews, also about the appearance of the preacher, the content of his sermon and his presentation. English, and for that matter, Scottish preaching, he argued, were characterized by a remoteness from the people. Preachers in the English style (and there were Welsh ministers, according to Matthews, who were adopting this style) were too given to wearing fashionable dress, assumed a too pious bearing and employed language which was half gentrified and rather abstruse. They would enunciate in a tone too prone to the monotonous and tended to lecture rather than exhort their congregations.[22]

The Welsh style, by contrast, was characterized by the preacher's physical presence that was at once imposing but not haughty or aristocratic, using language which was homely and familiar to the listeners. It was often observed that the Welsh language was less impaired or fissured by class usages than was English, that it remained a lingua franca for lord and peasant – assuming, of course, that the lord could actually speak any Welsh in the first place. Thus, in contrast to England, the preacher in Wales could with confidence preach to a wide audience, any audience, with no fear of having to adjust or modify his words.[23]

The use of commonplace similitude was a regular feature (Matthews himself was called 'the Dickens of the Welsh pulpit'[24]) and, although always serious-minded, the Welsh preacher habitually used a degree of wit to establish his points. The sermons were also less prone to pedantry. Moreover, since it was widely held that Welsh preaching was particularly inspirational, there was an element of the histrionic, or rather the passionate, of modulating the tone of voice and reaching natural climaxes of feeling. By these means the preacher was able to sway or possibly manipulate the sensitivities of his hearers.[25] The technique of *porthi'r gynulleidfa* (nurturing the congregation), of repeating or reiterating key words or phrases from the gospel or from theology – for example, *Edifeirwch, Colledigaeth, Achubiaeth, Y Groes, Y Gwaed* (Repentance, Damnation, Salvation, The Cross, The Sacrificial Blood) – would affect the psychology of the crowd and could drive congregations to emotional extremes, of hope or despair. It required a knowledgeable audience, of course, conversant with scripture and aware of the tenets of Calvin, to be sensitive to the preacher's nuances. It also reflected what was perhaps at the heart of the Welsh style, namely its extempore nature. Prior to the great preaching of Henry Rees, an older contemporary of Matthews, few of the Welsh preachers prepared their sermons in full, either in content or delivery. It meant that, while not exactly pursuing streams of consciousness, they could adapt to their hearers and modify the mood and content of the sermon accordingly.[26] Although the fervent and dramatic espousal of the doctrines of election and judgement were probably less prominent a feature of nineteenth-century Welsh preaching (compared, say, with that of Daniel Rowland, the early Methodist revivalist, in the eighteenth), it was by no means absent at all times, for example, from John Elias and Christmas Evans.[27]

Because of all this, preachers' performances became objects of day-to-day conversation among the people, though, as Dr Owen Thomas warned in 1857, this ran the risk of their judging merely the style of a sermon rather than its content. Even so, he concluded, a modicum of content would stick and some benefit emerge; the Welsh had become much more moral.[28]

Whether this Welsh style was specially Welsh is a moot point, but the fact was that it was believed to be so by the Welsh at the time. Matthews was able to trace common characteristics and identify major proponents of this Welsh way, dating from the early Calvinistic Methodists such as Daniel Rowland, but certainly including the major Nonconformist preachers of the early and mid-nineteenth century, drawn from all the denominations which had become 'methodized' into evangelical preaching. Christmas Evans, William Williams of Wern, John Elias, John Jones of Tal-y-sarn, Ebenezer Richard, Thomas Richard and Ebenezer Morris, were among those most frequently alluded to as the 'giants' of the Welsh pulpit. They were also referred to as 'yr hen bregethwyr' (the preachers of old), as if the times would change unless ministers and people alike were reminded of the qualities of true preaching.[29]

These men had been (and were to be) held in such high regard partly because they were self-made men drawn from modest social origins like most of their audiences.[30] Their eminence was also because they had been or were the most proficient conveyors of those forms or modes of sermonizing most prevalent during the nineteenth century, as the analysis of D. Ben Rees has shown.[31] The *celebratory sermon* was the type of sermon most frequently heard and preached at the preaching festivals which had become a regular part of the Nonconformist denominations' activities during the period and also at the various associations or conferences of denominational leaders. The *revivalistic sermon* was characteristic of those deliberate efforts to mobilize mass salvatory activity. Found especially during the first half of the century, this sort was probably the type that most fully displayed those features claimed as the Welsh style. The *evangelistic sermon* was more low-key, probably because it was more common and intimate. Whereas the first two modes were associated with very large audiences of many thousands and preached in the open air,[32] the evangelistic sermon featured in the regular Sunday and mid-week services of the local chapel or meeting-house. It represented the regular calling to sinners to come to repentance and it set out those elaborate stages by which the sinner or reprobate could find solace in the redemptive powers of Christ. Mostly, therefore, the preaching was Calvinist in theology but the emphases changed as the early nineteenth-century theological debate in Wales abated after about 1830, leading to the liberalizing of certain features and to the toleration of the Arminianism of the Welsh Wesleyans, all for the sake of evangelizing the country.[33]

The force of this Welsh preaching tradition was apparent in the frequency of very large gatherings compared with England. Edward Matthews and most of those who commented about Welsh preaching in the Welsh press hastened to add that there was more to the sermons than outward form or presentation. Sermons had to be of real substance, informed by learning and appropriate texts from the scriptures, and delivered by men whose personalities were wholly virtuous and supernaturally inspired.[34] Thomas Richard, whose biography by Matthews accompanied the essay on preaching, cautioned against those manipulative preachers who were not imbued with the Holy Spirit.[35] Similarly, Ieuan Gwynedd, though he gauged that congregations by the mid-century were sufficiently knowledgeable and intelligent to tell the difference, cautioned Nonconformists to be wary and watchful about such sermonizers.[36]

Such warnings were especially important since the Anglicans in Wales were all too ready to raise doubts about the competence and suitability of Nonconformist preachers, particularly the lay preachers. It was a sensitive matter because, of course, Nonconformists placed the utmost importance on preaching in worship compared, as they saw it, with the Anglicans. Moreover, attacking lay preachers was an implicit attack on the entire Nonconformist pantheon of great preachers since practically all the most famed ministerial pulpit orators had begun as raw and limited lay practitioners before being encouraged to seek ordination. It may be no accident that Matthews's essay and the biography of Richard appeared in the same year (1863) and followed the publication of what was probably one of the most biting satires of Welsh Nonconformity, *Wil Brydydd y Coed* (Wil the Woodland Poet) by David Owen (Brutus).

Owen went to great and riotous lengths to expose the worst type of preacher, the 'Jack', whose smattering of ill-digested learning and cobbled-together English phrases (to impress and give status) were sufficient to deceive most but not all among a largely gullible monoglot Nonconformist population.[37] Some years earlier, Owen had in fact published a more conventional and more detailed critique of Welsh preaching.[38] This, in the first instance, defended the Church from accusations that it paid no attention to preaching. Practically all the Nonconformist accounts of great preaching and great preachers had effectively denied any contribution by the Church, except for those few evangelical clergymen such as Daniel Rowland or David Jones of Llangan, who had been prominent in the Calvinistic Methodist movement before it broke away from the Church in 1811.[39] Owen argued that there was indeed a firm commitment by the Church to preaching, but preaching as a calling suitable only for learned and competent men.[40] Moreover, he added, preaching in the eyes of the Church should be a vehicle for instructing the flock and not exciting them through excessive extemporizing and dramatic effect. The Nonconformist denominations lacked what might be regarded as 'quality control' over whom they allowed into their pulpits. He absolved the Calvinistic Methodists and the Wesleyans from most of this, presumably because they were the most structured and hierarchical of the Nonconformists and could control and curb excesses at the local church level.[41]

Compared with the Anglican clergy, Owen asserted, Nonconformist preachers were too youthful (and therefore too immature) and lacked proper learning and education, while the sermons they preached were too often given for effect rather than instruction and showed a near blasphemous disrespect for the Word of God and the sanctity of the text. They chose stupid and idiotic topics for their sermons, often morcellating sentences from the scriptures and selecting words out of context. In sum, there were simply too many inane sermons, a case of 'never mind the quality feel the width'![42]

It is impossible to say how far Wales was affected by this, the worst type of preacher. It is certainly true that Nonconformist commentators were aware that there were less illustrious features to the Welsh pulpit and sought to remedy them by means of admonitory essays and biographies. The published biographies of the outstanding preachers all attempted to highlight the best qualities of their subjects and concentrated on those who had done credit to the Welsh pulpit. Matthews's analysis of a Welsh style was based on examining the careers of a few leading preachers. It did obliquely question what made a great preacher, whether it was wide learning or inspiration. Many giants of the Welsh pulpit before 1850 were autodidacts, whose merits had lain in their intense commitment to preaching the Bible, which in turn excited their intellectual curiosities. Christmas Evans, John Elias and John Jones of Tal-y-sarn were regularly mentioned as men to admire and emulate for these qualities.[43] They were also admirable for having achieved the moral regeneration of Wales, particularly among the lower orders, by having induced the populace to abandon immoral or unruly customs and sports.[44]

While a distinctive Welsh style of preaching had come into being, the intellectual substance behind it was less so. The Welsh evangelical and Nonconformist mind-set owed as much to the scholarly inheritance left by English Protestantism and Puritanism as to Welsh influences. By the first half of the nineteenth century, there was a common currency of literature to which aspirant and licensed preachers had to turn if they wanted to be effective. Much of their intellectual force was derived from the literature of the seventeenth century: from John Owen, Richard Baxter and William Gurnal (all in Welsh translations), and of Charnock and Goodwin among others, as well as the rich output of the Welsh Dissenting and Calvinistic Methodist literature of the eighteenth century.[45]

As the nineteenth century progressed, collections of really meaty sermons by the illuminati of the Welsh pulpit became available in print. These were intended to benefit not only the growing literate population but also to form templates which aspiring young lay preachers could copy, for example, the famous volume *Lampau y Deml* (1859).[46] David Williams of Caernarfon, its publisher, justified his issuing the volume by reference to the growing popular thirst for knowledge, particularly among the working class, a growing desire, as he saw it, for religion and the sentiment of the older generation to be reminded of the excitement they had experienced by hearing some of the great preachers of old. In an important observation, he added that such a volume was essential for those expatriate Welshmen such as mariners, who, by their absence, were deprived of hearing the Welsh pulpit.[47] Of course, the Welsh denominational press also paid attention to the careers and published the sermons of those English preachers who most closely resembled the Welsh style, such as C. H. Spurgeon,[48] Robert Hall or John Angell James, whose sermons were published as *Yr Eglwys o Ddifrif*, with the imprimatur of one of the contemporary giants of the Welsh pulpit, Henry Rees.[49]

Scotland, too, had begun to exercise some influence on Welsh Nonconformist thought and preaching, notably through the philosophical and metaphysical writings and teaching of Sir William Hamilton and the preaching of the eminent Edward Irving.[50] The Scottish influence played a significant part in the drive to improve the standards of instruction given to putative Welsh preachers and ministers, particularly among the

Calvinistic Methodists. Without the sound provision of higher education in Wales, for Nonconformists at least, Scotland became the provider for many adept aspirants to the Welsh pulpit. Lewis Edwards was among the first Welsh students to matriculate at Edinburgh University in 1833, where he came under the tutelage, and in many ways the patronage, of Dr Thomas Chalmers.[51] Chalmers, like Hamilton, came to be held in very high esteem in Wales, particularly since his preaching style resembled the Welsh style in many ways,[52] though Edwards thought him more intellectual than most Welsh preachers.[53] It is not surprising, therefore, that at the Disruption in 1843, much Welsh Nonconformist opinion was in sympathy with Chalmers and the Free Church since they seemed to represent a rejection of Establishment religion, similar to the anti-state church sentiment then emerging in Wales.[54]

The consequence of this association with Scotland was the emergence in the ranks of preachers of a new generation who were much better educated and more scholarly than their predecessors, including Edwards himself, John Phillips, Owen Thomas and John Parry.[55] Moreover, this association became a stimulus to improving arrangements in Wales for the training and education of ministers, again notably within the largest and least prepared of the Nonconformist denominations, the Calvinistic Methodists. It led to the establishment, largely through the efforts of Edwards, of what became the Methodist College at Bala and of which he was the first principal.[56]

It could be argued that the improvements in ministerial training, which were to be found in all the Nonconformist denominations by the 1840s and 1850s, paradoxically weakened the ties between the preacher and his congregation. Before this, there had been a social proximity between preachers and people based on the similarities of background, rural origins, economic circumstances and education (or lack of it). It has been argued that a closer analysis is required of the English ministry and their social networks[57] and the same is also required for Wales. For it is clear that, by the 1860s, the preaching ministry in Wales was becoming something of a self-perpetuating caste. Lewis Edwards was an example of this, being bound by ties of intermarriage and educational background to prominent Nonconformist families. Although Edward Matthews did not refer to this phenomenon directly in his essay, there is the implication that some preachers were becoming more gentrified or remote from their people by their imitating English fashions and speech patterns and nurturing an exaggerated sense of their own importance.[58]

At about the same period, starker warnings were given about the state of the Nonconformist preaching ministry. The leading Calvinistic Methodist layman, Morgan Richards, expressed concern about the risk of encouraging a professionally educated ministry. Self-made men, he argued, were better fitted for the calling and the pulpit than college men.[59] Education alone did not make a good preacher, and this was a point brought out forcefully over a generation later by the eminent preacher and scholarly Independent minister, Dr Thomas Johns of Capel Als, Llanelli.[60]

What had characterized the perceived tradition of Welsh preaching, too, during its high summer, was its peripatetic quality, with few settled ministries, particularly among the Calvinistic Methodists. Edward Matthews, indeed, stressed this as one of the features which distinguished preachers in Wales from those in England, that they faced fewer duties and distractions from their prime task of preaching evangelistically.[61] Nevertheless, for other reasons, he was favourable to nurturing cautiously the pastoral function (*Y Fugeiliaeth*) of the ministry within his own denomination, the Calvinistic Methodists, as he made plain in 1872.[62]

One could argue that this peripatetic nature of the ministry and lay preaching had contributed to the atmosphere of revivalism which permeated Welsh society from *c*.1790 to the early 1860s, the regular and rapid turnover of visiting preachers creating interest, excitement and anticipation among the congregations. This is not the place to rehearse the various arguments about the causes of the Welsh revivals, whether there were secular or supernatural impulses, for example, merely to stress how far powerful preaching played a part in the spiritual yearnings and anxieties which accompanied these outpourings.[63] Major revivals occurred approximately once per decade during these years while local revivals occurred about once in every six or seven years. They were occasions of special and determined evangelical effort and were characterized by the lessening of theological and denominational differences and rivalries within Nonconformity and even between the Nonconformists and the Established Church. The inspired preaching associated therewith accentuated the belief in a Welsh style, particularly as it included the commitment of those leading personalities identified by Matthews and other commentators.[64]

Were there adverse effects to this unremitting outpouring of evangelistic activity? The whole impact of preaching the gospel and the Protestant faith on the social psychology of the Welsh population has yet to be subjected to close examination and one might ask whether Welsh preaching induced a pattern of religious melancholy such as that identified in nineteenth-century America.[65] Indeed, the preaching ministry itself was susceptible.[66]

The degree to which inspired preaching kept Welsh people in the faith or indeed made them more serious about their faith is another area which requires further examination. Currie, Gilbert and Horsley have stressed the distinction between the full members or communicants of a denomination, coupled with the internal constituency of adherents, on the one hand and the external constituency of the *less committed*, those 'in the world', on the other.[67] Their delineation of the several and different modes or levels of attachment to religion sets out a scale of involvement ranging from deep belief in the supernatural at one end down to mere social attachment at the other. This has echoes of what some Welsh writers felt to be the case during the mid-nineteenth century. David Rees of Llanelli set out a tripartite division of commitment to religion, distinguishing between the chapelgoer who attended out of convention, the one who attended for reasons of respectability and the one who was truly enthusiastic about religion. It was only this last type which won Rees's approval.[68] Arguably, it was this type, too, which would really gain full spiritual fulfilment from the preaching and the attendant devotions. By the 1860s, it was probably the case that the Welsh style was less effective among the external constituency which began to contract.

Even so, evangelical religion permeated the lives of the great mass of Welsh people. The characteristics of chapel life as a social, communal phenomenon have already been well described.[69] Similarly, the influence of preachers in bringing sinners under the law was reflected in the campaigns to transform Wales morally, particularly to rid Wales of intemperance and incontinence and elevate the Sabbath Day.[70] More controversially, perhaps, was the intrusion of the Nonconformist pulpit into politics and social activism.[71] There was a conviction that the Welsh pulpit had made a great mark. However much English commentators might try to depict the deficiencies of Welsh life and culture, the sense of Welsh moral and spiritual superiority, as defined by Matthews and his like, remained strong. But its strength depended on the Welsh population being linguistically and culturally uniform.

By the 1850s, this situation had begun to abate. As W. T. R. Pryce has pointed out, the 1851 Religious Census revealed that religion was at its weakest in Wales in those areas and districts which were most subject to immigration and Anglicization, the borderland and industrial mining areas.[72] A combination of factors, rapid industrialization, linguistic and cultural alienation, endangered that confident view of the Welsh nation. Owen Thomas noted that the younger generation was becoming better educated and more mobile and had closer intercourse with England, all new features with which the ministry had to contend.[73] A better educated ministry would need to adapt its preaching but still, he hoped, retain that distinctive Welsh character.[74] These were the circumstances which lay at the heart of Matthews's warning in his essay against emulating English styles and habits of preaching (not to mention secular fashions), but by the 1850s and 1860s it was a process which was well under way.

This was accompanied or followed by progress towards establishing so-called 'English causes' in Wales, in order to bring the gospel to those thousands of English immigrants, an issue with which Lewis Edwards became especially associated.[75] It was an issue fraught with all manner of implications concerning Welsh religious identity. Preaching in English and instituting English-language ministries deflected all attempts to assimilate the migrants into the Welsh-language tradition and bore all sorts of social implications. Thomas Rees believed that English-language causes would keep those respectable Nonconformist English immigrants, who regarded the Welsh chapels as rather rough and ready, from deserting to the Anglican Church. He also urged his fellow Welsh preachers to volunteer to preach in English to these immigrants in the Welsh manner to sustain that moral national character built up by Christmas Evans and all those giants of the previous age.[76]

Thus, that happy ideal of the Welsh pulpit sketched by Edward Matthews was being eroded. He himself was to figure in the pantheon of great preachers in the 'Welsh style'. By the end of his life (he died in 1892) he, too, was associated with English causes, perhaps inevitably since his county of Glamorgan was the most heavily transformed by industrialism and population growth. It is certainly the case that the generation which followed him produced far fewer declaimers of biblical truths who possessed the dynamism and authority which he and his like had embodied.[77] In a way, asserting a distinctive national 'style' was an inevitable development in a nation such as Wales which had no state structure and hardly any institutional characteristics to identify it before the late nineteenth century. At a time of dominant imperial and British values, religion gave Wales one means of marking itself out as special, though for even as patriotic a writer as Edward Matthews that preaching style was ultimately a means to a superior loyalty, to evangelical truth and a spiritual unity which transcended all partisanship.[78]

Notes

[1] Edward Matthews, *Bywgraffiad y Parch. Thos. Richard, Abergwaen* (Swansea, 1863), p. xi. 'Do, do, gwelodd ein Harglwydd yn dda i fendithio Cymru â phregethu heb fod yn ail i un wlad dan haul. Eu llwch sydd yn gysegredig yn meddwl y genedl; ac y mae hi yn falch o'i meibion sydd heddyw yn chwythu yr udgorn, gan alw byddinoedd y Duw byw yn nghyd.'

[2] Thomas Charles Edwards, *Bywyd a Llythyrau y Diweddar Barch. Lewis Edwards, M.A., D.D.* (Liverpool, 1901), p. 43. '. . . nid wyf yn meddwl ei bod mor fanteisiol i fod yn ddefnyddiol; oherwydd bydd y cylch y bydd rhaid i chwi gerdded wrtho yn rhy gyfyng; oblegyd pregethu yw y peth lleiaf yn eu plith, a thyna'r ordinhad fawr y

mae'r Arglwydd wedi llwyddo fwyaf i achub eneidiau yn mhob oes; ond am fod yn ddefnyddiol, nis gwn pa le y gellwch fod yn fwy na chyda'r Methodistiaid tlodion. Nid wyf yn gweled un achos i chwi ymadael â'ch cyfeillion duwiol, filoedd ohonynt, ond yr ychydig sefyllfa yn y byd hwn ac esmwythdra i'r cnawd.'

3 Edward Matthews, *Bywgraffiad*, pp. ix–x. Other examples would be Roger Edwards, *Cofiant y Parch. Roger Edwards Yr Wyddgrug* (Wrexham, 1908), p. 26; Evan Jones (Ieuan Gwynedd), *Cofiant a Gweithiau Barddonol a Rhyddieithol Ieuan Gwynedd*, arr. R. O. Rees (Wrexham, n.d.), p. 10, on maternal instruction as well as play.

4 *Cofiant . . . Ieuan Gwynedd*, p. 104; J. Williams (ed.), *Digest of Welsh Historical Statistics*, I (Cardiff, 1985), for Welsh population figures.

5 Thomas Rees, *History of Protestant Nonconformity in Wales from its Rise to the Present Time* (1st edn., 1861), pp. 483–4; see also J. Williams, *Digest*, for population, and idem (ed.), II (1985) for (variable) denominational statistics of pastors, ministers and lay preachers from c.1870.

6 Rees, *History of Protestant Nonconformity*, indicates that members and/or communicants of the four major Nonconformist denominations, together with their adherents totalled some 706,000 people out of a Welsh population of 1.28 million.

7 See Ieuan Gwynedd Jones, *Explorations and Explanations: Essays in the Social History of Victorian Wales* (Llandysul, 1981), esp. ch. 6 for an overview of Welsh religion in 1851; also I. G. Jones and David Williams (eds.), *The Religious Census of 1851: A Calendar of Returns Relating to Wales*, 2 vols. (Cardiff, 1976, 1981). For the most recent estimates of attendances on Census Sunday 1851, see Michael Watts, *The Dissenters*, II: *The Expansion of Evangelical Nonconformity* (Oxford, 1995), pp. 22 ff. and appendix I, pp. 671 ff.

8 Matthews, *Bywgraffiad*, p. x; *Cofiant . . . Ieuan Gwynedd*, pp. 455–6.

9 Matthews, *Bywgraffiad*, p. xi. He denied that the English had any innate genius or superiority, asserting merely that the Welsh had been deprived of opportunities to shine in secular matters. English economic hegemony also formed a part of a more comprehensive and radical analysis of Welsh society, including also class and religious incongruities, laid out by the Independent minister Michael D. Jones during these years. See Glyn Williams, 'Nationalism in nineteenth century Wales: the discourse of Michael D. Jones', in idem (ed.), *Crisis of Economy and Ideology: Essays on Welsh Society, 1840–1980* (Bangor, 1983), pp. 180 ff.

10 *Reports of the Commissioners of Inquiry on the State of Education in Wales* (1847), part 3 (1848 ed.), 519, comments of Edward Vaughan Johnson, commissioner. For other 'official' depictions of Wales, see Ieuan Gwynedd Jones, *Mid-Victorian Wales: The Observers and the Observed* (Cardiff, 1992), esp. ch. 5; Gwyneth Tyson Roberts, *The Language of the Blue Books* (Cardiff, 1998).

11 *Commissioners of Inquiry*, part 1, p. 5, comments of R. R. W. Lingen, commissioner.

12 'Y Pulpud Cymreig', *Y Dysgedydd* (1858), 252–8; Keith Robbins, 'Religion and identity in modern British history', *Studies in Church History*, XVIII (1982), 472–3.

13 *Cofiant . . . Ieuan Gwynedd*, p. 455; Matthews, *Bywgraffiad*, pp. xvi and xxx, where he added that the secular reading material of the English – *The News of the World* – compared with the Welsh's devotion to scripture, made them inferior.

14 According to Ieuan Gwynedd, the lack of employment opportunities, confined social mobility and traditional behavioural practices had not made the Welsh bad or reprobate, just worse than they might have been. See *Cofiant*, p. 472.

15 As early as 1837–8, the young aspirant preacher Lewis Edwards had stressed this point; see his *Traethodau Llenyddol* (Wrexham, n.d.), p. 459.

16 Owen Thomas, *Cofiant y Parch. Henry Rees, Liverpool*, II (Wrexham, 1890), p. 907; Christmas Evans, 'Agwedd Crefydd yng Nghymru [1837]', *Y Traethodydd*, II (1846), 5–6; R.W. Jones (ed.), *Ysgrifau gan y Diweddar Barchedig John Puleston Jones* (Bala, 1926), pp. 122–3. John Lewis, *A Memoir of the Rev. William Griffith, Holyhead* (Caernarfon, 1934), p. 95, refers to the Welsh style of Griffith's preaching during his long pastorate at Holyhead, 1822–81.

17 Watts, *The Dissenters*, II, p. 179.

18 Matthews, *Bywgraffiad*, pp. xvii–xix, xxvii–xxix.

19 And repeated by Matthews, *Bywgraffiad*, p. xvii. 'English the language of our country's commerce, and the language of its courts, yes, the language of practically everything in our country; and it's a very good one too . . .'

20 Ibid., p. xxvii.

21 Witness Charles Dickens's experience when he attended the Calvinistic Methodist Association meeting at Bangor in 1852 and heard Owen Thomas preaching; see J. J. Roberts, *Cofiant y Parchedig Owen Thomas, D. D., Liverpool* (Caernarfon, 1912), p. 258.

22 Matthews, *Bywgraffiad*, pp. xxi, xxx.

23 Ibid., pp. xxx–xxxi. Because of the general intelligibility of the language, preachers would thereby remain memorable in people's minds.
24 J. Wyndham Lewis, 'Hanes a nodweddion y Parchedig Edward Matthews', in D. G. Jones (ed.), *Cofiant y Parchedig Edward Matthews o Ewenni* (Denbigh, 1893), p. 229.
25 E. Matthews, *Bywgraffiad*, pp. xxix–xxx; Owen Thomas, *Cofiant John Jones, Talysarn* (Wrexham, 1874), pp. 969–70.
26 Matthews, *Bywgraffiad*, pp. xxx–xxxii; Thomas, *Cofiant y Parchedig Henry Rees*, II, pp. 906–12.
27 Matthews, *Bywgraffiad*, p. xxxiii.
28 Owen Thomas, 'Rhagdraeth', in *Lampau y Deml: Sef Pregethau gan Weinidogion y Methodistiaid Calfinaidd* (Caernarfon, 1859), pp. vii–viii. It was not lost on Thomas that many of the Welsh attended chapel for entertainment alone, much as the English went to playhouses (the contrast of English secularism or worldliness again being drawn) to lap up the oratory and the turns of phrase.
29 Matthews's essay tried to place the subject of his biography, Thomas Richard, who had died as recently as 1856 (and Jones of Tal-y-sarn in 1857), in this tradition (*Bywgraffiad*, p. xix). Christmas Evans, 'Agwedd Crefydd yng Nghymru', looking back to the 1790s and early 1800s, identified up to fifteen seminal Nonconformist preachers who had built on the revival started by Daniel Rowland, including, rather partially, seven from his own denomination, the Baptists.
30 *Bywgraffiad*, pp. xxxii, xxxv, re Evans and Jones, Tal-y-sarn.
31 D. Ben Rees, *Pregethau a Phregethwyr* (Denbigh, n.d., but 1996), *passim*.
32 Matthews, *Bywgraffiad*, p. xxxii, recounts the preaching of Ebenezer Morris before 10,000 people.
33 Hugh Jones, *Hanes Wesleyaeth Gymreig*, I (Bangor, 1911), pp. 182–3, 391–2; John Roberts, *Methodistiaeth Galfinaidd Cymru: Ymgais at Athroniaeth ei Hanes* (London, 1931), pp. 112–21. The most exhaustive account is, of course, Owen Thomas, *Cofiant John Jones, Talysarn*, ch. 11. Christmas Evans reckoned that the debate within Calvinism over the 'new system' proposed by Andrew Fuller and Dr Edward Williams altered the language of preaching, making it less biblical or inspired. See 'Agwedd Crefydd yng Nghymru', pp. 9–10.
34 Edward Davies, 'Traethawd ar Bregethu', *Y Dysgedydd* (1858), 165–9, 'Cymhwysderau Pregethwyr' and 'Cyfansoddiad Pregeth'; Matthews, *Bywgraffiad*, pp. xv–xvi. Also, Henry Rees, 'Traethawd ar Bregethu', in J. Hughes (ed.), *Y Pregethwr: Sef Deg ar Hugain*

o *Bregethau gan Weinidogion y Methodistiaid Calfinaidd* (Caernarfon, 1864).
35 *Bywgraffiad*, pp. 132–3.
36 *Cofiant . . . Ieuan Gwynedd*, pp. 279, 280, in a tribute to David Williams, Llanwrtyd.
37 David Owen (Brutus), *Wil Brydydd y Coed*, ed. Thomas Jones (Cardiff, 1949), esp. perhaps pp. 70–7, the hilarious 'pregeth y "wheel"' and ch. 16, pp. 178–9 on Jackery. Matthews, *Bywgraffiad*, p. xxxviii, refers to 'quacks'. He was confident that the public was sufficiently tough-minded not to be deceived by them. R. Tudur Jones perceived an element of the 'Jack' in Matthews himself: *Ffydd ac Argyfwng Cenedl: Hanes Crefydd yng Nghymru 1890–1914*, I (Swansea, 1981), p. 158.
38 'Pregethu', in David Owen, *Brutusiana: Sef Casgliad Detholedig o'i Gyfansoddiadau* (Llandovery, 1855), pp. 40–8.
39 Only Jones of Llan-gan, Glamorgan, of the Anglicans features in Matthews's pantheon, partly perhaps because Jones was related to Thomas Richard by marriage and had been an inspiration during Richard's early preaching career. See *Bywgraffiad*, pp. xxxv, 78–9; also pp. 6, 30, 45, 46, 57, 58, 62, 69, 72–3, 98 ff. Christmas Evans (n. 29 above), in identifying the major evangelical preachers of the past, had included seven Anglican clergymen but they had all flourished before 1790.
40 *Brutusiana*, p. 40. On the evangelical tradition within the Anglican Church in Wales, see Roger L. Brown, *The Welsh Evangelicals* (Cardiff, 1986). It was no accident that Owen, a Low Churchman, should dedicate *Brutusiana* to one of the most prominent of the preaching clergy, David Parry, vicar of Llywel, Breconshire.
41 Owen, *Brutusiana*, pp. 41, 42. It is fair to say that the other main Welsh Nonconformist denominations, the Independents and the Baptists, were more radical politically, notably on the issue of Church disestablishment. This had been Owen's *bête noire* since he had become a member of the Anglican Church in the early 1830s, probably through David Parry, having unsuccessfully sought ordination with both these denominations before this.
42 Owen, *Brutusiana*, pp. 44–6.
43 Matthews, *Bywgraffiad*, p. xxxv, re John Jones especially. See also n. 34 above.
44 Matthews, *Bywgraffiad*, pp. xxxii–xxxv, including also Jones of Llan-gan.
45 That Welsh literature itself often reflected the earlier English tradition. Thomas Rees, *Miscellaneous Papers on Subjects relating to Wales* (London, 1867), p. 25.

46 See above n. 28; literally, 'The Temple Lights'.
47 *Lampau y Deml*, pp. v–vi.
48 A remembrance sermon for Spurgeon by James Owen at Swansea conveyed the preacher's evangelical fervour and in passing bracketed him with Christmas Evans; see Thomas Lewis, *Pregethau gan y Diweddar Barch. C. H. Spurgeon, cyfieithedig gan y Parch. Thomas Lewis, Casnewydd, Gyda Chrybwyllion helaeth o Fywyd Mr Spurgeon* (Carmarthen, 1892), pp. xl–xli. Spurgeon's visits to Wales largely centred on the south and east (ibid., pp. xxvii–xxix). He was also popular in Scotland, though Highland audiences, typically according to Lewis, were unresponsive (ibid., p. xiv).
49 *Yr Eglwys o Ddifrif, gan y Parch. J. Angell James: Gyda Rhagdraethawd gan y Parch. Henry Rees* (Denbigh, 1849). See also Edwards, *Traethodau Llenyddol*, pp. 464–7; Thomas, *Cofiant y Parchedig Henry Rees*, II, pp. 923–4, for Hall and other influences.
50 D. Ben Rees, *Pregethwr y Bobl: Bywyd a Gwaith Owen Thomas* (Liverpool and Pontypridd, 1979), pp. 64–5; Edwards, *Traethodau Llenyddol*, pp. 356 ff.
51 *Bywyd a Llythyrau y Parch. Lewis Edwards*, p. 136. Glasgow University, too, became a place for talented Welsh Nonconformists to attend.
52 Owen Thomas, 'Rhagdraeth', p. xiii, noted Chalmers in particular but also added the names of other contemporary Scottish preachers whose delivery resembled the vivid experiential 'Welsh' style: Thomas Guthrie, Robert Smith Candlish and Dr McCleod (*sic*) [Norman Mcleod, DD, the Younger] all significant figures in the Disruption. Thomas, in addition, noted in England the preaching of Henry Melvill, canon of St Paul's.
53 Edwards, *Traethodau Llenyddol*, pp. 359–60, identifying Chalmers's style with that of Daniel Rowland.
54 *Bywyd a Llythyrau y Parch. Lewis Edwards*, pp. 462–7.
55 Ibid., pp. 145–6.
56 Ibid., ch. 6, esp. pp. 175–7.
57 Robert Gray, 'The Nonconformist nation: cultural networks and social space in autobiographies of Victorian Nonconformist ministers', *Social History Society Bulletin*, XXIV/1 (1999), 39.
58 Matthews, *Bywgraffiad*, pp. xxi, xxiii–xxiv.
59 Henry Lewis, *Can-Mlwyddiant y Tabernacl, Bangor* (Conwy, 1907), pp. 124–5.
60 Gwilym Rees, *Cofiant y Parch. Thomas Johns, DD* (Llanelli, 1929), pp. 192–4, comments on the ministry made in 1905, including a condemnation of growing English values on congregations. Johns's own ministry had begun about the time (in 1864) of Matthews's

essay after attending the Independent College at Brecon (ibid., ch. 8 and p. 71).
61 D. D. Williams, *Llawlyfr Hanes y Cyfundeb* (Caernarfon, n.d., c.1940), pp. 206–7. Matthews regarded himself as one of the 'tramps' or 'wandering gypsies' among the preaching ministry. J. J. Morgan, *Cofiant Edward Matthews, Ewenni* (Mold, 1922), p. 382.
62 Williams, *Llawlyfr Hanes y Cyfundeb*, pp. 208–10. A fixed pastorate would secure proper maintenance for the ministry, thereby enabling a minister to concentrate on spiritual duties.
63 Cf. D. Densil Morgan, *Christmas Evans a'r Ymneilltuaeth Newydd* (Llandysul, 1991), pp. 167–75 and Christopher B. Turner, 'Revivalism and society in the nineteenth century', in J. Obelkevich *et al.* (eds.), *Disciplines of Faith: Studies in Religion, Politics and Patriarchy* (London, 1987), pp. 311–23.
64 The revivals were often associated with the special inspiration of hitherto insignificant local preachers, for example, Dafydd Morgan in the Great Revival of 1859, as well as the 'giants', see Turner, 'Revivalism and society in the nineteenth century', pp. 312–14.
65 J. Rubin, *Religious Melancholy and Protestant Experience in America* (Oxford, 1994). It is expected that the Wellcome project into the history of mental health in north Wales, centred at Bangor, will offer some observations on this psychosis.
66 See, for example, *Y Geninen*, VI (1888), 49; *Ysgrifau . . . John Puleston Jones*, p. 19, for 'errors of perfectionism'.
67 R. Currie, A. D. Gilbert and L. Horsley, *Churches and Churchgoers: Patterns of Church Growth in the British Isles since 1700* (Oxford, 1977), pp. 54–7, 118–210.
68 D. Rees, 'Ymneilltuwyr yr Oes', in Glanmor Williams (ed.), *David Rees, Llanelli: Detholion o'i Weithiau* (Cardiff, 1950), pp. 5–9.
69 Ieuan Gwynedd Jones, *Communities* (Llandysul, 1987); most recently, his 'Smoke and prayer: identity and religion, Cwmafon in the nineteenth century', *Journal of Welsh Religious History*, VI (1998), 13–44; A. H. Williams, *Cymru Oes Victoria* (Cardiff, 1973).
70 W. R. Lambert, *Drink and Sobriety in Nineteenth Century Wales c.1820-c.1890* (Cardiff, 1983); Huw Walters, 'Y wasg gyfnodol Gymraeg a'r mudiad dirwest, 1825–50', *National Library of Wales Journal*, XXVIII/2 (1993), 153–95; Matthews, *Bywgraffiad*, chs. 20 and 21, for the part played by Thomas Richard.
71 Jones, *Cofiant . . . Edward Matthews*, chs. 7–9; Morgan, *Cofiant Edward Matthews*, pp. 294–7, on his radicalism but eventual Liberal Unionism; D. W. Bebbington, 'Religion and national feeling in nineteenth-century Wales and Scotland', *Studies in Church History*, XVIII (1982), 489–503.

72 W. T. R. Pryce, 'Migration and the evolution of culture areas: cultural and linguistic frontiers in north-east Wales, 1750 and 1851', *Transactions of the Institute of British Geographers* (1975), 96–103. Also, most recently, Sian Rhiannon Williams, 'Y Gymraeg yn y Sir Fynwy diwydiannol *c*.1800–1901', in Geraint H. Jenkins (ed.), *Iaith Carreg Fy Aelwyd: Iaith a Chymuned yn y Bedwaredd Ganrif ar Bymtheg* (Cardiff, 1998), ch. 7.
73 'Rhagdraeth', pp. viii–ix. It also saw the rise of the higher criticism which threatened the biblical literalism of the Welsh pulpit. See Iorwerth Jones, *David Rees Y Cynhyrfwr* (Swansea, 1971), p. 59.
74 'Rhagdraeth', p. x.
75 Williams, *Llawlyfr*, pp. 219–20.
76 Thomas Rees, *Miscellaneous Papers*, pp. 90–3.
77 Morgan, *Cofiant Edward Matthews*, pp. 163–4, 381–2, 409, 419; Jones, *Ffydd ac Argyfwng Cenedl*, I, chs. 6 and 7.
78 Jones, *Cofiant . . . Edward Matthews*, ch. 16.

~ 4 ~
In Pursuit of a Welsh Episcopate

ROGER L. BROWN

It is hardly surprising that the new bishop of Llandaff, Alfred Ollivant, was invited to lay the foundation stone of the newly rebuilt Lewis's School at Pengam, about 12 miles north of Cardiff. Not only was Ollivant the bishop, he was also a prominent educationalist, having served as vice-principal of St David's College, Lampeter, and as Regius Professor of Divinity at Cambridge. Thus, on the 28 May 1850, as recorded for us by *The Monmouthshire Merlin*, Bishop Ollivant preached at a service held at Gelligaer church before laying the foundation stone of the school. The bishop preached in Welsh, the paper recording 'the great approbation [of this sermon] . . . by those who were competent to judge . . . the purity of pronunciation and the correct style of the preacher'. It continued:

> the discourse was also marked with fine flows of lofty evangelical sentiment. Seldom has a discourse, delivered in the pure vernacular of Wales, with oratorical correctness and appropriateness of diction, been more seasonably gratifying to a congregation, than that given by his Lordship . . .

The sermon concluded, the stone duly laid, an address was given by the bishop in English. The Revd George Thomas, a man of independent means and the principal trustee, then read an address in Welsh to the bishop. This thanked him for the part he had taken in the day's events, and added a warm eulogy on the Welsh sermon delivered by the bishop. The newspaper continued its account: 'His Lordship, expressing himself too diffident as to his acquaintance with the Welsh language to attempt an impromptu address in that tongue, acknowledged the compliment which had been paid him, in English ...'[1]

Some days later, one Mr Horsman, the member for Cockermouth, a man described by Geoffrey Best as 'the self appointed scourge of the Establishment',[2] and a particular scourge of the Ecclesiastical Commission, was holding forth on the floor of the House of Commons. He first noted that the new bishop of Llandaff was still living in Cambridge, and demanded of Lord John Russell, the Prime Minister, whether he could offer any 'justification of such a departure from ecclesiastical usage and the obligations of episcopal duties?' In fact, we may note, at the time of Ollivant's appointment there was no episcopal residence, and the Ecclesiastical Commissioners were at this time still negotiating with the Revd George Thomas, mentioned above, for the sale of his house in Llandaff for this purpose.

Worse was to come. The Prime Minister, declared Horsman, had received considerable praise 'for having taken especial pains' to select a man for the see of Llandaff who was familiar with the Welsh language. But, he continued:

> I find that last week the foundation stone of a church was laid in Wales, on which an address composed in the Welsh language was presented to the Bishop of Llandaff, who was present; to which that Right Rev. Prelate replied in English, stating he was unable to speak Welsh. It is true that the Bishop had previously gone through the form or task of preaching a Welsh sermon; but at the close of the proceedings he apologised for being perfectly unable to converse in that language. As the public was led to believe that the noble Lord was desirous of selecting a prelate to fill the see of Llandaff who was well acquainted with the Welsh language, the second question I intend to ask is, whether the supposed familiarity of the present Bishop with it was one of the reasons for his being selected, and, since a grave deception seems to have been practised on the noble Lord, whether he will state by whom that deception was practised?[3]

Though Horsman was simply giving notice of questions he intended to raise at a later date, Lord John Russell replied, protesting about the unfairness of Horsman's attack on the bishop. He went on to explain the reason for Ollivant's appointment. He had heard Welsh protests that no Welsh-speaking bishops had been appointed for a century and more, and during this vacancy he had made enquiries with many persons acquainted with Wales as to whether there was a clergyman who not only spoke Welsh but also possessed episcopal qualifications. He was continually referred to Ollivant. He had found that Ollivant had been head of a college in Wales and also a parish priest in a Welsh benefice, 'and in that manner had become acquainted with the language and habits of the people of the Principality'. The bishop of Winchester and the archbishop of Canterbury had given Ollivant the highest testimonials, and though others had told Lord Russell that the new bishop of Llandaff held different political opinions from the Prime Minister, Russell still felt that if he could obtain for Wales a man such as Ollivant he 'ought to waive any consideration of the kind'. Then, he added: 'I think that it is very likely to be the case with a person who is not a native of Wales, and therefore cannot be expected to speak the Welsh language with the ease and fluency of a native.' He had not been deceived and he believed that Ollivant would prove to be an ornament to the bench of bishops and to be of the greatest service as a spiritual instructor of the people. But Horsman was no fool, and though his allegations were carefully exaggerated, there was also some truth in them.[4]

The incident at Gelligaer revealed a number of issues relating to the appointment of Welsh bishops which need to be examined, namely the desire for Welsh-speaking bishops for the four Welsh dioceses and the difficulties of obtaining such men. Indeed, we might even say clergy, for there was an equal concern about English-speaking clergy being appointed to Welsh parishes, with the result that the ministry to the parishioners was generally conducted by an ill-paid, Welsh-speaking curate.

A challenge to this state of affairs had been mounted in 1770 by the (significantly) London-based Welsh society, the Cymmrodorion. This challenge related to the appointment of a distinguished schoolmaster, the English-speaking Dr Bowles, to the Anglesey parish of Trefdraeth. It was thought that only five of its 500 inhabitants spoke the language of their incumbent. His defence, that Wales was a conquered nation, that it was proper to introduce the English language into the principality and that it was proper for the bishops to promote English speakers to Welsh parishes, was not accepted by the Court of Arches. However, though the dean of that court offered ways and means of preventing such abuses before a man was instituted, he had to accept that Bowles was beyond his court's jurisdiction as he had been properly inducted into the living.[5]

Bowles was not alone in offering such a defence. Bishop Copleston of Llandaff said much the same kind of thing in the 1830s.[6] Others carefully noted that the 1562 Act which permitted the translation of the scriptures into Welsh had stated that this concession was in order to extend the knowledge of the English tongue into Wales by allowing a comparison to be made between the two languages.[7]

In fact no Welsh speaker had been appointed to a Welsh see since 1702, though this was due more to political considerations than to antipathy towards the Welsh language. Throughout the eighteenth century, a number of Welsh-born men were certainly appointed to Welsh and English sees,[8] although it might be argued that few of the Welsh-speaking clergy possessed the background or political leverage likely to endorse their candidature for episcopal office.

The arguments used for the appointment of Welsh-speaking bishops were generally pragmatic. Article 24 of the Thirty-Nine Articles was appealed to, for this spoke about the use of a foreign tongue as a thing plainly repugnant to the Word of God. It was repeatedly argued that, if missionaries abroad learnt the language of their people, then the same principle ought to apply to Wales, though this proved to be a two-edged argument. The absurdity of a bishop's words at a confirmation having to be translated by a chaplain who would also have to preach instead of the bishop – the proper teacher of his diocese – was emphasized. It was also argued that it was unfair that the Welsh-speaking clergy were denied the prizes of their own church. Further arguments related to the numerical superiority of the Welsh language in many parts of Wales.[9] The real argument, however, was hardly ever mentioned. This, I suggest, related to the whole question of nationality. It was assumed that Wales was a nation, but it was accepted that its distinction as a nation was not so much because of boundaries and frontiers[10] ('for Wales see England', said a celebrated cross-reference in the *Encyclopaedia Britannica*[11]), but rather that it possessed its own historic language and thereby a culture and heritage far older and more distinguished than that of the English. Pragmatic arguments were important, but behind those arguments was a question of pride and the growing birthpangs of nationalism. The same arguments were used with equal effect to secure Welsh chaplains for prisons and Welsh-speaking judges on the Welsh circuits.

As the years passed, so another argument in favour of Welsh-speaking bishops came to the fore. The Church in the four dioceses had failed to stem the advance of Dissent. Although we know now that parts of Wales were more 'Church' than many parts of England, the spread of Nonconformity had put the Establishment in the shade. Who was to blame? One school argued it was the poverty of the Church, another that it was the Anglican episcopate which had given no effective leadership, failed to understand the religious aspirations and cultural modes of its people, and introduced their English-speaking families and friends into Welsh livings.[12] A Welsh episcopate, it was argued, would win back Nonconformists to the Church and make Wales a safe nation again for the Establishment. It was an argument delicately tuned by William Ewart Gladstone.

The demand for Welsh-speaking bishops, now articulated by the prosperous bourgeois Welsh establishments of London, Liverpool and Manchester, was sufficiently strong to ensure a specific clause in the Established Church Bill of 1836. The clause required the newly appointed Ecclesiastical Commissioners to prepare schemes that would ensure that all those appointed to Welsh-speaking parishes and to the bishoprics in Wales were conversant with the Welsh language. The latter requirement, however, was lost by an amendment proposed by the archbishop of Canterbury who argued that it was not requisite for a Welsh bishop to possess the knowledge of the Welsh language, as the duty of a bishop was not to act as the shepherd of the flock, but as the superintendent of the pastors.[13] So we may note that the whole question was now being suffused into a wider question, namely, what is a bishop? The archbishop's brief probably came from Bishop Bethell of Bangor, a High-Church and aristocratic ruler of his diocese. It was Bethell who informed those who attacked the appointment of these so-called 'Anglo-Welsh' bishops that as they were made by the crown they were attacking the royal prerogative and presumably guilty of *lèse-majesté*.[14]

Bethell's remark clearly indicates the sense of insecurity within the Anglo-Welsh establishment. Its protagonists knew they were vulnerable and open to criticism. A Reformed Church was breaking its own foundation rules. Bethell's comments might have been the more dogmatic because of the ever-growing public concern and comment about these issues. The Association of Welsh Clergy in the West Riding of Yorkshire, for example, held public meetings in the 1830s and in 1835 requested Sir Robert Peel that the old policy of appointing native Welshmen to Welsh sees, 'so ancient and just, productive of such unquestionable benefits to the Principality', be restored. A. J. Johnes, an impassioned and not always accurate writer, joined in with an open letter to Lord John Russell.[15]

On the death of Bishop Jenkinson of St Davids in 1840, it seemed to many in Wales that the appointed day of recompense had arrived. It was generally believed that Lord John Russell had pledged his party to honour that clause lost in the House of Lords. There was a groundswell of support in south Wales for the appointment of Bruce Knight, who virtually ran the diocese of Llandaff for an absentee bishop and was a Welsh speaker.[16] But in an age of political appointments he had the misfortune to be known as a Tory, like another would-be candidate, Archdeacon John Williams of Cardigan and the first rector of the Edinburgh Academy (and declared by Sir Walter Scott as the first schoolmaster in Europe). Williams believed he had received assurances from his party that he would be appointed to the next vacant Welsh bishopric.[17] Alas, Lord Melbourne and the Whigs were in office and Sir Benjamin Hall made it clear that a Whig appointment was needed because the clergy of south Wales were sufficiently subservient to follow their bishops in their political opinions.

In a desperate attempt to undo the archdeacon's Tory antecedents, his brother-in-law, the royal physician, Sir David Davies, wrote to Melbourne. In this letter he made clear that he had heard from various quarters that it was the intention of Her

Majesty to appoint a Welshman to the see of St Davids. This was a rumour which triggered off petitions from the Welsh societies in London and the Welsh inhabitants of Liverpool, from all parts of Wales, prompted by the newspapers, all requesting a Welsh-speaking bishop, with some actually naming the man of their choice. A deputation from Liverpool, consisting mainly of Members of Parliament and one Liverpool cleric, met the Prime Minister in London and put their case. Melbourne was embarrassed, for he had already offered the bishopric to Connop Thirlwall, possibly because his strong Whig voice would be an asset in the upper chamber. But the letter had been misdirected and Thirlwall had still to reply. Melbourne, astute politician that he was, managed to get out of his difficulty by a counter-attack: if there was such a strong desire for Welsh-speaking bishops, he enquired, why was there no movement or campaign in the Principality and among the Welsh clergy on this subject? It was unfair and untrue, and the Prime Minister might well have known it was an untruth. Nevertheless the Welsh took it to heart, and felt that they had to put their house in order for the next appointment.[18]

There is one sequel. David James of Liverpool, later to follow John Williams as warden of the Welsh Collegiate Institute at Llandovery, wrote to Thirlwall pointing out the implications of his appointment and begging him not to accept it. Although Thirlwall did not take his advice, the letter impressed him so much that he learnt Welsh.[19] His written Welsh was good, his spoken Welsh less so. The story is told of Thirlwall preaching at the consecration of a Cardiganshire church. The local squire being rather ignorant of the language asked one of his servants for his opinion of the bishop's sermon, adding that it was a pity that he had preached in Welsh. The reply was quick and devastating: 'Well, it wasn't Welsh where I was sitting.' Another comment made was that when he entered the pulpit he was looked upon as a conjuror who was performing some wonderful tricks.[20] These were private comments. In public the bishop was lauded and commended by the Welsh press and his clergy, so much so that many Englishmen assumed that it was as easy to acquire a speaking knowledge of Welsh as it was to obtain a knowledge of a classical language. It is a pity that Thirlwall's own comment was not more generally known: 'there is an immense difference', he wrote in 1870,

> between a native Welshman and one who has only acquired the language as a foreigner. A little study and exercise will very soon bring the Welshman up to a mark which the Englishman will never reach as long as he lives.[21]

But the Welsh flattery of Thirlwall was to have dire consequences.

The next episcopal vacancy, that of St Asaph in 1846, came at a difficult time for the Welsh Church. The Ecclesiastical Commission had proposed to unite the two northern dioceses in order to establish a new diocese at Manchester. These proposals had been made at a time when it was assumed that bishops were peers of the realm and therefore members of the upper chamber. But it was also at a time when bishops were so unpopular that it was thought any increase in their number might cause civil unrest. A long opposition had been mounted to these proposals to unite the two sees, and the arguments ranged from that of church antiquity and solemnity to that of nationalism. Bishop Carey died at a time when matters had reached a delicate impasse. However, Bethell of Bangor came to the rescue, and noting that there was nothing in the various Orders of Council to compel him to accept another see, declined to do so. The matter could only be resolved by appointing a new bishop, and Bishop Short of Sodor and Man was appointed, mainly because he had looked after the see during the long illness of his predecessor. Although an influential lobby of Welsh clerics wanted to press for a Welshman, the delicacy of the situation was such that Lord Powis, who led the opposition to the uniting of the sees, persuaded them to desist. And by and large they did, grateful that the bishopric was at least preserved.[22]

As Bishop Copleston of Llandaff lay dying, the Welsh lobby pondered the possibilities. They remembered Melbourne's comment about the lack of support within Wales, and it was now asserted strongly, especially by Archdeacon John Williams, that the premier, Lord John Russell, had made a promise in 1836 that he would appoint a Welsh-speaking bishop. It was also understood that Palmerston, or at least his adviser in episcopal appointments, Shaftesbury, who had spent time in Wales and had studied Welsh, would have appointed a Welsh speaker had there been a vacancy. Furthermore, it was thought that the name he had in mind was Thomas Thomas, vicar of Caernarfon. Editorials in the local press, petitions, memorials, the Bath Church of England Lay Association, the Clergy in the West Riding, a public meeting in London attended by the Welsh Members of Parliament and peers, all made the same point. John Williams, MP for Macclesfield, who had instigated the celebrated 1847 educational report, made a comment that was echoed by many in claiming for his fellow countrymen the same privileges which were unhesitatingly accorded to the 'New Zealander and to the Hindoo', namely of having bishops who were required 'to possess a competent knowledge of the language of the distant people among whom they are appointed to minister.' It was a dangerous argument, for while the Welsh were arguing for a native Welshman, they appeared to be saying that they would be satisfied with a person who had learnt the language, as had Thirlwall.[23] And thus Alfred Ollivant was appointed bishop of Llandaff in 1849.

Manchester-born, Cambridge-educated, Alfred Ollivant had been vice-principal of the new Anglican training college at Lampeter, and sinecure rector of one of its livings. By 1849, he was Regius Professor of Divinity at Cambridge, chosen for his pastoral rather than his academic abilities. During his time in Wales he had acquired a sufficient command of the Welsh language to enable him to take Welsh services and occasionally preach from a manuscript text. There is some evidence that he was the second choice, and that Lord John Russell had initially wished to appoint the bishop of Sodor and Man, Lord Auckland, to the vacant diocese, but had desisted when he saw the strength of the Welsh lobby. But Ollivant's Welsh was never particularly good, and by the end of his long episcopate he had quite given it up. While he claimed that his Welsh clergy never asked him to use it, it seems reasonably clear that they felt that he was more intelligible to their Welsh congregations when he spoke in English rather than Welsh. Significantly, Ollivant's attempts to preach in Welsh were characterized as resembling 'the first attempts of a schoolboy to read Greek'.[24]

The same lobby was marshalled again during the vacancy in Bangor in 1859, though it is interesting that there was some dissent from south Wales that a Welsh speaker was an absolute requirement. But the Welsh lobby was only reinforcing the opinion of Lord Derby, the Prime Minister, that a Welsh-speaking bishop was required. He was clearly convinced about this necessity, and he noted his requirements in this way: he needed a man tolerably familiar with the Welsh language and able to converse and preach in it; one who was not a High Churchman and one who was not a rabid political opponent, though, as he pointed out more delicately to the bishop of Llandaff, he wished to give a preference to a man who would generally support his government. Writing to Lord Powis he agreed that the man appointed must be able to preach in Welsh and use the language colloquially, but by this time he was finding it difficult to select a Welsh cleric who came up to his expectations. Eventually his choice fell on a Scotsman, James Colquhoun Campbell, who had been appointed to the wealthy Glamorgan parish of Merthyr Tydfil by his relations, the Bute family, and was now archdeacon of Llandaff.

It was known that Campbell had acquired a knowledge of the Welsh language during his time in Merthyr, but the warnings that his Welsh was nondescript were ignored. A large number of people believed that the blame (as they put it) for Campbell's appointment lay with Bishop Ollivant. John Richards of Bron Menai, Caernarfon, thus wrote an open letter to Lord Derby accusing him of having taken the advice of Ollivant about Campbell's linguistic fitness. 'How came your lordship for a moment to suppose that Dr Ollivant was himself competent to give an opinion on the subject?' he asked. 'To know a language accurately, as a scholar, is one thing,' he continued, 'but to use it freely and idiomatically in conversation, public speaking, and preaching, like a native, is quite another thing.' Campbell was doomed to be a good man in the wrong place, and an alien appointed over the heads of the native clergy.[25] Campbell's first Welsh sermon in Bangor Cathedral was said to have been an awful disappointment.[26] It was not that Derby had been deceived, rather he had taken the advice of people who lived in Wales but whose knowledge of the language was fragmentary and whose assumed competence had been fuelled by the flattery of the Welsh people themselves. It is also probable that a further consideration had held sway, namely to ensure that the man eventually appointed reached the standard of the English episcopate.

When Bishop Short announced that he would take advantage of the recently passed Episcopal Retirement Act, in 1870, Gladstone was Prime Minister. He lived on the edge of Wales, at Hawarden, and his ecclesiastical concerns had caused him to take a lively interest in the Welsh Church. His chief adviser in Welsh affairs, H. A. Bruce, later Lord Aberdare, Home Secretary, was brother-in-law to Bishop Campbell. Although it has been argued that two polemical books, the Nonconformist MP Henry Richard's published letters on the social and political conditions of the Principality of Wales, and Dean Henry Edwards's open letter to Gladstone entitled 'The Church of the Cymru', had made a powerful influence on his thinking about the need for a truly Welsh episcopate, Gladstone's mind appears to have been made up by 1856 at least. In that year he had replied to Richard Williams Morgan, curate of Tregynon, a man of patriotic views who was to become the first and self-appointed patriarch of Caerleon, that he hoped the day would come when all the Welsh bishops 'might be able to communicate with the people in their own cherished language', though (he added significantly) 'I think it would be an error to recognise a knowledge of the Welsh tongue as dispensing with any other of the still more essential qualifications for the episcopal office.'[27] What those two works possibly made clear to Gladstone was that this latter qualification was no longer a working proposition.

By 1870 the situation had changed dramatically. Disestablishment was in the air, Nonconformity united on the warpath against the Church, and a new patriotic movement was surging forward. The Church was numerically weak compared to Nonconformity, concluded Gladstone, because it lacked bishops who either understood the Welsh character, or had the preaching abilities of the great Nonconformist preachers. The strength of Nonconformity was in its pulpit. If bishops were able to outpreach the masters of the Nonconformist pulpit then, Gladstone firmly believed, not only would the Church be strengthened but Dissent would collapse as Nonconformists would be attracted back to 'Mother Church'.[28] Gladstone's argument may have seemed naïve, but this alone could explain his subsequent statements and manœuvres during the St Asaph vacancy. He was well aware that Ollivant and Campbell, good as they were in some aspects of their episcopate, had failed to qualify as Welsh speakers and that the whole of Wales knew it.

Gladstone loved making bishops. His concept of episcopacy was high, and the men he appointed were meant to be reforming bishops in the mould of Samuel Wilberforce. Although political considerations were not so important to Gladstone as to other premiers, he still had to bear this in mind, along with other considerations, such as the throne (for Victoria took a strong interest in these appointments), the universities (for equity of appointments) and the needs of the vacant diocese itself. Equally, bishops were peers of the realm, with seats in the House of Lords and with public duties to perform.

Once again, the Prime Minister was inundated with letters arguing the claims of different candidates, and the situation was almost as bad as that depicted later by a newspaper columnist who wrote on the subject of how to make oneself a Welsh bishop. Get your friends to write letters to the press on your behalf saying what a wonderful bishop you would make, he advised would-be candidates. If you were unable get to Oxford let your friends spell out that that was to the loss of that place rather than to yourself. There are numerous examples of such a practice.[29]

The appointment to St Asaph became for Gladstone one of acute concern. It was the weightiest episcopal problem which he had ever had to face, he wrote to Bruce, and writing to Bishop Browne of Winchester he exclaimed that he was anxious to obtain a Welshman who was not gravely deficient in any other requirement for a bishop. Such an admission must have caused Gladstone great anxiety: his great love of ecclesiastical appointments was turning sour. By contrast Bruce and many others were horrified by his stance. Bruce argued that he had often enquired whether there was any Welshman suitably qualified for episcopal office, even after making a large deduction from the average English standards of eminence, 'and I have utterly failed to discover what I sought'. Those Welsh clergymen who were regarded as leaders in the Welsh Church were men like James of Panteg, Thirlwall's former opponent, whom Bruce described as 'shallow, pretentious and wanting in honesty and dignity of character'. When Bruce learnt of some of the men Gladstone was actively considering he became almost speechless with horror. The need, he wrote, was not for impassioned oratory, but to improve the qualities of the clergy. A man of the popular preacher type would cause retrogression in the good work already being done in Wales by the other bishops. His arguments were crystallized in a newspaper cutting found in the Gladstone papers which Bruce possibly sent him: 'It would be a mistake to choose a man, however eloquent in Welsh, who could not on occasion address the House of Lords in intelligible English.' A Welshman, gentleman and scholar was required, whose appointment would be acceptable to local feeling and conducive to the good of the Church. It would not be to the honour of Wales to be represented in Parliament or convocation by bishops who could not hold their place on a perfect equality with their brethren from all parts of the kingdom.[30]

But how was such a man to be found? The same newspaper article noted the dilemma. The men within the Welsh Church most fitted for the episcopal bench by their upbringing and education were English-speaking, or had just a sufficient smattering of Welsh to take a service. But the Welsh speakers came mainly from the *gwerin* clergy, the peasant stock of the land, whose road to ordination lay through the provincial seminaries at Lampeter or St Bees rather than the universities, and whose social refinements were sadly missing.

Much could be made of the numerous men on Gladstone's lists of possibilities. At least two short lists were drawn up. H. T. Edwards, then vicar of Caernarfon and later dean of Bangor, was soon rejected on Bishop Ollivant's advice, who argued he was young and comparatively untried, though his social position and scholarship were identical to those of his younger brother who became bishop of St Asaph in 1889.[31] The person whom Gladstone preferred, though with some distaste, was John Griffiths of Llandeilo. He had achieved the rather dubious distinction of a Lambeth DD, the only reason for which appears to be that, as many Welsh Nonconformist ministers were collecting theirs from America, it seemed good to Archbishop Tait that he should return the compliment for the Welsh clergy. His background was *gwerin*, he was Lampeter-trained, and while Tait was impressed by his style of preaching but could not understand it, Thirlwall described it as 'miserably poor and commonplace'.[32] Even worse, Gladstone felt he was appointing a man who had masterminded his own campaign for the bishopric, asking influential people known to him to write to the Prime Minister seeking his appointment. He had moved too much in this matter, concluded Gladstone, even to the extent of informing people that the premier had urged him to present his claims and qualifications before he disposed of the vacancy.[33] But nevertheless Griffiths was a noted Welsh preacher, known throughout Wales and it was accepted that his appointment would be greeted with applause by the Welsh lobby, though not by the English establishment. Thirlwall wrote with an acid chill that if Gladstone wanted a popular Welsh preacher 'and would be content with something rather below the average, I think you would be safe in the choice of Dr Griffiths'.[34] But when Gladstone was about to nominate Griffiths to the crown for the vacant bishopric, a problem occurred and a rumour developed which possibly reached the ears of the queen herself. It appeared that the widowed Griffiths had entered into another relationship which was highly suspect. Griffiths was dropped like a brick, though he let it be known that his name had stood high on Gladstone's list.[35]

The eventual choice fell on Joshua Hughes, vicar of Llandovery. Knowing the kind of man Gladstone was looking for, Ollivant recommended him: Hughes had been his pupil at Lampeter. As a proctor in convocation he had spoken with sense and ability, he was a gentleman and his wife was a baronet's daughter. Though he was neither a university graduate nor a scholar, Hughes was nevertheless a man who could bear himself well in any society in which he might be placed. Others, however, noted his strong Welsh accent, disagreeable to English ears, or suggested he was respectable but little known in Wales, though Archbishop Tait felt he was the more important of the candidates on Gladstone's shortlist. There is little doubt that

Hughes was a good bishop in his diocese, but had little effect in the House of Lords or in the higher councils of the Church. Equally, it is unlikely that he would have achieved an archdeaconry in England. But Gladstone was more concerned to find a pastoral man for the vacant diocese than a peer of the realm, and had other considerations in mind than merely social. The tragedy was that Hughes found himself in the most aristocratic of the Welsh dioceses, where his taste for Welsh matters was resented and his social origins rather despised. But the real question raised by this election concerns what is a bishop, and here surely Gladstone got it right.[36]

By 1870, it was widely held that a Welsh bishop needed to be an indigenous Welsh speaker, although Disraeli's appointment in 1874 of Basil Jones, a Welsh landowner and archdeacon of York, to the diocese of St Davids reverted to the earlier policy. The appointments which followed were all of native Welsh speakers, though by this time the restructuring of secondary education in Wales and the provision of educational funding enabled increasing numbers of Welshmen to proceed to a university education. Many went on to holy orders. Nevertheless prejudices took time to die. John Owen, bishop of St Davids from 1897, of Nonconformist stock, had such a pronounced Welsh accent that Dean Vaughan considered he was 'absolutely unintelligible in English'.[37] But the real tragedy was that, by the 1890s, though the policy of native speakers was adhered to faithfully, some of those appointed saw their role in more ambivalent terms. Alfred George Edwards, elected bishop of St Asaph in 1889, faced the almost imminent prospect of the disestablishment of the Church in Wales, and reacted accordingly. It was not for him to compromise and accept a settlement with the Nonconformity he resented; rather his task was to fight disestablishment and keep his Church intact as the Church of England in Wales. And so he called in the old world of England to assist the new world of Wales. An emphasis was placed on the union between the churches, and it was argued incessantly that the four Welsh dioceses were simply part of the province of Canterbury rather than a semi-indigenous church.

Edwards's own relationship to the Welsh language was equally ambiguous, for though he used it, he clearly despised it. In this he was not alone, for the Welsh people had accepted the myth that the way to progress was through the English language, and the Church continued its role as one of the promoters of this myth. The influence of Edwards and his colleagues on the bench, whose preferment he promoted by ways which were often dubious, ensured that the Church of England in Wales remained precisely that.[38] A bishop was always to be addressed in English. Parry Jones, a Gwent clergyman who wrote some delightful books on the folk history of Wales, relates in one of these books how in the 1960s, almost at the end of his life, he actually spoke to a bishop in Welsh for the first time. Both he and his bishop were Welsh speakers from infancy, both used it within their own homes, and yet he spoke that day in their own native language with fear and trepidation lest his familiarity be rebuffed. It was not, but that incident reveals all too clearly the legacy of the past.[39] What Gladstone had done in identifying the Welsh Church with the nation and its language in 1870 had been undone within thirty years. And we still live in Wales with this strange ambiguity: can the Church in Wales be a national church and pay lip-service to the language?

I thus end with some questions. I have taken the view that 'nationality' in Wales was seen more in a linguistic than a geographical sense by the Victorians, or at least by the Church. The boundaries of the four dioceses were certainly not coterminous with the thirteen counties. But when did the concept of nationality become geographical rather than linguistic? Did it occur because of the diminishing use of the Welsh language, or because the thirteen counties were identified as an entity in late Victorian legislation, such as the 1881 Act to prohibit sales of intoxicating liquors on Sundays in Wales? I also wonder if Gladstone's choice of Joshua Hughes for St Asaph in 1870 helped further the concept of the bishop as a pastoral leader of his diocese rather than a great officer of state. They are interesting questions, but a wider context is needed to answer them than this particular chapter.

Notes

[1] *Monmouthshire Merlin* (1 June 1850).
[2] G. F. A. Best, *Temporal Pillars* (Cambridge, 1964), p. 386.

3. *Hansard*, 3rd series, III (1850), cols. 899–903.
4. Roger L. Brown, 'Laying the foundation stone of Lewis' School, Pengam: an episcopal sequel', *Gelligaer*, XIII (1990), 12–17.
5. Idem, 'Pastoral problems and legal solutions in the Established Church in Wales', in Norman Doe (ed.), *Essays in Canon Law* (Cardiff, 1992), pp. 9–13; *Depositions and Arguments in the Case of the Churchwardens of Trefdraeth against Dr Bowles* (London, 1773); Geraint H. Jenkins, ' "Horrid unintelligible jargon": the case of Dr Thomas Bowles', *Welsh History Review*, XV (1991), 494–521.
6. Edward Copleston, *Charges to the Diocese of Llandaff* (1836), pp. 23–4; also (1845), p. 9.
7. 5 Elizabeth c. 28, s. 3.
8. John Evans, appointed bishop of Bangor in 1702, was translated to Meath in Ireland in 1716. Bishop Wynne of St Asaph, 1715–27, possibly understood but did not speak Welsh, while John Harris of Llandaff, 1729–38, and Richard Trevor of St Davids, 1744–52, were both born in Wales but do not appear to have been Welsh-speaking. Trevor was later bishop of Durham.
9. Joseph Morgan, *The Rev. David James of Panteg* (Pontypool, 1925), pp. 14–15; Daniel Jones, *Welsh Bishops for Wales: An Essay on the National and Scriptural Claims of the Established Church in Wales to be Governed by Welsh Bishops* (Llandovery, 1851); The Association of Welsh Clergy in the West Riding of Yorkshire, *Reports* (1852), p. 31; (1854), pp. 38–41; (1856), pp. 55–6.
10. Compare Bishop Basil Jones's assertion in his 1886 *Charge to the Clergy of the Diocese of St Davids* that Wales was no more than a 'geographical expression' (p. 23). Jones was speaking in the context of the proposed disestablishment of the Welsh Church and sought to emphasize its identity with the Church of England.
11. Quoted in Kenneth O. Morgan, *Rebirth of a Nation: Wales 1880–1980* (Oxford and Cardiff, 1981), p. 3.
12. The first school is typified by Archdeacon Bevan of Hay, a wealthy squarson, and the second by the Welsh patriot, A. J. Johnes, and many of the Welsh clergy such as Dean Edwards of Bangor or David Howell, later dean of St Davids.
13. The clause relating to Welsh parochial appointments was enacted by 6 & 7 William IV c. 77, s. xi, but clarified by the 1838 Pluralities Act (1 & 2 Victoria c. 106, s. ciii–civ).
14. Christopher Bethell, 'A letter to the clergy of the county of Anglesey' (unpublished, London, 1837), pp. 5, 8.
15. Evan Evans, *Diwygiad yr Eglwys Sefydledig yn Nghymru* (Liverpool, 1837); Association of the Welsh Clergy, *Report* (1855),

p. 24; A. J. Johnes, *A Letter to Lord John Russell on the Operation of the Established Church Bill* (London, 1836), *passim*; Morgan, *David James*, pp. 12–20.

16 *Carmarthen Journal* (24 July 1840), 3; *Cardiff and Merthyr Guardian* (25 July 1840), 2; (1 August 1840), 3; *Welshman* (7 August 1840), 2; *John Bull* (12 February 1848), 103.

17 Maxwell Fraser, 'Sir Benjamin Hall and Lady Hill in the 1840s', *National Library of Wales Journal*, XIV (1965), 35; Letter from Lord Bute to J. B. Bruce, 7 October 1836, NLW Bute Papers, L79/126.

18 J. C. Thirlwall, *Connop Thirlwall* (London, 1836), pp. 108–14; letter from Benjamin Hall to Lord Melbourne, 11 July 1840, and letter from Sir David Davies to Lord Melbourne, 18 July 1840, in the Melbourne Papers, Windsor Castle, items 74/109 and 72; *Cardiff and Merthyr Guardian* (25 July 1840), 3.

19 Morgan, *David James*, pp. 32–9.

20 David Evans, *Atgofion* (Lampeter, 1904), p. 143.

21 Letter from Thirlwall to Gladstone, 17 January 1870, Gladstone MSS, British Library, 44424/20.

22 Roger L. Brown, *Lord Powis and the Extension of the Episcopate* (Cardiff, 1989).

23 Letter from John Williams to David James, 27 September 1849, in Letters from the Llanbadarnfawr Parish Chest, NLW, typescript, p. 24.

24 *Carnarvon and Denbigh Herald* (18 June 1859), 6; cf. (30 April 1859), 6; *Western Mail* (18 December 1882), 3.

25 Letters from Lord Derby to Lord Newport, 25 April 1859; Derby to Ollivant, 25 April 1859 in Derby Papers, Liverpool Records Office, 188/1, fos. 34, 9–12.

26 *Carnarvon and Denbigh Herald* (30 April 1859), 6; *Yr Haul* (1896), 1; letters from Derby to Powis, 2 and 4 May 1859, City of Liverpool Library, Letter Books of the 14th Earl of Derby, 920/DER/188/1, fos. 36–7, 40–1.

27 Quoted in *Cardiff and Merthyr Guardian* (1 November 1856), 7.

28 Letters from Gladstone to Tait, 7 January 1870, Gladstone MSS 44220/144; Gladstone to Thirlwall, 5 January 1870, Gladstone MSS 44538/41; cf. Bruce to Gladstone, 14 January 1870, Gladstone MSS 44086/86.

29 *Western Mail* (11 June 1874), 8.

30 Letters from Gladstone to Bruce, 12 January 1870, Gladstone MSS 44086/82; Gladstone to Bishop Browne of Winchester, 24 February 1870, Gladstone MSS 44115/16; Bruce to Gladstone, 8 January 1870, 14 January 1870, Gladstone MSS 44086/70, 86; newspaper cutting at Gladstone MSS 44425/127.

31 Letter from Ollivant to Gladstone, 20 January 1870, Gladstone MSS 44424/129.
32 Letters from Tait to Gladstone, 10 February 1870, Gladstone MSS 44330/153; Thirlwall to Gladstone, 26 January 1870, Gladstone MSS 44424/182.
33 Letters from Gladstone to Cawdor, 13 January 1870, 1 February 1870, Gladstone MSS 44424/92, 221; Gladstone to Ollivant, 18 January 1870, Gladstone MSS 44424/115; cf. Griffiths to Campbell, 17 January 1870, Gladstone MSS 444086/102.
34 Letter from Thirlwall to Gladstone, 26 January 1870, Gladstone MSS 44424/182.
35 Letters from Thirlwall to Gladstone, 15 February 1870, Gladstone MSS 44424/182; T. Thirlwall to Thirlwall, 25 February 1870, Gladstone MSS 44425/138.
36 Letters from Ollivant to Gladstone, 7 February 1870, 8 February 1870, 22 February 1870, 2 March 1870, Gladstone MSS 44424/256, 262, and 44425/78, 168; Tait to Gladstone, 10 February 1870, Gladstone MSS 44330/153. See also Matthew Cragoe, 'A question of culture: the Welsh Church and the bishopric of St Asaph 1870', *Welsh History Review*, XVIII (1996), 228–54.
37 Letter from Randall Davidson to Lord Salisbury, quoting a letter of Dean Vaughan, 19 January 1897, Salisbury Papers, Hatfield House.
38 G. Hartwell Jones, *A Celt Looks at the World* (Cardiff, 1946), pp. 19–20, 74–5; Roger L. Brown, *David Howell* (Denbigh, 1998), pp. 201–9, 232–3, 235; idem, 'Traitors and compromisers: the shadow side of the Church's fight against Disestablishment', *Journal of Welsh Religious History*, III (1995), 35–53.
39 D. Parry Jones, *A Welsh Country Parson* (London, 1975), pp. 83–4.

~ 5 ~
Welsh Nationalism and Anglo-Catholicism: The Politics and Religion of J. Arthur Price (1861–1942)

FRANCES KNIGHT

John Arthur Price was a man for whom the themes of religion and national identity were always intimately connected. First and foremost, J. Arthur Price was a Welsh nationalist. He took up the cause while at Oxford in the early 1880s and ended his days as a supporter of the newly founded Welsh Nationalist Party, later to become Plaid Cymru. His political beliefs dovetailed neatly with his Anglo-Catholicism. This was the creed to which he was deeply devoted, believing that it was essential for the spiritual health of the Welsh Church that it be invigorated by Anglo-Catholicism once it had thrown off the shackles of Canterbury. Price was not, however, a priest or a politician, although as a young man he had been attracted to the possibility of a political career, and he did once consider standing as the Liberal candidate for Denbigh Boroughs.[1] He earned his living as a chancery barrister, and supplemented it with regular journalism. He became an expert on canon law, and played a significant part in drawing up the constitution of the disestablished Church in Wales. His journalistic output would have made his writings familiar to the late nineteenth- and early twentieth-century readers of *The Saturday Review*, *The Church Times*, *The Manchester Guardian*, *The South Wales Star* and *The Welsh Outlook*.

Arthur Price never became a central figure in either Welsh politics or the Welsh Church. He was close to many who were at the centre, and felt some bitterness about the extent to which he was sidelined. He remains an obscure man, not famous enough even to merit an entry in *Who's Who*,[2] although he is mentioned briefly in the standard works on early twentieth-century Welsh politics, most noticeably those by Kenneth Morgan.³ Perhaps it is the fate of lawyers to be forgotten, even when their legal work lives on, and of journalists to be disregarded almost as soon as the ink is dry on their final article. Yet Arthur Price is an intriguing figure; a nationalist who maintained faith in that cause when many around him abandoned it, and a churchman who vigorously worked for disestablishment when most of his fellow Anglicans were either doubtful or hostile. As an apparently monoglot English speaker and long-term resident in England, he made a strange advocate of Welsh language and culture, but that is part of the paradox that made him the person he was. Price was certainly not all that he appeared on the surface; in the view of his nephew, who wrote his obituary for *The Church Times*, 'this sedate barrister was a revolutionary at heart'.⁴

Arthur Price was in many ways an unlikely revolutionary. He was born on 20 November 1861, the son of a Shrewsbury solicitor. On his father's side, the family came from Shropshire. But his mother was from Meirionnydd, and so was his future wife, Emily Foster. Due to his mother's connections, it was Barmouth that Price regarded as his Welsh home. Yet Price only ever lived in Wales in the twilight of his life, moving from London to escape the bombing in 1941, and dying at Trawsfynydd on 4 June 1942. For the whole of the rest of his life, Wales remained a holiday destination, and he kept a house for that purpose in Barmouth.⁵

Price had been educated at Shrewsbury School, where he was regarded as sufficiently responsible to be appointed a praeposter. He went from there to Balliol College, Oxford, where he spent five years, reading classics and modern history. He became vastly knowledgeable in both subjects, and was a lifelong devourer of new history books. He was hugely disappointed with his second-class degree, and after a period of uncertainty, during which he failed to obtain a job on a London newspaper, he went to London to read for the bar.⁶

He was called to the bar in 1890, and continued to practise law at Lincoln's Inn until he was well into his seventies. As a young man, Price had hoped that a law school might be founded at Aberystwyth, and that this would give rise to a Welsh bar.⁷ He also hoped that he would be able to join the north Wales law circuit, but was advised against it by a leading Wrexham solicitor, probably because of his lack of Welsh. 'Shall the sons of the soil be as strangers in the land of their forefathers' graves?'[8] Price wrote vexedly to his friend, the historian, J. E. Lloyd, after it had become clear that there were no legal openings for him in north Wales. In the end, Price made his home in Muswell Hill. He became part of the London Welsh élite, keeping in close touch with Welsh Liberal MPs at the New Reform and the National Liberal Club, and regularly attending and speaking at the meetings of the Honourable Society of the Cymmrodorion. He regarded himself as one of the best friends that Wales had in London, and it rankled that, although he was often asked for subscriptions, he was not always invited to major Welsh events.[9]

What was it that turned Arthur Price into a Welsh nationalist? In part, it may have been a reaction against his education as an English gentleman. In an article he wrote in 1918 he blamed Oxford University for making a young Welshman or a young Scotchman (*sic*) look at the political problems of his own country through the eyes of a cultured Englishman.[10] Equally important was his conversion to the cause of Welsh home rule, which forced him to abandon the Tory politics that he espoused in his early twenties, when he spoke at Primrose League meetings.[11] Price's Tory phase seems to have waned in the spring of 1890, when Liberal fortunes rose as David Lloyd George was returned at Caernarfon.[12] Before this, however, Price had made something of a name for himself on Tory platforms. His first public-speaking engagement in Wales was in December 1887, when he addressed the Newtown Workingmen's Conservative Club on the theme of 'Conservative policy and Welsh radicalism', a title that hints at something of Price's future direction. Much of the hour-and-a-half long speech was an attack on the Welsh Liberal Tom Ellis, whom at this period Price detested. 'I continued to make my audience more bitter against Ellis than I am myself, which is saying something.'[13] Ellis, nicknamed the 'Parnell of Wales', was one of the two leading lights in the late nineteenth-century Liberal Party in Wales (the other being Lloyd George).[14] Nine months later, Price heckled Ellis when Ellis spoke at a radical meeting in Barmouth. 'I shouted "stuff" in the midst of one of his sentences, whereat he glared at me and hurled some sentences at my devoted head.'[15] Over the next few days Price tried to organize a Tory counter-demonstration, and was urged by local Tories to learn Welsh so that 'I should really be a power in my fatherland.'[16]

During the 1890s, J. Arthur Price's antipathy towards Ellis was somewhat unexpectedly transformed into a lively friendship, although there were strains.[17] Ellis was MP for Price's 'home' constituency of Meirionnydd; by 1891 Price was writing to him affectionately as 'my own dear MP'.[18] They were by this time both closely involved in Cymru Fydd, the Young Wales movement, which formed its first branch in London in 1886, and flourished across Wales during the next decade.[19] Price had become involved with Cymru Fydd while he was still a Tory, when the editor of the Cymru Fydd journal asked him for a contribution, 'as he is going to give the other side a hearing'.[20] Soon, however, Price was converted to the cause, and he remained a regular contributor. His change of political allegiance was, however, by no means unproblematic. He wrote to Lloyd about it on National Liberal Club notepaper, with the address crossed through.

> The crossed out address indicates a terrible change in my political views, does it not! But though I am with the radicals, I am not of them. Let me tell you that though I am thoroughly with them politically none exhibits a more hearty contempt than I do for the South Wales Radical MPs . . . brought up . . . in the narrowest sectarianism, they cannot rise to the level of statesmanship . . . of course there are exceptions, and I do except Ellis and Lloyd George whom I like very well.[21]

This new regard for Ellis was to be severely strained, however, by Ellis's decision, in July 1892, to accept the post of Junior Lord of the Treasury and Deputy Whip in Gladstone's last administration. Ellis's action provoked much comment in Wales, for acceptance of a government post inevitably compromised the extent to which he could continue to press his nationalist claims.[22] Price was horrified at this betrayal of the cause; he wrote to Lloyd that 'all hope of Welsh Nationalism doing anything for some time ended when Ellis grasped the Saxon gold'.[23] Not unnaturally, Price played down this episode in the appreciation he wrote of Ellis in 1907. He commented circumspectly that a few of Ellis's young admirers had considered that the leader of Cymru Fydd should not identify himself with the government, but that they were not noticed.[24] In fact, he always regarded Ellis's decision as marking the eclipse of nationalist fortunes. It is unlikely that he ever forgave Ellis for failing to share his own belief that, whether in print or on the platform, all other questions should be subordinated to making the case for home rule.[25] With Ellis's acceptance of a government position, it seemed to Price, as to others, that Wales had lost its Parnell.

As is well known, Ellis's early death in 1899 was a considerable blow to Welsh nationalism, coinciding more or less with Lloyd George also turning his back on the cause.[26] Despite the tensions that had marked their relationship, for the rest of his life Price did his best to keep the memory and the political legacy of Ellis alive. Many of his articles pay homage to Ellis, and also to Ellis's great political influences, the Italian nationalist Joseph Mazzini and the Irish nationalist Thomas Davis. Price seems to have persuaded himself that Ellis was the greatest politician that Wales had ever produced, and that he had preached 'the most startling political gospel that [Wales] had heard since the days of Owen Glyndwr [sic]'.[27] His veneration of Ellis increased as his disillusionment grew with the next generation of Liberal politicians. Towards the end of his life, however, Price's doubts about Liberal politics resurfaced, and he claimed that 'nothing in my youthful days surprised me more than Tom Ellis' pathetic belief that a complete measure of Welsh Home Rule would be granted to Wales by a Liberal Government'.[28]

Price's own political beliefs were, however, much moulded on those of his hero. Like Ellis, Price was a passionate advocate of Irish as well as Welsh home rule, which he wished to see achieved with continued allegiance to the crown. He thought the monarchy important because the Welsh had freely chosen to give their allegiance to it.[29] Like Ellis, he believed strongly in the disestablishment of the Welsh Church. He was a supporter of European co-operation, and the rights of small nations. Price was also a passionate campaigner for women's suffrage, and considered that Mrs Pankhurst was a saint.[30] He wanted to see the development of a distinctively Welsh ethos within Welsh education,[31] the promotion of the language and equality of opportunity for every boy and girl in Wales. He had strong views about the writing and teaching of history, and lambasted the history departments of the University of Wales for being tied to the historical theories of Oxford and Cambridge. Like Ellis, he had a vision of Wales that embraced cultural, literary, philosophical and spiritual dimensions.[32] But Price's vision, and his primary argument for nationalism, was always largely based on history. He stated his case in an article for *The Welsh Outlook* in 1921.

> The great argument for Welsh Home Rule is that Wales is a nation with a language and traditions different from those of England, and that past history has proved that, under the centralized system of English Government, Welsh national character will not have full (or fair) development . . . We are told that the Poles, the Czechs and the Magyars are ancient nations. But not one of them is as old as the Welsh. By the side of the Welsh, the French and Scotch [sic] are modern nations. Cymru had all the essentials of a political nation except a united government, before England in any sense existed.[33]

History was the principal weapon in the armoury of Price's writings about Wales. He promulgated the remarkably common approach to Welsh historiography which emphasized lost glories, a difficult present and a glorious future.[34] Price tended to plunder the past in order to make political points about the present. He was silent on other, more practical aspects of the home rule question, for example its economic implications, which were being discussed at this period by politicians like E. T. John.

Up until December 1921, Price never missed an opportunity to put the case for Welsh home rule in the journal to which he was most devoted, *The Welsh Outlook*.[35] Initially, believing that the war was being fought to secure the right of small nations to self-determination, he had been optimistic that home rule would be achieved after its conclusion. By October 1916, however, he was expressing unease about the likely outcome, in a tone that was grimly prophetic. 'Is the War really tending to a greater liberty, to a more vigorous realisation of the principles of nationalism, to a greater respect for the tender conscience,' he wrote, 'or are we drifting into a reaction which will enthrone the militarist state above nationality and conscience alike?'[36] Price was a sharp critic of what he saw as the unchecked rise of state power, something he associated with Protestantism. It had come into being in England when Henry VIII broke with Rome, he contended, and in Germany when 'Luther magnified the rights of small German princelings against the canon law of the Church and the customary law that safeguards the peasant's homestead.'[37] Now it was resurgent everywhere under the influence of Hegel, and the assertion of the rights of nationalities against the despotism of states offered, he believed, one of the few effective checks to safeguard the future.

By September 1918, with the end of the war just weeks away, Price was forced to admit in print that the whole subject of nationalism in the British Isles was under a cloud. Nor did it appear that Irish home rule was to be delivered; indeed Price was vitriolic on the opposition coming from Ulster: 'a group of renegade Gaels in the north east of Ireland, whose one aim is to oppress their fellow Celts and to pretend to be Anglo-Saxons'.[38] Although the fortunes of Welsh home rule appeared to rally briefly in the summer of 1919, with a well-attended conference on the subject at Llandrindod Wells, by the early 1920s the Welsh political agenda was moving in other directions. Furthermore, the growing strength of Labour in south Wales was leading to fears in the north that the projected Welsh parliament would hand over control to the 'Bolsheviks of the South'.[39]

It seems likely that Arthur Price's excessive and repetitive treatment of the home rule theme, as well as the changing political climate, caused his work to be used rather less frequently by *The Welsh Outlook* in the years after 1922. His proposed series on 'Great nationalists' never progressed further than the first article.[40] The journal's editorial stance was becoming decidedly less sympathetic. A leader of February 1921 seems to contain a veiled attack on Price: 'A few enthusiasts have for a generation been talking about Welsh Home Rule, but the fact remains that they are very generally regarded as foolish, if harmless dreamers, whose facts and arguments are hardly worth attention.'[41] *The Welsh Outlook* had traditionally been a Liberal organ, and this distancing of itself from the nationalist cause, reflecting as it did the deeper strains within the Liberal Party, no doubt caused Price's disillusionment with the party to crystallize.

From about this time Price's Liberal Party allegiance began to be severely tested. Lloyd George had long forsaken the nationalist cause, in Price's view abandoning a place in history with Llewelyn the Great and Owain Glyndŵr to become instead 'a great English reforming statesman'.[42] Price's long-time friend, Llewelyn Williams, the former editor of the nationalist newspaper *The South Wales Star*, had joined the Asquithian Liberals after falling out with Lloyd George over the issue of conscription in 1916. Meanwhile, E. T. John, the person whom Price regarded as 'the best Welsh Home Ruler alive',[43] had joined the Labour Party in 1917. It seems doubtful that Price, as a former Tory who held old-fashioned beliefs about class harmony, and whose economic views were regarded by at least one of his friends as 'mildly reactionary',[44] ever seriously considered throwing in his lot with socialists.

It was the Welsh Nationalist Party, Plaid Genedlaethol Cymru, founded at Pwllheli in August 1925, that was to become J. Arthur Price's final political resting place. Price was, as D. Hywel Davies has pointed out, the link between Cymru Fydd and Plaid Cymru.[45] By the early 1930s (probably earlier), he had become an assiduous attender of the Nationalist Party's summer schools. In January 1930, Saunders Lewis, the party's president, invited him to join a committee of the party's legal experts to consider how the objective of dominion status for Wales should be attained.[46] 'The Welsh Nationalist Party stops Welsh politics from growing absolutely grey,'[47] he told his friend the former Liberal MP Ellis Davies in 1935. He wrote a lengthy letter to J. E. Lloyd about levels of alcohol consumption among Plaid Cymru members. Whilst Saunders Lewis, Ambrose Bebb, and the rest were not total abstainers, as Lloyd was, 'they drink far more mildly than do the older Welsh Liberals. I do not think that from what I saw of them at Machynlleth that any of them drink spirits.'[48] Price must, however, have been regarded with ambivalence by some in the party, who were anxious to dissociate themselves from the failed nationalist movements of the past.⁴⁹ After his conversion to the Welsh Nationalist Party, Price announced that it was this party that stood for the ideals of Tom Ellis and, the by then also deceased, Llewelyn Williams. In 1929, after the intervention of a Liberal MP whom he particularly despised – Hopkin Morris – in the Prayer Book debate, Price unleashed a fierce attack on the University of Wales-educated Liberal MPs, whose politics, he suggested, had 'sunk to the level of an Orange Lodge'.⁵⁰ It evidently pained Price that the University of Wales, founded as it had been on nationalist principles, should be producing graduates who placed religious bigotry before nationalism. Four years earlier he had described Sir Harry Reichel, the principal of the University College of North Wales, Bangor, as 'a wild Orange dog . . . this man hates Christian civilisation with a deadly hatred and you have the result in modern Wales'.⁵¹ He urged the university to rally to Saunders Lewis, the prospective candidate for the University of Wales's parliamentary seat.

Privately, however, Price was less enthusiastic about Saunders Lewis, and his letters to Ellis Griffiths sometimes betrayed signs that he disapproved of the party leader. Like others in the party, he did not share Lewis's view that if there was no Plaid Genedlaethol Cymru candidate standing, one should abstain from voting.⁵² The 1935 general election was the last that Price lived to see. In London he voted Liberal, presumably feeling that the London Liberals were not as bad as the Welsh ones. He used his Oxford University vote, where no Liberal was standing, in favour of his old adversary in the disestablishment debate, the Conservative Lord Hugh Cecil, and of the Independent candidate, a Mr Herbert. He consoled himself at the poor showing of Plaid Genedlaethol Cymru's only candidate in the election, J. E. Daniel (who polled 6.9 per cent in Caernarfonshire⁵³) by pointing out to Ellis Davies that Daniel had doubled his share since 1931. He rejected Ellis Davies's scepticism about whether the party would ever return an MP.

> You say that the Nationalist Party will have to wait seventy years before they return a member. I may remind you that that opinion was widely expressed in 1910 after the suffragette agitation had begun that women would have to wait twenty or even forty years for the vote.⁵⁴

In fact, neither Ellis Davies's pessimism nor Price's optimism was well founded; Welsh nationalism, in its new guise, had to wait a further thirty-one years for success at the Carmarthen by-election.

Price, now aged seventy-five, was somewhat ambivalent about Saunders Lewis's controversial decision, in company with Lewis Valentine and D. J. Williams, to start a fire at the RAF Bombing School on the Llŷn peninsula early on the morning of 8 September 1936, and then report their action at the local police station.[55] Price explained his position in letters to Ellis Davies. 'Had I been asked my opinion I should have advised them not to do it. But then I am old fashioned. At any rate they acted finely by not putting up some people to do the business on the sly.'[56] He hoped that the government would not rebuild the aerodrome 'since to do so is to offer a temptation to excited youths again to set it on fire . . . the government ought not to put temptation in people's way'.[57] When the retrial of Lewis, Valentine and Williams was moved to the Old Bailey, Price made an unsuccessful attempt to act for them. He was thwarted by another London-Welsh barrister, Alun Pugh, who told him that he 'could do no good by interfering in anyway . . . as Pugh is a close personal friend of Saunders Lewis and a generous subscriber to the Party's funds, I could of course do no more.'[58] Price evidently considered that the defence at the Old Bailey trial, which resulted in the defendants serving nine-month sentences in Wormwood Scrubs, had been mishandled. He chose, however, not to dwell on legal failure, but to draw a parallel with the 'blood of the martyrs as the seed of the Church'; the sufferings of the nationalists would, he believed, sow the seed of nationalist revival.[59]

It hardly needs to be said that, during the lifetime of Arthur Price, religion was a hotly contested topic of public discussion in Wales, and that it impinged directly on the political agenda. Price had been born and raised in the Church of England. As was perhaps inevitable for a late nineteenth-century product of Jowett's Balliol,[60] he experienced some degree of religious doubt in his early twenties, but this passed off by the end of the 1880s. He read Edward Gibbon and became 'most impressed with early Christianity, even under his sarcastic description. What a comfort to human life an *unnationalized* Christianity must have been.'⁶¹ This liberal in politics did not however become a liberal in theology, and certainly in later life he tended to chastize those whose religious opinions he regarded as indefinite. He remained committed to the Anglo-Catholic position, was a worshipper at St Albans, Holborn, and was an associate member of both the Holborn and the Highgate, Finchley and Muswell Hill branches of the English Church Union.⁶² Price remained until his death on the editorial staff of *The Church Times*, which was then an Anglo-Catholic newspaper.⁶³ He was *The Church Times*'s legal correspondent, reporting the proceedings of consistory courts in which issues of importance to Anglo-Catholics were being discussed. He reviewed, wrote special articles on English and Welsh religious history, and leading articles, particularly on the Welsh Church, under various pen names which included 'Aligius' and 'Cambrensis'.

The religious views of the thirty-year-old Price are conveyed well in a letter that he wrote to Tom Ellis in 1891, a year when they were on good terms. Ellis, like many of Price's associates, was a Calvinistic Methodist.

> Don't also think too hardly of Welsh ritualism. I hate its narrowness, its semi-restriction of salvation to its own path as much as you do. I think it loathsome. Still it has this good in it. It is making the Welsh curate a democrat (at least in his own Church) and it is giving him an enthusiasm – a belief that he has a real mission to the people and a feeling of superiority to the squire . . . It is also in a way helping disestablishment because it makes him feel that the Church is superior to the state . . . I feel that ritualism is necessary to give a force to the Church to enable it to outlive disestablishment. A Church founded by sixteenth century Englishmen of doubtful theology and more doubtful morals would have jolly little chance of outliving disestablishment; but a Church whose members truly or partly have persuaded themselves that they are the old British Church must in the end be a *national force* in Wales.⁶⁴

Even during the Cymru Fydd days, when on the surface, at least, they were supposed to be pulling in the same direction, Price found Lloyd George's religious attitudes offensive, and the seeds were sown for the antipathy that he would later feel towards the future Prime Minister. He poured out his disgust at

Lloyd George's mockery of Anglicanism in another lengthy letter to Tom Ellis in November 1891, written after Lloyd George had made a speech at Rhyl.

> I think the way he ridiculed the doctrine of Apostolic Succession was grossly insulting . . . my dear Ellis . . . unless I tell you how I feel on religion I fear I cannot show you how George's remarks affect me. Naturally I believe I am a Presbyterian. I like the Presbyterian form of Church government, as in Scotland and among the Welsh CM [Calvinistic Methodists]. In many points I think it more scriptural than the Church. Unfortunately, I say it with regret, I cannot accept the scriptures as Nonconformists do. I feel the difficulties too much and therefore I am bound either to give up religion or to look to a Church to justify my belief in scripture. Believing in the validity of Anglican orders I can myself accept the scriptures through the Church. I dare say you will think this a coward's creed. I dare say it is. At any rate I am no bigot. To me subjectively this doctrine religiously appeals; but I can almost envy the man who does not need it. At any rate I am convinced that to confine salvation to a Church with valid orders is an absurdity and judging from results heaven's blessing would seem to be far more on Welsh Presbyterianism than on the Welsh Church. Still for better or worse I hold my creed and it is very maddening for me to hear George tell me that the whole of my religious system is a great imposture.[65]

Price welcomed the gradual extension of Anglo-Catholic practice within the Welsh Church, even if it never became the democratic force of which he had once dreamed. In later life he blamed the Anglo-Welsh bishops for never giving it a fair trial, and mused on how different the history of the nation might have been if the Tractarian Isaac Williams had been appointed principal of Lampeter.[66] As it was, St David's College, Lampeter, produced generations of Low Church clergy, and Ritualism made little impact in the college until about 1910.[67]

In January 1895, Price attracted public notoriety when, with four Anglo-Catholic clergy from north Wales, he advocated what became known as the Bangor scheme. The proposal, drafted by Price with the support of Lloyd George, was made in the wake of the first Welsh Disestablishment Bill of 1894, a measure which inspired a massive church defence campaign among most

Anglicans.[68] Price suggested that what was needed was a compromise over disendowment, as a sweetener to make disestablishment more palatable to churchpeople. He tried (unsuccessfully) to convince ardent church defenders such as the future Bishop Owen, then principal at Lampeter, that as disestablishment was only a matter of time, they might as well settle on the best terms possible. The 'Bangor scheme' involved disestablishment, the better distribution of existing endowments, the abolition of lay patronage, a greater share in church management for the laity and a reform of the cathedral system. Most important was the constitution of the Church in Wales as a separate province under its own archbishop, with the restoration of its ancient national character.[69] Much of the Bangor scheme was put into effect when disestablishment was finally achieved in 1920, but in 1895 the scheme was ahead of its time, and attracting the ire of the bishops, it was submerged beneath the weight of church defence opposition. At that time, its importance lay in drawing public attention to the fact that there were articulate Welsh churchmen who actively favoured disestablishment.

The wholesale rejection of the Bangor scheme by Welsh Church leaders seems to have delivered a severe, if temporary, blow to Price's Anglican allegiance. In September 1896, whilst staying at St Davids, he gave serious thought to conversion to Rome. The publication of *Apostolicae Curae*, the papal rejection of the validity of Anglican orders, added further fuel to his spiritual crisis. He confided his difficulties in a twelve-page letter to J. E. Lloyd, a Congregationalist, whose counsel on previous occasions he believed had been a means for bringing him back to orthodox Christianity. Price's passionate advocacy of disestablishment was making continued membership of the Established Church a difficulty, and was causing him to doubt whether he was part of the true Church, and whether its sacraments were valid. The difficulty with Rome, however, lay in the doctrine of papal infallibility, which he could not reconcile with his knowledge of the papacy both past and present. Was he, he wondered, held back from joining the Church of Rome by worldly motives; the fear of losing the reputation that he was making as an ecclesiastical lawyer, the loss of influence in Wales, his mother's heartbreak?

I quite admit that worldly motives do weigh with me and this reminds me of the terrible text about gaining the world and losing my soul . . . on the other side if I deliberately choose to remain in the Anglican Communion, dissenting as I may do from some of its details . . . am I so dishonest as to have no right to a share in our Saviour's promises?[70]

It is not clear how Lloyd responded to Price's spiritual dilemma, but in a letter written a few weeks later, Price assured him that the crisis had passed.

The road to disestablishment was a long and slow one, and in the end the Church would call upon the legal skills of the barrister whose efforts it had repudiated in 1895. When the long-awaited event was finally brought about in 1920, Price was nearly sixty. He was undoubtedly excited by the newly disestablished Church, and fervently hoped that it would usher in an era of spiritual and national renewal. In the early 1920s, he made a visit to St Davids, a place he had not seen since his spiritual crisis of 1896. Then, he had been disheartened by its chilly, Low-Church ambience, and what he termed 'the common ban placed alike on the faith of the invader, and the tongue of the invaded'.[71] Now, under the friendly, Welsh-speaking, High Church Dean William Williams, all was different. Price wrote: 'As I entered the Cathedral I could not help feeling a thrill. I seemed at last to be on free ground.'[72] To his delight, in the nave of the cathedral he saw a Welsh flag, and in the Vaughan chapel, a new bust of Giraldus Cambrensis. Price became lyrical as he teased out the significance of this. 'Giraldus has returned to his cathedral to enjoy a posthumous victory. The cause for which he fought has triumphed after a weary waiting of seven hundred years.'[73] For all campaigners for an independent Welsh Church, the wait had indeed been weary.

Despite his high churchmanship, Price had strong ecumenical hopes for Wales, and usually treated Nonconformists with respect and courtesy, though he did not disguise his dislike of narrow-minded Protestants. He nursed the hope that some kind of reunion might be possible between Welsh Churchmen and Welsh Nonconformists, and that a disestablished Welsh Church would establish friendly relations with Welsh Nonconformity. In

1917, he suggested that the prospect was 'much easier now that the Welsh Nonconformists have happily shaken themselves free of the English Free Church Council.'[74] As in other matters, he believed that the Welsh must put aside their religious differences for the greater good of their nation. That did not mean, however, that they should abandon dogmatic thinking for indefinite opinions, but rather that they should be honest about their differences. 'Nondenominationalism is a dishonest thing,' he wrote to D. R. Daniel in 1906.

> It is an attempt to shirk difficulties instead of settling them . . . men like Henry Richard were strong men because they thought dogmatically . . . [but] a Welshman who goes to Bangor University College is trained undogmatically, believes himself in nothing and consequently no one believes in him.[75]

Price did not expect to convert Welsh Nonconformists to Anglo-Catholicism, but in the 1920s he came to see Christianity as the only bulwark that Europe possessed against Communism. It did not much matter whether Christians believed in an inspired book or an infallible church, the important thing was that they should hold to absolute, not relative, values.[76] In 1935, Price now aged seventy-four, reported happily to his friend Ellis Davies, a Calvinistic Methodist, that at the Church Assembly meeting at Llandrindod Wells, the President of 'your Church' had been in the gallery, and that 'some interesting things' were said about reunion by the bishop of Monmouth.[77] This was what Price relished most, Welshmen from different traditions showing willingness to explore their common ground on the basis of their shared national identity.

It can be argued that in Price were blended to perfection the twin themes of religion and national identity. His principal devotion was nationalism; he once wrote that 'Welsh patriotism for a Welshman is not an amicable sentiment for a locality: it is a duty, the neglect of which is an act of moral treason.'[78] Despite (or perhaps because) of his many years in London, he hated England and the English, and the most insulting thing that he could say about a person was that they were infected with the spirit of the English middle classes. He accused the Welsh

Liberal MPs of the late 1920s of this sin, and also the historians of the University of Wales.

In religion, Price was as consistent as he was in his nationalist politics. He believed that Anglo-Catholicism was a democratic force, and that its adoption would, in the first instance, make disestablishment more likely, and thereafter revitalize a disestablished Church as a truly national institution. Anglo-Catholicism appeared to provide the perfect cultural idiom for his politics, and he was as committed to explaining his religion to his political friends as he was to explaining Wales to the readers of *The Church Times*. The Church appears to have found it difficult to trust him after his youthful involvement in the Bangor scheme, and never made the most use of his undoubted talents. In the final year of his life, when he was eighty, he was appointed chancellor of the diocese of Bangor. He accepted after some hesitation, and wrote to Lloyd about it, inviting Lloyd to his installation. He commented sadly that 'almost everyone who would really have been interested in the matter has passed away'.[79] This final official recognition from the Church may have pleased him, but the pity was that he was too frail to carry out any of the duties.[80] Was he a disappointed man? He was not, because he never stopped believing that Wales's hour would come.

Notes

[1] National Library of Wales (NLW): Thomas Edward Ellis 1699, 22 November 1891.

[2] Even more curiously, he does not appear in *Who's Who in Wales*, a book that noted many Welsh people residing outside Wales. I am grateful to Dr Densil Morgan for drawing my attention to a short appreciation of Price by E. Morgan Humphreys, which appeared in *Gwŷr Enwog Gynt* (Llandysul, 1950).

[3] He merits a string of references in Kenneth O. Morgan, *Wales in British Politics, 1868–1922* (Cardiff, 1991 edn.), and is also mentioned in the same author's *Modern Wales: Politics, Places and People* (Cardiff, 1995), and in Professor Morgan's article 'Tom Ellis versus Lloyd George: the fractured consciousness of fin-de-siècle Wales', in Geraint H. Jenkins and J. Beverley Smith (eds.), *Politics and Society in Wales, 1840–1922: Essays in Honour of Ieuan*

Gwynedd Jones (Cardiff, 1988). Price is also briefly mentioned in D. Hywel Davies, *The Welsh Nationalist Party, 1925–1945: A Call to Nationhood* (Cardiff, 1983).

4 *Church Times* (12 June 1942), 335. Price had no children, and was particularly close to this nephew, the Revd Seiriol Evans, minor canon of Ely and future dean of Gloucester. See University of Wales Bangor Archives (UWBA) J. E. Lloyd 318/.64, 9 June 1942.

5 The house, Bryn Egryn, Llanaber, near Barmouth, originally belonged to his wife, and was managed by Mrs E. Nichols as a bed-and-breakfast establishment.

6 UWBA: J. E. Lloyd 314/.414, 25 March 1887, and 314/.415, 3 November 1887. Price wrote to Lloyd, whom he had known at Oxford, at regular intervals from the time of his graduation up until his death. I am grateful to Elen Wyn Hughes, assistant archivist at Bangor, for locating Price's letters in the voluminous Lloyd archive, and for practical help during my visit to Bangor.

7 UWBA: J. E. Lloyd 314/.418, 25 December 1887.

8 UWBA: J. E. Lloyd 314/.422, 7 August 1888.

9 UWBA: J. E. Lloyd 314/.456, 5 July 1903.

10 'Nationality and Welsh home rule', *The Welsh Outlook* (April 1918), 117.

11 UWBA: J. E. Lloyd 314/.417, 3 December 1887. The Primrose League was formed in 1883 in memory of Benjamin Disraeli, to promote Conservative principles.

12 See Morgan, *Wales in British Politics*, pp. 111–19, for an account of this period.

13 UWBA: J. E. Lloyd 314/.418, 25 December 1887.

14 Morgan, 'Tom Ellis versus Lloyd George'.

15 UWBA: J. E. Lloyd 314/.423, 29 September 1888.

16 Ibid.

17 It was Price who contributed the chapter on 'Thomas E. Ellis, M.P.' to J. Vyrnwy Morgan's *Welsh Political and Educational Leaders of the Victorian Era* (London, 1908), pp. 373–405. The chapter provides a useful insight into Price's views on Ellis.

18 NLW Thomas Edward Ellis 1696, 4 July 1891.

19 For Cymru Fydd see W. Llewelyn Williams, 'Cymru Fydd', *The Welsh Outlook* (May 1919), 124–5; Morgan, *Wales in British Politics*, pp. 104–6, 160–5 and Wyn Jones, *Thomas Edward Ellis 1859–1899* (Cardiff, 1986), p. 25 and *passim*.

20 UWBA: J. E. Lloyd 314/.425, 7 June 1889. Price's first article appeared in the August 1889 issue, and was entitled 'Welsh nationalism and revolutionary politics'.

21 UWBA: J. E. Lloyd 314/.444, 10 February 1891.

22 Morgan, *Wales in British Politics*, p. 121.
23 UWBA: J. E. Lloyd 314/.449, 14 October 1892.
24 Price, 'Thomas E. Ellis M.P.', p. 397.
25 Ibid., p. 396.
26 Morgan, 'Tom Ellis versus Lloyd George', p. 109.
27 Price, 'Thomas E. Ellis M.P.', p. 374.
28 NLW: Ellis W. Davies 30/71, 14 March 1937.
29 This appears to echo the beliefs of Howell Harris. See Geraint Tudur's contribution to this volume for more on Howell Harris's view of monarchy.
30 Price provided an interesting account of a memorial service at St John's Westminster for Mrs Pankhurst that he attended on 16 July 1936. The bishop of London, A. F. Winnington Ingram, preached a fulsome tribute, parts of which even Price found difficult to swallow. 'Of course I quite approve of Prayer for the Departed,' he told his friend Ellis W. Davies, 'but the assumption that Mrs Pankhurst already beholds the beatific vision of the Blessed Trinity struck me as a little presumptuous.' NLW: Ellis W. Davies 30/49–50, 12 July 1936 and 17 July 1936.
31 This seems to have been a source of tension in his relationship with the eminent Welsh historian Professor (later Sir) John Lloyd, who taught first at University College Aberystwyth, and then became a major figure at Bangor. Price told Lloyd in no uncertain terms that he considered that the Welsh University was doing nothing to save the language. UWBA: J. E. Lloyd 314/455, 4 December 1902, and 456, 1 July 1903.
32 Morgan, 'Tom Ellis versus Lloyd George', p. 98.
33 'The historical case for Welsh home rule', *The Welsh Outlook* (December 1921), 272.
34 This subject is taken up by E. Wyn James in his contribution to this volume.
35 'State, nationalism and conscience', *The Welsh Outlook* (October 1916); 'Is Welsh home rule coming?', *The Welsh Outlook* (July 1917); 'Nationality and Welsh home rule', *The Welsh Outlook* (April 1918); 'Welsh nationalism and Mr Lloyd George's speech', *The Welsh Outlook* (September 1918); 'Anti-nationalism', *The Welsh Outlook* (July 1919); 'Four men and a moral' (about the Paris Peace Conference), *The Welsh Outlook* (November 1919); 'The premier and Ireland', *The Welsh Outlook* (February 1920); 'Some national rebirths of today', *The Welsh Outlook* (March 1920); 'Great nationalists I: Grattan', *The Welsh Outlook* (November 1920); 'The historical case for Welsh home rule', *The Welsh Outlook* (December 1921).

36 'State, nationalism and conscience', p. 311.
37 Ibid.
38 'Welsh nationalism and Mr Lloyd George's speech', p. 274.
39 Morgan, *Wales in British Politics*, pp. 292–3.
40 'Great nationalists I: Grattan' (November 1920).
41 *The Welsh Outlook* (February 1921), 28.
42 'The Premier's heyday', *The Welsh Outlook* (March 1919), 75.
43 'Anti-nationalism', p. 181.
44 E. Lloyd Owen, 'Plaid Genedlaethol Cymru', in *The Welsh Outlook* (August 1925), 218.
45 Davies, *The Welsh Nationalist Party 1925–1945*, p. 32.
46 Ibid., p. 83.
47 NLW: Ellis W. Davies papers 30/29, 15 January 1935.
48 UWBA: J. E. Lloyd 316/.294. This letter provides a fascinating insight into the relationship between politics, religion and alcohol in early twentieth-century Wales.
49 Morgan, *Wales in British Politics*, pp. 302–3.
50 'The Welsh University in Parliament', *The Welsh Outlook* (June 1929), 171. Harry Reichel was an Ulsterman by birth, and his father had been bishop of Meath.
51 UWBA: J. E. Lloyd 315/.363, 13 June 1925.
52 John Davies, *The Green and the Red: Nationalism and Ideology in Twentieth Century Wales* (Aberystwyth, 1980), pp. 6–7.
53 Davies, *The Welsh Nationalist Party*, p. 271.
54 NLW: Ellis W. Davies 30/35, 4 December 1935.
55 See Davies, *The Welsh Nationalist Party*, pp. 154–66, for an account of this incident.
56 NLW: Ellis W. Davies 30/68, 4 February 1937.
57 NLW: Ellis W. Davies 30/58, 25 October 1936.
58 NLW: Ellis W. Davies 30/69, 15 February 1937.
59 NLW: Ellis W. Davies 30/71, 14 March 1937.
60 Benjamin Jowett (1817–93) was master of Balliol College. He helped to revive the study of classics in the university and encouraged his students to study Hegel and other recent German philosophers.
61 UWBA: J. E. Lloyd 314/429, 21 July 1889.
62 Lambeth Palace Library: English Church Union membership lists.
63 Bernard Palmer, *Gadfly for God: A History of the Church Times* (London, 1991), pp. 116–17.
64 NLW: Thomas Edward Ellis 1698, 21 October 1891.
65 NLW: Thomas Edward Ellis 1699, 22 November 1891. According to Morgan, Ellis had 'some sympathy for the aesthetic and cultural visions of high Anglicans like Arthur Price'. 'Tom Ellis versus Lloyd

George', p. 100. Price recorded that when at Oxford, Ellis regularly worshipped in New College chapel, came to appreciate the liturgy of the Book of Common Prayer and the historical continuity of the Church of England. Price, 'Thomas E. Ellis M.P.' p. 387.

66 'The Oxford Movement and Wales', *The Welsh Outlook* (August, 1933), 207–9.
67 This was the time that the Society of St David was founded, a student society that later had branches in other parts of Wales and in some English towns. The SSD had existed in an earlier form as the Guild of St David in the 1890s. Price was evidently a supporter of the SSD, and may well have been a member. The SSD still exists at Lampeter.
68 Morgan, *Modern Wales: Politics, Places and People*, p. 159.
69 Eluned E. Owen, *The Early Life of Bishop Owen* (Llandysul, 1958), pp. 179–81.
70 UWBA: J. E. Lloyd 314/.451, 27, September 1896.
71 'The Home of St David', *The Welsh Outlook* (March 1917), 113.
72 'St David's revisited', *The Welsh Outlook* (March 1923), 80.
73 Ibid.
74 'The awakening in the Welsh Church', *The Welsh Outlook* (October 1917), 363.
75 NLW: D. R. Daniel 2151, Price to Daniel, 13 April 1906.
76 'The political and moral effects of an indefinite creed', *The Welsh Outlook* (February 1925), 47–8.
77 NLW: Ellis W. Davies 30/39, 26 August 1935.
78 'State, nationalism and conscience'.
79 UWBA: J. E. Lloyd 318/.206, 7 May 1941.
80 *Church Times* (12 June 1942), 335.

~ 6 ~
Continuity and Conversion: The Concept of a National Church in Twentieth-Century Wales and its Relation to 'the Celtic Church'

TRYSTAN OWAIN HUGHES

Celtic Christianity has been a vehicle through which people have chased their dreams.[1]

The notion of ecclesiastical continuity with the ancient Welsh Church, or the Celtic Church as it is sometimes called, has long been an issue in Wales.[2] Since the Reformation, members of almost all Welsh denominations have at one time or another attempted to define themselves as being the rightful heirs to the Celtic Church. Such a claim was not confined solely to Wales, but was also made in Scotland and Ireland.[3] Yet such enchantment with the early Celtic saints and the Christianity they practised has not been, by and large, driven by a desire for correct history or serious scholarship, no matter how much denominations claimed this to be the case. Instead, pretensions to the mantle of continuity were largely the consequence of specific events and times, when the need to reassert or win spiritual dominion was most potent. Although the history of Celtic Christian revivalism in Britain as a whole has been addressed by scholars such as Ian Bradley, no attention has hitherto been paid to twentieth-century Welsh Anglican and Roman Catholic claims to continuity with the Celtic Church and the subsequent claims to the title 'the national Church of Wales'.

At the root of Welsh claims to continuity lay the question of the Celtic Church's relationship with Rome. Had the Celtic Church been part of the larger universal Catholic Church, accepting the primacy of the bishop of Rome, or had it been an independent institution, anti-Roman in its attitude and proto-Protestant in its teaching? At the Reformation, with the need to persuade the Welsh people of the national and indigenous character of the new religion, the Anglican Bishop Richard Davies of St Davids claimed that his church represented the native Welsh religion.[4] The Anglican Church was not, as its name might suggest, an alien imposition, but was the restoration of the ancient Welsh Church. The thesis was later to be developed along Dissenting lines by Welsh Nonconformists.

The Celtic card was played by both sides in the nineteenth-century debate surrounding the proposed disestablishment of the Anglican Church in Wales.[5] Nonconformist liberationists charged the Established Church with Anglicization, and presented themselves as representing the independent and tribal Celtic Church. In reaction, the publication of numerous histories of the Anglican Church aimed to reassert its claim to continuity.[6] With disestablishment becoming a certainty, the link between conversion and continuity was explicitly presented. A number of Welsh Anglicans warned their fellow-religionists that if the Church was to survive, and indeed grow, they had to present themselves as the spiritual ancestors of St David, not Queen Elizabeth. Even if the Church's established status had now to be relinquished, its position as the mother church of Wales was secured.[7]

Another link forged by Anglicans at this time was that between continuity and national identity. Bishop Richard Davies had used nationality in his 'Address to the Welsh nation' of 1567, and a sense of patriotism was conspicuous amongst an influential group of pro-continuity Anglican clerics in the early 1800s.[8] The extent of the late nineteenth-century fusion of continuity and cultural duty was, however, unprecedented. The Church was encouraged, not only to present itself as being in the descent of the Welsh saints, but also to show itself to value the culture which they had nurtured.[9] Tainted by the charge of Anglicization, it now had to reinvent itself as the national Church in Wales.

By the time the Church was disestablished in 1920, the earlier prophetic warnings had finally received attention. The crisis of disestablishment had compelled Welsh Anglicanism to find its own identity, independent of Canterbury. The early Welsh Church presented the opportunity to establish this new identity. At the acceptance of the church's constitution in April 1922, Lord Sankey stated emphatically that

> the Church in Wales is a Catholic and National Church . . . As a national church we are the old Christian Church in these islands. The saints of the Church of God are sons of the race. They sleep in Welsh soil, hard by the shrines they loved and served so well. The self-same prayers which moved their lips move ours. Today we are the heirs of their beliefs and of their traditions.[10]

Henceforth, this would not be the theory of an academic minority, but would be established as a virtual fact within the Church, accepted without question by the great majority of its members.

Unlike past Anglican advocates of the theory, however, these new Celtophiles rarely referred to the ancient Welsh Church as a Protestant institution.[11] It was now a widely held belief that the Celtic Church was truly Catholic and that the Anglican Church had inherited its apostolic catholicity. This conviction did not, however, lead to a uniformity of belief. Even after disestablishment, Welsh Anglicans held differing views concerning continuity.[12] There were those who held that an independent Celtic Church was eventually forced to succumb to Rome, regaining its independence at the Reformation. Others, however, combined their insistence on the independence of the Celtic Church with the general Anglican theory of unbroken continuity. It was suggested that the Church of Rome had never at any time held authority over the Welsh Church. 'Up to the reign of Elizabeth there were no Roman Catholics in this country,' wrote Norman E. Martin of Port Talbot in 1933, 'and it was under Elizabeth [that] the Papal party broke away from the real Catholic Church and so became the first dissenters.'[13] The Anglican Church was therefore not 'a new Church at the time of the Reformation' but rather 'the old Church reformed'.[14] These views, however, were not exclusive and there was no tension between advocates of the different theories. The important fact was that their Church was in continuity with the ancient and Catholic Welsh Church.

By the 1920s, Nonconformist interest in the Celtic Church had waned. The political, financial and religious aim of forcing disestablishment had now been attained. The Anglican Church's new-found status, however, was not to be left uncontested. Although the post-Reformation Roman Catholic Church had traditionally been weak in Wales, by this time its fortunes had changed. Largely as a result of immigration, but also through winning prominent converts, the Church of Rome found itself thriving. The resulting self-assurance and confidence found voice in a movement which saw the conversion of Wales to Rome as a realistic possibility.[15] If this was to be accomplished, it was held that Rome had to present itself as the ancient Church which moulded Wales into a nation. Thus, an ever more explicit link between continuity and conversion was forged. Likewise, the connection with national sentiment was also developed, as Rome consolidated its claim to the ancient Welsh Church by its fervent efforts to nurture the language and culture of the nation.[16]

The dawn of the twentieth century, then, saw both Anglican and Roman Catholic Churches, out of their own particular historical circumstances, presenting themselves as heirs to the Christianity of the early Welsh saints. The result of this, however, was largely negative. There was deep hostility between the factions, and mutual polemic clouded any serious historical discussion. Criticism of opposing viewpoints was far more frequent than positive evaluation, and debates more often than not degenerated into a competition for one-upmanship and point-scoring. At the root of this conflict was the fact that this was clearly a denominational struggle based on contemporary aims and objectives. 'The exact position of the Early British Church is a subject of considerable importance,' wrote the Catholic J. E. De Hirsch-Davies in 1926. 'The subject is not merely an academic one: it affects present-day problems.'[17] It was no coincidence that the Anglican Church relied on such claims at times of financial need. To counterbalance the monetary losses of disendowment in the 1920s, the Church distributed circulars emphasizing the 'historical fact' that it was 'the oldest branch of the Catholic Church in this island' and was 'in unbroken continuity from the ancient British Church'.[18] Likewise in the 1950s, with the launch of another financial appeal, the Celtic card was again played.[19]

It was believed, however, that the ancient and national Welsh Church could lead to far more than fiscal affluence. In 1933, the Anglican Dean J. L. Phillips of Monmouth claimed that, with Nonconformity declining, its successor as the religion of Wales depended upon 'a correct presentation of history' and 'the conception of which Church is best adapted to express national spirit and national righteousness'.[20] Thus the Celtic Church came to be regarded as an essential evangelistic weapon. Both Anglicans and Roman Catholics were certain that any success which the other was securing resulted from false historical and nationalistic 'propaganda' which was being disseminated successfully.[21] This hypothesis seemed to be supported by contemporary evidence. Both the poet D. Gwenallt Jones's conversion to Anglicanism and the playwright Saunders Lewis's conversion to Catholicism were seen to result from their conviction that their respective churches represented Wales's ancient tradition.[22] Gwenallt even stated that 'no issue will rival this in importance for the religious destiny of Wales'.[23] The testimony of other converts produced further evidence. Whilst serving as an Anglican minor canon at Bangor Cathedral, Archimandrite Barnabas claimed that he had come to the conclusion that he 'could not honestly believe that this was the ancient Catholic Church of Wales, and again my gaze turned longingly to the Roman Church'.[24]

The question of the early British Church, then, did have some practical effect at this time. This was, however, confined largely to the minority intellectual sphere. Mostly, the sole outcome of the issue was to incite hostility. Ian Bradley claims that most Celtic Christian revivals in Britain were 'inspired and driven by denominational and national rivalries, ecclesiastical and secular power politics and an anti-Roman Catholic agenda'.[25] Prejudice and polemic were certainly common on all sides in the twentieth-century Welsh debate. Anglicans were particularly scathing of Roman Catholics, who themselves were not beyond belittling and taunting the 'modern heresy' of Anglican continuity.[26] '*Every single* Bishop of the Anglican Church is a *heretic*', claimed the *Welsh Catholic Times* in 1932, 'and they cannot be Catholic and Anglican at the same time.'[27] Generally the chapels stayed out of the controversy, content to allow their two archenemies to chip away at each other's foundations. On occasions, however, Nonconformists did venture into the fray, either to defend their own position,[28] or merely to support Anglican anti-Roman sentiment. In *Y Cymro* in 1953, for example, D. E. Rees of Bangor used the debate as an opportunity to reproach Catholicism as idolatrous and persecutory. In light of this, he concluded, 'David was never a Papist, nor were his contemporaries Dunawd, Deiniol, Cybi, nor any other of the Celtic fathers of that age. They were anti-Catholic.'[29] Another Nonconformist correspondent questioned the right of Roman Catholics to call themselves Christian by suggesting that 'St David was a Christian and not a Papist'.[30] It was hardly surprising that, later that year, one *Western Mail* contributor wrote that 'pride, egotism, prejudice, falsehood and misrepresentation are the basis of the anti-Papal view'.[31]

The anti-Catholic element which tinged the controversy was even criticized by some less conservative Welsh Anglican scholars. These rejected the historical basis of Anglican continuity and accused their fellow churchmen of using the Celtic Church as a vehicle for anti-Roman sentiment.[32] The Revd A. W. Wade-Evans, for example, indicted his Church for a so-called 'ecumenical' service to commemorate the Council of Nicea. Held at the Anglican St Davids Cathedral on 14 July 1925, it was attended by representatives of Welsh Nonconformist denominations[33] and the Eastern Orthodox Churches.[34] At the celebrations, Archbishop A. G. Edwards presented the Church in Wales as the heir to an early Welsh Church, which had its origins in the East and not in the Latin West. Wade-Evans pointed out the hypocritical inconsistency of an archbishop who had previously campaigned to prevent Wales from seceding from the orbit of Canterbury. He wrote that 'only till yesterday Wales was being told, year in and year out, that the four Welsh dioceses were merely a portion of the Province of Canterbury, and what a wicked, wicked thing it was to sever so sweet a connection'. Following Edwards's address at the service, the Nicene Creed was recited in Welsh, English, Greek and Russian. The absence of Latin was conspicuous and deliberate. Wade-Evans noted that even the creeds which were recited were *not* the same as each other (because of the *filioque* clause), and so joy at the unity of

East and West was false. 'They had indeed met as one, but only to say that they were two', he concluded, 'two in their views about God, but One in their opposition to Rome. They were united only on a negation. Their gathering was but an anti-Roman gesture.'[35]

No matter how much a minority of Anglicans recognized the inconsistencies and prejudices within their Church's historical arguments, the vast majority of their fellow-religionists unquestionably accepted continuity. The result was a bitter war of words with the Roman Catholic Church which lasted in press and on platform up until the 1960s. The crux of the problem remained the question of whether the Celtic Church was independent of Rome. It was believed that whosoever could prove this one way or the other, had won the right to be called the national church. In reality, both sides were quite literally 'making myths and chasing dreams'[36] and conclusions reached from historical research were tenuous. The basis of the debates concerned differences in practice between Rome and the ancient Welsh Church, and early Celtic disagreements with Augustine's Saxon Church. Did the Welsh Church's refusal to change the date of Easter to accommodate Rome's calendar suggest hostile relations between the communions? What of the differences in the shape of the bishop's tonsure or in the form of baptism? What about the reconsecration of St Chad by the Saxon Church?[37] It was believed that the spiritual heir to the Celtic Church could be deduced from these questions. In recent scholarship, even the concept of a Celtic Church has been shown to be flawed, and to superimpose past realities on present-day institutions is simply an anachronism. Still, the right to be called 'the national Church' became the staple diet of twentieth-century Welsh Anglican and Roman Catholic ecclesiastical controversies.

From the 1920s onwards, then, the subject was aired repeatedly. In *The Welsh Outlook* in 1926 a debate on continuity rumbled on for months.[38] In the initial article, De Hirsch-Davies insisted that the key to understanding the disagreements between Augustine of Canterbury and the early Welsh Church was 'to be found in the attitude which may be called – anti-Saxon, anti-English, anti-Canterbury, anti-Innovation, anti-anything-else, according to the nature of the dispute, but not anti-Roman'. The Celtic Church may have disliked the arrogant attitude of the Saxon Church, but it was still in full communion with the Church of Rome.[39] The Anglican Lewis Davies retorted that Hirsch-Davies's article should have carried the heading 'The Romance of the Roman Position',[40] while Wade-Evans launched another attack on his fellow Anglicans' belated and vain attempt to shake off their 'sham-English pose'.[41] Lengthy and hostile correspondences in the inter-war years were also found in the *West Wales Guardian*[42] and the *Western Mail*, where Roman Catholics were accused of 'cultivating a persistent hostility in every direction against the National Church . . . and its continuity'.[43]

The Anglican Dean William Williams of St Davids was particularly zealous in his espousal of Celtic-Anglican continuity. Having always encouraged devotion to the early Welsh saints at his cathedral, by the 1920s Williams's Celtophile attitudes had taken a new twist. This came as a result of the dawn of the ecumenical movement. Across Britain, the movement had embraced the Celtic Church as its focal point.[44] While Williams likewise saw the Celtic Church as having a part to play in ecumenism, his views were far from being all-embracing. These were aimed exclusively at Welsh Nonconformists whom he believed to have forsaken the presence and protection of the (Anglican) mother church. Although he invariably maintained that his exclusion of Rome was due to its arrogant, unscriptural and superstitious dogmas,[45] his real motives were betrayed by his incessant cavilling at the Catholic view of early Welsh history. For him, the ecumenical movement meant reconciliation with the Church of the early Welsh saints. The Roman Catholic Church therefore stood as a direct and potent threat to the validity of Anglican pretensions to national superiority. 'Where shall we in Wales look for a centre of unity?' he asked, 'Not in the Church of Rome, with its false claim to infallibility and supremacy, and its many errors of belief . . . The eyes of many are just now turned towards the old Mother Church of Wales.'[46]

Following the Second World War, further articles and correspondence reflected the importance which continued to be placed on the position of the Celtic Church. In 1953, the editors of both the *Western Mail* and *Y Cymro* had to close correspondence on the theme of continuity, such was the length and fervency of the debates in their respective letter-pages.[47] Catholics dealt with the question directly in the pages of the *Menevia Record*,[48] *Western Mail*,[49] *Review*,[50] *Blackfriars*[51] and *Welsh Catholic Times*.[52] 'If the faith of St David be made the touchstone of religion's metal,' noted the latter publication, 'our case alone will stand the test.'[53] Anglicans put forward their claim to continuity in *Y Faner*,[54] *Y Cymro*[55] and on numerous occasions in *Province*.[56] 'Anglicans must dwell on this point,' wrote Ewart Lewis, 'because they believe it to be true, and fundamental to their whole position.'[57] The Church in Wales also fostered traditional Catholic practices such as devotion to saints,[58] pilgrimages,[59] the celebration of Masses and the hearing of confessions,[60] aiming to promote identification with the ancient Church. Even delegates to conferences were briefed on the alleged historical facts of their Church's background.[61]

Most of all, however, it was the hierarchy of both the Roman Catholic and the Anglican churches which incessantly emphasized continuity. On the Roman side, Archbishop Mostyn of Cardiff reacted fervently to the increasingly vocal claims of the Church in Wales. A year after disestablishment he dedicated a well-publicized pastoral letter to the matter[62] and was later to incite controversy by claiming that Anglican cathedrals 'stood as cold and empty shells awaiting the time when new life would be infused into them, and they would be once more used for the purpose for which they were erected'.[63] Likewise, Bishop Vaughan of Menevia wrote, rather poetically, that 'in vain has Imagination's uncharted sea been sailed again and again by our romantic Madocs in search of [the independent Celtic Church]; their quest was always doomed to failure'. Wales, he continued, owed a far more extensive debt to Rome than she realized, as it was the sixth-century Roman Catholic monks who 'welded that motley collection into one homogeneous whole, and made them a people who took the national name of "Cymru"'.[64] The Anglican bishops advanced almost identical claims. Archbishop Edwin Morris was particularly zealous in his insistence on continuity. His Church alone was the Catholic Church in Wales.[65] In his *Primary Visitation Charge* as bishop of

Monmouth in 1946, he caused scandal by suggesting that Roman priests and Nonconformist ministers were 'intruders' in Wales, with only a 'historical excuse' for being in the country.[66] His incessant critique of the Church of Rome in fact revealed what his biographer admitted to be 'anti-Roman not historical' views. In one letter to Archbishop Fisher of Canterbury he even suggested 'that we should now even go over to the offensive and call in question Rome's right to the title Catholic'.[67]

Perhaps the one positive outcome which complemented claims to continuity and the desire to be regarded as the national Church of Wales was the fostering of Welsh consciousness. In their efforts to be taken seriously as heirs to the early saints, both Anglicans and Roman Catholics began to show a sincere dedication to the Welsh heritage, language and culture. Within the Roman Catholic Church, a succession of bishops, priests and prominent laypeople struggled to present the Church as being in tune with national sentiment. For the conversion of modern Wales to take place, it was suggested that the present-day Catholic Church had to become as devoted to Welsh culture as the Celtic Church had been. Catholic devotion to St David soon began to take on a nationalistic tinge[68] and many priests were taught Welsh in their seminary training. With the conversion of a number of prominent Welshmen (including Saunders Lewis, a founder member and early president of the Welsh Nationalist Party, later Plaid Cymru), the Church even found itself to be an integral part of the Welsh nationalist scene. Likewise, Anglicans complemented their insistence on continuity with a zeal for Welsh culture. 'If the Church in Wales is to play her full part her leaders must realise that she is a Welsh Church, not an English one imported into Wales', *Province* noted in 1954. 'She must not give the impression that she is lukewarm about the Welsh language and Welsh culture.'[69] Anglicans were urged to take a special interest in the preservation of the native tongue[70] and Welsh-language services were encouraged.[71]

While efforts to foster Welsh consciousness may have been praiseworthy in themselves and not without success, both churches faced criticism and disillusionment in their endeavours. No matter how much they strove to present themselves as a national church, their struggle seemed ultimately in vain. As well as facing criticism from Nonconformists,[72] both Churches ironically accused each other of Anglicization. This indictment was far stronger than the minority efforts to foster national identity. Roman Catholics saw the Church in Wales as an Anglicizing institution imposed on an unwilling Wales in the sixteenth century. In 1916, *The Tablet* enthused that 'disestablished and disendowed, Anglicanism in Wales steps down from its pedestal, and is now universally recognised as the alien Church it has always been'.[73] For the next forty years, Catholics repeatedly presented Anglicanism as 'a strange and alien faith, the "ffydd y Saeson", "the faith of the Saxons" '.[74] Its status as an English importation was presented as the reason why there were so many Welsh martyrs at the Reformation[75] and the reason why the Welsh nation eventually embraced Nonconformity. At the 'great and inglorious Deformation' of the sixteenth century,[76] the Anglican Church stood guilty of destroying the soul of the Welsh nation and the chapels were simply an attempt to fill the resulting spiritual and national vacuum.[77] 'What can we say of a Church which began life as an imported schism,' asked Fr Ivor Daniel in 1946, 'and now thinks that the recent restoration of Mass vestments and episcopal regalia prove its continuity with the ancient Faith of Wales?'[78] In response, however, Roman Catholics were themselves denounced as being an Anglicizing force in Welsh society. The vast majority of them were, after all, immigrants with little or no interest in the culture and language of the nation. In the *Western Mail* in 1936, the Church was described as a 'modern, wholly alien, cult' and a blunt conclusion was reached, that 'today there is no such thing as Welsh [Roman] Catholicism'.[79] Likewise, throughout the 1950s, the Anglican periodical *Province* continually derided Roman Catholics for 'the foreign accent of their religion'.[80]

During the 1960s, denominational propaganda surrounding the position of the ancient Welsh Church rapidly decreased. With the move towards ecumenical dialogue and the general consensus against inter-Christian proselytization, discussions surrounding continuity became confined to the academic sphere.[81] Yet in the early decades of the twentieth century, and particularly during the 1920s, the Church in Wales, which faced the threat and then reality of disestablishment, and the Roman

Catholic Church, which experienced significant growth in the context of hostility, both had their own particular needs and problems. Both responded to their situations by alleging continuity with the Celtic Church and therefore claiming the mantle of the national church. 'Men of every age', wrote Glanmor Williams, 'tend to rewrite history in the light of their own needs and experience.'[82] It was truly believed that whoever secured recognition as heir to the early Welsh saints would reap conversions from among native Welshmen. In reality, the issue had limited effect or influence. Its only real achievement was to incite controversy and hostility from all quarters. Historical evidence was rarely treated impartially, and misrepresentation was frequent. In describing the current revival of Celtic Christianity in Britain, Ian Bradley echoes the unfortunate position in which the Celtic Church found itself in early twentieth-century Wales. For the vast majority of Welsh Anglicans and Roman Catholics, the ancient Welsh Church was simply 'the projection of all kinds of dreams about what should and might be'.[83]

Notes

1. Ian Bradley, *Celtic Christianity: Making Myths and Chasing Dreams* (Edinburgh, 1999), p. vii.
2. The phrases 'Celtic Church', 'early Welsh Church' and 'early British Church', are used loosely to constitute the band of Christian churches, all belonging to the 'Catholic' Church, which were to be found in 'Celtic' Britain and Ireland before the Saxon invasions. They subsequently survived those invasions.
3. Cf. Donald E. Meek, 'Between faith and folklore: twentieth-century interpretations and images of Columba', in Dauvit Broun and Thomas Owen Clancy (eds.), *Spes Scotorum: Hope of Scots* (Edinburgh, 1999); Bradley, *Celtic Christianity*.
4. Cf. Glanmor Williams, *Welsh Reformation Essays* (Cardiff, 1967), p. 207; Bradley, *Celtic Christianity*, pp. 94–5.
5. Cf. Saunders Lewis, 'Damcaniaeth Eglwysig Brotestannaidd', *Efrydiau Catholig*, 2 (1947), 36–55; Bradley, *Celtic Christianity*, p. 134.
6. Cf. Robert Camber Williams, *Penodau yn Hanes yr Eglwys yng Nghymru* (Lampeter, 1905), p. 12; Lemuel James, *The Historic Continuity of the Church* (Bangor, 1907); Joseph Maddocks and

W. J. Waterhouse, *The Continuity of the Church in Wales* (Llandrindod Wells, 1910); A. G. Edwards, *Landmarks in the History of the Welsh Church* (London, 1912), pp. 91–2 and *passim*.

[7] Cf. J. W. Bund, *The Celtic Church of Wales* (London, 1897).

[8] The group included Bishop Thomas Burgess of St Davids, Thomas Price, and Rice Rees; cf. Glanmor Williams, *Religion, Language, and Nationality in Wales* (Cardiff, 1979), pp. 122–3.

[9] Many prominent Anglicans, e.g. Dean H. T. Edwards, J. Arthur Price and David Jones, emphasized the mutuality of continuity and nationality; see *The Welsh Church and Nationality* (Bangor, c.1900); cf. Bradley, *Celtic Christianity*, p. 134. J. Arthur Price is the subject of Frances Knight's chapter in this volume.

[10] D. T. W. Price, *A History of the Church in Wales in the Twentieth Century* (Penarth, 1990), p. 22.

[11] The word Protestant was generally out of vogue within the Church at this time.

[12] Cf. *Welsh Catholic Times* (15 July 1932), ii.

[13] *Western Mail* (22 June 1933), 11.

[14] *Pembroke County and West Wales Guardian* (13 December 1929), 4.

[15] Cf. Trystan Owain Hughes, *Winds of Change: The Roman Catholic Church and Society in Wales 1916–62* (Cardiff, 1999), pp. 44–50.

[16] Cf. Trystan Owain Hughes, '"No longer will we call ourselves Catholics in Wales, but Welsh Catholics": Roman Catholicism, the Welsh language, and Welsh national identity in the twentieth century', *Welsh History Review*, 20/2 (2000), 336–65.

[17] J. E. De Hirsch-Davies, 'Wales and Catholicism I', *The Welsh Outlook* (February 1926), 43; cf. *Menevia Record*, III/2 (1955), 9; V/2 (1957), 21.

[18] *The Tablet* (21 July 1923), 83.

[19] Edward Lewis, *John Bangor, the People's Bishop: The Life and Work of John Charles Jones, Bishop of Bangor 1949–56* (London, 1962), pp.145–7.

[20] *Western Mail* (8 June 1933), 5; cf. 'Let the Welsh Bishops base their appeal on National grounds, and they will reap a hundredfold' (Anglican Bishop Timothy Rees of Llandaff), *Welsh Catholic Times* (8 January 1932), I.

[21] *Province,* IV/1 (1953), 139; cf. VIII/3 (1957), 73–4; XIII/3 (1962), 86–91; *The Tablet* (8 September 1934), 291; Michael McGrath, 'Wales and monasticism: a brief review', *Blackfriars* (March 1948), 115–16: 'As long as the Welsh people are fed on material of this kind it is vain to hope for the rapid progress of Catholicism amongst them.' See *Menevia Diocesan Yearbook 1957*, p. 102.

22. Although Saunders Lewis denied that this was strictly true, Bruce Griffiths claims that his conversion 'is not entirely to be divorced from his discovery of an older Welsh tradition to which he felt Wales should return for inspiration'. See Bruce Griffiths, *Saunders Lewis* (Cardiff, 1989), p. 80.
23. Quoted in Catherine Daniel, 'Wales', in Adrian Hastings (ed.), *The Church and the Nations* (London, 1959), p. 122.
24. Archimandrite Barnabas, *Strange Pilgrimage* (Welshpool, 1985), p. 30; see also Catherine Daniel, 'Paham yr wyf yn aelod o Eglwys Rufain', *Llafar* (1957), 47–9.
25. Bradley, *Celtic Christianity*, p. ix.
26. *Welsh Catholic Times* (15 July 1932), ii.
27. Ibid. (6 May 1932), ii.
28. Cf. *Western Mail* (10 September 1946), 2.
29. *Y Cymro* (16 January 1953), 13.
30. Ibid. (30 January 1953), 13.
31. *Western Mail* (26 March 1953), 6.
32. Cf. D. Ambrose Jones, *A History of the Church in Wales* (Carmarthen, 1926), p. 20; Arthur W. Wade-Evans, *Welsh Christian Origins* (Oxford, 1934).
33. A 'special invitation' was offered to the Baptist minister and author David Davies, 'a Champion of the Ancient British Church as against the See of Rome'. It was of no consequence that Davies also believed that this early Church was a primitive Nonconformist establishment and that the modern Church in Wales could claim no continuity from it.
34. The patriarchs of Jerusalem and Alexandria were both present.
35. *The Welsh Outlook* (January 1926), 9–10.
36. Taken from the title of Ian Bradley's book, *Celtic Christianity: Making Myths and Chasing Dreams*.
37. There was doubt over the historical accuracy of Anglican claims that St Chad was reconsecrated by the 'Saxon' church. The Roman Catholic counter-claim was either that St Chad's original 'Celtic' consecration was merely supplemented by the 'Saxon' church or that he had not been consecrated a 'Celtic' bishop in the first place. See *St Peter's Magazine*, III/1 (1923), 12–17.
38. *The Welsh Outlook* (May 1926), 137–8; (June 1926), 165–6, 166–7; (August 1926), 216–18; see also (February 1927), 46; (March 1927), 84.
39. De Hirsch-Davies, 'Wales and Catholicism I', pp. 43–5.
40. *The Welsh Outlook* (April 1926), 109–10.
41. A. W. Wade-Evans, 'Wales and the Church of Rome', *The Welsh Outlook* (December 1926), 320–2.

42 *Pembroke County and West Wales Guardian* (20 December 1929), 4; (27 December 1929), 4; (3 January 1930), 4 etc.
43 *Western Mail* (16 August 1930), 9; cf. (23 July 1930), 12; (26 July 1930), 9, etc.
44 Ian Bradley suggests that in Scotland at this time Celtic Christianity appealed to those of 'a more eirenic and ecumenical disposition'. See *Celtic Christianity*, p. 178.
45 *Western Mail* (21 July 1930), 11.
46 Ibid. (15 October 1929), 9.
47 Cf. *Western Mail* (1 April 1953), 6; *Y Cymro* (27 February 1953), 17.
48 *Menevia Record*, I/3 (1954), 9.
49 *Western Mail* (22 November 1957), 6.
50 *Review*, I/3 (1957), 5; V/4 (1962), 14: Etienne Raven urged his fellow Catholics to visit Llandaff Cathedral by claiming 'however at home its present tenants seem, we are the rightful owners!'
51 Catherine Daniel, 'Wales: Catholic and Nonconformist', *Blackfriars* (March 1957), 101.
52 *Welsh Catholic Times* (8 January 1932), i; (29 January 1932), i, etc.
53 Ibid. (26 February 1932), i.
54 *Baner ac Amserau Cymru* (10 January 1951), 8.
55 *Y Cymro* (16 January 1953), 13.
56 *Province*, IV/2 (1953), 175; V/4 (1954), 143; VIII/3 (1957), 74–5.
57 Ibid., III/1 (1952), 19.
58 *Western Mail* (17 April 1936), 12; the Church in Wales's Calendar of Saints was finally adopted in September 1944, cf. Ewart Lewis, *Prayer Book Revision in the Church in Wales* (Penarth, 1958), pp. 25, 55–6.
59 See *Province*, I/3 (1950).
60 Daniel, 'Wales', p. 121.
61 *The Provincial Youth Council of the Church in Wales: Preparatory Study Notes (for Aberystwyth 1959) for the Use of Church in Wales' Delegates to Ecumenical Conferences* (Penarth, 1959), pp. 9, 12.
62 Francis Mostyn, Cardiff Advent Pastoral 1922. Apart from Anglicans, the Baptist minister David Davies also condemned Mostyn's assertions as 'utterly unhistorical', *Western Mail* (5 December 1922), 10; cf. *The Welsh Outlook* (January 1926), 9; *St. Peter's Parish Magazine*, III/1 (1923), 12–16 and Bishop Louis Casartelli of Salford's reaction to the newly disestablished Church's claims in *The Tablet* (21 July 1923), 83.
63 *Western Mail* (15 October 1929), 10. Referring to the archbishop's 'most astounding assertion', Dean William Williams reacted by stating that it was 'difficult to believe that anyone who possessed a certain amount of knowledge and a grain of charity could be capable of perpetrating such a travesty of history, on the one hand,

and a parody of Christian love on the other', *Western Mail* (18 October 1929), 7.
64 Francis Vaughan, 'Foreword', in T. P. Ellis, *The Catholic Martyrs of Wales* (London, 1933), p. xv; cf. McGrath and Petit, *Joint Advent Pastoral for Cardiff and Menevia 1950*; Michael McGrath, 'Wales and monasticism: a brief review', *Blackfriars* (March 1948), 115–16.
65 'Rome was incensed by Morris's deliberate omission of the word "Catholic" in describing them'; see John S. Peart-Binns, *Alfred Edwin Morris: Archbishop of Wales* (Llandysul, 1990), p. 86.
66 *Western Mail* (2 September 1946), 3; cf. earlier statements by an Anglican correspondent in reaction to the official constitution of Roman Catholic parishes in Wales, *Western Mail* (4 February 1928), 9.
67 Peart-Binns, *Alfred Edwin Morris*, pp. 93–4; cf. Bishop John Charles Jones of Bangor's similar claims, see Lewis, *John Bangor*, pp. 145–7.
68 *Welsh Catholic Times* (26 February 1932), i.
69 *Province*, V/4 (1954), 110; cf. III/2 (1952), 39.
70 Owain W. Jones, *Glyn Simon: His Life and Opinions* (Llandysul, 1981), p. 66.
71 Theomemphus, *Bilingual Bishops and All That* (Llandybïe, 1958).
72 Cf. *Western Mail* (24 February 1960), 4.
73 *The Tablet* (12 February 1916), 200; cf. (26 February 1916), 267.
74 Ellis, *Catholic Martyrs of Wales*, p. xix.
75 Ibid; R. O. F. Wynne, 'Y Cymru a'r Diwygiad Protestannaidd', *Efrydiau Catholig*, 6 (1954), 17; 'Detholiad o Englynion Hiraeth am yr Hen Ffydd', *Efrydiau Catholig*, 6 (1954), 5–12.
76 *Welsh Catholic Times* (15 July 1932), ii.
77 Cf. *Welsh Catholic Times* (29 January 1932), i; *Western Mail* (10 September 1946), 2; Daniel, 'Wales: Catholic and Nonconformist', p. 103; *Western Mail* (8 March 1960), 4; Vaughan, 'Foreword', p. xiv.
78 *Western Mail* (10 September 1946), 2.
79 Ibid. (12 February 1936), 11.
80 *Province*, VII/2 (1956), 72.
81 Compare Glanmor Williams, *Reformation Views of Church History* (London, 1970), p. 70, with Leslie Hardinge, *The Celtic Church in Britain* (London, 1972), pp. 17–28.
82 Glanmor Williams, *Welsh Reformation Essays* (Cardiff, 1967), p. 207.
83 Bradley, *Celtic Christianity*, p. vii.

~ 7 ~
'The Essence of Welshness'?: Some Aspects of Christian Faith and National Identity in Wales, c.1900–2000[1]

D. DENSIL MORGAN

The Historical Background

It may be too sweeping a generalization, but it could be said (and I would venture to do so) that Wales emerged from its Romano-Celtic past during a religious revival. If the birth of the nation is dated during the fifth century, that too was the time of the vast missionary surge which we still delight in calling the 'age of the saints'. It was then, in *c.* AD 450–600 that Dyfrig, Illtud, David and their companions fulfilled a ministry which blended monasticism with evangelization in a uniquely potent fusion. In the short time between that juncture and the dawn of the seventh century, Christianity and the life of the emerging nation had become so tightly interlaced as to be virtually indistinguishable, and for nearly a millennium-and-a-half Welsh identity and religious affiliation became totally intertwined. Not for nothing has it been claimed that: 'Of all the associations between religion and social values in Wales the most intriguing and longest lasting has been that between religion and nationality. From the outset the Christian religion seemed to be part of the essence of Welshness.'[2]

What was true of early and high medieval Wales was also true of modern Wales where the native pattern developed differently from that prevalent in other lands. Whereas the onset of modernism and later the presuppositions of the Enlightenment threatened to sever the unity between religious affiliation and citizenship, in Wales that unity was preserved. Modern Wales no less than Celtic and medieval Wales remained openly Christian.

Even more remarkable was the fact that industrialism, far from being a harbinger of secularization, *strengthened* the hold which Christianity held on the mass of the people. The lead which Wales took in the industrial revolution first with the production of iron then of coal, steel and slate, did nothing to lessen the influence and appeal of faith, by now in its Nonconformist guise. If Victorian Christianity in England was a bourgeois and a minority affair, in Wales it remained sturdy, proletarian and popular. Such was the degree of interpenetration between faith, life and national consciousness that 'by 1890 being a Welshman and being a Christian were virtually synonymous'.[3] Even in industrial and increasingly urban Wales, for the majority of the people being Welsh still meant being Christian.

During the Edwardian era, Welsh Christianity was at its most ebullient. 'There is good reason to believe that the sun will yet shine brighter on our land, and its religious life will show forth even more glory during the twentieth century than ever it did during the nineteenth,' wrote one Nonconformist minister in 1900. 'Thus we can look forward with utter confidence to the even greater success of the Kingdom of God in tomorrow's Wales'.[4] The naïveté of this prognosis only struck subsequent generations as being foolish. To many at the time it must have seemed quite reasonable. Institutional religion was massively influential. The 'four great Nonconformist denominations', the Calvinistic Methodists, the Congregationalists, the Baptists and the Wesleyans, had a shared communicant membership of some 535,000 to say nothing of the huge phalanx of 'listeners' (*gwrandawyr*) or adherents, as many as 950,000, who though not members were officially attached to the chapels and regularly attended services. Along with 500,000 children in Sunday schools, Nonconformity commanded the loyalty of nearly 1.5 million Welsh adults in a population of 2.5 million. Two out of every five Welsh people were Protestant Dissenters. Anglicanism was also growing in confidence and numbers at the time. During 1914, 24,500 infants and adults were baptized in the four Welsh dioceses of Bangor, St Asaph, St Davids and Llandaff; 17,000 candidates were confirmed by their bishops; 155,500 worshippers attended Easter communion and 169,000 children were taught in the Church's Sunday schools. In all, 13.78 per cent of the population belonged to the Established Church. If this was less than the total number of Nonconformists, it represented considerably more than any other single denomination. Whatever separated the different religious traditions during these years, the presence and influence of mainstream Christianity, whether Dissenting or Established,[5] was taken as a fact. 'We think that from the evidence advanced before us', wrote the authors of the *Report of the Royal Commission on the Church of England and Other Religious Bodies in Wales and Monmouthshire* (1910), 'that the people of Wales show a marked tendency to avail themselves of the provision made by the churches of all denominations for their spiritual welfare.'[6] Between the turn of the century and the onset of the Great War, Wales remained a remarkably Christian country.

The Disestablishment of the Church of England in Wales, 1890–1914

Despite the impression current at the time, there was nothing specifically Welsh about the chapel religion of Protestant Nonconformity. Three of the larger Nonconformist bodies, the Congregationalists, the Baptists and the Wesleyans, had come into Wales from England, the first two during the seventeenth century and the third at the beginning of the nineteenth. Only the Calvinistic Methodists, who had seceded from the Established Church in 1811, had explicitly Welsh roots. The specifically Welsh character of Protestant Dissent was unselfconscious and pragmatic rather than being a matter of principle. For most of the nineteenth century preaching, worship and spiritual fellowship were conducted through the medium of Welsh for the simple reason that that was the language of the people and the only language which many of them could understand. Yet by the 1870s it was clear that a genuine Welsh national consciousness was growing and that questions concerning the relationship between religion and national identity were being asked.

Although by the mid-century Nonconformity had displaced Anglicanism as the principal form of Welsh Christianity, it was certain representatives of the Established Church who had shown themselves to be most theologically sensitive to the particular claims of Welsh nationality. For Dean H. T. Edwards of Bangor a commitment to Welsh nationality was not a matter of pragmatism but of deep principle. The episcopal church in Wales was the linear descendant of the early church of David, Teilo, Seiriol, Beuno, Cybi and all the Celtic saints whose existence long predated the see of Canterbury and the political union between England and Wales which was sealed in 1536.[7] For centuries it was this church, Celtic, Catholic and Reformed, which had been the *one church* of the Welsh nation and it would have remained so had it not been for the erastianism of the Tudor, Stuart and especially Hanoverian state. 'The policy which arrayed all the forces of nationality against the Church was not adopted in Wales until the eighteenth century', he claimed. 'At that point its effect was to make the Welsh people not Romanist, but Nonconformist.'[8] The alienation of the mass of the Welsh people from their ancient church had occurred not because of their spiritual apostasy but due to the politically motivated policy of appointing English clergy to principal Welsh benefices. Throughout the eighteenth and early nineteenth centuries not a single Welshman had been appointed bishop in the Welsh Church.[9] It was no wonder, claimed Edwards, that the ordinary men and women whose forefathers and mothers had been so staunchly loyal to their national church had forsaken what they had come to regard as an alien institution. 'The regeneration of the Church of the Cymry, by the restoration of the masses to her fold, can assuredly be effected by none other than native bishops and native clergy.'[10] With verve, erudition and a sincere patriotism, Dean Edwards staked his claim that, despite everything, it was the Established Church which was the true church of the Welsh people and still best placed to renew the nation's spiritual and national life.

The elegant logic of H. T. Edwards cut little ice either with the majority of Welsh Nonconformists or with those of the greatest influence among his own communion. His death in 1884 coincided both with the increasing politicization of Welsh Dissent and with the deepening intransigence of the Anglican hierarchy against the current spirit of national resurgence. Even before the widening of the franchise in 1868 to include tenant farmers and workers as well as landowners, Welsh Nonconformity had become a political force. Thereafter its radicalization was apparent to all. Toryism collapsed to be superseded by the ideologies of the Liberal Party with which virtually all of the newly enfranchised Nonconformist Welshmen were identified. By the mid-1880s land reform, tithe abolition, the plea for a non-sectarian scheme of general education and the disestablishment of the Church of England had become the issues of the day. Whereas the first generation of Nonconformist politicians, exemplified by Henry Richard MP, had entered politics for religious reasons, the spiritual sincerity of their successors was more suspect. David Lloyd George who had been returned for the Caernarvon Boroughs in 1889, although nominally a Baptist, was in fact totally secular in outlook and by the later Victorian period his values were becoming commonplace. By then the policy of the Welsh parliamentary party was to play the nationalist card. Trading on the grievances of their overwhelmingly Nonconformist constituency, Lloyd George focused on the intertwined questions of national and religious identity. As the party of privilege and the landed élite, the Tories, they claimed, had always been inimical to the needs and aspirations of ordinary Welsh people, while the Established Church, far from being the guarantor of the nation's spirituality, was in fact nothing but the Church of *England* in Wales. By its long subservience to its 'alien' masters, the Anglican Church had forfeited its claim to be the one authentic church of the people. It was a politicized Nonconformity, therefore, which seized upon the glaring ecclesiastical weaknesses which patriotic Churchmen had revealed with such candour to forward its own aims. In short it suited Lloyd George to reinforce the claim that Christianity (in its Nonconformist guise) and Welsh national identity were one.

Though many of the lower clergy were in substantial agreement with Dean Edwards's thesis (and appalled by the rabble-rousing of Lloyd George's radical Dissent), there were significant elements within Victorian Anglicanism which gave credence to the Nonconformist claim that the Church was an alien body. By a bitter irony it was Dean Edwards's younger brother, A. G. Edwards, who did more than anyone to perpetuate the view that episcopalianism was inimical to the national aspirations of the rising generation. Appointed bishop of St Asaph in 1889, A. G. Edwards made an immediate impression as the leading 'Church Defender' of the day. His strategy for preventing the disestablishment of the Anglican Church in Wales was to emphasize its superior social status and links with the Anglicized ruling class. Unlike his brother, Bishop Edwards's attitude to his own Welshness and that of the common people was deeply ambiguous: 'I am half an Englishman and half a Welshman and have been labouring between the two all my life'.[11] His identity problem became the basis of the Welsh Anglican campaign to preserve the Church's established rights.[12] Under his leadership 'Church Defence' became an out-and-out war against popular Nonconformity and the voluntary, democratic and proletarian Welsh-speaking culture from which it had grown. Nonconformist reaction was to emphasize further its own character as being unambiguously Welsh (which in fact it was not) while patriotic Churchmen were put in the invidious position of appearing to endorse the Anglicizing policies of the hierarchy.

The disestablishment campaign resulted in victory for Nonconformity when, in August 1914, the Liberal government finally passed the bill declaring an independent Anglican church in Wales shorn of many of its ancient endowments, privileges and all of its links with the state. Yet it was a hollow victory. Public concern had moved away from narrowly ecclesiastical matters, and the mutual vilification in which the most zealous of the protagonists had indulged had only served to cause popular disenchantment with Christianity generally. By 1914 it had become clear that the burning issues would be material rather than spiritual: housing, poverty, unemployment and the like. The battle lines would no longer be drawn simply between patrician and hierarchical Tories supported by the Anglican Church, and chapel-going, Welsh-speaking common folk (*gwerin*), but instead a class-based political culture would rapidly evolve. If, during the Victorian and Edwardian eras, Nonconformist Wales had been overwhelmingly Liberal, after the Great War the major political influence would be that of the Labour Party. By then, a specifically Welsh identity would be less bound up with religion and more with an increasingly secularized scheme of socialist politics.

ASPECTS OF CHRISTIAN FAITH AND NATIONAL IDENTITY

Religion, Identity and Labour, 1920–1939

As was true elsewhere, the First World War had an adverse effect on religious faith and affiliation in Wales, though its nature and extent would not become explicit for some time.[13] Following the trauma of war came the pain of depression. The two decades which divided the Great War from the conflict of 1939–45 were quite excruciating for the Welsh people. Social dislocation and economic collapse were catastrophic in their effects, and hunger, hardship and suffering became widespread. During the 1920s the heavy industry which had been south Wales's mainstay for a century-and-a-quarter went into steep decline. With changes in shipping technology and developments in transport generally, the previously insatiable foreign demand for Welsh steam coal ceased virtually overnight. European markets began to be serviced by coal mined more cheaply in Italy, Spain and Poland, while France and Belgium, which had formerly been among Wales's best customers, began to be supplied (ironically) with German coal as war reparations in accordance with the stipulations of the Treaty of Versailles. Former South American markets were also importing United States coal at a cheaper rate. Just as the coal industry, which employed 271,000 colliers or 35 per cent of the total Welsh population, was collapsing, south Wales's second largest industry, steel, was also being destroyed. Wales's oldest industrial heartland, on the north-eastern rim of the coalfield between Merthyr Tydfil and Pontypool, was being made desolate. The closure of the iron and steel works at Cyfarthfa in 1921, Blaenafon in 1922, Ebbw Vale in 1929 and Dowlais in 1930 – all names redolent of the industrial past – was a knockout blow to an area which was already reeling. Ancillary industries such as railways and shipping, even clothing and house-building, also suffered, while those which avoided the worst effects of the slump, anthracite mining and tinplate manufacture in the south-west, slate quarrying in north Wales, and agriculture, hardly flourished. The national situation was exacerbated by a world-wide recession, while the lessons of low investment, an inability to respond quickly to changing markets and a vast over-dependence on a single industry economy, were bitter ones to learn.

By December 1925 unemployment in Wales was 13.4 per cent of the insured population; two years later it was 23.3 per cent and in 1930 27.2 per cent. (The comparable percentage in England for 1930 was 15.8.) If the 1920s were dire, the 1930s were even worse. In December 1930 the eastern valleys of Rhymney and Tredegar registered unemployment at the rate of 27.5 per cent of the adult population, Pontypridd and Rhondda at 30 per cent, while the proportion in Newport was as high as 35 per cent. By August 1932 when the depression reached its lowest point, 42.8 per cent of all Welsh insured working men were idle. The cost of maintaining the unemployed was in itself crippling. In September 1931 state benefit was cut and all prospective claimants were means-tested. Those who were in a position to leave Wales did so, in their thousands and tens of thousands, to find work elsewhere. The rest had no alternative but to stay. The trauma which this left on the national psyche was immense and its recollection would remain emotively bitter for years to come:

> Do you remember 1926? That summer of soups and speeches,
> The sunlight and the idle wheels and the deserted crossings,
> And the laughter and the cursing in the moonlit streets? . . .
> . . . 'Ay, ay, we remember 1926', said Dai and Shinkin,
> As they stood on the kerb in Charing Cross Road,
> 'And we shall remember 1926 until our blood is dry'.[14]

The switch of allegiance from the Liberal Party to Labour was swift. For the twenty-one Welsh Liberals returned in Lloyd George's 'coupon election' in 1918, Labour gained ten seats and the party won nearly 31 per cent of the Welsh vote. Before the war its active support in Wales had been desultory. Following the collapse of the coalition government in 1922, the Liberals' popularity began to decline; only eleven members were returned for Welsh seats during the 1922 election, twelve in the election a year later, eleven in 1924, ten in 1929 and only nine in 1931. Even these were split between the different factions of Liberal, Independent Liberal and National Liberal. By 1935, Labour controlled every single seat in the industrial south, polling 400,000 votes or over 45 per cent of the Welsh total. By the 1930s most of Wales had rejected the individualism of its Liberal past in favour of a collectivist and more class-based Labour future. This would have profound effects on the way in which Welsh people perceived their own identity and the way in which that identity was linked with the Christian faith.

Long before the deep dislocation of the 1930s, Christianity and the Labour movement had striven to accommodate one another.[15] Early socialists such as Keir Hardie, founder of the Independent Labour Party, had used biblical language and a religiously inspired idealism in order to convince Welsh chapelgoers of socialism's compatibility with their faith. For Hardie socialism was Christianity at work, the practical application of the Sermon on the Mount in order to usher in God's kingdom on earth. It was above else a moral code rather than an economic dogma and was commended as such not least by the Revd T. E. Nicholas of Glais in the Swansea valley, the ILP's most effective propagandist among the workers of south Wales before the Great War. If Nicholas, a neo-Marxist poet-preacher in the romantic style, was a skilled populist, there were other young Nonconformist leaders like the Baptist, the Revd Herbert Morgan, and the Presbyterian, the Revd Silyn Roberts, whose apologia for the socialist creed was much more intellectually astute. James Griffiths, leader of the west Wales anthracite miners, later MP for Llanelli and a minister in successive Labour governments, recalled Silyn's immense influence on young men who were keen to reconcile Nonconformity with socialism during the early years of the century.

> He preached God and Evolution. He was a minister and a Socialist . . . he became our inspirer and our justification. We could tell our parents, who feared this new gospel we talked of, 'but Silyn Roberts believes as we do'. How many devout but dubious fathers became reconciled to Socialist sons by that assurance? He linked the South Wales of Evan Roberts [the religious revivalist] to the South Wales of Keir Hardie.[16]

Even into the 1920s there were Welshmen and their families whose national identity was bound as closely with Nonconformist Christianity as with the socialism of the Labour movement. 'It is rather late in the day to utter this nonsense [concerning the incompatibility of Labour with the chapels]', wrote one observer in 1923, 'for there are thousands of Welshmen today who can find no inconsistency in singing *Diolch iddo* and *Ar ei ben bo'r goron*, with the Welsh hwyl at one meeting, and then proceeding to another meeting to sing *The Red Flag* with the same enthusiasm.'[17]

Late in the day or not, by then the problems implicit in this assumed reconciliation had come well to the fore. Those who were keenest to forge the combination tended to see Christianity in terms of socialist ideology or a humanitarian faith. T. E. Nicholas had claimed that 'true Christianity recognizes the divinity of man . . . not as a fallen being but one who is continually advancing to higher levels and who is endowed with unlimited possibilities'.[18] Even less radical Nonconformist socialists sat very loosely to orthodox formulations of the creed. Whereas the outward trappings of chapel culture were being preserved in the guise of attendance at worship, hymn-singing and often an appreciation of a well delivered sermon, specifically religious convictions were weakening daily. Basic theological truths concerning the holiness of God, the reality of human sinfulness, the deity of Christ and the unique nature of his birth, death and resurrection were being refashioned according to the canons of humanitarian socialism. Rather than devising a doctrinally robust Christian socialism which was faithful to the gospel, the tendency in Wales was to spiritualize a basically materialist ideology according to Nonconformist *mores*.[19] In every compromise it was traditional Christianity and not the Labour movement which lost out.

Even more threatening to the link between religion and national identity was the fact that chapel-going itself was in decline. Chapel statistics reached their high point in 1926 when the four major Nonconformist denominations recorded a joint membership of 536,000.[20] Yet this still huge number representing baptized communicants masked the fact that the previously extensive class of 'listeners', and even more ominously, many children formerly present in Sunday schools, were no longer attending. There was a growing conviction that Protestant Dissent was losing its grip on the hearts, minds and imagination of the people.[21] During each succeeding year the chapels lost more members than they gained, and for every Welsh worker who succeeded in combining a Christian commitment with Labour politics, there was another for whom religion and socialism were wholly inimical and still more who simply drifted away. Despite the earlier attempt to yoke the Labour movement to Welsh language and Nonconformist culture, socialism came to be associated increasingly with progress and the English language whilst Welsh, especially in the valleys of the industrial south, became identified with Puritanism and the Liberal past. For proponents of the class struggle, of course, the perpetuation of national identity was detrimental to the solidarity of the workers' international for which English was deemed to be a much more appropriate means of expression. By the 1930s, Welsh identity was perhaps more popularly represented not by the moderate chapel-going James Griffiths, but by Aneurin Bevan, the openly atheistic, non-Welsh-speaking Member for Ebbw Vale.[22] Welshness, the language and religious affiliation were going their separate ways.

A Catholic National Identity, 1920–1939?

However large the chapel loomed in the popular mind, Christianity was not commensurate with Protestant Nonconformity. On 1 April 1920 the newly disestablished and autonomous Welsh Anglican Church, soon to be entitled the Church in Wales, became a fact. The mean-spirited political *imbroglio* which had been the disestablishment campaign came to an end in 1914, but the creation of the new church had to be postponed until after the war. Having been cushioned from the worst effects of disendowment by the government's financial guarantee, Welsh Anglicans began to accustom themselves to their new status. Though disestablished, the new church was still hierarchical in nature, in many places gentrified and ambivalent about its status. The old hostility to the Welsh language persisted; many of its senior clergy and middle-class laity despised Welsh as an uncouth throwback to the past, 'the last refuge of the uneducated' according to A. G. Edwards[23] who had been unanimously elected its first archbishop. Yet confidence was steadily growing and Churchmen began to appreciate, if not to relish, their new-found independence. The Church soon created two new dioceses, Monmouth in 1921 and Swansea and Brecon in 1923. If the senior clergy remained for the most part Anglicized and still establishment-minded Tories, there were many among the parish ministers for whom Anglicanism was no bar to being wholly Welsh. Their cause was strengthened by two totally unexpected occurrences: the appointment, in 1923, of Dr Maurice Jones as principal of St David's College, the Church's seminary-university at Lampeter, and the even more surprising election, in 1931, of Timothy Rees, a monk of the Community of the Resurrection at Mirfield, Yorkshire, as bishop of Llandaff. Jones, a native of rural Meirionnydd and former military chaplain, was impervious to the social snobbery, the anti-Welsh bias and anti-Dissenting antipathy of the hierarchy. His influence on successive generations of prospective clergy throughout the inter-war years did a significant amount to restore respect for the Welsh-language culture of the common people within the Church in Wales.[24] Like Jones, Rees's career in England led his sponsors to think of him as an appropriate choice for a senior position in the Church in Wales. It became apparent from the outset, however, that this most unassuming of men was less a prelate and autocrat than an evangelist and pastor whose Anglo-Catholic social radicalism blended perfectly with an evangelical piety to which Nonconformists warmed. He was, in fact, H. T. Edwards reincarnate, a keen Welsh-speaking patriot with a social conscience to boot.[25] His death aged sixty-five in 1939 deprived the bench of bishops of its most attractive personality, one who had made a specifically Welsh Anglican identity a possibility once more.

These years also witnessed the consolidation of Roman Catholicism within the land.[26] In 1916 Pope Benedict XV had announced that henceforth Wales's two dioceses of Cardiff and Menevia be afforded the status of a separate ecclesiastical province with its own archbishop. The appointment in 1921 of Francis Mostyn, bishop of Menevia and fourth son of Sir Piers Mostyn, baron of Talacre in Flint, as archbishop betokened the beginnings of a rapprochement between the see of Rome and the Welsh people. Bereft of any indigenous working-class tradition such as that of Lancashire and other parts of the north of England, and possessing only three landed, recusant families (of which the Mostyns of Talacre were one), Catholicism was viewed in Wales with hostility and fear. Its *mores* were strange, its rituals mystifying and the presence among its faithful of thousands of virtually peasant Irishmen and their rough families put the church well beyond the pale. For most Welsh Christians it was a foreign and vaguely sinister institution. Mostyn, however, was keen to convince his fellow countrymen that Roman Christianity represented the continuation of the classic Welsh tradition of which the poets of the princes and medieval noblemen, and the Welsh Catholic humanists of the Renaissance, had embodied with such distinction. This was part of the appeal which the church had for a number of exceedingly gifted Welsh converts of whom Saunders Lewis was the most brilliant. In 1925 Lewis, the son and grandson of Calvinistic Methodist ministers of renown and fast gaining the reputation of being the *enfant terrible* of Welsh literature, helped form Plaid Genedlaethol Cymru, the Welsh Nationalist Party. Its political manifesto which diverged radically from the *laissez-faire* individualism of contemporary Liberalism and what Lewis and his colleagues saw as the rootless collectivist materialism of the socialist movement, reflected the social teaching of the Catholic Church.[27] Although small and unrepentantly élitist, the Nationalist Party had an influence well beyond its numbers especially in the flourishing intellectual life of inter-war Wales. Accusations of (among other things) fascism, anti-Semitism and a blind subservience to ultramontanist Rome did nothing to prevent the stimulation which its ideals provided for the younger Welsh-speaking generation at least. Whereas Labour-dominated industrial Wales was being progressively Anglicized, and the still predominantly Liberal rural areas were stagnating, nationalism presented a radical political alternative. For many young members of Plaid Genedlaethol Cymru, the renewal of Christianity, often in a fairly dogmatic and catholicized form, would be essential if Welsh identity was going to survive.

ASPECTS OF CHRISTIAN FAITH AND NATIONAL IDENTITY

Nonconformity and the Crisis of Identity, 1920–1962

Despite its Romanist hue, the Nationalist Party attracted many more Nonconformists and even Welsh Churchmen than Catholics. If Nonconformity, whose institutional presence was still hugely influential in inter-war Wales, was in decline, there were signs that its theological base was at least being strengthened. The doctrinal liberalism which had become almost a prerequisite for denominational leadership after the war (especially but by no means exclusively, among the Congregationalists), was being challenged by a renewal of confessional orthodoxy inspired chiefly by the thought of Karl Barth. By the 1930s more and more Nonconformist ministers were rejecting the theology of morals and experience for that of revelation and the Word of God. Preaching began to be thought of again more in terms of proclamation and not moral uplift, while a new urgency gripped Welsh evangelical Dissent generally.[28]

For Welsh Christians who had long accepted the mutual interpenetration of faith and national identity, there was much in this confessional renaissance which could be condoned. In the light of the extreme hardship and deprivation which were currently being experienced, especially in the industrial south, the need for national renewal was patent. Despite everything, neither political nor religious idealism had been extinguished, and it was equally apposite for the Welsh to see their dilemma in religio-national terms as in socio-economic ones. For liberal-minded, Labour-supporting Nonconformist clergy such as Morgan Watcyn-Williams, an English-speaking Presbyterian, in Merthyr Tydfil, and the Barthian Baptist Lewis Valentine, a Welsh-speaking leader of the Nationalist Party in the north, the redemption of the Welsh nation would only come about on the basis of a shared commitment to the Christian faith.[29] It was left to J. E. Daniel, a leading nationalist and professor of Christian doctrine at the Bala-Bangor Congregational College, to provide a specifically Barthian combination of revelational theology and Christian nationalism. His highly perceptive wartime essays including 'The secular idea of man' and the influential '*Gwaed y Teulu*' (The family's blood) constitute a sturdy and original contribution to our understanding of the nature of the relationship

ASPECTS OF CHRISTIAN FAITH AND NATIONAL IDENTITY

between Christianity and national identity in twentieth-century Wales.[30]

From the standpoint of the Christian faith, the post-war era was at best mixed. The 1939–45 conflict was much less traumatic than the Great War had been, and consequently there was less idealism about the need or the ability to build 'a land fit for heroes to live in'. Having been disappointed once, both Christian and secular confidence was much more chastened than it had been a quarter of a century before. Following the austerity of the late 1940s, the 1950s formed a period of social and economic stability and growing affluence. Having been restored, the traditional heavy industries of south Wales were by now working to full capacity, unemployment was low and social dislocation seemed to have been checked. A healthy economy allowed people to purchase luxuries which soon became essentials for modern life: washing machines, televisions and their own small family cars. Huge local council projects provided post-war Wales with cheap but adequate rented housing, while the extension of mortgage facilities allowed more and more families to purchase their own homes. The standard of public health improved, especially following the establishment of the National Health Service in 1945, while by 1947 the popular measures to nationalize coalmining and steel manufacture allowed the people what they believed to be a stake in their own future. Though weaker than of old, institutional Christianity still played a significant role in Welsh national life. In 1955, for instance, the chief Nonconformist denominations could still boast a joint membership of 370,000 baptized communicants, representing as many as one in seven of the total Welsh population.[31] In some areas, especially those in which the Welsh language was the general means of expression, chapel culture was still strong, while even in the more Anglicized districts Protestant Dissent was yet a living force. As part of the Festival of Britain activities of 1951, W. J. Gruffydd could still state with little incongruity that 'by the end of the first quarter of the nineteenth century, Wales had become what it substantially is today, a nation of Evangelical Christians'.[32]

Yet all was not well within this purported nation of believers. Anglicization and secularization were marching on apace. The Census Returns for 1951 noted the sharp downward trend in the people's ability to speak Welsh. In the short span of ten years the total number of Welsh speakers had declined by nearly 100,000 to 715,000. Native speakers tended to be in the older age group while there was little vision as to how 'the language question' might be addressed. The received wisdom was that Welsh could be preserved on the hearth rather than by any official or political measures. Inevitably, appeals to preserve the language were often thoroughly pessimistic and forlorn. It would not be until after 1962, with Saunders Lewis's famous radio broadcast 'The fate of the language' and the opening of the first Welsh-medium secondary school in south-eastern Wales, that radical measures for linguistic renewal would begin to be implemented and made effective. Before then there was a feeling of inevitability about the demise of Welsh and the chapel culture and Nonconformist value system which it was perceived to embody. The tercentenary of the ejection of the Puritan ministers from the Established Church in 1662, the event which had created Protestant Nonconformity, was celebrated in Wales not with jubilation but with a sense of foreboding. Post-war Dissent saw itself to be in a state of perpetual 'crisis',[33] and denominational leaders felt that there was little they could do to allay its effects. In the most perceptive analysis of contemporary chapel life published at the time, R. Ifor Parry showed how Nonconformity was suffering due to its cultural captivity to 'the Welsh way of life' which was currently in decline; that it was tied to 'the Nonconformist Conscience', the Puritanism of which was everywhere regarded as being antiquated and hypocritical; that the plainness of its worship had bred a manichean negativity towards beauty and the senses; and that growing economic affluence had led to a materialism which dissolved the moral seriousness on which Dissenting conviction was built: 'This is the atmosphere in which Nonconformity is having to exist and today it is fighting for its very existence.'[34]

Christian Faith and the Renewal of National Identity, 1950–1979

The gloominess which characterized Welsh Nonconformity stood in contrast to the sense of rejuvenation which permeated

Welsh Anglicanism during these years. After having experienced its first quarter-century of disestablished independence, the Church in Wales was at ease with itself and confident about its future. By the 1950s a world-affirming catholicism, in tune with the tenor of the times, had come to represent 'central' Welsh churchmanship while the Church was becoming increasingly sensitive to the national aspirations of the Welsh people. Whereas chapel religion was seen to be oppressive and Puritanical, Anglicanism, with its Prayer Book liturgy, sacramentalism and rounded doctrines of creation and incarnation, provided a very appealing version of Christian faith. Unencumbered by the negativities of sabbatarianism and teetotalism, it presented a viable spiritual alternative for those who were offended by Nonconformity but chose not to succumb to secularism and irreligion. Not a few of its most distinguished lay members and senior clerics were former Nonconformists. Yet perhaps the most interesting contemporary development involved the change of attitude within the Church to Welsh nationality and identity.

With the appointment of J. C. Jones to the see of Bangor in 1949, Glyn Simon to Swansea and Brecon in 1953 and thence to Llandaff four years later, and G. O. Williams as J. C. Jones's successor in 1957, much of the ambiguity which had coloured the bishops' attitude to Welshness was repudiated. If Jones was a popular and warm-hearted patriot and Williams, an exceedingly able former warden of Llandovery College, was virtually a Welsh nationalist, the most unexpectedly zealous advocate of a pro-Welsh policy was Glyn Simon. A cradle Churchman (unlike the other two who had been brought up as Calvinistic Methodists) whose first language was English, Simon made his patriotic credentials plain in 1957 by sharply criticizing the election of Edwin Morris, an Englishman who had served the Church in Wales as bishop of Monmouth, as archbishop. 'The recent elections,' he claimed, 'have revealed an anti-Welsh and pro-English trend, and in some cases a bigotry as narrow ... as any to be found in the tightest and most remote of Welsh communities.'[35] Given the historical ambivalence which the Church expressed towards its own Welshness, the continued existence of a pro-English trend was hardly exceptional. What was extraordinary was the virulent and public way in which a senior member of the hierarchy chose to express his disapproval of the status quo. Simon's own tenure as archbishop between 1968 and 1971 coincided with a renewed sense of national consciousness throughout Wales. Cardiff had been proclaimed the Welsh capital in 1958, the central government's Welsh Office had been established in the capital in 1964, while the campaign to prevent the Tryweryn valley from being drowned to provide water for the English Midlands had been fought throughout the late 1950s and early 1960s. In 1966 Gwynfor Evans was returned as Plaid Cymru's first MP, for Carmarthen, while the investiture of the Prince of Wales at Caernarfon Castle in July 1969 had provided a focus for significant anti-establishment dissension. When Dafydd Iwan, president of the radical Welsh Language Society, was imprisoned for the non-payment of fines imposed for his part in the campaign for bilingual road signs, Simon ruffled not a few establishment feathers by visiting him in prison. 'There is nothing unscriptural or un-Christian in nationalism as such', he claimed.[36] Simon's policies were continued by his successor, G. O. Williams, and by the 1970s the perception of the Church in Wales as being an alien body had changed dramatically. The old dichotomy between an Anglicized Church and a thoroughly Welsh Nonconformity was ringing increasingly untrue. In the popular mind the contention that 'the Anglican church is the proper spiritual home for a patriotic Welshman'[37] had much to commend it.

The theological ferment which affected Western Christianity generally during the 1960s did not bypass the Welsh churches. The Second Vatican Council, John Robinson's *Honest to God* (1963), the 'Death of God' movement and various secular theologies had their devotees within the land. A particularly vigorous theological discussion took place in the influential monthly *Barn* (Opinion) between J. R. Jones, a Calvinistic Methodist layman and professor of philosophy at the University of Wales, Swansea, and H. D. Lewis, also a Calvinistic Methodist and professor of the philosophy of religion at King's College, London. Heavily influenced by Tillich's 'Protestant Principle' and some of the most enigmatic sections of Bonhoeffer's *Letters and Papers from Prison*, Jones championed a highly idiosyncratic existential humanism which was openly antagonistic to Christian orthodoxy. As well as reflecting faithfully each of the religious predilections of the 'secular sixties', this altercation was intensified by being linked to the concurrent crisis of nationhood and that within Welsh Dissent.[38] Despite its apparent malaise, Nonconformity was sufficiently healthy to fuel such an intellectually distinguished discussion and to provide work for renewal movements of both evangelical and ecumenical hues. It was still common for Welsh Nonconformists to link the renewal of nationhood with spiritual revival and a rediscovery of Christian faith. The most weighty contributions to a Christian theology of nationhood during these years were produced not by Churchmen but by Nonconformist scholars of the calibre of Pennar Davies, R. M. (Bobi) Jones and most notably R. Tudur Jones.[39]

Pluralism and Multiple Identities: 1979 to the Millennium

The confidence which accompanied the renewal of national consciousness during the 1960s and 1970s and which led to the establishment of an effective system of Welsh-medium primary, secondary and higher education, a much higher public profile for the language and eventually a Welsh-language television channel in S4C, evaporated somewhat with the rejection of the Labour Party's plans for devolution in the 1979 referendum and the advent of Thatcherism soon after. Yet even under a Tory regime it was obvious that at least some of the previous gains were being consolidated rather than lost. The cultural pessimism which had characterized the 1950s was not repeated and an undercurrent of hope was still perceptible in Welsh life despite the wholesale transformation which the nation was forced to face. The most obvious change was in Wales's industrial base. By the mid-1980s the heavy industries of coal and steel which had fuelled Welsh life for a century-and-a-half had been dismantled. The formerly bustling steel centres of Port Talbot and Shotton became strangely silent, and following the defeat of the miners after the stoppage of 1984–5, production ceased in virtually every Welsh pit. The Rhondda valleys would soon return to their pre-industrial shades of green. Religiously it was completely obvious that traditional Christianity, whatever its complexion, was losing ground and that Anglicanism as well as Nonconformity was in decline. Even Roman Catholicism was only holding its own rather than advancing.[40] The anxiety, gloom and dejection which denominational leaders felt was replicated even among some historians. 'Humanly speaking, at this rate of decline . . . it seems as if the end of distinctively Welsh expressions of Christianity may be in sight,' wrote Glanmor Williams, 'as those religious values dearest to earlier generations are being more and more abandoned in a lingering but painfully inexorable process.'[41]

Yet if mainstream, denominational Christianity was declining, even in post-industrial and post-modern Wales other forms of Christianity, religion and religiosity were flourishing: pentecostalism, house fellowships (in the larger towns and cities), evangelical groups of different types and worship styles as well as some individual congregations in each of the older churches.[42] However bad the situation seemed all round, shafts of light were still visible through the gloom.

What had become incontrovertible by the 1980s, even if it was covertly true long before, was that there was not one single and specific Welsh identity but many, the validity of which did not depend on stereotypes concerning social class, locality, language or religious affiliation but on a shared experience of life in a late twentieth-century pluralist Wales. It was, admittedly, a novel situation which caused some consternation: apart from a shared popular interest in rugby football, what were the ties which bound the Welsh together as a single people? The semblance of an answer was provided, unintentionally it seems, by the central government's progressive devolution of power to the Welsh Office. The Secretary of State found himself responsible for a wide variety of powers such as primary, secondary, further and some higher education, industrial planning and agricultural policy which had previously been the prerogative of Westminster alone. Wales was being afforded powers which set it apart from the other regions of the United Kingdom: it now had the wherewithal to begin developing a civic culture of its own. The creation of such bodies as the Welsh Land Authority, the Welsh Development Agency and the Development Board for Rural

Wales, as well as the passing of specific legislation on broadcasting, the National Curriculum and the status of the Welsh language, underscored a separateness which, in turn, fortified the nation's rapidly evolving identity. Following the narrowly won devolution referendum of 1997, this process culminated in June 1999 with the establishment of the Welsh Assembly. This new brand of Welsh citizenship seems destined to provide a shared basis for the nation's identity well into the twenty-first century. Whereas in the past Welshness had been a social and cultural phenomenon, it is now a civic and political reality within the context of a devolved and perhaps ultimately federal British state.

Just as there is no longer a single Welsh cultural identity, pluralism has become an undoubted characteristic of the religious life of the new Wales. Rastafarianism, Hari Krishna, Hinduism, Sikhism, Buddhism, much Islam to say nothing of the run-of-the-mill secularism of everyday life, are all to be found in a contemporary and spiritually diverse Wales.[43] The Christian verities may still abide, but they are now compelled to do so in competion with the faith claims of many other sects and religions. This may be an unprecedented situation. 'For the first time since the sixth or seventh centuries AD, when the Welsh could he said to have come into existence as a separate people, being Christian is not, for the majority of them, an essential part of being Welsh.'[44] It does, though, present as much a challenge as a threat. Whereas in the past Welsh Christians liked to think that they enjoyed a privileged position due to the intertwining of Christianity and culture within their history,

> Duw a'th wnaeth yn forwyn iddo,
> Galwodd di yn dyst,
> Ac argraffodd Ei gyfamod
> Ar dy byrth a'th byst.[45]
>
> God made you his maidservant,
> He called you to be his witness,
> And He impressed his covenant
> On your posts and gates.

they now realize that they are being called to forgo this special status and live by faith alone:

> There is no point in pretending that in the divine economy, Wales has a special place not given to other nations. On the contrary, we must take the political economy of our nation seriously enough to want to make a new Wales in which the divine economy can hold sway.[46]

The challenge of the new millennium has to do with mission and evangelism, spirituality, politics and culture, in fact the renewal of all things under the sovereign grace of God. However the relationship between nation and identity will be formulated in the years to come, the long history of Wales's Christian past will still provide inspiration and hope.[47]

Notes

1. A fuller version of this chapter has appeared as 'Christianity and national identity in twentieth century Wales', in *Religion, State and Society*, 27 (1999), 327–42.
2. Glanmor Williams, *The Welsh and their Religion* (Cardiff, 1991), p. 14; idem, *Religion, Language and Nationality in Wales* (Cardiff, 1979); Pennar Davies, 'The fire in the thatch: religion in Wales', in R. Brinley Jones (ed.), *Anatomy of Wales* (Peterston-super-Ely, 1972), pp. 105–16.
3. R. Tudur Jones, *Ffydd ac Argyfwng Cenedl: Hanes Crefydd yng Nghymru, 1890–1914*, I (Swansea, 1981), p. 15.
4. David Powell, *Y Greal* (July 1900), 170.
5. There were some 90,000 Welsh Roman Catholic communicants at the time, while the smaller Protestant bodies had a membership of some 20,000; cf. D. Densil Morgan, *The Span of the Cross: Christian Religion and Society in Wales, 1914–2000* (Cardiff, 1999), ch. 1.
6. *Report of the Royal Commission on the Church of England and Other Religious Bodies in Wales and Monmmouthshire*, I (London, 1910), p. 19.
7. For a discussion of the way in which the early Celtic Church was appropriated by the Roman Catholic and the Anglican Churches see Trystan Owain Hughes's contribution to this volume.
8. H. T. Edwards, *Wales and the Welsh Church* (London, 1889), pp. 318–19.

9. For a discussion on the development of a Welsh-speaking episcopal bench, see Roger L. Brown's contribution to this volume.
10. Edwards, *Wales and the Welsh Church*, p. 162.
11. George Lerry, *Alfred George Edwards: Archbishop of Wales* (Oswestry, n.d.), p. 54.
12. See Roger L. Brown, 'Traitors and compromisers: the shadow side of the Church's fight against disestablishment', *Journal of Welsh Religious History*, III (1995), 34–53.
13. See Morgan, *Span of the Cross*, ch. 2.
14. Idris Davies, 'Gwalia Deserta', in Dafydd Johnson (ed.), *The Complete Poems of Idris Davies* (Cardiff, 1994), p. 6.
15. See Robert Pope, *Building Jerusalem: Nonconformity, Labour and the Social Question in Wales, 1906–1939* (Cardiff, 1998), *passim*.
16. Quoted in David Thomas, *Silyn (Cofiant Silyn Roberts)* (Liverpool, 1957), p. 77.
17. *The Labour Voice* (14 April 1923).
18. Quoted in David Howell, *Nicholas of Glais: The People's Champion* (Clydach, 1991), p. 29.
19. Cf. Robert Pope, *Seeking God's Kingdom: The Nonconformist Social Gospel in Wales, 1906–1939* (Cardiff, 1999), *passim*.
20. John Williams, *Digest of Welsh Historical Statistics*, II (Cardiff, 1985).
21. See Morgan, *Span of the Cross*, chs. 4 and 5.
22. Kenneth O. Morgan, *Modern Wales: Politics, Places and People* (Cardiff, 1995), pp. 443–53.
23. Quoted in Owain W. Jones, *Glyn Simon: His Life and Opinions* (Llandysul, 1981), p. 55.
24. William Price, *A History of St David's University College, Lampeter*, II (Cardiff, 1990), pp. 68–104.
25. See J. Lambert Rees, *Timothy Rees of Mirfield and Llandaff: A Biography* (London and Oxford, 1945).
26. Trystan Owain Hughes, *Winds of Change: The Roman Catholic Church and Society in Wales, 1916–1962* (Cardiff, 1999), *passim*.
27. See esp. Dafydd Glyn Jones, in Alun R. Jones and Gwyn Thomas (eds.), *Presenting Saunders Lewis* (Cardiff, 1973), pp. 23–78.
28. Cf. Iain H. Murray, *D. Martyn Lloyd-Jones: The First Forty Years, 1899–1939* (Edinburgh, 1982), pp. 57–225.
29. Morgan Watcyn-Williams, *From Khaki to Cloth: The Autobiography of Morgan Watcyn-Williams MC* (Caernarfon, 1949); D. Densil Morgan, 'Y Proffwyd ymhlith y Praidd: Lewis Valentine (1893–1936)', *Transactions of the Honourable Society of Cymmrodorion*, new series IV (1998), 188–215.
30. See D. Densil Morgan, Introduction to *Torri'r Seiliau Sicr: Detholiad o Ysgrifau J. E. Daniel* (Llandysul, 1993); and idem,

'Basel, Bangor a Dyffryn Clwyd: mater y genedl yng ngwaith Karl Barth ac eraill', in Gareth Lloyd Jones (ed.), *Cenadwri a Chyfamod: Cyfrol Deyrnged i Gwilym H Jones* (Denbigh, 1995), pp. 149–72.

31 Williams, *Digest of Welsh Statistics*, I and II.
32 'A portrait of south Wales', in Geoffrey Grigson (ed.), *South Wales and the Marches* (London, 1951), p. 57.
33 Cf. Ambrose Bebb, *Yr Argyfwng* (Llandybïe, 1955).
34 R. Ifor Parry, *Ymneilltuaeth* (Llandysul, 1962), p. 175.
35 Quoted in John S. Peart-Binns, *Edwin Morris: Archbishop of Wales* (Llandysul, 1990), p. 119.
36 Owain Jones, *Glyn Simon*, p. 58.
37 John Davies, *A History of Wales* (London, 1993), p. 539.
38 See Morgan, *Span of the Cross*, ch. 7.
39 Pennar Davies, 'Y Genedl yn y Testament Newydd', in D. Eirug Davies (ed.), *Gwinllan a Roddwyd* (Llandybïe, 1972); and idem, 'Towards a theology of language', in Paul Ballard and D. Huw Jones (eds.), *This Land and People* (Cardiff, 1979); R. Tudur Jones, *The Desire of Nations* (Llandybïe, 1974); idem, 'Crist: Gobaith Cenedl', in Davies (ed.), *Gwinllan*; and idem, 'Christian nationalism', in Ballard and Jones (eds.), *Land and People*; Bobi Jones, *Crist a Chenedlaetholdeb* (Bridgend, 1994).
40 See Morgan, *Span of the Cross*, ch. 8.
41 Williams, *The Welsh and their Religion*, p. 72.
42 Morgan, *Span of the Cross*, p. 272.
43 See D. P. Davies, 'A time of paradox among the faiths', in David Cole (ed.), *The New Wales* (Cardiff, 1990), pp. 206–18.
44 Williams, *The Welsh and their Religion*, p. 69.
45 D. Gwenallt Jones, *Ysgubau'r Awen* (Llandysul, 1939), p. 27.
46 Gethin Rhys, 'The divine economy and political economy: the theology of Welsh nationalism', in Roger Hooker and John Sergant (eds.), *Belonging to Britain: Christian Perspectives on a Plural Society* (London, 1990), p. 71.
47 For some stimulating assessments of this subject, ibid., pp. 55–74; D. P. Davies, *Against the Tide: Christianity in Wales on the Threshold of a New Millennium* (Llandysul, 1995), and Noel Davies, *Wales: Language, Nation, Faith and Witness* (Geneva, 1996).

~ 8 ~
Civic Religious Identities and Responses to Prominent Deaths in Cardiff and Edinburgh, 1847–1910[1]

JOHN WOLFFE

On 31 May 1847 Thomas Chalmers, the pre-eminent leader of the Free Church of Scotland, was found dead in bed at his home in the Edinburgh suburb of Morningside, the victim of a sudden heart attack.[2] The shock resounded around the Christian world. From Albany, New York, a prominent minister, William B. Sprague wrote of the 'deep emotion' that he felt and of the 'universal mourning' that had been stirred. He had preached a memorial sermon that had drawn 'one of the largest congregations that I have ever seen assembled on any occasion'.[3] Grief was not only international, but also national: 'the lowest depths of every true Scottish heart' were reportedly stirred by the death of a man who was 'the property not of a sect, but of broad Scotland'.[4] In the opinion of the *Scotsman*, 'Thomas Chalmers was a man whom Scotchmen of all opinions and of many coming generations will regard with pride and reverence as one of their country's great names.'[5] The *Inverness Courier* saw the death of Chalmers, 'the pride of a Presbyterian Scotland', as a striking counterpoint to the recent demise of Daniel O'Connell, 'the champion of Ireland and of Catholic Europe' and suggested that 'an important cycle of time had been completed'.[6]

During the next few days such sentiments were focused on Edinburgh itself, where the news broke 'like the shock of an earthquake'. When it was relayed to the Free Church General Assembly, which was in session, many were in tears. The funeral was held on 4 June. All shops closed for the day. The proceedings began with a procession headed by the General Assembly of the Free Church to the home of the deceased. As the procession passed along the Lothian Road numerous other groups fell in, including the magistrates, town council and large numbers of other clergy, including some from other denominations. At the house devotions were conducted. The body was then brought out and taken in procession back through the city and past the university on its way to the recently opened Grange cemetery, which, in the opinion of the *North British Daily Mail*, was thereby being established as the '*Père la Chaise* of the Modern Athens'. Although this place of burial was less than a mile from the house the chosen circuitous route was some three miles long, and was evidently intended to enhance the impact of the spectacle. Numbers in the procession were estimated at 2,000 and it was calculated that there were as many as 100,000 spectators. The Free Church General Assembly organized the proceedings, and the whole impressive spectacle clearly held great significance for them. The Church had only been in existence for four years at the time of Chalmers's death: the loss of their greatest leader was a cause of great emotional distress and insecurity, but it also provided them with an opportunity for a very public show of strength and demonstration of status and support.[7] Their newspaper, *The Witness*, claimed that 'It was the dust of a Presbyterian minister which the coffin contained, and yet they were burying him amid the tears of a nation, and with more than kingly honours.'[8] Another newspaper report described the occasion as a 'protestant pilgrimage'.[9]

Ten months later in March 1848 another fatal heart attack, this time suffered by the second marquess of Bute at his home in Cardiff Castle, stirred a comparable, albeit more localized, state of mourning. Bute had been the predominant landowner in the area, and his decision in the 1830s to develop the docks had laid the foundations of the subsequent economic prosperity of the town. He was also the dominant influence in local political and social life, and is justly recognized as the 'maker of modern Cardiff'.[10] According to the *Cardiff and Merthyr Guardian*, his sudden death was followed by a 'consternation, a panic which must have been witnessed to be understood'.[11] The borough council later recorded its 'deep regret on an event that has deprived this Town of its most powerful and Munificent Friend whose purse was always open to every call for its improvement and for the promotion of every Charity'.[12] There was a sense that Cardiff was mourning its own creator.

Bute's funeral, like Chalmers's, provided an opportunity for a conspicuous expression of strength and solidarity by those who otherwise greatly regretted his loss. Although the actual interment was to be in Cambridgeshire, there was nevertheless a grand funeral procession through Cardiff. The ceremonial began with a reading of part of the Burial Service before the coffin left the castle drawing room. The procession from the castle to the docks (where the coffin was embarked for Bristol) was a mile and a half in length, and took three-quarters of an hour to pass a stationary spectator. It was made up of Friendly Societies, gentry, the corporation, the militia, the dead man's tenants and Anglican clergy, led by the dean of Llandaff. Two bands played the 'Dead March'. All businesses were closed, blinds were drawn and ships flew their colours at half mast. The dense orderly crowds of onlookers were estimated as amounting to double the numbers present at local observance of the funerals of George IV and William IV. The *Cardiff and Merthyr Guardian* judged that 'the "Majesty of the People" never shone so conspicuously than it did upon this occasion'.[13] In contrast to the Presbyterian and Scottish tone of Chalmers's funeral, the proceedings in Cardiff reflected the Tory and Anglican values with which Bute himself had imbued the political culture of the town. These were, however, to be successfully challenged during the ensuing years.

Both in the funerals and memorials of their own most distinguished and prominent members, and in the commemoration of national figures, the towns and cities of Victorian and Edwardian Britain and Ireland more or less consciously sought to assert their essential unity and status as communities. Such concerns mingled with often sincere expressions of public grief to produce very extensive local observance at times of prominent bereavements. A comparison of the experiences of Cardiff, as the emerging capital of Wales, and Edinburgh, as the long-established capital of Scotland, provides a basis not only for exploring the role of religion in civic life but also for gaining insights into the wider interactions between religious and national identities.

The distinction between official Christianity and the quasi-religion of civic consciousness is analogous to that made by Robert

Bocock between *religious* ritual, involving some sense of contact with the transcendent; and *civic* ritual, which merely affirms group consciousness. Bocock, criticizing Durkheim, sees the analytical distinction as crucial, but recognizes that empirically many rituals combine the two.[14] Such overlap and association is inherent in the material to be surveyed in this chapter, which ranges from explicitly mainstream religious activities such as church services, to primarily secular ones such as the erection of statues.

The aftermath of Thomas Chalmers's death was exceptional in the extent to which it prompted the articulation of a Scottish religious patriotism. The main focus in the analysis that follows will be on responses in Cardiff and Edinburgh to the deaths of individuals of overarching 'British' significance, as a basis for direct comparison between the two cities, and the exploration of interplay between British, Scottish and Welsh national consciousness. The main cases under consideration will be those of the duke of Wellington (1852), Prince Albert (1861), Disraeli (1881), Prince Albert Victor, duke of Clarence, the elder son of the Prince of Wales (1892), Gladstone (1898), Victoria (1901) and Edward VII (1910).

It is first necessary as a basis for comparison to give some idea of characteristic English civic responses to such occurrences. The central ceremonial event was usually a procession to a memorial service at the cathedral or other principal Anglican church. The indications are that Nonconformists were generally willing to give at least tacit support to such observance, in recognition of the primacy of the Established Church on national occasions. For example, in Leeds on the day of the funeral of the duke of Wellington a local holiday was kept and there was a civic procession from the courthouse to the parish church, watched by a crowd estimated at between 20,000 and 30,000. Nonconformist town councillors attended the parish church with their Anglican counterparts and were treated with notable courtesy by the vicar, the leading High Churchman Walter Farquhar Hook.[15] In both Cardiff and Edinburgh, however, sharper denominational divisions and more ambivalent precedents meant that the form of arrangements was initially much more uncertain.

At the time of the Census of 1801 Cardiff was only, in effect, a large village, with a population of 1,870. Even in 1851, although its population had increased nearly tenfold in fifty years, it was still a relatively small place with a population of 18,351. By 1901, however, continued rapid growth combined with an extension of the borough boundaries in 1875 to produce a further massive increase to 164,333, a proportionate rate of expansion in the later nineteenth century that was second only to Middlesbrough among major British towns. This rise in population was founded on Cardiff's role as the major port and commercial centre serving the south Wales coalfield, with an occupational structure dominated by workers in transport and manufacturing, but also with a substantial prosperous middle-class element.[16] When Victoria came to the throne, it was a small pocket borough strongly under the influence of the Butes; by the time she died it had become a proud and independent-minded place, recognized as a city in 1907, and increasingly regarded, as least by its own citizens, as the *de facto* capital of Wales. Its own development was thus bound up with the process that Kenneth Morgan has characterized as the 'rebirth of a nation'.[17] The town council, which had been a passive and inactive institution in the years of the Bute ascendancy, became in the late 1860s a focus for more active local politics. Liberals dominated it for much of the late nineteenth century, although the Conservatives were to gain control between 1904 and 1909.[18] Attendances at religious worship in 1851 amounted to an estimated 56.3 per cent of the population. Of these attendances only an estimated 20.5 per cent were Anglican (although the proximity of Llandaff Cathedral, then outside the borough, somewhat strengthened the Anglican presence in the area as a whole), while 14 per cent were Roman Catholic, reflecting the large Irish immigration into south Wales in the preceding decade. Nonconformists accounted for 59.2 per cent of attendances, the balance being made up by one congregation of Latter Day Saints.[19]

Cardiff was changing so fast that each prominent bereavement tended to generate a distinctive response, in which past precedents were as frequently discarded as followed. Shortly before the duke of Wellington's death in 1852, the town had in a hard-fought contest elected as its Liberal MP Walter Coffin, a Unitarian coalmaster and railway proprietor, thus defeating the interest of the Bute family.[20] In this context the question of how to mark the duke's funeral was a matter of some debate in the town council. Alderman Morgan proposed a procession to church, but Coffin himself seemed much more uncertain as to the appropriate means of commemoration. John Batchelor, a leading opponent of the Bute influence, opposed the closing of shops on the day of the funeral.[21] The eventual resolution was an open-ended one: 'That some mark of respect should be paid by the Council to the memory of the late Duke of Wellington on the day of his Funeral which was left to the Mayor to carry out in the best manner he should think fit.'[22] The mayor opted for a strongly Anglican observance, attending St Mary's church on the morning of the funeral, and 'respectfully' inviting his fellow townsmen to join him in a procession to the other Anglican church, St John's, in the afternoon. The latter event attracted substantial crowds, but the indications are that the form it took expressed something less than a general consensus.[23]

The people of Cardiff appear initially to have been profoundly moved by Prince Albert's death in 1861: flags were halfmasted, minute guns fired and bells tolled. Many were observed to be in tears when the news was communicated by clergy and ministers at the Sunday services on the following day.[24] A correspondent of the *Cardiff Times* suggested that the day of the funeral would be a fitting occasion for an interdenominational service of 'prayer and humiliation'.[25] Such an event did not materialize, but most places of worship held special services or prayer meetings, and there were military processions to Llandaff Cathedral and St John's church. Significantly, however, the council, although later passing an eloquent address of sympathy to the queen, does not appear to have participated in any official way in these Anglican services, and the involvement of the military at St John's was a matter that gave rise to 'many criticisms'.[26] A subsequent attempt to raise money for a local memorial to Albert fell flat, an indication that in Cardiff there was not yet a fully developed sense of civic identity associated with commemoration, which translated immediate grief into statues or memorial buildings in other towns.[27]

Indeed, in the mid-nineteenth century, Cardiff's response to national mourning failed to manifest the degree of collective self-consciousness already apparent in a major English town such as Leeds in 1852 and 1861. The Liberal *Cardiff Times* did not record any local commemoration at all for Palmerston in 1865. Disraeli's death in 1881 was noted in some Anglican Sunday sermons, and the Tory *Western Mail* claimed that 'even the most fierce Radical' expressed respect for him, but observance on the day of the funeral was limited to halfmasted flags and the ringing of a muffled peal at St John's.[28] Llandaff Cathedral and several other Anglican churches held memorial services for General Gordon in 1885, attracting large congregations, but no civic recognition.[29]

From the 1890s, however, Cardiff rapidly made up lost ground, in a manner that reflected its own predominant Nonconformity, though articulation of a Welsh identity remained limited. On the day after the duke of Clarence's death in 1892 there was a succession of speeches of condolence in the general purposes committee of the council and an agreement to invite the people of Cardiff to join in mourning on the day of the funeral. However, the mayor said that they 'had no desire to appear to dictate to the public in the matter'. The *Western Mail* took satisfaction in a perceived unity of Radical and Tory in grief and loyalty to the throne.[30] On the following Sunday funeral sermons were preached at numerous churches and chapels. A special interdenominational service at the Park Hall was crowded with a reported attendance of more than 3,000.[31] On the day of the funeral thousands of people were observed on the streets wearing mourning insignia, and a packed memorial service at the recently enlarged St John's was attended by the mayor and a large number of the corporation. In his sermon the vicar, Charles John Thompson, under whose ministry since 1875 the Anglican Church in Cardiff had enjoyed a notable renaissance, took the opportunity to flatter the corporation.[32] He regretted that the town's growing importance was receiving inadequate recognition and suggested that Clarence (who would have become prince of Wales had he lived) would have had a life bound up with 'something of the fulness of the future of Cardiff'. On the other hand the limits to the preacher's Welsh identification were very evident when he went on to describe the deceased as English to his 'heart's core', which was obviously intended as a compliment.[33] Even in Nonconformist Sunday sermons there was no articulation of a consciously Welsh response to Clarence's death, and copious inclusive references to 'England' were made without any apparent sense of incongruity.[34]

When Gladstone died six years later, the council, on which the parties were then finely balanced, passed a particularly effusive but politically and religiously neutral resolution of regret and sympathy. They noted that he had been 'an Honorary Freeman of this ancient Borough'; praised his 'disinterested public service' and 'broad-minded statesmanship'; and expressed gratitude for his 'noble example of sublime Christian faith and calm resignation in the hour of death'. Whereas in 1892 the corporation's attendance at St John's had appeared to favour the Anglican Church, it now adopted an impartial stance, noting with satisfaction that both Anglican and Nonconformist services were to be held and resolving that its own members 'should attend such place of worship as they may desire'.[35] A number of councillors were present at St John's, but the deputy mayor was on the platform party at a joint Nonconformist memorial service at the Park Hall, which was reportedly broadly representative of all denominations and of 'officialdom . . . the tradespeople and the masses'.[36]

When news of Queen Victoria's death reached Cardiff in the evening of 22 January 1901 and was communicated to the town by the sounding of the *Western Mail* siren, the immediate public reaction was remarkable:

> the sight in St Mary Street was one never to be forgotten. Shops, hotels, restaurants and other places of business in the neighbourhood were literally emptied into the street. Thousands of people came running from all directions, and in a few seconds the roadway was packed from the Great Western corner to Wood Street.

At the Empire Theatre a picture show was suddenly interrupted with the news. A portrait of the queen was projected on to the screen while the band started to play the 'Dead March'. Unfortunately boys in the gallery had not heard the announcement and started to cheer, but were quickly 'sh-shed' by the adults, and the whole audience rapidly subsided into a sombre silence broken only by the band.³⁷ The next day a special meeting of the full town council was convened and recorded unanimously its 'most profound and heartfelt grief at the death of the most illustrious and venerable Sovereign who has ever adorned the British throne'.³⁸ On the following Sunday morning church and chapel services generally assumed a memorial character, and were unusually well-attended.³⁹

Official arrangements for the day of the funeral were again left to the personal discretion of the mayor, who this time formally announced that he would be attending service at St John's and 'kindly asked' members and officials of the corporation to join him.⁴⁰ An unspecified number duly did so. A civic procession was formed and made its way to a packed church in front of a large, orderly and solemn crowd. Meanwhile a service at Llandaff Cathedral was similarly filled to capacity, and Volunteer companies paraded for a service at their own drill hall, while others marched to St Andrew's church. Nevertheless, the largest congregations of all were to be found at Nonconformist services, notably at the Park Hall and at Wood Street Congregational Church. The Welsh-language Anglican church, Dewi Sant, also held a service, as did the synagogue, but no Roman Catholic services were recorded. It was observed that 'every place where services were announced were [sic] crowded out long before the hour of service'. Indeed, it would appear that this was an occasion when the supply of religious observance in Cardiff was generally insufficient to meet the public demand. The one exception was at St Mary's church where the choral requiem service only drew between 500 and 600 people, less than half the capacity of the building. In Cardiff at least, more Protestant expressions of mourning had a much greater appeal.⁴¹

Edward VII's death gave rise to a similarly intense public mood, finding expression in widespread and well-attended religious observance. Events on the day of the funeral showed a swing back to greater official recognition of the predominance of Nonconformity in the life of Cardiff, while also seeking to convey a sense of underlying solidarity. Following a military parade in Cathays Park which then marched to attend a brief service at St John's, the civic and official procession walked from the City Hall to the Free Church service at the Park Hall. The crowd watching the proceedings in Cathays Park was estimated at 50,000, more than a quarter of the population of the city. Simultaneous services were held at St John's, Llandaff Cathedral and at Pembroke Terrace Chapel, for Welsh-speaking Nonconformists, the latter addressed by the archdruid of Wales. Later in the day there were two further processions to St John's, by the Masons in the afternoon and by the Boys' Brigade, Church Lads' Brigade and Boy Scouts in the evening. Meanwhile, services were held at the synagogue, and various other churches and chapels, this time including crowded Roman Catholic ones. 'It will thus be seen', concluded the *Western Mail*, 'that all sections of the religious, civic, and military life of Cardiff united with one accord in giving expression to that sense of irreparable loss which is felt by the whole of the civilised world.'[42]

By this time Cardiff was showing an increasing consciousness of its status as 'the metropolis of Wales', a phrase first appearing in connection with commemorative observances in 1898. In July 1898 the Public Works Committee of the Council received a circular proposing the erection of monuments to Gladstone 'in the capitals of England, Scotland and Ireland' and responded with a unanimous resolution to the effect that a similar memorial should be erected in Cardiff 'as the capital of Wales'.[43] Local comment in 1901 and, more particularly 1910, reflected a similar sense of a developing Welsh identity linked to the growing local civic pride. Such identity presented itself as fundamentally consistent with wider loyalty: the 'good government' of Victoria had, according to the *Cardiff Times*, 'finally won the reverence and love of the Welsh people for the British throne'.[44] On Edward VII's death his long association with the principality as prince of Wales was recalled and he was praised as having been 'always a friend of Wales'.[45] Local observance of his funeral was described as 'inspiring . . . evidences of the universal and deep-rooted loyalty of Wales to the Throne'.[46] The presence of the lord mayor of Cardiff at the funeral itself at Windsor was perceived as an honour in which the 'Welsh nation' as a whole was sharing.[47] Subsequently a conference with representatives from all parts of Wales was held at Cardiff City Hall to initiate a movement for a national memorial to the king. The form of the memorial was left for further discussion but one suggestion given a prominent airing well illustrates the manner in which civic pride, national identity and loyalty to the Crown were becoming woven together in the process of mourning and commemoration:

> that the University Gardens, Cathays Park, should be transformed into a 'Forum' in which representations of all that was greatest and most inspiring in Welsh History, grouped with gardens round the personality of the late King, and blended with architectural adornments, should form a fitting image of Welsh Nationality.[48]

Cardiff was thus becoming increasingly confident in finding forms of commemoration that reflected its own distinctive sense of civic community. The degree of caution and experimentation that remained evident indicates, however, that the development of such ritual was uncertain. Nevertheless beneath various attempts to bridge the religious and cultural divisions of the town and to express a sense of unity in bereavement lay recognition of the widespread fundamental religiosity of public attitudes. If civic ritual was to have any prospect of achieving an overall sense of group consciousness, it had to build upon religious ritual rather than attempt to replace it. Cardiff's eventual success in establishing forms of collective mourning which expressed a wider consensus was a necessary corollary of its own gradual emergence during this period as the acknowledged capital of Wales.

Edinburgh, in contrast to Cardiff, had long enjoyed the status of a capital city, and its responses to prominent deaths reflected a self-conscious awareness of its wider representative function in relation to Scotland as a whole. Examination of them therefore suggests significant insights into the development of Scottish national consciousness. The population (including Leith) was 194,000 in 1851, more than ten times the size of Cardiff at the same date. Subsequent relative growth, however, was proportionately much slower, and in 1901 Edinburgh, with 395,000 people, was only two and a half times the size of Cardiff. It had a particularly numerous legal, commercial, academic and ecclesiastical middle class, in 1881 employing the high proportion of 20.51 per cent of the occupied population in domestic service.

The working classes were spread among a wide variety of small-scale artisan and service industries. There were great extremes of wealth and poverty: between the splendid Georgian terraces of the New Town and the more recent middle-class developments of Morningside and Newington lay the crowded slums of the Old Town, with their population swelled by a significant recent Irish influx.[49] Liberalism was politically dominant until the home rule split of 1886, but the Tories were not wholly eclipsed.[50] Church attendance on 30 March 1851 was very similar to that in Cardiff, amounting to 55.4 per cent of population, of which only 16 per cent of the total were at Church of Scotland services. The massive impact of the Disruption in 1843 was apparent in the 33 per cent of attendances at the Free Church, while the United Presbyterian Church, at 27 per cent, also substantially exceeded the Established Church. The largest contributors to the balance were the Congregationalists, the Episcopal Church and the Roman Catholic Church, all with 5 per cent of attendances apiece.[51] The membership of the town council in 1856 comprised only seven members of the Church of Scotland, but seventeen members of the Free Church, fourteen Dissenters, and one Episcopalian.[52]

Graeme Morton has recently aptly encapsulated the prevailing sense of identity in nineteenth-century Edinburgh as one of 'unionist nationalism'. This frame of mind was well illustrated in responses to the death of Sir Walter Scott in 1832, mourned as a universal genius, a literary figure of European stature and as an articulator of Scottish identity and history, but not as a symbol of potential political independence. In fund-raising for the grandiose monument in Princes Street, erected between 1840 and 1844, the author's Scottishness was not particularly emphasized. 'Rule Britannia' was played at the laying of its foundation stone.[53]

Such ambivalences were also apparent in more specifically religious forms of memorial observance. In John Knox's *Book of Common Order*, the basis on which the worship of the Church of Scotland developed, it was stated that 'the corpse is reverently brought to the grave, accompanied with the congregation, without any further ceremonies'.[54] A traditional Scottish funeral therefore proceeded straight from prayers at the house of the deceased to the place of interment, without any intervening service in church. If prayers were held in church this was a matter of convenience rather than liturgical necessity. In a contribution to a pamphlet controversy generated by the services held in Scotland on the day of Princess Charlotte's funeral in 1817, Thomas McCrie, a Presbyterian Dissenter and church historian, argued that burial services (and by implication parallel memorial services) had been condemned by the Church of Scotland at the Reformation, and remained inconsistent with true Presbyterianism. According to McCrie, they were a superstitious practice, unknown to early Christianity, and the holding of them by the Church of England was but one symptom of how vestiges of 'Popery' had been retained south of the Border.[55] Even in 1817, as McCrie noted with concern, the 'highly excited sympathy' of the people[56] had led the Scottish churches into compromising the consistency of this position: the subsequent development of observance of this kind in Scotland is therefore a revealing touchstone of the erosion of a traditional Presbyterian stance in favour of broader religious expressions of distinctive Scottish identity.

Although Thomas Chalmers's obsequies in 1847 saw a strong assertion of the links between Presbyterianism and Scottish national identity, it is significant that no extensive posthumous national and religious cult materialized. No statue to him was erected in Edinburgh until the 1870s, and the eventually successful campaign to remedy the omission stemmed primarily from embarrassment that such an eminent figure should have been left without a public monument for so long.[57] It is probable that, once the immediate shock of his death had passed, the memory of him as both the scourge of Voluntaryism in the 1830s and the 'betrayer' of the Established Church in 1843 meant that he was to seem too divisive a symbol for consensual commemoration.[58] In the event the Scottish religious patriotism temporarily evoked by Chalmers's death and funeral was to prove a less characteristic response to prominent deaths than did endeavours to express local dignity and status in the context of a wider British whole.

Initially, however, civic or religious responses of any kind were relatively limited. Following Wellington's death, it does not seem to have occurred to the town council to arrange any significant events in Edinburgh to mark the occasion of the funeral. They were preoccupied rather with arrangements relating to attendance of a deputation at St Paul's Cathedral in London and with safeguarding their claims to precedence over Dublin 'on the ground of their being the older Corporation of the two, and also as representing Scotland which was united with England nearly a century before the Union with Ireland'. Not only did they carefully record the outcome of the seating arrangements made after an altercation with the Dublin councillors in St Paul's, but they subsequently took steps to ensure their names were recorded in the *Gazette* 'immediately *after* those of the Corporation of London and *before* those of the Corporation of Dublin'.[59] They did recommend the closing of places of business on the day of the funeral, and there was general compliance in the centre of the city, although not in the suburbs. Otherwise in noticeable contrast with processions and church services that were widely held south of the Border, Edinburgh's formal tribute was limited to the firing of minute guns from the castle and the tolling of church bells.[60] Traditional Presbyterian suspicion of memorial services and the impossibility, in the aftermath of the Disruption, of finding a location and format that would have commanded general support were no doubt unspoken factors behind this relative passivity.

During ensuing decades there was a continued pattern of limited response in which civic and ecclesiastical strands were kept more distinct than in England. On Prince Albert's death the council passed an eloquent address of condolence, and on the subsequent Sunday the lord provost and members attended St Giles's Cathedral in official robes. Participation in a Church of Scotland service on this occasion indicates that, in Edinburgh, Free Church and Dissenting councillors were now prepared to acknowledge the national role of the Established Church at such times. On the day of the funeral itself, however, public observance was limited to the tolling of bells and the firing of minute guns from the castle, and the churches held prayer meetings rather than full services. Subsequent council discussion of monuments to the prince well illustrated their wish to uphold Scottish distinctiveness within a framework of underlying loyalty: they gave moral support to plans for the London memorial, but noted that, before they had even heard of this, steps had been already taken to provide by subscription for a Memorial in Scotland, and, while they are confident that the wealth of England will enable her to dispense with contributions from this part of the Country, they have no doubt that a Memorial will also be provided in Scotland not unworthy of the Prince to whose Memory it is to be erected or of this portion of the Kingdom which desires to give expression in this form to its profound and universal feeling.[61]

The subsequent process of raising money and erecting the monument was involved and protracted, but it was eventually unveiled in Charlotte Square in 1876.[62]

In the meantime Palmerston's death in 1865 was followed by a resolution of sympathy, but no recorded public observance, although the council was concerned that the lord provost should represent it at the funeral at Westminster.[63] In 1881 muffled peals were rung for Disraeli from St Giles's and the Tron, and for the duke of Albany in 1884 minute guns were also fired from the castle.[64] Meanwhile James Cameron Lees, who was appointed minister of St Giles's in 1877, led the restoration of the cathedral's fabric and sought to develop its role in Scottish national life, in a manner modelled on the work of Dean Stanley at Westminster Abbey.[65] Following Lord Iddesleigh's death in 1887 he initiated a new development in respect of a service at St Giles's on the day of the funeral, prompted particularly by the deceased's personal association with Edinburgh as lord rector of the university. In his address Lees articulated a sense of participation in a wider national community:

We are met to-day, brethren, in this house of prayer, to join our devotions with those, and to express our deep sympathy with those, who at this hour in far-off Devonshire are laying in the grave the remains of that honoured statesman who was personally known to so many of us, and whose death has caused a thrill of sadness to vibrate throughout the whole land.[66]

Such a sense of seamless solidarity with Anglican mourners implied a significantly different blend of civic, national and ecclesiastical sentiment from that apparent earlier in the century.

Indeed, during the period between 1890 and 1910 observance of mourning and funerals in Edinburgh began strongly to resemble the practice of major English towns and cities. The duke of Clarence's death in 1892 stirred an 'immense sensation' in the Scottish capital.[67] The lord provost and magistrates met to decide what form local ceremonies should take, an indication that there was now demand for more extensive public display than hitherto, but that both precedent and appropriate practice were still uncertain. The *Scotsman* reported that 'it seems to be the feeling that a funeral service in St Giles's should form the central feature of the celebration',[68] a scheme that was duly implemented simultaneously with the ceremony at Windsor. The council first met to adopt addresses of condolence and then proceeded in state to a service at St Giles's, to hear an address in which Lees dwelt on the closeness of the royal family to the life of the people of Scotland, and an anthem by John Stainer, the organist of St Paul's Cathedral. Meanwhile businesses were closed, blinds drawn and minute guns fired.[69] Cameron Lees wrote: 'I never saw anything like the feeling Scotland has displayed. Edinburgh . . . was a sight I will never forget . . . Thousands went away who could not get into the church [St Giles's] and the whole scene was most impressive.'[70]

When Gladstone died in 1898, the lord provost delivered an eloquent speech to the council, placing particular stress on the local and Scottish connections of the deceased, and suggesting that there was a temporary hushing of 'the strife of tongues' in the face of 'the great fact of his departure'.[71] He asked St Giles's to hold a service on the day of the funeral and the cathedral duly obliged with a format intended to be 'as simple and non-official as possible'. Nevertheless, the town council attended in their robes.[72] Meanwhile in a revealing counterpoint to their emphasis on consensus and their increasing acceptance of English-influenced ceremonial, they continued jealously to uphold their claims to precedence over Dublin, seeing it as a question of 'precedency between countries represented by their capitals'. Some discreet lobbying before Gladstone's funeral in Westminster Abbey led to satisfactory seating arrangements from the point of view of the Edinburgh representatives.[73]

The trend towards increasing ceremonial and assimilation between civic and ecclesiastical ritual reached its culmination in

1901 and 1910. Following the deaths of both Victoria and Edward VII the town council held special meetings, which were opened in prayer by the minister of St Giles's, after which the lord provost moved an address of condolence.[74] Large formal services were held in St Giles's on both the funeral days, and seen as representative of a cross-section of local and national Scottish life. Lees, still in harness in 1901 and recalled from retirement in 1910, gave both memorial sermons, eloquently evoking his idealized perception of common feeling and sentiment between the royal family and the Scottish people. There was a reciprocity here, that had been apparent since 1861, with the royal family's warm personal feelings towards the Church of Scotland. Mourning draperies were widely displayed by businesses while sombre and reverent crowds gathered outside the cathedral and in other public places. On both occasions a general consensus was perceived by the *Scotsman*, which commented in 1901:

> It was natural that multitudes should seek admission to St Giles's where the proceedings were accompanied by a certain amount of pageantry, but it was even more significant of the true feelings of the people that they should have turned out in so large numbers to the quiet unostentatious services in their own churches, where there was no excitement, no bands of music, no ritual or none to speak of, and only their own familiar hymns to sing, and their own clergymen to lead the devotions. This was a particularly gratifying feature in connection with the opening of the churches in the working-class districts, and testimony has been borne by one and all to the deep feeling with the memorable event of the day evoked among all classes of the community.

The newspaper supported this description with the information that during the day the local police had made only two arrests, whereas the average Saturday figure was 'about 80 or 90'. Even if this circumstance was in part attributable to the closure of public houses, it was still suggestive of far-reaching acceptance of the consensual mood that the circumstances of the day required a particularly decorous standard of behaviour. Nine years later, at one o'clock, the time of Edward VII's funeral at Windsor, all the trams were stopped for a quarter of an hour and a solemn stillness descended on the city's normally bustling streets, broken only by the sound of psalm-singing from the churches and by the tolling of bells.[75]

Thus at the beginning of the twentieth century, in Edinburgh, as elsewhere, the forms and symbols of official religiosity constituted the dominant expression of the mood of communal grief. If Presbyterian suspicion of such rituals lingered at all, it was overwhelmed by public pressure to express grief in a manner that since the mid-nineteenth century had moved much closer to English customs. The Scottish capital remained very conscious of its own civic dignity and its wider national role, but in the context of a wider British whole in which thoughts were drawn inexorably to the invisible ceremonies in London and Windsor.

It is instructive briefly to compare the Welsh and Scottish experience, as represented by Cardiff and Edinburgh, with the Irish one, as represented by Dublin. The funeral of Daniel O'Connell in August 1847 was a striking Catholic and Irish parallel to the Scottish and Presbyterian obsequies of Thomas Chalmers in Edinburgh a few months earlier. The central event of O'Connell's funeral was a pontifical High Mass attended by eighteen prelates and over 1,000 clergymen, while a lengthy street procession drew large crowds amidst an atmosphere of mingled nationalistic and religious fervour.[76] In subsequent decades responses to death gave rise to much more division in Dublin than in either Cardiff or Edinburgh. In 1891 the funeral of Charles Stewart Parnell was, in striking contrast to that of O'Connell, an essentially secular – but very well supported – occasion held in defiance of the Roman Catholic Church, which had dissociated itself from the deceased because of his adultery with Kitty O'Shea. Meanwhile the very decision to mark the death of prominent British figures could be divisive. This was apparent in the prolonged controversy associated with a proposal to erect a statue of Prince Albert on a prime site in College Green, and a dispute in the municipal council regarding a resolution of condolence on the death of Queen Victoria. Nevertheless, even in Dublin general consensus was apparent on occasions such as the tragic death of the duke of Clarence, or following the death of Edward VII, hailed as a friend of Ireland, for whom a votive Mass was held at the Catholic pro-cathedral.[77]

In both Cardiff and Edinburgh the paradoxical trend over the period was for forms of memorial observance to assume an increasingly close resemblance to those in England, even as verbal assertions of distinctive Welsh and Scottish identity tended to become more apparent. Both the small-town deference of Bute's funeral and the traditional Presbyterianism of Chalmers's had become wholly outdated long before 1910. Both cities sought to observe national grief in a manner that reflected their own increasing size and complexity as urban communities, and their evolving wider national roles. In the age of the railway and the electric telegraph, the examples of cities in other parts of the United Kingdom became much easier to observe and hence to emulate. Nonconformist and Presbyterian worship of course enjoyed a higher status as a focal point for civic observance than was the case in England, but an older tradition of Protestantism in which memorial services were regarded with caution or even hostility had been wholly eclipsed by the early twentieth century. Cardiff and Edinburgh also came to resemble English towns in that the forms of the commemoration of national figures became uncontentious in a manner that they had not been in the mid-nineteenth century. Meanwhile, religious changes supported this process. In Scotland the progress of Presbyterian reunion passed its first major milestone with the formation of the United Free Church in 1900. In Wales, although the Anglican Church was to remain legally established until 1920, its days had seemed numbered since the early 1890s. Before the turn of the century local practice in Cardiff was showing a recognition that the Free Churches were entitled to at least an equal status on national occasions. The easing of denominational conflict in the late Victorian period facilitated the rise of a strong civic religiosity beneath which continuing underlying tensions could be obscured.

Notes

[1] This chapter is a revised version of part of chapter 4 of J. Wolffe, *Great Deaths: Grieving, Religion and Nationhood in Victorian and Edwardian Britain* (London, 2000). Grateful acknowledgement is made of the permission of the British Academy for its

re-publication in this volume, and of its support for the research on which it is based.
2. Stewart J. Brown, *Thomas Chalmers and the Godly Commonwealth in Scotland* (Oxford, 1982), pp. 370–1.
3. New College Library, Edinburgh, Chalmers Papers, CHA 2.5.97, MS letter from Sprague, 12 July 1847.
4. *Macphail's Edinburgh Ecclesiastical Journal*, XVIII (1847), 477.
5. *Scotsman* (2 June 1847).
6. Reprinted in *Free Church Magazine*, XLII (June 1847), 189–90.
7. New College, Edinburgh, Chalmers Papers, CHA. 6.26.86 (Printed) 'Programme of Arrangements of the Funeral of the Rev. Dr. Chalmers'; Anon., *Funeral of Dr. Chalmers, In A Letter to a Friend by an Englishman* (1847); *North British Daily Mail* (5 June 1847).
8. Reprinted in *Free Church Magazine*, XLII (June 1847), 187.
9. Cutting from *People's Journal* in collection of tributes to Thomas Chalmers, New College Library, Edinburgh X13b 4/1.
10. M. J. Daunton, *Coal Metropolis: Cardiff 1870–1914* (Leicester, 1977), p. 24; D. Cannadine, *Lords and Landlords: The Aristocracy and the Towns 1774–1967* (Leicester, 1980), p. 41.
11. *Cardiff and Merthyr Guardian* (25 March 1848). Bute's heir was an infant, who was not to come of age until 1868, so his death left a major local power vacuum.
12. Glamorgan Archive Service (GAS), Cardiff Borough Council (CBC) Minutes, B/C 4/2, 3 May 1848.
13. *Cardiff and Merthyr Guardian* (1 April 1848).
14. R. Bocock, *Ritual in Industrial Society: A Sociological Analysis of Ritualism in Modern England* (London, 1974), pp. 60–2.
15. *Leeds Mercury* (20 November 1852); *Leeds Intelligencer* (20 November 1852).
16. Daunton, *Coal Metropolis*, pp. 1–14, 182.
17. Ibid., pp. 17–18; J. Davies, *Cardiff and the Marquesses of Bute* (Cardiff, 1981), p. 143; K. O. Morgan, *Rebirth of a Nation: Wales 1880–1980* (Oxford and Cardiff, 1981), pp. 126–7.
18. Davies, *Cardiff and the Marquess of Bute*, pp. 106–37; Daunton, *Coal Metropolis*, pp. 170–1.
19. I. G. Jones and D. Williams (eds.), *The Religious Census of 1851: A Calendar of the Returns Relating to Wales*, 2 vols. (Cardiff, 1976, 1981), I, pp. 137–40. This calculation for Cardiff depends on an estimated figure for one of the two Anglican churches (St John's), which failed to make a return of attendance. It has been assumed that attendance there was in the same proportion to seating capacity as at the other Anglican church (St Mary's), but if it was actually lower, then the Nonconformist predominance was even

greater than the stated figures suggest. Figures returned to the Welsh Church Commission in 1906 would put total adult church affiliation at that date at 45.4 per cent of the population, with Nonconformist Sunday scholars amounting to a further 17.4 per cent. Nonconformists made up 63.8 per cent of the adult total, Anglicans 25.5 per cent and Roman Catholics 10.7 per cent. All these figures should be treated with caution, but are indicative of substantial ongoing Nonconformist predominance.

[20] Davies, *Cardiff and the Marquess of Bute*, pp. 133–4.
[21] *Cardiff and Merthyr Guardian* (25 September 1852). On Batchelor, see Daunton, *Coal Metropolis*, pp. 169–70.
[22] GAS, CBC Minutes, B/C 4/2, 20 September 1852.
[23] *Cardiff and Merthyr Guardian* (20 November 1852).
[24] Ibid. (21 December 1861).
[25] *Cardiff Times* (20 December 1861).
[26] Ibid. (27 December 1861); GAS, CBC Minutes, 30 December 1861.
[27] *Cardiff Times* (14, 21 February 1862).
[28] *Western Mail* (25, 27 April 1881).
[29] Ibid. (16, 17 March 1885).
[30] Ibid. (16 January 1892); Cardiff Central Library (CCL), CBC Minutes, 1891–2, pp. 155–6 (15 January 1892).
[31] *Western Mail* (18 January 1892).
[32] On Thompson and St John's, see J. C. Read, *A History of St John's Cardiff and the Churches of the Parish* (Bridgend, 1995).
[33] *Western Mail* (21 January 1892).
[34] Ibid. (18 January 1892).
[35] CCL, CBC Minutes, 1897–8, p. 565 (23 May 1898); *Cardiff Times* (28 May 1898).
[36] *Cardiff Times* (4 June 1898).
[37] *Western Mail* (23 January 1901).
[38] CCL, CBC Minutes, 1900–1, p. 189 (23 January 1901).
[39] *Cardiff Times* (2 February 1901).
[40] CCL, lithographed notice, 30 January 1901.
[41] *South Wales Daily News* (4 February 1901).
[42] *Western Mail* (21 May 1910).
[43] CCL, CBC Minutes, 1897–8, p. 727 (28 July 1898).
[44] *Cardiff Times* (26 January 1901).
[45] *Western Mail* (7 May 1910).
[46] Ibid. (21 May 1910).
[47] Ibid. (20 May 1910).
[48] CCL, Cardiff City Council Minutes 1910, p. 249 (13 July 1910). The scheme does not appear to have got off the ground, and the site apparently envisaged was subsequently used for the Welsh National

War Memorial. The central roadway in the monumental development of Cathays Park was however named King Edward VII Avenue.
49 R. Q. Gray, *The Labour Aristocracy in Victorian Edinburgh* (Edinburgh, 1976), pp. 9–27.
50 W. H. Marwick, 'Municipal politics in Victorian Edinburgh', *The Book of the Old Edinburgh Club*, XXXIII/1 (1969), 31–5.
51 C. G. Brown, *Religion and Society in Scotland since 1707* (Edinburgh, 1997), pp. 45, 59.
52 Marwick, 'Municipal politics', p. 35.
53 G. Morton, *Unionist Nationalism: Governing Urban Scotland 1830–1860* (East Linton, 1999), pp. 156–72.
54 Quoted in A. I. Dunlop, 'Burial', in N. M. de S. Cameron (ed.), *Dictionary of Scottish Church History and Theology* (Edinburgh, 1993), pp. 110–11.
55 Scoto-Britannicus [ie Thomas McCrie], *Free Thoughts on the late Religious Celebration of the Funeral of HRH The Princess Charlotte of Wales* (Edinburgh, 1817), pp. 9–23.
56 Ibid., p. 36.
57 *Proposed National Monument to Dr. Chalmers*, printed report of meeting on 30 November 1869 (Chalmers Papers, CHA 6.26.87). The statue, by John Steell, was eventually erected at the intersection of Castle Street and George Street in 1878. M. T. R. B. Turnbull, *Monuments and Statues of Edinburgh* (Edinburgh, 1989), pp. 48–9.
58 I am indebted to Professor S. J. Brown for this observation. For further discussion of Chalmers's impact see S. J. Brown, 'Thomas Chalmers and the communal ideal in Victorian Scotland', in T. C. Smout (ed.), *Victorian Values: Proceedings of the British Academy*, LXXVII (1992), 61–80.
59 Edinburgh District Council, Town Council (ETC) Minutes, vol. 258, pp. 426–8 (1 November 1852); vol. 259, pp. 121–4 (28 December 1852).
60 *Scotsman* (20 November 1852).
61 ETC Minutes, vol. 283, p. 393 (4 February 1862).
62 E. Darby and N. Smith, *The Cult of the Prince Consort* (New Haven and London, 1983), pp. 67–70.
63 ETC Minutes, vol. 291, pp. 226, 291 (24, 31 October 1865); *Scotsman* (28 October 1865).
64 Ibid. (27 April 1881); *The Times* (7 April 1884).
65 Norman Maclean, *The Life of James Cameron Lees* (Glasgow, 1922).
66 *Scotsman* (19 January 1887).
67 Ibid. (15 January 1892).
68 Ibid. (16 January 1892).

[69] ETC minutes 1891–2, pp. 115–6 (20 January 1892); *Scotsman* (21 January 1892).
[70] Royal Archives, Windsor Castle, VIC/Z 93/59, Cameron Lees to Miss McNeill, 21 January 1892, quoted by gracious permission of Her Majesty Queen Elizabeth II.
[71] ETC minutes 1897–8, pp. 379–81 (24 May 1892).
[72] *Scotsman* (26, 27, 30 May 1898).
[73] ETC minutes 1897–8, pp. 431–3 (14 June 1898).
[74] Ibid., 1900–1, pp. 161–2 (24 January 1901); 1909–10, pp. 427–8 (9 May 1910); *Scotsman* (25 January 1901, 10 May 1910).
[75] Ibid. (4 February 1901, 21 May 1910).
[76] W. B. MacCabe (ed.), *The Last Days of O'Connell* (Dublin, 1847), pp. 206–52.
[77] Wolffe, *Great Deaths*, pp. 123–35.

~ 9 ~
The Fluctuating Fortunes of 'Old Mortality': Identity, Religion and Scottish Society

DOUGLAS ANSDELL

The idea for this chapter came partly from some words that were written by John MacLeod, who was principal of the Free Church College, Edinburgh, from 1927 to 1943. He wrote that, 'the Disruption is the great epoch in the church life of the Highlands. Its memories furnish them with the heroic materials that Scotland as a whole finds in the Covenanting struggle.'[1]

When MacLeod first wrote these words in 1919, he would have presumed that the Scottish public were aware of the impact of the Covenanting period on Scottish history and society. Another writer, in 1892, had described the events of the Covenanting period as being 'imprinted on the memory of every reader of our history'.[2] In his statement, MacLeod was giving the Disruption period in the Highlands similar weight to that of the Covenanting period in the rest of Scotland and thereby affirming that it was momentous, memorable and formative. It is this comparison that I would hope to explore in the following pages, and ask to what extent these periods, Covenanting and Disruption, provided 'heroic materials' for Lowland and urban Scotland and for the Highlands. I would understand the term Disruption to include the period of evangelical expansion in the Highlands which immediately preceded the Disruption of 1843.

The Covenanting and Disruption periods were indeed significant for both regions. However, it is the impact that these 'heroic materials' were allowed to have in shaping the subsequent notions of identity in the Highlands and Islands and in Lowland and urban Scotland that I would like to consider in this chapter.

In a recent review of William Ferguson's *The Identity of the Scottish Nation*[3] and of a collection of essays edited by Broun, Finlay and Lynch entitled, *Image and Identity*,[4] Professor David McCrone noted that remembering is crucial to the shaping of national consciousness,[5] and with regard to identity this can often be a selective remembering. This observation suggests, as other writers have done, that the creation of identity can be regarded as myth and as construct. However, identity should also be seen at the same time as device, or as a mechanism for reinforcing a particular social arrangement. Identity has to do with remembering; it also has to do with reminding.

In his review, Professor McCrone opened with a quotation from the French historian, Ernest Renan, who said, 'To have common glories in the past, a common will in the present, to have accomplished great things together, to wish to do so again, that is the essential condition of being a nation.'[6] It is, of course, possible to extend this definition to include a number of non-national, distinct groups. It would be quite straightforward to replace nation with community, clan or indeed a whole range of social, religious or ethnic groups. Strong and distinct identities are not only the possession of nations, and many communities certainly would not relinquish this prerogative.

As such, the notion of identity can be employed by groups in society that are large and small, dominant and marginal. It enables certain groups to maintain and strengthen their position within society in relation to other groups; it enables them to establish their distinctiveness and provides a focus for adherence and aspiration. Identity varies depending on the context, and the expression of one identity does not necessarily negate the simultaneous expression of others. From a historical point of view, a sense of identity can answer questions concerning who we are and from whence we have come.

However, I have no wish to dispute Renan's understanding of what constitute the raw materials or the essential requirements for the creation of a national or group identity. If we look closely at this statement we can see a concern with community and collective action, a concern with history and, in particular, a glorious past, the need for repetition and sharing a common cause in the present. A group or nation with a sense of identity will thus be able to answer the following questions. Who are they? In what stream of history do they stand? What is their present duty? What qualities and values should they adopt? When were these best displayed?

MacRae and Old Mortality

Before proceeding any further, I would like to return to my concern with two important periods of Scottish history. I would like to introduce two characters as a means of demonstrating how the past can be used to shape a sense of identity in Scottish history. The first is Kenneth MacRae, born in Dingwall in 1883 and died in 1964. He was a Free Church Minister in Lochgilphead, Argyll, in Kilmuir, Skye, and in Stornoway. At one stage in his ministry, in 1936, he was released from his church and pastoral duties by the Free Church General Assembly. His task was to travel around Free Church congregations to seek 'to persuade the young people of the church to a greater interest in and zeal for the message and testimony which had been given to the Free Church'.[7]

Essentially, his task was to remind Free Church congregations who they were and what historical events had produced them. MacRae's view was that the distinctive position of the Free Church was not sufficiently understood. As MacRae toured and lectured, he distributed leaflets that summarized the principles of the Free Church and its mission. The leaflet made the claim that Free Church teaching came out of 'the best days that Scotland ever saw' and suggested that 'a return to the old paths can alone secure the Divine favour for our beloved land'.[8] It was, of course, a concern with identity.

The image of Kenneth MacRae moving around Free Church congregations seeking to remind them who they were brought to mind *Old Mortality*. This was the title of one of Sir Walter Scott's novels and was the nickname of an itinerant who moved around the graves of Covenanters, clearing the moss from the gravestones and renewing the inscriptions and emblems. *Old Mortality* was of course a work of fiction, but, in appendices, Scott provides some detail concerning the person after whom this book was written.

Scott writes of this character, 'he considered himself as fulfilling a sacred duty, while renewing to the eyes of posterity the decaying emblems of the zeal and suffering of their forefathers, and thereby trimming, as it were, the beacon light, which was to warn future generations to defend their religion'.[9] This, then, was also a concern with identity, a reminder to succeeding generations of the rock from which they were hewn.

There is a similarity between Old Mortality and Kenneth MacRae. Both represented different traditions and communities, yet both were seeking to preserve a distinct identity in the communities to which they belonged. Both MacRae and Old Mortality focused on specific periods in history in which the qualities they valued were, as they thought, best displayed. The periods they would have considered important were, for Old Mortality, the late seventeenth century, the period of Presbyterian resistance under the later Stuarts, and for MacRae the first half of the nineteenth century, identified with the expansion of evangelical Christianity in the Highlands leading up to the Disruption of the Church of Scotland in 1843.

These were certainly remarkable periods in Scottish religious history and would appear to carry the potential for providing those who followed with a distinct self-understanding and a strong sense of their place in history. The qualities of sacrifice, zeal, commitment and triumph featured strongly in the memory of those who sought to keep alive the values they considered to be demonstrated at these times.

There is considerable evidence within the Presbyterian tradition to suggest that the late seventeenth century and the early nineteenth century were glorious times to which later generations should aspire. There are several examples from within this tradition which demonstrate how these periods were viewed. Concerning the Covenanting years, reference could be made to texts such as J. Howie's *Scots Worthies* (1797), James Stewart's *The Wrestlings of the Scottish Church* (1721), J. Thomson's *Cloud of Witnesses* (1714) and R. Wodrow's *History of the Sufferings of the Church of Scotland* (1841), all of which documented the troubles experienced by the church and the remarkable qualities demonstrated by many in the late seventeenth century.[10]

One later church historian referred to these books just mentioned and said

> over wide districts of Scotland, there were many even of the humblest classes to whom the names and principles connected with Covenanting times had long been familiar. Weavers at the loom, artisans at the workshop, ploughmen in the field and shepherds out among the hills, cherished these memories.[11]

It certainly was not uncommon for Scottish Presbyterians to be reminded of the sacrifices made in Covenanting times, of the principles they stood for and the commitment they demonstrated. This was for the purpose of encouraging the present generation, whoever that might be, to cling to the principles for which they believed their forefathers had bled and died.

Similarly, in the Highlands much was committed to print to protect the memory of the individuals who contributed to this 'glorious' age of the church. The Highland church in the nineteenth century recorded the deeds and sayings of the men and ministers who participated in the dramatic period of evangelical awakening. Many, writing from within the Highland tradition, saw these events as a new beginning, a turning point and a break with the past.

It is not uncommon for evangelical histories dealing with certain areas in the Highlands and Islands to identify the precise point at which evangelical Christianity was introduced, the preacher who first brought the message and those who initially responded. One anonymous writer, in the 1820s, claimed that as far as he could ascertain 'the first time these doctrines, called the doctrines of grace, were preached in Skye is not further back than 1805'.[12]

Those taking this view contended that the memory and influence of these times should not be forgotten and this resulted in a highly productive period of recording Highland church history, most writers being conscious that they were writing to reaffirm a particular set of priorities and to provide an example for future generations. Although there are many examples of this genre, a typical example is MacCowan's account of *The Men of Skye*, in which he states that his main desire was to 'perpetuate the memories of the worthy fathers of Skye, and that the examples of their lives may serve as a stimulus for many'.[13]

This enterprise which is concerned with the selective remembering of Covenanting and Highland evangelical traditions, has to do with the question of identity. The past is being used to inform communities who they are, what stream of history they stand in, what qualities they should adopt and when these were best displayed. In the way that these two traditions used history, we can see a selective remembering and we can see a reminding in order to reinforce a particular social arrangement.

The Covenanting period and the evangelical expansion in the Highlands both had the raw materials or 'heroic materials' to shape a sense of identity. Yet they operated in social settings that were very different, thus having implications for the extent to which these 'heroic materials' could shape society.

Scottish Identity in the Early Eighteenth Century

There has been considerable writing recently about the question of identity in Scottish history.[14] In this, perhaps not surprisingly, there has emerged a focus on the period between 1690 and 1750. Indeed, much that has been written on the question of Scottish identity, 1690–1750, enables us to understand why a distinct Covenanting identity did not assume a more prominent role in Scottish society at this time.

There is a fair degree of consensus among Scottish historians as to the forces that were at work in the early eighteenth century. For example, historians writing about Scotland at this point have drawn attention to the inclusion of Scots in the English upper classes and the opportunities which became available to them therein. Professor Smout has also noted that 'the Union provided material opportunity which' the Scots intelligensia and the bourgeoisie 'were not prepared to pass up for a few insults'.[15]

There were opportunities in administration, politics, the army, medicine, architecture, engineering and in the Empire. This was, of course, nothing new, but historians have commented that this trend was more marked in the early eighteenth century and in particular following the Union with England in 1707. Scots had indeed 'been going south in search of greater opportunities for centuries, but not in such numbers, and rarely with the advantage . . . of having fellow countrymen sufficiently highly placed in politics to act as influential patrons'.[16]

Another feature of this period that has been commented on fairly widely by historians is the softening of Presbyterianism. The picture that emerges from commentators on this period is that the Presbyterian Church, having gained much, began to distance itself from its more violent past and thus the ideals of the Covenanting period found little favour.

A new emphasis on politeness and tolerance has been observed and this was combined with a rejection of the religious enthusiasm of the seventeenth century. This drift, it has been argued, reached its high point and is perhaps best demonstrated by William Robertson, clergyman, historian and principal of Edinburgh University, who succeeded in distancing the Presbyterian establishment from much of its past. Colin Kidd has suggested that 'Robertson broke the spell of the Covenants' and that he 'fashioned a new whig Presbyterian patriotism out of the remnants of the old to meet the needs of a North British province'.[17] Similar views can be found in the writing of Smout, Keith Brown, David Allan and in Drummond and Bulloch.[18]

In this, the church was not acting in isolation, and commentators on this period have suggested that support for this position can also be found within the Scottish intellectual community, who kept fanatical Presbyterianism at arm's length and thus helped to defuse the 'explosive potential' which could be found in Scotland's recent religious past.[19]

Another emphasis that historians have identified in this period is the formation of a new British identity. Of this period, Richard Finlay has suggested that 'the Scots had to accommodate their national identity to the changed political circumstances following the Treaty of Union in 1707 . . . from now on Scottish national identity would have to be formulated within the parameters of the emerging British state'.[20] Similarly, Keith Brown has said that 'the successful re-orientation towards a unionist and British perspective was completed between 1707 and 1760'.[21] This would have profound consequences for the formation of an identity based mainly on the Scottish past.

Yet another emphasis of this period is the strong commitment to the Protestant succession, which was seen, by some, as the triumphant outcome of the Covenanting struggle. Wodrow, who wrote in great detail about the sufferings of the Scottish church, emphasized Williamite deliverance and the Hanoverian succession and it was suggested that the message contained in his works was 'to endear to our hearts the blessings secured to us by the Revolution Settlement and the Hanoverian Settlement'.[22] As the Protestant succession was grafted on to the Presbyterian tradition it is likely that this would have had the effect of locating a distinct Scottish identity within a larger British identity. Again, this would have consequences for the development of a distinctly Scottish sense of identity.

Indeed, it has also been argued that the Jacobite threat reinforced this attachment, by confirming the Presbyterian attachment to the Protestant succession and, consequently, Scotland's location within a larger national identity. Keith Brown has emphasized this by noting that 'the most enduring effect of the survival of Jacobitism was to push eighteenth-century Scots lowlanders, in particular, into a closer sense of identity with the English and loyalty to the Whig regime that governed Britain'.[23]

Thus the legacy of the later Covenanting era was handed over to a period that provided it with little prominence. There is some agreement among historians that Scottish self-understanding was now to be seen within the context of British identity, that the larger nation, especially after 1707, offered improved opportunities for aspiring Scots, that there was a moderating of Presbyterianism in which the recent past was held at arm's length and that the Protestant succession was regarded as a fitting conclusion to the Covenanting struggle. This located Scotland within the larger British picture and the adoption of an identity shaped by the Covenanting years was unlikely to be a route to prominence in urban and Lowland society in the early eighteenth century.

Evangelicalism and Highland Identity in the Early Nineteenth Century

In the late eighteenth century and early nineteenth century a variety of mission groups focused their attention on the

Highlands and Islands. It was a diverse impulse involving churches, voluntary societies, mission groups and individuals. It was, in many communities, successful, and intense spiritual movements resulted from the activity of itinerant evangelists. It was a remarkable movement that succeeded in many communities and much of it fed into the Free Church in 1843.

Many communities in the Highlands and Islands at this time did not have the resources to resist or counter the advance of evangelical Christianity, which came through the agency of Gaelic-speaking highlanders. It came with education, literacy and with a compelling certainty. The initial success of the evangelicals brought about a change in the social structure and institutions of Highland society.

A new group was introduced and quickly became dominant. Its network of ministers, elders, teachers and catechists enabled it to penetrate every family. Thus we find a new prestigious group in Highland society and this was combined with a rigorous enforcement at grass-roots level. Consequently, a remarkable degree of consensus was achieved allowing evangelicals to provide leadership, define acceptable behaviour and, of course, to shape identity.

The contrast with Lowland and urban Scotland of an earlier period is instantly obvious. In both cases the raw materials were there to construct a distinct identity but as the social arrangements varied so did the fortunes for the church in these two periods. Evangelical success resulted in its domination in many Highland communities where, often, it was associated with status and prestige. Evangelicalism was left unhindered to shape the identity of these communities. The prominent members of Highland and Island communities in the nineteenth century, elders, ministers, teachers and catechists, would have shared an identity that was produced by the 'heroic materials' of the evangelical awakening and Disruption period. They were Gaelic-speaking, Presbyterian and evangelical.

However, in the eighteenth century in urban and Lowland Scotland, as Richard Finlay has suggested, 'the period is characterised by cultural confusion and the historian has a great many varieties of Scottishness and Britishness to choose from'. He regards this plethora of identities in the eighteenth century as a 'reflection of the complexities of the nature of social change experienced by Scottish society at this time'.[24] It is unlikely that such a description could be extended to the Highlands and Islands in the first half of the nineteenth century.

In Lowland and urban communities in the early eighteenth century, prominent members of society were unwilling to reinforce an identity emerging from the Covenanting past and it remained a marginal concern as other alternatives located Scotland within a British identity. In the Covenanting struggle, one would imagine there was enough 'heroic material' to give birth to a new nation and sustain it for generations, but the legacy of this era was handed over to a period that had other views on national identity and did not welcome an identity drawn from, and driven by, Scotland's Covenanting past. It might have been this that Christopher Harvie was referring to when he wrote that, 'granted certain conditions, the intellectual and emotional material'[25] for a revival of Protestant sectarianism may still be inflammable in Scotland.

There is a need for some caution in order to avoid drawing the distinction too sharply between Lowland and urban, and Highland and Island society. It is probably at this point that it could be suggested that the argument in this chapter has been somewhat over-stated. However, an important question to ask is how should Highland society be viewed? Was it simply another example of rural Scotland or should it be seen as in some way distinct? The argument advanced in this chapter would favour the latter and this leads to the conclusion that in Lowland and urban Scotland there were, undoubtedly, people whose sense of identity was shaped by Scotland's religious past, but they would have been at variance with the sense of identity being promoted by prominent individuals and significant structures within that society. Similarly, there were individuals in the Highlands and Islands whose sense of identity *was not* shaped by the Highland evangelical past, but they would have been at variance with the sense of identity being promoted by prominent individuals and significant structures within that society.

IDENTITY, RELIGION AND SCOTTISH SOCIETY

MacRae and Old Mortality

Let us now return to the two characters mentioned earlier. Both Old Mortality and Kenneth MacRae sought to remind communities who they were and what tradition they stood in, and thereby aimed to reinforce a preferred social arrangement. Old Mortality, and those who would have shared his concerns, focused on a period that carried great potential, but this was not shared by prominent individuals in a society and in a time that provided a range of other answers to the question of Scots identity. Kenneth MacRae belonged to a different tradition that also carried great potential, and this tradition had been dominant in many Highland and Island communities for some time and, in some areas, had few challenges to the question of identity.

For characters such as Old Mortality, there would have been little chance of succeeding in providing Lowland and urban Scots with a single sense of identity derived from a Covenanting past and inspired by the zeal of that period. Yet when Kenneth MacRae visited Highland congregations he would still have found Highland communities that could be described as Gaelic-speaking, evangelical, Presbyterian. The task he set himself perhaps betrays his awareness that times were changing and things were not as they had been.

Many of the points put forward in this chapter concerning Highland society were expressed forcefully in a letter written by Finlay MacLeod to the *Herald* in 1996. In this letter he described the level of control that the church managed to achieve in some Highland communities. He wrote,

> It is not difficult to make sense of how the Calvinist church introduced itself into Gaelic society early in the last century. But it is a more demanding task to explain how it came to inhabit every facet of life from birth to death for everyone in that society. For the institution itself it was a triumph. Once it had achieved this inordinate level of societal success its continuation across time was secure, and it could afford to continue in immutable form.

If this position is accepted, it would have clear consequences for the way these communities saw themselves.

MacLeod, however, proceeds to suggest that 'Gaelic society is no longer traditional and now contains significant elements of modernity'.[26] Thus, the 'inordinate level of societal success' that has been identified in earlier stages was now, he suggests, being eroded and replaced by other influences. To the same extent, the Highlands and Islands have witnessed the erosion of a distinct identity drawn from evangelical Christianity. Richard Finlay's observation of the eighteenth century concerning the availability of a plethora of identities can increasingly be applied to Highland and Island communities. Thus, it could be argued that the predicament that Covenanters would have confronted in the early eighteenth century, and that Kenneth MacRae feared, was now also shared by Highland evangelicals. As the predominance of the evangelical church gave way to other forces and influences, so would come a greater range of answers to the question of identity in Highland communities.

The task taken on by Old Mortality and Kenneth MacRae (and others) is essentially a concern with identity. In them we can observe identity being employed as a device to reinforce a particular social arrangement which they believed was best exemplified in particular periods of Scottish history. With regard to the Presbyterian identity resulting from the Covenanting struggle, recent scholarship has demonstrated that the forces at work in eighteenth-century Scotland and Britain provided little encouragement for the Covenanting legacy to define Scottish identity.

In the Highlands and Islands it was different, and a certain identity resulting from a period of evangelical awakening achieved a measure of success. However, the social arrangements that allowed this no longer prevail, and with this comes, inevitably, an erosion of the identity that many would claim had characterized Highland and Island communities since the early nineteenth century, when, in a time, real or imagined, communities were more static, influences were less diverse and identity was more homogeneous.

Despite both periods containing the essential ingredients or 'heroic materials' to shape a distinct identity, this did not necessarily guarantee success in society. Thus the task taken on by Old Mortality and Kenneth MacRae will depend, not so much on the enthusiasm of those doing the reminding, or on the magnificence of their message but, at the end of the day, on the social context in which their message was received. This is the factor upon which, I believe, the fortunes of an Old Mortality or a Kenneth MacRae would ultimately depend.

Notes

1. J. MacLeod, *By-Paths of Highland History*, ed. G. N. M. Collins (Edinburgh, 1965), p. 41.
2. M. MacDonald, *The Covenanters of Moray and Ross* (Inverness, 1892), p. 11.
3. W. Ferguson, *The Identity of the Scottish Nation: An Historical Quest* (Edinburgh, 1998).
4. D. Broun, R. J. Finlay and M. Lynch (eds.), *Image and Identity: The Making and Remaking of Scotland through the Ages* (Edinburgh, 1998).
5. D. McCrone, 'History and national identity', *Scottish Affairs*, XXVII (Spring 1999), 97.
6. Ibid.
7. I. H. Murray, *The Diary of Kenneth MacRae: A Record of Fifty Years in the Christian Ministry* (Edinburgh, 1980), p. 439.
8. *What the Free Church Stands for* (Free Church of Scotland, n.d.).
9. W. Scott, *Old Mortality* (London, 1974), pp. 64–5.
10. J. Howie, *Scots Worthies* (Edinburgh, 1797); J. Stewart, *The Wrestlings of the Scottish Church* (Glasgow, 1721); J. Thomson, *A Cloud of Witnesses* (Edinburgh, 1714); R. Wodrow, *The History of the Sufferings of the Church of Scotland from Restoration to the Revolution*, I (Glasgow, 1841), p. vi.
11. T. Brown, *Annals of the Disruption* (Edinburgh, 1893), p. 2.
12. Lay Member of the Established Church, *An Account of the Present State of Religion throughout the Highlands of Scotland* (Edinburgh, 1827), p. 48.
13. R. MacCowan, *The Men of Skye* (Glasgow, 1902), p. viii.
14. The texts below either deal with or contain significant reference to the subject of Scottish identity. Ferguson, *Identity of the Scottish Nation*; C. Kidd, *Subverting Scotland's Past: Scottish Whig Historians and the Creation of an Anglo-British Identity, 1689–1830* (Cambridge, 1993); idem, *British Identities Before Nationalism: Ethnicity and Nationhood in the Atlantic World, 1600–1800* (Cambridge, 1999); M. Pittock, *Inventing and Resisting*

Britain: Cultural Identities in Britain and Ireland, 1685–1989 (London, 1997); A. Murdoch, *British History, 1660–1832: National Identity and Local Culture* (London, 1998); Broun, Finlay and Lynch (eds.), *Image and Identity*; T. Claydon and I. McBride (eds.), *Protestantism and National Identity: Britain and Ireland, c.1650–c.1850* (Cambridge, 1998); S. J. Connolly (ed.), *Kingdoms United: Great Britain and Ireland since 1500* (Dublin, 1999); S. G. Ellis and S. Barber (eds.), *Conquest and Union: Fashioning a British State, 1485–1725* (London, 1995); T. M. Devine and J. R. Young (eds.), *Eighteenth Century Scotland: New Perspectives* (Edinburgh, 1999); B. Bradshaw and P. Roberts (eds.), *British Consciousness and Identity: The Making of Britain, 1533–1707* (Cambridge, 1998).

[15] T. C. Smout, 'Problems of national identity and improvement in later eighteenth century Scotland', in T. M. Devine (ed.), *Improvement and Enlightenment* (Edinburgh, 1989), p. 8.

[16] L. Colley, *Britons: Forging the Nation, 1707–1837* (London, 1994), p. 124.

[17] C. Kidd, 'The ideological significance of Robertson's "History of Scotland"', in S. J. Brown (ed.), *William Robertson and the Expansion of Empire* (Edinburgh, 1997), pp. 143–4.

[18] T. C. Smout, 'Problems of national identity', in Devine (ed.), *Improvement and Enlightenment*; K. M. Brown, 'Scottish identity in the seventeenth century', in Bradshaw and Roberts (eds.), *British Consciousness and Identity*; D. Allan, 'Protestantism, Presbyterianism and national identity', in Claydon and McBride (eds.), *Protestantism and National Identity*; A. L. Drummond and J. Bulloch, *The Scottish Church, 1688–1843* (Edinburgh, 1973).

[19] Kidd, 'The ideological significance of Robertson's "History of Scotland"', p. 122.

[20] R. J. Finlay, 'Caledonia or North Britain? Scottish identity in the sixteenth and seventeenth centuries', in Broun, Finlay and Lynch (eds.), *Image and Identity*, p. 143.

[21] K. M. Brown, 'Scottish identity in the seventeenth century', in Bradshaw and Roberts (eds.), *British Consciousness and Identity*, p. 236.

[22] Wodrow, *The History of the Sufferings of the Church of Scotland*, p. vi.

[23] Brown, 'Scottish identity in the seventeenth century', p. 239.

[24] Finlay, 'Caledonia or North Britain?', p. 143.

[25] C. Harvie, 'The Covenanting tradition', in G. Walker and T. Gallagher (eds.), *Sermons and Battle Hymns: Protestant Popular Culture in Modern Scotland* (Edinburgh, 1990), p. 10.

[26] F. MacLeod, 'A danger to itself and society', *Herald* (29 June 1996).

~ 10 ~
Revival:
An Aspect of Scottish Religious Identity

KENNETH B. E. ROXBURGH

The concept of identity is difficult to define, although most writers would agree that aspects of culture, language, ethnicity and religion all have central roles to play. The eighteenth century was a crucial period in the development of Scottish national identity. Within this period, religion played an important part in national, as well as individual experience, of what it meant to be Scottish at a time when many political, economic and cultural changes were taking place. Religion, in the form of Presbyterianism, continued to influence the lives of most Scots as it pervaded the whole of Scottish society in the eighteenth century.

The impact of the Enlightenment upon eighteenth-century Scotland has generated a great deal of discussion in recent years, focusing primarily on the influence of the Literati upon university and ecclesiastical life,[1] without necessarily asking how the ordinary Scot was affected. Indeed, although many leaders of the Popular party within the Established Church could adopt many aspects of the Enlightenment ethos,[2] there is evidence that popular piety within Presbyterianism criticized the strong affiliation of Moderate Enlightenment perspectives with the spiritual malaise of the Church of Scotland.

Politics and Religion

Presbyterianism experienced a great deal of turmoil in the eighteenth century. The 'Glorious Revolution' of 1688, which caused the flight of James VII (James II of England) and the accession of William and Mary to the throne, was perceived by probably the majority of the Scottish population (certainly in the Lowlands) as a rejection of James VII's attempts to reintroduce the practice of Roman Catholicism and the beginning of a triumph of popular Presbyterian doctrine and piety. The reinstatement of 'the antediluvians', sixty Presbyterian ministers who had been deposed since 1661, and their restoration to their parishes, whether held by someone else or not, led to the beginnings of an expulsion of Episcopal ministers and the abolition of Episcopacy. This was followed in 1690 by the re-establishment of full Presbyterian government in the Church of Scotland. The whole sequence of events was celebrated by the General Assembly as an act of God's providence.[3] In March 1703, Elizabeth West attended the opening of the General Assembly to hear David Williamson, one of the Covenanters and minister of the West Kirk in Edinburgh, preach the opening sermon in which he had spoken of 'what a great Plague Prelacy had been to the Church of Scotland and what a mercy it was to be delivered from it'.[4]

On the political field, the Union of the Parliaments in 1707 was not proving to be a popular decision within Scotland.[5] In an unusual and yet powerful alliance between the Jacobites and radical Presbyterians, there were many dissenting voices to the proposed treaty. Although many Scots believed that the Union of Parliaments would bring economic prosperity, others maintained that they were mortgaging their future to England. Within the Church of Scotland, there was apprehension that the hierarchy of the Church of England would exert undue influence on spiritual matters. In his final sermon to the people of Simprin on 15 June 1707, Thomas Boston urged his parishioners to continue in their opposition, 'against popery, prelacy, superstition and ceremonies. And mourn for this, that by the union, a nail is sent from Scotland, to fix the Dagon of the English hierarchy in its place in our country.'[6]

Thomas Boston may be seen to be a representative of many people within the Church of Scotland at this time who were opposed to the Union. He later recalled how the failure of the Church of Scotland clergy to oppose the Union had alienated the people of his parish of Ettrick, the spirits of the people of that place being embittered on that event against the ministers of the Church; which was an occasion of much heaviness to me, tho' I never was for the Union, but always against it from the beginning unto this day.[7]

Elizabeth West wrote in 1705 of how she heard

> word of an union betwixt the two nations, Scotland and England. O this afflicted me very much, knowing how treacherous England had always been to us in former times; especially in Breach of Covenant . . . confederacy with such a deceitful and cunning people, who would, if it lay in their power, ruin all their neighbour nations, to advance their own interest. But that which of all troubled me was, that this Union of theirs would prove a snare to our Covenanted Church of Scotland; for they that would ruin our State, would also ruin our Church.[8]

Religion and Popular Piety

Many members of the Popular party believed that the spiritual fortunes of the Church in Scotland in the 1730s were anything but enviable. In fact, men like James Robe of Kilsyth and William McCulloch of Cambuslang, who would be among the leaders of the evangelical awakening in Scotland, very clearly perceived a religious decline in the society of their day. The evangelicals within the Church of Scotland had become deeply divided over the issue of the Secession of Ralph and Ebenezer Erskine from the Established Church over the issue of patronage. After several years of trying to win them back over into the life of the church, the early 1740s marked a turning point when evangelicals joined with others finally to depose them from the ministry. Such division would have serious repercussions during the evangelical revival as the Erskines became severe critics of George Whitefield and the events of Cambuslang.

Whereas the leaders of the emerging Moderate party within the Church of Scotland would devote their time and energy to gaining positions of influence within the General Assembly of the Church of Scotland in order to effect change, members of the

Popular party believed that only a spiritual awakening could reverse the spiritual malaise that prevailed within the country. In an age when various social changes were taking place, many people sought a refuge in religious identity in harking back to past experiences of religious fervour associated with the familiar security of past generations of spiritual vitality such as the Scottish Reformation and the Covenanting movement.

Scotland's Revival Tradition

The revival tradition in Scotland was one which was intimately woven into the experience and expectation of evangelicals in the Church of Scotland. Accounts of the Scottish Reformation under John Knox, as well as later spiritual awakenings in Stewarton and Irvine in 1625 and Kirk of Shotts in 1630[9] were recalled in the early 1740s as news of a fresh awakening in New England through the ministry of George Whitefield and Jonathan Edwards was eagerly received on the Scottish side of the Atlantic.[10] By 1741 expectations were nourished that Scotland could also experience a similar outpouring of the Holy Spirit,[11] one which would recapture the glorious days when the Scottish experienced the blessing of God.

The subject of revival seems to fascinate a whole variety of different people. Sociologists, psychologists and theologians, as well as ecclesiastical historians, have all contributed major studies to revival in general and the evangelical awakening in the eighteenth century in particular. The evangelical revival, far from being a merely localized upsurge in religious interest, was international in scope. The dramatic response of churchgoers in Bristol and London in 1737, and of the Kingswood colliers with white gutters on their cheeks caused by tears in 1739 under the preaching of George Whitefield, is usually reckoned as marking the genesis of the English awakening. But in fact these events had been preceded by similar developments in Wales some years earlier, predated again by a movement of God's Spirit in New Jersey in 1719 and 1726 and in Easter Ross, Scotland, in 1724. In Scotland, although there was an awareness of the wider impact of revival in England, Wales and New England, the fresh experience of revival at Cambuslang in 1742 was used by members of the Popular party to vindicate their adherence to the Church of Scotland against the attacks of the Seceders who refused to believe that what was happening in Cambuslang and Kilsyth could ever be described as a work of the Holy Spirit.

The Secession Movement and the Revival Tradition

Paradoxically, the early days of the Secession movement attracted the attention of George Whitefield who wrote to Ralph Erskine in May 1739 detailing events surrounding his own ministry in England and Wales.[12] By 4 August 1739, Ralph Erskine was satisfied with the enquiries he had made concerning Whitefield and wrote in his diary that he was praying for him and his colleagues, thanking God 'for what he has done to them and by them'.[13] The correspondence between Ralph Erskine and Whitefield enabled Whitefield to come to a distinctively Calvinistic understanding of the *ordo salutis*.[14] With hopes that Whitefield could be persuaded to identify himself with the Secession movement, the Associate Presbytery invited him to come to Scotland.

By the time Whitefield arrived in Scotland in July 1742, the Secession movement had established itself as a growing movement in urban areas like Stirling, Perth and Dunfermline, setting up a structure which mirrored the Established Church and made enterprising plans for expansion into new areas. The strength and appeal of the early Secession movement can be seen in the visit of William Wilson, one of the original Seceders, who was involved on 22 March 1738 in a service at the Braid Hills in Edinburgh when he baptized ten children, some of the attenders having travelled twenty or thirty miles for the baptisms. According to the *Caledonian Mercury* 'there were about 5,000 hearers at each service (there being three in all) besides an ungodly audience consisting of many thousands, some of whom set fire to the furze'.[15] In April 1737, 3,000 communion tokens were made for the celebration of the sacrament in Stirling. It appears that Ebenezer Erskine 'drew about one third of the population of St Ninians and about one half of that of Stirling, together with a substantial number from other parishes'.[16] By 1742 the Secession movement had twenty ministers and thirty-six congregations and by 1745 it had a synod and three presbyteries.

One of the striking features of the Secession movement was its identification with the Covenanting tradition. The Covenanting tradition, with its emphasis on Scotland as a covenanted nation, in a special relationship with God, resonated with popular piety in the seventeenth and eighteenth centuries.[17] In 1738, the Kirk session in Logie received a paper that alluded to the apostasy of the Church of Scotland from the Covenanting principles of the previous century.[18] The Secession movement, characterized by outdoor conventicles and fierce denouncements of unfaithful ministers, brought the message of the gospel and the Covenanting tradition together in a powerful way, especially in areas of the country which had a strong link to the seventeenth-century movement.[19] The fact that the leader of the Moderates, William Robertson, referred to the Covenanting movement as banditry and unworthy of the new age of the Enlightenment[20] indicates the feeling of alienation that many ordinary Scots felt within the Established Church.

Furthermore, the Secession movement's strong opposition to patronage, with an accompanying encouragement of the right of ordinary believers to call their own minister, led many people, especially in the central belt of Scotland, to identify themselves with a group that claimed to be following the principles of the early reformers. In October 1732, Ebenezer Erskine, moderator of the Synod of Perth and Stirling, preached a blistering sermon against restricting the call of a minister to the heritors and elders of a congregation. In his sermon he asserted that

> the Call of the church lies in the free choice and election of the Christian people. The promise of conduct and counsel in the choice of men that are to build the church, is not made to patrons, heritors, or any other particular set of men; but to the church, the body of Christ.[21]

Referring to the new Act, he declared that 'whatever church-authority may be in that act, yet it wants the authority of the Son of God'. 'By this act,' he continued,

Christ is rejected in his authority, because I can find no warrant from the word of God, to confer the spiritual privileges of his house upon the rich beyond the poor . . . this act will place the power of electing ministers . . . in the hands of a set of men who are generally disaffected to the power of godliness.[22]

This strong identification of the movement with the spiritual rights and privileges of ordinary believers encouraged many people to identify themselves with the Seceders as those who were faithful to a past spiritual heritage.

Revival and Societies for Prayer

One of the major precursors of the spiritual awakening of 1742 was the resurgence of interest in, and commitment to, religious societies for prayer. In sociological terms, the beginning of the revival can be discerned, not only in the preaching and publication of men like Whitefield and McCulloch, but also in the popular piety of ordinary men and women who longed for a more intense religious experience. In 1731, when McCulloch became the minister of Cambuslang, a parish which had a population of 934 persons, there were three societies in his parish meeting weekly for prayer, a number which would increase to more than a dozen by the end of 1742.[23] McCulloch believed that the groups which had met for prayer on three consecutive evenings in the manse at Cambuslang in February 1742 had been instrumental in engendering a spirit of anticipation for the forthcoming weekly lecture, where the significant spiritual awakening first became manifest.[24]

Religious societies, meeting for prayer, Bible reading and Christian fellowship, were encouraged by John Knox as early as 1557. In a letter of 7 July 1557, written from Geneva, he urged his fellow countrymen to hold weekly meetings, and gave many practical suggestions as to how they might arrange the meetings in the absence of any Protestant clergy.[25] They were encouraged by Samuel Rutherford[26] during the General Assembly of 1640.[27]

During the troubled years of the 'killing times', the Covenanters advocated the use of such house meetings as a means of strengthening the faith and spiritual resolve of their people. Many of these societies became the *United Societies* of the Cameronians, although there were many less extreme groups who chose to remain within the Church of Scotland in 1689, and continued to hold their regular meetings in private houses on weekdays.[28] The meetings were normally regulated by a set of rules to avoid any dangers of divisiveness. Although it was certainly usual in smaller rural communities for men and women to meet together in these societies, it became the custom for the sexes to be segregated. Further divisions on the basis of age, marital status and even social class were not unusual.[29] John Erskine, during his student days at Edinburgh University, was connected with a society which consisted of about twenty members.[30] One of the features of the revival in Kilsyth and elsewhere was the way in which children, between the years of ten and sixteen, often met in their own meetings, under the supervision of the minister.[31]

Each society normally met on a weekly basis and, if there were several meeting in the same locality, they would combine their numbers for a special monthly meeting called the 'association'. Delegates from the associations met on a yearly basis, when the assembled company was called the 'correspondence'.[32] When the Secession occurred in 1733, it was from many of these groupings that the four 'brethren' (namely Ebenezer Erskine, James Fisher, Alexander Moncrieff and William Wilson) derived their support, and which eventually formed the basis of new congregations.[33]

Fellowship meetings were often used as a thermometer to evaluate the spiritual health of the church and community. John Willison refers to the attitude of Thomas Boston that 'in parishes where the gospel begins to thrive, these meetings are set up as naturally as birds draw together in spring'.[34] Religious societies flourished during the revival. Willison was delighted to hear about the increase of societies around Edinburgh in 1740, 'especially among college students . . . which revives our hopes concerning the church, and the promoting of Christianity in the rising generation'.[35] In 1742 James Robe was similarly encouraged that 'there were proposals among the hearers of the gospel for setting up societies for prayer which had long been intermitted'.[36]

The societies were encouraged to meet regularly during the week,[37] for the purpose of scripture reading, prayer, fellowship, discussion of theological and practical subjects and the sharing of spiritual experiences.[38] They were designed for the members' spiritual nourishment and discipline. Membership was taken seriously, and was based on an examination by two or three who would speak with the applicants about 'God's work on their souls' as well as inquiring into their performance of 'secret and family worship'.[39] Although societies were to take care not to 'encroach on the ministry or church-censures' they were to take responsibility for excluding members who were guilty of sinful activity until they were able to satisfy both 'the kirk-session and the meeting about it' and give evidence of true repentance.[40] The influence of the societies can be measured from the way McCulloch, on receiving the suggestion of holding a second communion, took 'care . . . to acquaint the several meetings for prayer with the motion, who relished it well'.[41] It was only after he had sought *their* approval that he made the suggestion to the Kirk session. Prior to the second communion being celebrated several days were set aside 'for a general meeting of the several societies for prayer in the parish', the general design of these meetings being 'to ask mercy of the God of heaven to ourselves . . . that the Lord would continue and increase the blessed work of conviction and conversion'.[42]

By 1743, the practice of united prayer had extended beyond the boundaries of any one parish. A report was printed that 'a Proposal from the Praying Societies at Edinburgh' desired 'to set apart Friday 18th now past for Thanksgiving . . . and Prayer.'[43] In these events, a seed was sown which would eventually grow into the Concert for Prayer which was suggested at a meeting of Scottish ministers in October 1744.[44] The initial outcome was that for two years individual Christians were encouraged to spend some time on Saturday evening and Sunday morning in prayer for revival, and that the first Tuesday of February, May, August and November would be set aside for special prayer 'either in private praying societies, or in public meetings, or alone in secret'.[45] The societies for prayer gave the concert for prayer their wholehearted support.[46] When the original two-year period came to an end, a new proposal was signed by twelve

Scottish ministers, suggesting that the Concert for Prayer be renewed for a further seven years.[47] The proposal was taken up by Jonathan Edwards who published *An Humble Attempt to Promote Explicit Agreement and Visible Union of God's People in Extraordinary Prayer* in 1747.[48] Thus a movement which was characteristic of Scottish piety had an influence on the wider world of evangelicalism.

Revival and the Common People

The message which Whitefield and others preached was well received by several people of 'great rank' particularly Lord Rae, the earl of Leven and the marquis of Lothian.[49] However, it was among the ordinary people of Edinburgh, Glasgow, Aberdeen and Dundee that the revival had its greatest impact. Thomas Davidson spoke of how 'many real Christians have been revived by his means . . . some of the most notorious and abandoned sinners . . . have a promising concern upon their minds about religion'.[50] It is hardly surprising, given the extraordinary circumstances, that the youthful John Erskine should draw the conclusion that Scotland was on the verge of the 'latter day Millennial glory'.[51] Although the revival eventually reached a number of towns and villages throughout Scotland, the early hope that it was the herald of some millennial 'latter day glory' was never realized. McCulloch and Robe faced several disappointments in the lives of professed converts,[52] although in 1751 James Robe could testify that the vast majority of those who had been converted continued to be 'good Christians'.[53] Indeed, almost twenty years after the revival began, the church at Cambuslang kept a day of fasting and thanksgiving 'in commemoration of the Reformation Work . . . in this place . . . about twenty years ago'.[54]

Thomas Gillespie, founder of the Presbytery of Relief in 1761, believed that 'when the Lord God is to do any great and mighty work in the church and the world, he stirs up his people to pray for it and about it'.[55] Looking back on the revival, in the midst of the critical days of the '45 rebellion, Gillespie believed that it had been 'one of the most remarkable effusions of the Spirit on some corners of the land ... since the Reformation'.[56] He was equally convinced that the only hope for peace was for the Church to turn once again to God in prayer for his blessing upon 'King George ... the Parliament ... our armies ... to give us an honourable peace and put an end to the present disturbances and ... pour down his Spirit to dwell among us and cause His glory to dwell in our land'.[57]

Revival Experiences

From the very beginning of the revival, William McCulloch compiled a written record of those who had been converted.[58] He was convinced that one method of securing an endorsement of the revival as a work of the Holy Spirit was to publish evidence of the revival's transforming influence on individual lives.[59] McCulloch's examinations record the spiritual experiences of 108 people from Cambuslang and the surrounding area,[60] representing about a quarter of the final number of converts.[61] They provide a wealth of material about the religious experiences of ordinary men and women who came under the influence of the revival.[62]

Converts spoke of various 'means of grace' which brought relief and comfort to their spiritual distress. For many, it was verses from scripture, which appeared to come into their minds 'with great light',[63] 'with a strong impression',[64] 'with greater power and light than almost any word ever I had met with', which brought a conviction that 'it was from the Spirit of the Lord'.[65] On other occasions the singing of Psalms[66] not only played a part in convicting some people of their sins,[67] but was also a means of attaining spiritual joy.[68] Although most of the narrators neither experienced visions nor heard voices, there were several who found comfort from this source, some even believing that they heard the voice of Christ speaking to them.[69] It was a vision of the crucified Christ 'standing with outstretched arms of mercy, ready to receive' which brought comfort to Catherine Cameron.[70] Several of these, almost superstitious, sensations came under the editorial pen of Alexander Webster, John Willison, Thomas Gillespie and James Ogilvie, to whom

McCulloch sent the manuscripts for their comments and suggestions prior to any possible publication.[71] The editorial comments made by these Church of Scotland ministers indicates different perspectives on what could be viewed as being acceptable religious experiences.

Strangely enough, the vivid, almost erotic, language which the narrators used to speak of their communion with Christ was rarely censored by the eagle eye of the editors.[72] The reason for this is undoubtedly because of the way in which the Song of Songs and other scripture passages were used, both by the Seceders and leaders in the revival, to describe the intimacy of fellowship between Christ and the believer.[73] For this reason, the love for Christ which Catherine Cameron experienced was expressed in terms of ravishing love in which she was willing to 'give up my whole soul and body to him . . . and my heart was in a flame of love to him . . . I came home from that Sacrament with Christ in my arms'.[74]

One feature of the conversion associated with the revival was the vivid impression of a crucified Saviour. The leaders of the revival believed that it was necessary for the mind to be stimulated by such images of Christ's suffering in order for conviction of sin and conversion to Christ to take place. That the revival took place within the context of communion seasons emphasized this theme. The vivid description of the suffering of Christ was well known in Scottish devotional piety. Duncan Campbell, in his *Sacramental Meditations on the Sufferings and Death of Christ*,[75] described the passion of Christ graphically, in order to transport his readers back to the Cross of Calvary.[76] One of the narrators in the McCulloch MSS speaks of

> a most lively and affecting representation made to my mind, of the Sufferings of Christ: I thought I saw Jesus Christ evidently set forth before my Eyes as Crucified . . . and that my Sin had procured his Sufferings . . . I found the tears rushing down my Cheeks.[77]

The claim to see visions, to have verses impressed on their minds and to experience premonitions of future events were issues with which the editors felt no sympathy whatsoever, and they consistently marked such passages for removal.[78] They were afraid that scripture, which they believed was the only 'object and ground of all divine faith', would be displaced by 'immediate revelations', which, they were convinced, were nothing more than 'human fancy'.[79] Furthermore, they feared that many Christians recognized the authority of scripture only when they perceived that the Spirit had impressed particular verses on their minds with light and power.[80]

Almost from the very beginning, the revival came under the critical eye of ministers within the Established Church[81] and especially from the Seceders.[82] The Seceders saw the revival movement in the Church of Scotland as a special threat to their identity. John Willison was convinced that they 'had given it out that the Spirit had left the Ministers and Ordinances of the established Church at your Secession'[83] and therefore the popular piety being expressed through the testimonies of the converts could not be accepted as genuine.

One aspect of the revival which the Seceders criticized was the physical phenomena which were reported at Cambuslang and Kilsyth. On behalf of the Seceders, Ralph Erskine condemned the effects of the Cambuslang revival on the bodies of those who came under conviction of sin as being

> nothing else, but the Effects of a strong Impulse upon the Imagination, and cannot possibly be the immediate Effects of any Acting of the superior Faculties of the Soul, such as the Understanding and Will; These can produce no such Effects as are mentioned here.[84]

The Seceders knew that such bodily manifestations had been recorded in earlier examples of revival, although they maintained that such instances attended the ministry of those 'who were honoured to be most instrumental in carrying on *Reformation Work*'.[85]

The leaders of the revival, while not denying the presence of such phenomena, tried to play down their significance by implying that the numbers of those affected were not as great as was claimed.[86] Furthermore, they argued that the work of the Holy Spirit in convicting men and women of their sin was not limited to the mind and will, but also included the emotions. It was to be expected that these convictions would 'produce fears and sorrows' which would 'in some constitutions naturally produce such outward effects as are now objected to'.[87] Gillespie believed that the 'uncommon symptoms with which the trouble of some is attended, do flow from the clear and deep discovery they receive of the evil of sin, and the danger and misery of one's being without interest in the Saviour'.[88] Whereas the Seceders used these instances of enthusiasm to oppose the revival, James Robe never claimed that 'convulsions, bitter outcryings . . . are . . . considered in themselves as Evidences of Persons being under any Operations of the Spirit of God'. Rather, he simply maintained that 'they are not inconsistent with a Work of the Spirit of God upon the Soul . . . and even flow naturally from it'.[89]

Finally, critics focused on the frequency with which meetings were being held, and the resultant temptation for workers to neglect their employment. Adam Gib contended that 'there is no Value in any Length or Frequency of religious duties beyond the divine Demand' of the Lord's Day.[90] Alexander Moncrieff estimated that the loss of work which was occasioned by the revival amounted to eight million sixpences a week,[91] an indication of the vibrant piety within the country at the time.

The significance of revival, as an aspect of Scottish religious identity, has never received the attention that it merits within the history of Scotland. Yet, as we have seen, the expectation and experience of revival were viewed by many ordinary people within Presbyterianism as a vital aspect of their spiritual, as well as national heritage. Times of revival awakened within their minds the memory of significant periods of Scottish history such as the Reformation and Covenanting periods which they identified as high points in the spiritual pilgrimage of their nation. These memories encouraged them to believe that their identity as Scots could not be divorced from their spirituality as Presbyterians and evangelicals.

Notes

[1] Richard B. Sher, *Church and University in the Scottish Enlightenment* (Edinburgh, 1985).
[2] See Kenneth B. E. Roxburgh, *Thomas Gillespie and the Origins of*

the *Relief Church in Eighteenth-Century Scotland* (Bern, 1999), esp. pp. 241–51.
3   *Acts of the General Assembly of the Church of Scotland 1638–1842* (Edinburgh, 1843), pp. 222–3.
4   Elizabeth West, *The Exercises of Elizabeth West* (Edinburgh, n.d.), p. 178.
5   William Ferguson, *Scotland: 1689 to the Present* (Edinburgh, 1987), pp. 48 ff. See T. M. Devine and J. R. Young (eds.), *Eighteenth Century Scotland: New Perspectives* (Edinburgh, 1999), ch. 3, pp. 24–52.
6   Thomas Boston, *Complete Works*, IV (London, 1853), p. 465. Opposition to the Union did not only come from Scotland. There were those, like William Beveridge (1637–1708), bishop of St Asaph, who spoke vehemently against the Act of Union on the grounds that the Presbyterianism of Scotland would endanger the national Church of England. See article on W. Beveridge in the *Dictionary of National Biography*, II (Oxford, 1963), p. 448.
7   Thomas Boston, *A General Account of my Life*, ed. G. Low, (London, 1908), p. 169. In a similar vein, John Willison, of Dundee speaks of the Church of Scotland's 'degeneracy and defection' which he believes 'have of late years become too visible; and our union with England, in 1707, may be looked upon as the chief source thereof, next to the corruption of our hearts'. See John Willison, *Practical Works* (Glasgow, 1844), p. 899.
8   West, *Exercises*, p. 215. She goes on to say that 'the most part of the godly in Scotland were against it', p. 219.
9   Accounts of the earlier Scottish revivals can be found in R. Fleming, *The Fulfilling of Scripture*, II (Edinburgh, 1850), pp. 95–9. See also W. J. Cooper, *Scottish Revivals* (Dundee, 1918), pp. 26–39.
10 Ian Muirhead comments that 'revivals occurred frequently throughout a period of more than 150 years of Scottish church history, were widespread across the country, and were of significance as the continuing source of much that was effective in the life of the Scottish church'. See Ian A. Muirhead, 'The revival as a dimension of Scottish church history', *Scottish Church History Society Records*, XX (1980), 179.
11 M. J. Crawford, 'New England and the Scottish religious revivals of 1742', *American Presbyterians*, LXIX/1 (Spring 1991), 25. *The Weekly History* (London, 1741), XXII/2–3; XXVI/2 ff.
12 Ralph Erskine replied on 6 July 1739; see *National Library of Wales Journal*, XXVI/3 (Summer 1990), 251–80.
13 Donald Fraser, *The Life and Diary of the Rev. Ralph Erskine* (Edinburgh, 1834), p. 287.

14 Arnold Dallimore, *George Whitefield*, I (London, 1970), p. 504.
15 Robert Small, *History of the Congregations of the United Presbyterian Church from 1733 to 1900*, I (Edinburgh, 1904) p. 426.
16 Andrew T. N. Muirhead, 'A Secession congregation in its community: the Stirling congregation of the Rev. Ebenezer Erskine, 1731–1754', *Scottish Church History Society Records*, XXII (1986), 221–2.
17 One of the questions which prospective candidates for their ministry were asked was, 'Do you own the binding obligation of the national covenant of Scotland, particularly as explained in 1638, to abjure prelacy, and the five articles of Perth; and of the solemn league of the three kingdoms, particularly as renewed in Scotland in 1648, with an acknowledgement of sins; and will you study to prosecute the ends thereof?' See John McKerrow, *Secession Church History* (Edinburgh, 1841), p. 123.
18 R. M. Ferguson, *Logie: A Parish History*, I (Paisley, 1905), pp. 164–8.
19 See Richard J. Finlay, 'Keeping the Covenant: Scottish national identity', in Devine and Young (eds.), *Eighteenth Century Scotland*, pp. 121–33.
20 Colin Kidd, *Subverting Scotland's Past: Scottish Whig Historians and the Creation of an Anglo-British Identity, 1689–c.1830* (Cambridge, 1993), pp. 185–204.
21 E. Erskine, *Works*, I (Edinburgh, 1981), p. 544.
22 Ibid., p. 558.
23 James Robe, *A Short Narrative of the Extraordinary Work of the Spirit of God at Cambuslang* (Glasgow, 1790), p. 316. McCulloch himself had 'for a considerable time bypast, been praying fervently for a Revival to decay'd Religion'. *A True Account of the Wonderful Conversion at Cambuslang* (Glasgow, 1742), p. 3. During 1742 the number of societies increased to more than a dozen, although by 1752 they had decreased to six.
24 Robe, *A Short Narrative*, p. 3.
25 D. Hay Fleming, 'The Praying Society of St. Andrews', *The Original Secession Magazine*, XIV (1879–80), 38–9. The letter is printed in full in Thomas McCrie (ed.), *The Life of Knox* (Edinburgh, 1855), pp. 349–52.
26 Samuel Rutherford (1600?–1661), principal of St Andrews University. He was appointed as one of the commissioners of the Church of Scotland to the Westminster Assembly in 1643.
27 *Records of the Kirk of Scotland*, I (Edinburgh, 1838), pp. 285–7, 294, 303, 304.
28 A. Fawcett, *The Cambuslang Revival* (Edinburgh, 1971), p. 66.

29 Ibid., pp. 66–8.
30 *Christian Repository* (1819), 420–5. The numbers who attended societies probably varied considerably, although a letter from A. Bowre to A. Muire, dated 6 August 1743 from Edinburgh, speaks of 'two societies . . . of twenty five or twenty six persons each', and this may well have been the average number at the height of the revival. *The Christian History for 1743* (Boston, 1744), p. 274.
31 Robe speaks of how he was 'informed that several young girls in the town of Kilsyth, from ten to sixteen years of age, had been observed meeting together for prayer', *A Short Narrative*, p. 72. George Murie from Edinburgh speaks of there being between twenty-four and thirty societies in and around Edinburgh and of how among that number 'there are several meetings of boys and girls'. *The Christian History for 1743*, p. 271.
32 W. MacKelvie, *The Annals and Statistics of the United Presbyterian Church* (Edinburgh, 1873), p. 2. See also D. Hay Fleming, 'The Praying Society of Cameron', *The Original Secession Magazine*, XX (1892), 797–806; 3rd ser. I (1893), 36–46, 154–65.
33 A. L. Drummond and J. Bulloch, *The Scottish Church 1688–1843* (Edinburgh, 1973), pp. 48–9. William MacKelvie, *Annals*, pp. 1–4.
34 Willison, *Religious Societies* (Kilmarnock, 1783), p. 9.
35 Ibid., p. 3.
36 James Robe, in giving his description of Kilsyth prior to the revival makes the comment that around the year 1733 the state of religion declined and 'our societies for prayer came gradually to nothing'. *Narrative*, pp. 66, 70. At the height of the revival in Kilsyth there were twenty-two societies. *The Christian History*, p. 343. Willison speaks of how 'there is a great increase of praying societies in Edinburgh and other towns and villages'. Letter of 28 February 1742 in *The Christian History for 1743*, pp. 86–7.
37 Ibid., p. 243. Hepburn commends the practice of meeting on the Lord's day if no sermon has been provided. See *Rules and Directions*, p. 5.
38 John Hepburn, *Rules and Directions for Fellowship-Meetings* (Edinburgh, 1756), p. 3. George Whitefield was particularly concerned that the societies did not content themselves with 'reading, singing and praying together; but set some time apart to confess your faults and communicate your experiences one to another' for acquainting 'each other with the operations of God's Spirit upon their souls . . . was the great end and intention of those who first began these societies'. *A Letter*, p. 16.
39 Hepburn, *Rules and Directions*, p. 4.
40 Ibid., p. 6.

REVIVAL: AN ASPECT OF SCOTTISH IDENTITY

41 Robe, *A Short Narrative*, p. 33.
42 Ibid., p. 34.
43 *An Account of the Most Remarkable Particulars Relating to the Present Progress of the Gospel*, III/1, p. 18.
44 J. Edwards, *Apocalyptic Writings* (New Haven, 1977), p. 321.
45 Ibid. The concept of the Concert for Prayer occupied the whole of the *Christian Monthly History* for April 1745; see the *Diary of George Brown* (Glasgow, 1856), pp. 10–11, for an illustration of a layman who was involved in the Prayer Concert during November 1744.
46 Fawcett, *Revival*, p. 224.
47 This was dated 26 August 1746; see James Robe, *A Second Volume of Sermons in Three Parts* (Edinburgh, 1750), p. xi.
48 Although Edwards acknowledges the initiative taken by the Scottish ministers to set up the Concert for Prayer, the initial idea may well have come from his own book, *Some Thoughts concerning the Present Revival*, published in 1742 and widely read in Scotland. In the concluding pages, Edwards, giving suggestions as to how to promote the work of revival, specifically mentions the importance of Christians storming 'heaven with their humble, fervent and incessant prayers'; see J. Edwards,*The Great Awakening*, ed. C. C. Goen (New Haven, 1972), pp. 518 ff.
49 G. Whitefield, *Works*, I, pp. 311, 320, 322–3, 324, 333, 335, 338, 340, 345, 347, 369, 400, 455, 467.
50 Letter to a friend in London, dated 24 October 1741, in *Glasgow Weekly History*, IX, p. 7. In another letter dated 5 November 1741, a friend in Edinburgh told Whitefield that at the Tolbooth Church there were more than an extra hundred communicants, 'eighteen of whom were found to be converted by your ministry'. John Lewis, *London Weekly History*, XXXIV, p. 3.
51 J. Erskine, *Signs of the Times Considered, or the high PROBABILITY that the present APPEARANCES in New England, and the West of Scotland, are a PRELUDE of the Glorious Things promised to the CHURCH in the latter Ages* (Edinburgh, October 1742).
52 Fawcett, *Revival*, pp. 166–70. Minutes of the Cambuslang Kirk Session, SRO CH2/415.2, p. 120 where we are told that 'some opposers have triumphed in the matter of backsliders that were concerned in the work'.
53 Kilsyth Kirk Session Records, 19 March 1751, quoted by Fawcett, *Revival*, p. 171. Minutes: Cambuslang Kirk Session, p. 120.
54 Minutes: Cambuslang, p. 431.
55 MSS Sermons for 1771, Aberdeen University Library, MS159, p. 137.

56 Gillespie Sermons, Dunfermline Library, vol. 1, fo.80^r.
57 Ibid., fos.97^v–98^r.
58 Robe, *A Short Narrative*, p. 312.
59 In a letter from Lord Grange to McCulloch, dated 5 December 1743, 'I have much the greater concern for the success of your book because I am fully of your opinion, that instances in fact of the power and influence of the Holy Ghost by the gospel on the hearts and lives of men is needful to convince the world of the truth of Christianity . . . And such are the subjects of your book.' *Edinburgh Christian Instructor* (1838), p. 68.
60 Fawcett identified 106 cases, see *Cambuslang Revival*, 6; Smout identified 110 cases, see T. C. Smout, 'Born again at Cambuslang: new evidence on popular religion and literacy in eighteenth-century Scotland', *Past and Present*, XCVII (November 1982), 116. Leigh Schmidt notes that 'five cases in the first volume of the manuscripts are repeated in the second; three of the narratives in the first volume are fragments. These cases have led in the past to some confusion in tabulating how many cases there are. For the record, I have not counted duplicate cases, but have included the three fragmentary cases in my calculation.' *Holy Fairs* (Princeton, 1989), p. 248 n. 6.
61 McCulloch speaks of 'a fourth part of the persevering subject' in Robe, *A Short Narrative*, p. 312.
62 Several studies have examined the documents in some detail including Ned Landsman, 'Evangelists and their hearers: popular interpretation of revivalist preaching in eighteenth-century Scotland', *Journal of British Studies,* XXVIII (April 1989), 120–49; Stewart Mechie, 'The psychology of the Cambuslang Revival', *Records of the Scottish Church History Society*, X (1950), 171–85.
63 McCulloch MSS, 1: 123.
64 Ibid., 1: 128.
65 Ibid., 1: 323.
66 John Willison had encouraged this because it 'helps excite and accentuate the graces; it is the breath of love or joy; it is the eternal work of heaven'. *A Sacramental Directory* (Edinburgh, 1716), p. 100.
67 McCulloch MSS, 2: 9–15 (Janet Barry); 2: 447 (Margaret Clark).
68 Ibid., 2: 351ff. (Mary Colquhon) 2: 480–1 (Jean Wark).
69 Ibid., 1: 325; 1: 339.
70 Ibid., 1: 320.
71 Arthur Fawcett suggests the order of Webster, Gillespie, Willison and Ogilvie. *Cambuslang Revival*, p. 7. However the order in which the marginal editorial marking occurs is consistent with the above

order. See especially 1: 514 where there is an indication that Webster, Willison and Gillespie edited the MSS and then Webster once again read them over before finally handing them on to Ogilvie.

72 One exception which Gillespie alone marked for excision was that of Catherine Cameron who spoke of having 'great delight in prayer when I would sometimes have gone to bed, I thought I would have Christ between my arms: He was as a Bundle of Myrrh to me and sweet to my soul'. 1: 327.

73 See sermon by Ralph Erskine on 'The best match: the incomparable marriage between the Creator and the creature', in *The Practical Works of the Rev Ralph Erskine* (Glasgow, 1776), I, pp. 145ff. Sermon by Ebenezer Erskine on Song of Songs 8:5 in *Whole Works*, III, pp. 117ff. Whitefield preached on 'thy maker is thy husband' (Is. 54: 5) during the revival, see McCulloch MSS 1: 230. The sermon is in G. Whitefield, *Sermons on Important Subjects* (London, n.d.), pp. 151ff.

74 McCulloch MSS, 1: 327, 335, 343.
75 (Edinburgh, 1703).
76 See Schmidt, *Holy Fairs*, pp. 142–3.
77 McCulloch MSS, 1: 292–3.
78 Ibid., 1: 10–11; 1: 32–3; 1: 47; 1: 131; 1: 137–8; 1: 220; 1: 237.
79 Thomas Gillespie, *An Essay on the Continuation of Immediate Revelations of Fact and Future Events in the Christian Church* (Edinburgh, 1742), p. 5.
80 Ibid., p. 19.
81 John Bissett, *A Letter to a Gentleman in Edinburgh containing Remarks upon a late Apology for the Presbyterians in Scotland* (Glasgow, 1743).
82 Act of the Associate Presbytery anent a Publick Fast at Dunfermline, the fifteenth Day of July 1742 (1742).
83 John Willison, *A Letter from John Willison* (Edinburgh, 1743), p. 23.
84 R. Erskine, *Fraud and Falsehood* (Edinburgh, 1743), p. 25.
85 Fisher, *A Review of the Preface to a Narrative of the Extraordinary Work at Kilsyth* (Glasgow, 1742), p. 26.
86 James Robe, *Third Letter to Mr James Fisher* (Edinburgh, 1743), p. 7.
87 Ibid., p. 15.
88 Robe, *A Short Narrative*, p. 153.
89 James Robe, *Third Letter*, pp. 4–5, 14; Alexander Webster, *A Letter to Ralph Erskine containing a Vindication of Mr Webster's Postscript to his second Edition of Divine Influences in answer to*

Mr Erskine's Charge of Fraud and Falsehood (Edinburgh, 1743), p. 17.
[90] Adam Gib, *A Warning against Countenancing the Ministrations of Mr George Whitefield* (Edinburgh, 1742), pp. 17–18.
[91] John M. Gray, *Memoirs of the Life of Sir John Clerk* (Edinburgh, 1892), p. 248.

~ 11 ~
Unity and Disunity: The Scotch Baptists, 1765–1842

BRIAN TALBOT

The Scotch Baptists are the oldest of the three streams of Baptist life in Scotland. They established their first society in 1765 in the city of Edinburgh. At the end of the eighteenth century, Scotch Baptist churches contained around 400 members and 1,000 adherents.[1] At the beginning of the nineteenth century, Scotch Baptists could claim the allegiance of approximately 90 per cent of Baptists in Scotland.[2] The name 'Scotch Baptist' was given to them to distinguish between those individuals who had adopted Baptist principles in Scotland and the Particular (Calvinistic) Baptists in England. It was not merely a national distinction because these Scottish Baptists differed from their Particular colleagues in their understanding of the constitution of a church of Christ.

> The appellation *Scotch* Baptists is assumed merely to distinguish them from the two classes of Baptists in England, known as *General* or Arminian; and *Particular* or Calvinistic Baptists; with neither of which have they any communion; as they differ materially from both the bodies above named in their views of the Gospel, and especially in regard to church order.[3]

The reason for the differences between the two Baptist traditions arose in part from the distinctive origins of the Scotch Baptists. Their first Scottish historian, Patrick Wilson, noted that many of their ecclesiological ideas were influenced by John Glas, the leader of the Glasite movement. Scotch Baptists, though, were even closer in theological ties to another Christian denomination, the Old Scotch Independents. They were 'with the exception of baptism . . . nearly allied in sentiment to the Old Scotch Independents – the followers of Mr David Dale', the industrialist from New Lanark. It was from the latter group that many of the earliest members of this connexion emerged to play a prominent part in shaping the future direction of the wider Baptist life and witness in Scotland, in the first four decades of the nineteenth century.[4]

At the end of the eighteenth century, churches of this connexion had also been formed in England and Wales.[5] The Welsh Scotch Baptist movement was led by John Richard Jones of Ramoth. Jones, in 1793, became acquainted with Robert Roberts, a member of the open-membership Baptist Church in Wrexham, who introduced the Ramoth minister to the works of Archibald McLean, leader of the Scotch Baptist movement in Scotland.[6] Over the next five years controversy ensued among north Wales Calvinistic Baptists until, in 1798, the churches associated with Jones broke away from the older movement. Details are unclear, but it is likely that around twelve Meirionnydd, Caernarfonshire and Denbighshire churches adopted Scotch Baptist principles.[7] The circumstances of the emergence of Scotch Baptists in Wales were quite different from those of their brethren in Scotland. In 1765 there was no functioning 'English' Baptist body north of the border, for only in the late 1820s did this stream emerge as an influential force to rival the Scotch constituency. The Particular Baptists of north Wales, by contrast, had no desire to see a secession in their ranks over ecclesiological issues. It was, however, the growing intolerance of J. R. Jones that made a separation inevitable.[8] The division had disastrous consequences for Baptists in north Wales, as their energies were consumed by internal conflict rather than evangelism and both communities became inward-looking and saw little numerical growth in the next fifteen years.[9]

It is important to note the beliefs and practices that united this association of Baptist congregations. William Jones, a leading Scotch Baptist elder, then in Liverpool, described their opinions in his monthly magazine, *The Theological Repository*, in two articles in March and April 1808. The first article was concerned with a defence of believer's baptism. This was of particular significance in Scotland because the Scotch Baptists alone among Christian denominations north of the border held to that belief in the late eighteenth century. The second article discussed the other tenets of their faith. The opening section referred to beliefs held in common with other Calvinistic Baptists regarding the Godhead and salvation. It was, however, the second section of Jones's article which revealed the distinctive features of their position.

> They also hold it their indispensable duty to follow entirely the *pattern* of the primitive apostolic churches, as recorded in the New Testament, and to attend to all the directions given them, which they consider to be inseparably connected with genuine love to the truth, and steadfastness and liveliness in the faith and hope of the gospel . . .[10]

In practice, the New Testament was believed to teach that each congregation of believers had a plurality of elders and deacons. 'English' Baptists, by contrast, could accept a plurality of deacons, but preferred a sole elder or pastor. Church discipline had to be exercised 'on all proper occasions'. Scotch Baptists were not unique in advocating this principle, but its use was probably more wide-ranging than in other Baptist circles. It was stated that 'the Rule of forbearance *is divine revelation*, and not the fancies of men'. This rule was, however, qualified in the statement that 'no precept given by Christ can be a matter of indifference, they act upon this principle, that his authority can never clash with itself by giving laws, and at the same time a dispensation to neglect them'. In addition, 'they consider it their duty to be all of one mind in every thing that regards their faith and practices as a body, agreeably to the unanimity which was exemplified in the Church in Jerusalem and is most solemnly inculcated upon other churches'.[11] The observance of this statute was in due course to be the cause of damaging conflicts which drained their enthusiasm for evangelism and weakened the ties between their congregations.

At the time when William Jones wrote his article, in 1808, Scotch Baptists could have foreseen only benefits from the promulgation of this teaching, for example, in the successful resolution of the Socinian disputation, considered later in this chapter. The weekly observance of the Lord's Supper, regular participation in 'the feast of charity' and the abstinence from 'eating of blood, and things strangled' were other practices observed by this group of Christian believers.[12] Jones was correct in laying the emphasis on their 'order and practices'. It was the church order of Scotch Baptists that marked them apart from other British Baptists. It is ironic that the Baptist tradition with which they shared this excessive biblical literalism in ecclesiological matters, the Old Connexion of English General Baptists, differed from them more than the other Baptist traditions, in doctrinal matters, holding to an Arminian rather than a Calvinistic theological perspective.

There were only a few theological opinions resulting from a strict adherence to New Testament language that marked them out from other Calvinistic Baptists. One such belief, promulgated by Archibald McLean, was the necessary denial of the eternal sonship of Jesus on the grounds that such terminology could not be found in the Bible. McLean probably held this opinion as a result of his association with the Old Scotch Independents. James Smith, former parish minister of Newburn, Fife, and one of the founders of that body, taught that Jesus in the scriptures 'is never said to be eternally begotten'.[13] McLean concluded his discussion of that subject by declaring:

> Christ is eternal, but not as the Christ; the Son of man is eternal but not as the Son of man. Emmanuel is eternal; but not as Emmanuel; even so the Son of God is eternal in his divine person, but it does not follow that he is so as a Son.[14]

The impact of such a viewpoint in the other Baptist streams would have been modest, due to the willingness to tolerate a measure of theological diversity within a conservative theological framework. The Scotch Baptists, by contrast, long after McLean's death, used this doctrinal shibboleth as a test of orthodoxy for aspiring church members.[15] It is significant here to note that the Scotch Baptists had set out a clear statement of their opinions regarding beliefs and practices to which allegiance must be given by all who sought to remain within their ranks.

The presence of this Edinburgh elder overshadowed all other leaders in the Scotch Baptist connexion in his lifetime. McLean was undoubtedly the main focus for unity within their ranks. Amongst Scotch Baptists in Wales, at least in the first decade of their existence, even their strong-willed leader J. R. Jones acknowledged McLean's supremacy.[16] During the first forty-four years of Scotch Baptist witness, McLean's pronouncements on an issue served as a definitive statement of their beliefs or practices. These declarations on such issues as the Socinian controversy tended to reinforce his authority within the movement. There were individuals, however, who could not tolerate the Edinburgh elder's excessive influence over the connexion, such as Charles Stuart and George Grieve, but the vast majority of Scotch Baptists accepted the guidance he offered to them without question.[17]

It is important to consider next the other factors that contributed to the internal cohesion of this movement. Unity in doctrine and church practices was assumed amongst the Scotch Baptists. This issue was almost as important to the maintenance of harmony in the connexion as was their leader Archibald McLean. It was a policy that provided the essential framework for relationships between the local congregations. They had no doubts in their minds that unity, even unanimity, was essential in their ranks. A church wishing to be received into fellowship faced a process that was lengthy and thorough. Samuel Swan, an elder of the congregation meeting at Wellington Road, Wortley, near Leeds, made this clear in a letter, in 1835, to James Everson, one of the pastors of the Beverley church. 'I admit the independent right of each church to judge, but surely when a number of churches are associated, *none* ought to be received into the association without the concurrence of the whole . . .'[18] This had been practised by the Scotch Baptist churches when Haggate Baptist Church in Lancashire sought fellowship with them in 1834. The correspondence between Swan and Everson that year records in great detail the process by which approval was granted. The initial contact was between the Leeds and Haggate churches and involved the exchanging of statements of faith and practice for mutual inspection.

> We deemed it our duty to open correspondence with them with a view to fellowship. We gave them a brief statement of our faith and

practice requesting one from them in return. The subjoined letter No.1 is a copy of their statement which we hand for your inspection and approval. The question they propounded led to an explanation on both sides and the whole correspondence was brought to a favourable issue by the reception of the following letter No.2.

We received them with greater confidence from the report of one of our brethren who visited them last July and who was perfectly satisfied with what he saw and heard amongst them.[19]

Swan noted that in reply to a letter from his church the Haggate friends had declared: 'with respect to what is said of the Institutions of Christ our views exactly agree with yours . . . Indeed we can truly say that we agree with every sentence in your letter.'[20] This outcome was remarkable considering that the Leeds letter contained a full statement of their beliefs and practices. The Haggate church was accepted as a sister church at the end of this process.

Great care was also taken before accepting someone as a member of a Scotch Baptist church. The candidate's previous church was required to give its support for such a transfer of membership. The case of Andrew Bruce may be exceedingly thorough, but it illustrates the extremely diligent consideration given to requests for admission to the membership of a congregation. Complications arose over his request to join the Clyde Street congregation in Edinburgh. Clyde Street records show that correspondence was entered into with the Tabernacle Church, Edinburgh, where Bruce had been an adherent; Thurso Baptist Church where he had been a member; Thurso magistrates; and various other individuals in different parts of Scotland of whom some were ministers or elders.[21] This example was not an isolated case of extraordinary thoroughness in considering an application for membership. It is surprising that anyone was willing to endure such an ordeal, but it did indicate the seriousness with which Scotch Baptists took the links with their sister churches. Even a visit to a town in which one of their congregations was located, by a member on private business, could be the occasion of a letter assuring that church of his good character. In one particular case the visit was midweek and the man in question had no plans to attend a service, but should he come into contact with any members of that church they would be aware of his commendation by his own fellowship.[22] It is difficult to overestimate the importance of the letters exchanged between Scotch Baptist leaders for directing the opinions and conduct of their congregations, especially communications from the senior elder in Edinburgh. J. R. Jones, in a letter dated March 1800, indicated an earnest desire to have a theological difficulty explained by McLean. 'My Dear Brother, I exceedingly long to hear from you. I had no answer to my former letter which was dated sometime in August last.'[23] The regular maintenance of a consensus of views and practices by written correspondence, and occasional visits, was a time-consuming process, but it was a unifying hallmark of the Scotch Baptist connexion in Britain.

Scotch Baptists also sought to be united in evangelistic efforts. The significance of this factor is seen in that the periods of greatest mission activities were also those of harmony in the connexion, for example, in the late 1790s.[24] The 1830s, by contrast, the era of the greatest disunity in the ranks, saw little co-operative effort in evangelism. The Bristo Place Church, Edinburgh, sent annual letters to its sister churches in this period with a view to increasing evangelistic activity, though with little success.[25] It was only to be expected that the Edinburgh Church would take the lead in urging the churches to co-operate in raising funds, and in sending out workers as home missionaries, as it had done earlier in support of the work of the Particular Baptist Missionary Society. After the 1834 division in the ranks of Scotch Baptists, discussed later in this chapter, the small breakaway group that moved to Minto House took the lead in directing the affairs of the stricter party in the constituency. The problem that Scotch Baptists faced was that, as the network of churches with which they associated grew smaller, so the amount of evangelistic activity they could accomplish also diminished.

One other, though less important, factor in maintaining union amongst Scotch Baptists was the determination to work diligently to overcome problems that arose between the churches. The detailed interest in the affairs of each other's congregations was bound to throw up issues which caused profound disagreement, but this was not allowed to be an excuse for failing to maintain 'the unity of the Spirit in the bond of peace' (Eph. 4: 3). Andrew Duncan, an elder of the Glasgow congregation, described in a letter to John Charlton, an elder of the Beverley church, how a reconciliation had been achieved between his own congregation and another smaller Scotch Baptist church in the city in 1825.

> We had a baptism last Saturday morning and a small church attended who were formerly in fellowship with us, but who withdrew from us on a matter of discipline. They have again applied for admission to our communion. After some correspondence it was effected last Lord's Day . . .[26]

Scotch Baptists have gained historical notoriety for the extent of their divisions during the nineteenth century. However, it is important to record a balanced picture that includes some successful reunions such as that in Glasgow. The achievement in healing a local division led the Glasgow church to attempt unsuccessfully to bring about a reunion with Scotch Baptist churches which had left the connexion, for various reasons, in the preceding decades.

Overseas mission work conducted by Particular Baptists in India came to McLean's attention during his regular journeys to England.[27] Support for evangelistic activities in other countries was not as important as home evangelism in uniting Scottish Baptists, but it played its part in widening their horizons, especially those of Scotch Baptists. In his *Memoir* of McLean, in 1823, William Jones, an elder of the Windmill Street Scotch Baptist Church in London, stressed the lively interest of McLean in this subject:

> This indeed was only the legitimate consequence of his own views of the nature of the Gospel, and of our Lord's Commission to 'Go into all the world, and preach (or proclaim) it to every creature' . . . He considered it to be his duty to assist the society which had been established for the support of the mission, to the utmost of his ability.[28]

McLean was probably the first minister in Scotland to announce publicly the need to obey the 'Great Commission'

(Matt. 28: 19-20). At the end of 1798 he delivered a stirring discourse to his Edinburgh congregation based on Psalm 22: 27-8. He persuaded them to support the Particular Baptist Missionary Society. This was soon followed by *An Address to the People of God in Scotland, on the Duty of Using Means for the Universal Spread of the Gospel of Christ*, which affirmed the need to engage in evangelism in Scotland. McLean had no difficulty in persuading fellow Scotch Baptists to follow the lead from Edinburgh. They responded generously to his appeal. McLean was able to reveal the level of this generosity to Andrew Fuller in a letter sent in April 1796:

> Sir, enclosed you have a banker's bill for £151.11.0 for your missionary society, to be applied to the purpose of propagating the gospel among the heathen. It was collected as follows:
>
> | | |
> |---|---|
> | From the church at Edinburgh | £58.04.0. |
> | From the hearers at Edinburgh | £19.10.0. |
> | | £77.14.0. |
> | From the church and hearers at Glasgow | £41.00.0. |
> | From the church and hearers at Dundee | £10.06.0. |
> | From the church and hearers at Paisley | £10.10.0. |
> | From the church and hearers at Largo | £05.05.0. |
> | From some brethren at Wooler | £04.11.0. |
> | From a few brethren at Galashiels | <u>£02.05.0.</u> |
> | | £151.11.0. |
>
> Since the above collections were made, we have received about £24 more, and having published two small pamphlets on the subject, if any thing comes from the sale of them it shall be appropriated to the same use.[29]

Scotch Baptists in England and Scotland were consistent not only in their continued support for the Baptist missionary work in India, but also in their advocacy of other Baptist work overseas. The more insular brethren in Wales, however, chose not to support the work of the Particular Baptist Missionary Society, displaying a consistent separation from the activities of mainstream Particular Baptists.[30]

Scotch Baptists showed great caution in their relationships with other Baptists. There were some who were quick to associate, but others that appeared to want almost no contact at all. J. R. Jones, in 1801, made plain his desire for the latter position at a joint conference in Ramoth Baptist Chapel of Scotch and Particular Baptists in north Wales. The gathering was broken up by the extraordinary spectacle of the Ramoth elder taking the pulpit Bible in his hands and declaring in a loud voice (in Welsh), 'In the name of the Lord I separate myself from the Babylonian Welsh Baptists and from their errors in doctrine and practice, in order that I may unite myself with my brethren in Scotland who have received the truth.'[31] The majority of church members would have been somewhere in the middle between these two positions. It is likely that many of them would have agreed with the sentiments expressed by Robert Anderson, elder of Bristo Place Church, alongside Henry Dickie, in a letter sent to James Everson in 1836:

> I feel as you do, that in general our conduct should be such as to make it appear that we remain separate from the English Baptists from principle. At the same time I think that opportunities of preaching the Gospel in any of their churches or elsewhere occasionally may be embraced consistent with strict Scriptural views.[32]

Unity with fellow Scotch Baptists was the first priority of those within that particular connexion. There were varying degrees of willingness to work with other Baptists, but the primary focus regarding union was to preserve it within their own ranks. The problem of disunity within Scotch Baptist ranks regularly engaged their attention. It was not surprising, though, that those individuals who set such high standards for the maintenance of church purity in doctrine and practice should fail to live up to them.

There was one major external cause that produced divisions amongst the followers of Archibald McLean, that is, the rise of the Campbellites. This new denomination came into being through the preaching of Alexander Campbell. This Ulsterman, in association with his father Thomas, established a congregation at Brush Run in America in 1813. Campbell aimed to restore 'the ancient order of things', that is, a return to the original pattern of church life found in the New Testament. He argued for congregational autonomy, the weekly observance of the Lord's Supper, a plurality of elders and deacons in each congregation and a simple pattern of worship. New Testament preaching began with a testimony to the gospel facts; this testimony, without any other supernatural agency, produced faith.[33] It was abundantly clear that there were marked similarities between Campbell's teaching and the opinions of the Scotch Baptists, who faced this new challenge from the followers of Alexander Campbell at a time when their connexion was at its weakest. The loss of some of its most conservative members, such as the churches in Saltcoats and Stevenson in Ayrshire,[34] however, would probably have removed some of the strongest opponents of closer ties with the Particular Baptists.

The external threat posed by the Campbellites had caused serious difficulties for Scotch Baptists, but it did not compare to the challenge posed by internal divisions. The principal problem was raised by Andrew Liddel of Edinburgh in a letter to James Everson of Beverley dated March 1836. Officially Scotch Baptists believed both in forbearance and unanimity in belief and church order. Such a position could be maintained in principle, but not in practice. This letter majored on the theme of the futility of compromise on doctrinal and ecclesiological issues. Liddel spent the first part of his letter recording his grief at the divisions caused in Scotch Baptist ranks in the 1830s over the issue of whether elders are required at the Lord's Table to celebrate communion. He saw that forbearance on this issue would lead to acceptance of an open table and then an open membership amongst Baptist churches. He stated:

> It cannot now be denied, I think, that the sentiment about the Lord's Supper, the avowed cause of division, leads into other and more evident disorders. From this I humbly think that the most timorous might see that such a sentiment and practice cannot be of God.[35]

Liddel was correct to discern the likely direction of compromises between churches in order to strengthen or to establish unity between them.

It was easier to remain within the safety of one's own ecclesiastical circles. Robert Anderson, of Bristo Place Church, took this viewpoint in his letters, in the mid-1830s, to James Everson. In March 1836 he wrote:

> We are endeavouring to prevail (in conjunction with other churches of our connexion) with some others around us who are much assimilated to us to give up the practice of receiving into occasional fellowship such persons, though themselves baptized, [who] are members of free communion Churches.[36]

Later that year in reply to a letter from Everson, dated 20 October, Anderson was quick to deny that his church was serious about uniting with 'English' Baptists. Everson was making it plain that, should this be the case, they would be disfellowshipped by the Beverley church. 'You are mistaken,' said Anderson, 'in supposing we are hankering after Union with the English Baptists as presently constituted, or throwing down the things which distinguish us from them.'[37] Schism within Scotch Baptist ranks had been extremely painful for all concerned. The inability to exercise forbearance with each other over one or two issues of doctrine or church practice was a fatal flaw in their bond of union. It also had resulted in the fragmentation of a once united body.

One important issue that Scotch Baptists faced was the persistent problem of mutual mistrust. It was, ironically, their own insistence on mutual exhortation, that is the opportunity for any male member to bring a sermon or contribution in worship services without prior approval from the eldership, that left them vulnerable to the promulgation of strange ideas. As early as March 1774 a group within the church in Edinburgh persistently challenged the official line on a number of points. One individual argued that only real Christians had a duty to pray to God; that the office of elder was not a special position, but that the work of ruling, public teaching and dispensing the ordinance belonged equally to all the brethren; that neither the apostolic prohibition of blood-eating, nor the observance of the first day of the week were binding upon Christians. This party of eight people appears to have been more interested in drawing attention to themselves than in presenting a considered theological position. After they had left the church they began to advance even more radical ideas, including a denial of the deity of Christ.[38] The regular presentation of contrasting opinions in congregational worship cannot have assisted either with the harmony or edification of the membership.

These problems were an irritation to the Edinburgh congregation. Other problems were much more serious, especially the doctrinal errors advanced by Neil Stuart, an elder of the Glasgow congregation. He had been promoting the Sabellian belief that there are no hypostatic distinctions in the Godhead. Glasgow Scotch Baptist Church accepted Stuart's ideas as correct doctrine in the spring of 1776. Archibald McLean received news of this development and requested clarification of their beliefs concerning the doctrine of the Trinity. The written response duly arrived and received an even quicker reply from McLean. In his reply, McLean quoted extracts from Stuart's letter, including this description of the Trinity:

> You say That the three names Father, Son (Word), and Holy Ghost, are not expressive of three distinct subsistences [sic] in the same Godhead; but of the one undivided Godhead dwelling bodily in the man Christ Jesus – and thus acts in all the characters, relations, and offices implied in these and in every other appellation which he condescends to bear for our complete salvation and consolation.[39]

McLean, using the scriptural passages recommended by Stuart, convincingly destroyed the case that the Glasgow elder had advanced. The church at Glasgow recognized the strength of McLean's case and changed their view to Socinianism, admitting that the Father and the Son are distinct persons, but affirming that the Godhead is the person of the Father, and the manhood of Christ is the person of the Son. The logic of their case forced them to deny that the Son of God was a divine person or had any existence at all prior to his conception in the Virgin Mary.

A conference was organized in Edinburgh to sort out this matter. George Begg and Neil Stuart, the Glasgow elders, committed a breach of a previously agreed protocol by visiting the churches at Dundee and Montrose prior to the conference to argue their case with a view to gaining their support in Edinburgh. It appears that they had some measure of success because 'they were not altogether disappointed, for they unsettled the minds of several of the brethren at both places, and not a few were entirely subverted'.[40] When they arrived in Edinburgh the elders were allowed to state their case. McLean countered the arguments presented with a convincing refutation.

> Neil Stuart exposed himself sufficiently by such arbitrary and unnatural glosses as flatly contradicted the plain sense and scope of the sacred text; but, being closely pressed with these and similar passages, he found himself shut up and was at last sunk into silence.

George Begg later admitted the error of his ways, as did many of the other members of the Glasgow church. The Dundee and Montrose churches also regained most of the members who had adopted the views of Neil Stuart. In the end there were only three people, one of whom was Stuart, who remained outside the connexion after the resolution of this controversy.[41]

Baptists in Wales also faced controversy over the deity of Christ. A secession in south Wales from Particular Baptist ranks, in 1798, led to the setting up of a short-lived rationalist body, the General (Arminian) Baptist Association, which soon became avowedly Unitarian, certainly by 1805.[42] This development occurred at the same time as the English General Baptists agreed to welcome self-proclaimed Unitarians into their ranks.[43] North Wales Baptists were almost immune from this controversy. There was only one case of Sabellianism arising in this period. Joseph Richards, an elder at Dolgellau Scotch Baptist Chapel, together with the majority of his congregation, withdrew from fellowship with the Scotch Baptists after Richards had been invited to withdraw his advanced opinions by J. R. Jones in the spring of 1800.[44]

The practice of making the sonship of Christ the test of doctrinal orthodoxy for prospective members gave rise to a further controversy in the Edinburgh congregation in 1777. Was Christ the eternal Son of God or just the Son of the eternal God? Robert Walker advanced the view that Christ was the eternal Son of God – but to no avail. The influence of McLean was decisive. He insisted that Christ was not the Son until He appeared in the flesh. His congregation dutifully accepted the position he propounded.[45] This view was maintained by Scotch Baptists long after McLean's death. James Williamson in his reminiscences of life in the Pleasance church from the 1820s recorded the interview of a friend who had made an application for church membership.

> An old Aberdonian weaver, Mr T. – always took the 'opportunity' of putting the question, 'What did the candidate think of the "pairson" [person] and "dig-nae-tee" [dignity] of Christ?' This was a poser to a chum of mine, Walter Wilson, who having been brought up a Presbyterian, answered, that He was the 'eternal Son of God'. This answer was quite heterodox, according to McLean theology; so Walter, like Apollos, had to be instructed in the way more perfectly.[46]

This unfortunate episode between McLean and Walker deprived the church of the valuable services of their elder Robert Walker who continued to hold firmly to his beliefs.

One very important issue and probably the 'Achilles' heel' of Scotch Baptists was the question of the relationship between the Lord's Supper and the eldership. The answers to the following questions were sought very carefully, especially over the situation at Newburgh, in the period 1780 to 1810. Is an elder required for an act of communion to take place? What number of people are required to constitute a church for this purpose? Is a church set in order if there is only one elder? These were important issues, not merely academic questions, as they had a practical bearing upon life in the churches. Small societies not set in church order were permitted to receive communion only at the Edinburgh church. Naturally the distance was a major obstacle to attendance in Edinburgh on Sundays. So the question began to be raised, why could Christians observe every part of divine worship in their locality except communion?

William Hynd, a member at Newburgh, claimed that it was the duty of disciples to observe the Lord's Supper wherever two or three of them could meet together, although they were not furnished with elders or set in church order. Several people in Newburgh were convinced by his arguments; others, though, were persuaded that there was a need to examine this matter. As a result of this discussion in Newburgh a letter was sent to the

Edinburgh church for its deliberation. At the Edinburgh church meeting Charles Stuart and George Grieve, two members who were former ministers, argued that the position of Hynd was weak, but in any case it ought to be a matter of forbearance. A local church had the responsibility to make up its own mind on this matter. This flexible approach was similar to that which Andrew Fuller had recommended in his exchange of letters with McLean in 1796.[47] The senior elder, McLean, and the rest of the church, however, maintained that the Lord's Supper belonged only to a regular constituted church.

The decision was strongly contested by those who held the opposing viewpoint. Hynd was requested on three occasions to come to Edinburgh and argue his case, but he refused to accept the invitations. As a result he was excommunicated by a majority vote of the Edinburgh church. Charles Stuart and one other person were also put out for objecting forcefully to the decision to expel Hynd. George Grieve then withdrew from the church because he felt the whole situation had been handled unwisely. It appeared as though the matter was now settled in the connexion. The departure of some valuable members, whom they could hardly afford to lose, appeared to be the only long-term consequence of this controversy. This vexatious affair was concluded in April 1784.[48] J. Idwal Jones, a twentieth-century Scotch Baptist elder in north Wales, discussed the various arguments put forward in Scotch Baptist journals and concluded that a great deal of energy was wasted on futile attempts to insist that the Bible spoke conclusively in favour of either case.[49]

In the period 1765 to 1842 the Scotch Baptists made considerable progress. They appeared to lay a strong foundation for the future by measures aimed at maintaining the union of the churches within the connexion. Archibald McLean was the major bond of union between the different congregations. Great care was taken over the reception of new members into local congregations and churches into their wider fellowship. McLean sought to broaden the horizons of the churches by urging them to co-operate in evangelism at home and by supporting the English Particular Baptist Mission in India. There had been problems in and between the churches, but it did appear that the difficulties were being overcome prior to 1834.

There were many obstacles that prevented Scotch Baptists from formally uniting with other Baptists in Britain. The most important reason was an inability to exercise forbearance on almost any matter by a large minority of the connexion. J. R. Jones's relationship with McLean is a good example of this problem. The Ramoth elder was devoted to the Scottish leader for a number of years, but he became increasingly intolerant of the minor differences which arose between them, for example, over the understanding of the millennium in Revelation 20. As early as February 1806 the tone of Jones's letters to the Edinburgh patriarch became increasingly critical. In a lengthy critique of McLean's view on the millennium Jones declared: 'I rather wonder at the lame shift you made to turn away the force of my objections to your view of the Millennium and the final resurrection.'[50] Eventually McLean's patience ran out and he requested an end to the correspondence from Jones.

An additional factor that served as a barrier between Scottish and Welsh Scotch Baptists was language. There were only four or five Welsh brethren who could read English, and so communication with the wider connexion was filtered through J. R. Jones. When the Ramoth elder strained his relationship with the Edinburgh Church, in practice the entire Welsh movement was affected by this problem.[51] The ties between Welsh and Scottish Scotch Baptists appeared to weaken further over the following decade until the breach became complete.[52] The date of the final separation was certainly prior to 1822. In that year William Scott of the Edinburgh church issued a circular containing the names of the churches in their connexion, but no Welsh churches were included.[53] Scotch Baptists had increasingly turned inward, focusing on their differences at the expense of evangelism. This critical intolerance of their colleagues was destroying the very fabric of their bond of union.

This unresolved problem, of a lack of forbearance, had been raised on a number of occasions without a satisfactory answer. It was not too difficult for the connexion to stand firm against Socinianism, but the mistake was made in assuming that all other contentious matters could also be brought to a swift conclusion. In the 1830s, some Scotch Baptists were keen to work with the 'English' Baptists in Britain while others were drawn to the even more conservative Churches of Christ. This led to a loss of identity within the movement as different sections of it were pulling in opposing directions. The inevitable result was division between Baptists who no longer had 'all things in common'. The final blow to any pretence of unity amongst Scotch Baptists came with division in 1834, officially over the necessity of elders presiding at the Lord's Table. It was, in reality, an acknowledgement that their basis of union could not survive in an era of changing theological opinions. Scotch Baptists had been imprisoned by their past and had consequently been unable, as a body, to come to terms with a changing religious environment in Britain. There were some conservative Scotch Baptists like John Cowan, an elder of the Galashiels church, who had come to regret the opportunities that the connexion had failed to grasp in earlier years. He stated:

> Our churches will never be what they have been, I fear – if indeed they long survive. Other connexions are occupying the fields which I am convinced we might have occupied had we been properly alive to our duty. But let us not despair nor faint in the Lord's work. His end will be secured independently of man.[54]

The Baptists who had striven hardest to maintain unity with one another ended up losing the grounds of their own unity. The Scotch Baptist tradition contributed much to Baptist life in Britain, especially in Scotland. It was, however, destined to play only a minor part in the future due to disunity within its own ranks.[55]

Notes

[1] J. Rippon (ed.), *Baptist Annual Register*, II (London, 1795), pp. 373–4.
[2] Ibid. Also, Brian R. Talbot, 'The origins of the Baptist Union of Scotland', unpublished Ph.D. thesis, University of Stirling, 1999, p. 163.
[3] James Everson, 'The Scotch Baptist Churches', *The Christian Advocate and Scotch Baptist Repository*, I/1 (March 1849), 1.
[4] P. Wilson, *The Origin and Progress of the Scotch Baptist Churches from their Rise in 1765 to 1834* (Edinburgh, 1844), pp. 3–4.

5. D. B. Murray, 'The Scotch Baptist tradition in Great Britain', *Baptist Quarterly*, XXXIII/4 (1989), 188–9.
6. D. Densil Morgan, 'The development of the Baptist movement in Wales between 1714–1815 with particular reference to the evangelical revival', unpublished D.Phil. thesis, University of Oxford, 1986, p. 242.
7. Ibid., pp. 194–5.
8. T. W. Davies, 'The McLeanist (Scotch) and Campbellite Baptists of Wales', *Transactions of the Baptist Historical Society*, VII (1920–1), 158–69.
9. Morgan, 'The development of the Baptist movement', pp. 195–6.
10. 'A compendious account of the principles and practices of the Scottish Baptists', *The Theological Repository*, IV/23 (April 1808), 199–200.
11. Ibid., p. 201.
12. Ibid., pp. 200–5.
13. 'The case of James Smith, late minister at Newburn and Robert Ferrier, late minister at Largo, truly represented and defended' (1768; Glasgow, 1816), cited by H. Escott, *A History of Scottish Congregationalism* (Glasgow, 1960), p. 25.
14. W. Jones (ed.), *The Works of Mr Archibald McLean*, I (London, 1823), p. 451.
15. J. Williamson, *Some Reminiscences of the Old Baptist Church Pleasance* (Edinburgh, 1901), p. 15.
16. Davis, 'McLeanist and Campbellite Baptists', p. 159.
17. Wilson, *Origin and Progress*, pp. 19–23.
18. Samuel Swan, Leeds, to James Everson, Beverley, 15 February 1835. MS Letters relating to the Scotch Baptist Churches, National Library of Scotland, Edinburgh.
19. Swan to Everson, 7 October 1834.
20. Haggate letter sent by John Hudson to Samuel Swan, 6 April 1834, cited in Samuel Swan to James Everson, 7 October 1834, MS Letters.
21. Andrew Bruce's Case, 14 July 1828, Clyde Street Hall, Waugh Papers, Baptist House, Glasgow.
22. Letter to a church in Kendal, Cumbria, 16 January 1838, concerning John McNeil from Clyde Street Hall, Waugh Papers.
23. J. R. Jones, Ramoth, to A. McLean, Edinburgh, March 1800, in D. Williams, *Cofiant J. R. Jones, Ramoth* (Carmarthen, 1913), pp. 805–6.
24. For example, *Edinburgh Quarterly Magazine*, I (Edinburgh, 1798), 68–73.
25. For example, 'From the Church Meeting in Bristo Place, Edinburgh, to the Church in [Beverley]', a circular letter, Edinburgh, 9 February 1838, MS Letters.

26 Andrew Duncan, Glasgow, to John Charlton, Beverley, 7 September 1825, MS Letters.
27 Wilson, *Origin and Progress*, p. 29.
28 Jones (ed.), *Works of Archibald McLean*, IV, p. lxxiii.
29 W. Jones (ed.), *The New Evangelical Magazine*, II (London, 1816), p. 76.
30 Davies, 'McLeanist and Campbellite Baptists', p. 158.
31 Williams, *J. R. Jones*, p. 376; Davies, 'McLeanist and Campbellite Baptists', p. 166.
32 Robert Anderson, Edinburgh, to James Everson, Beverley, 1 March 1836, MS Letters.
33 C. L. Allen, 'Alexander Campbell', in D. M. Lewis (ed.), *The Blackwell Dictionary of Evangelical Biography 1730–1860* (Oxford, 1995), pp. 188–9.
34 D. M. Thompson, *Let Sects and Parties Fall* (Birmingham, 1980), pp. 26–7.
35 Andrew Liddel, Sheffield, to James Everson, Beverley, 12 March 1836, MS Letters.
36 Anderson to Everson, 1 March 1836, MS Letters.
37 Anderson to Everson, 8 December 1836, MS Letters.
38 Wilson, *Origin and Progress*, pp. 10–11.
39 Letter III, 'On Sabellianism', in Jones (ed.), *Works of Archibald McLean*, III, p. 499.
40 Rippon, *Baptist Annual Register* (1795), pp. 365–6.
41 Wilson, *Origin and Progress*, pp. 15–17.
42 D. Densil Morgan, 'Smoke, fire and light: Baptists and the revitalisation of Welsh Dissent', *Baptist Quarterly*, XXXII/5 (1988), 229–30.
43 R. Brown, *The English Baptists of the Eighteenth Century* (London, 1986), pp. 107–9.
44 J. R. Jones to A. McLean, March 1800, in Williams, *J. R. Jones*, pp. 805–6.
45 Wilson, *Origin and Progress*, pp. 17–18.
46 Williamson, *Some Reminiscences*, p. 15.
47 J. Belcher (ed.), *The Complete Works of the Rev. Andrew Fuller*, III (reprint, Harrisonburgh, VA, 1988), p. 480.
48 Wilson, *Origin and Progress*, pp. 19–23.
49 J. Idwal Jones, 'Essay on early doctrinal differences amongst Scotch Baptists mainly in the period 1780–1810 and largely revolving around the question of the Celebration of the Lord's Supper', MS Letters.
50 J. R. Jones to A. McLean, 5 February 1806, Waugh Papers.
51 J. R. Jones to William Braidwood, 7 October 1796, in Williams, *J. R. Jones*, p. 801.

52 R. D. Mitchell, 'Archibald McLean, 1733–1812, Baptist pioneer in Scotland', unpublished Ph.D. thesis, University of Edinburgh, 1950, pp. 154–6; Davies, 'McLeanist and Campbellite Baptists', p. 159.
53 T. W. Davies, 'A Scotch Baptist Circular', *Transactions of the Baptist Historical Society*, V (1916–17), 251–7.
54 John Cowan, Galashiels, to James Everson, Beverley, 11 December 1848, MS Letters.
55 Two clusters of Scotch Baptist churches survive in Wales but none in Scotland.

~ 12 ~
'Our Mother and our Country': The Integration of Religious and National Identity in the Thought of Edward Irving (1792–1834)

LIAM UPTON

Edward Irving is probably best known to students of British church history for the dramatic manner in which he parted company with the Church of Scotland. He was minister to the Caledonian Chapel in Hatton Garden, London, from 1822 to 1827, and of the National Scotch Church in Regent Square from 1827 to 1832. Within a year of his arrival in London, he became the most celebrated preacher of his day. The cream of society fought to gain admittance to the Caledonian Chapel to hear him.[1] On one occasion, the Prime Minister, Lord Liverpool, was said to have climbed in through a window in his anxiety not to miss one of Irving's sermons.[2] In 1825, Irving embraced the radical pre-millennialism of James Hatley Frere, and confidently predicted that the Second Coming would occur in 1868.[3] In 1832, he and his congregation were locked out of the National Scotch Church because he had permitted members of it to interrupt his services by speaking in tongues.[4] This locked-out congregation became the first congregation of a new pentecostal, pre-millenarian denomination, the Catholic Apostolic Church. In 1833, Irving was deposed from the ministry of the Church of Scotland for preaching what his opponents condemned as the 'heresy' of 'the sinfulness of Christ's humanity'.[5]

Irving's public career was almost entirely spent in London. The greater number of those who came to hear him preach, and those who read his books and articles, were English, and members either of the Church of England or of other English Protestant denominations. Yet, throughout his life, Edward

IDENTITY IN THE THOUGHT OF EDWARD IRVING

Irving was passionately devoted to his mother church and his native country. As far as he was concerned, they were one and the same; the Church of Scotland and the Scottish nation were co-extensive. He believed that the doughty character of the nation had been formed by its epic struggle, from the Culdees down to the Covenanters, to preserve the Presbyterian purity of its religion against the incursions of Romanism and Episcopalianism. As a minister in London, he was particularly concerned that Scottish expatriates should not lose this integrated identity. However, his Scottish Presbyterian identity did not prevent him from participating in another broader, equally integrated religious and national identity, that of British Protestantism.

Edward Irving was born in Annan, in Dumfriesshire, in 1792. As far as he was concerned, the Scottish nation into which he was born was Lowland, Scots- and English-speaking, Presbyterian, and Hanoverian. Although he was born well within living memory of the '45 rebellion, that other Scottish nation, Highland, Gaelic-speaking, Episcopalian or Roman Catholic and Jacobite, which had met its nemesis on Culloden Moor, and the persistence of Jacobite and Episcopalian sympathies amongst many of the Lowland aristocracy and gentry, never appeared to impinge on his consciousness. It was in 1814, when Irving was already twenty-two, that Sir Walter Scott published *Waverley*, and began to apply his romantic wizardry to what one nineteenth-century commentator described as 'the strange perversion of facts which induced good Lowland Scots to fancy themselves more nearly allied to the semi-barbarous wearers of the tartan than to their English blood-relations'.[6]

The Scottish nation into which Irving was born was at ease with its place in Great Britain. Annan was to thrive during the Napoleonic Wars on the high prices paid for the sloops of corn and droves of cattle which it sent across or around the Solway Firth into England. National consciousness and national pride were not concerned with nostalgia for the centuries of independence before the Union of 1707, or with pining for the king across the water, but with the remarkable economic and cultural progress which the country had made within the Union since the middle of the eighteenth century. The agricultural revolution had transformed the Lowland countryside from a stagnant, backward, subsistence economy, often teetering on the edge of famine, to a dynamic, forward-looking, free-market economy, where innovative and efficient farming produced ever greater yields for buoyant domestic and export markets.[7] The first industrial revolution had quadrupled the populations of towns like Glasgow, Paisley and Dundee as they became major exporters of factory-manufactured textiles.[8] The Scottish Enlightenment had moved Lowland Scotland from the periphery to the centre of European cultural and intellectual life. While such jewels in the Scottish cultural crown as David Hume, Adam Smith, William Robertson and Robert Burns belonged to the recent past, Irving grew up in the period during which Francis Jeffrey published the *Edinburgh Review*, Sir Walter Scott published his poems and novels and the Scottish universities could boast such polymathic purveyors of 'Scotch Knowledge' as Dugald Stewart and John Playfair.[9]

Irving was a contemporary and perhaps the most intimate friend of another famous product of the late Scottish Enlightenment, Thomas Carlyle. Like Carlyle, he was a provincial cosmopolitan, rooted in the folk culture of the Lowlands, but reading omnivorously in English, French and Italian. But he was also rooted in a Scottish tradition that was antecedent, and directly opposed, to that of the Enlightenment. In his childhood in Annandale, he was surrounded by the graves and the memories of the Covenanters, who had suffered martyrdom for their Presbyterian principles in 'the killing times' after the Battle of Bothwell Brig in 1679 rather than submit to the imposition of episcopacy on the Church of Scotland. Thus Irving was as much an heir to the sectarian, theocratic fervour of the seventeenth century as he was to the Enlightenment of the eighteenth. In his boyhood in Annan, he visited, by his own account, 'almost every one' of the Covenanters' graves 'in the moors and solitudes where they fell martyrs to the doctrine of Christ's sole supremacy in His house'.[10] His biographer, Mrs Oliphant, paints a colourful, but plausible, picture of Irving as a boy, eagerly drinking in, from old men and women in high-backed chairs at cottage firesides, the stirring tales of the Covenanters' sufferings and martyrdoms for 'the preservation and confession of the truth'.[11]

Irving published one of these tales in 1828. He had heard it during his time as an assistant to Thomas Chalmers in Glasgow (between 1819 and 1822) from an old woman who was a friend of his great-aunt. It was about William Guthrie, a nephew of James Guthrie, the minister from Stirling who was amongst the first to be executed for the Covenanter cause in 1661. William Guthrie was obliged to flee to the Continent after he had risked death to recover the head of his martyred uncle from the pole over the West Port in Edinburgh, on which it was displayed. He left behind a betrothed sweetheart who died within twelve months 'of a blighted and withered heart'. Guthrie returned to Scotland with William of Orange in 1688 and was devastated by the news of his sweetheart's death. He resolved to leave Scotland forever, and go into England. On the way south, he paused for some time to meditate amongst the communion tables of Irongray, a parish near Dumfries. These were tables cut out of stone where, as Irving had it, 'the famishing saints were fed with heavenly food' at secret Covenanter communion services during the 'killing times'. The parishioners begged him to stay and minister to them. He did so, and after many years of faithful mourning for his dead sweetheart, married a local girl. At the end of the tale, the woman from whose lips Irving heard it revealed that she was the fruit of that marriage, that William Guthrie was her father.[12]

Alas, this stirring tale of God's providence for his persecuted saints in the Kirk of Scotland is a total fabrication. James Guthrie's head stayed up on the Netherbow Port (not the West Port) for twenty-nine years, until the sentence of forfeiture on Guthrie was rescinded by Parliament on 22 July 1690, and the skull was taken down by a divinity student named Alexander Hamilton. However, the woman who told Irving the story was a real person, Mary Lawson, who was really the daughter of the minister of Irongray from 1694 to 1756, who was called, not William, but James Guthrie. As this James Guthrie was probably a divinity student in Edinburgh when his namesake's skull was taken down from the Netherbow in 1690, my theory is that he made up this story, in which he was a Covenanter hero, to impress his children, and that Mary either continued to believe it all of her life, or began to believe it again in second childhood, and told it to Irving in good faith sometime between 1819 and 1822. Irving may have changed the name of the hero because he was aware that James Guthrie of Stirling had a real Covenanter cousin called William. The fact that Irving chose to publish this tale as an accurate transcription of a piece of oral history, without alerting his readers to its historical falsity, of which he must have been aware, suggests that for him the myth of the Covenanters' struggle for the national Kirk, as it was preserved in the nation's folklore, was more important than the historical reality.[13]

It was perhaps in emulation of the Covenanters' heroic and uncompromising piety that the ten-year-old Irving sometimes joined his schoolmaster, Adam Hope, and a pious band of local members of the Burgher Church, on a six-mile Sunday pilgrimage to hear the true Word of God at the Burgher meeting-house at Ecclefechan.[14] The Burghers were among the spiritual heirs of the Covenanters. They were a branch of the Seceders who had left the Church of Scotland in 1733 because they felt that the main body of that Church, in submitting to the Patronage Act of 1712, had strayed from strict adherence to its Presbyterian principles; Thomas Carlyle, who attended the Ecclefechan meeting-house at the same period as Irving, claimed that what distinguished the Burghers from their brethren in the Church of Scotland was 'a stricter adherence to the National Kirk in all points'.[15] While Irving's adherence to the Burgher Church was short-lived, it undoubtedly reinforced the deep commitment to the principles of the Scottish Reformers and the Covenanters which persisted throughout his life.

Irving's first pastoral post, from 1819 to 1822, was as assistant to the celebrated Thomas Chalmers in Glasgow. Chalmers believed that by restoring the all-embracing parish system of the Scottish countryside to the teeming slums of Glasgow, he could recreate the social cohesion which had been lost in the mass migration from the countryside to the city. The concentration of the labouring masses in the inner-city slums, and the middle-class exodus to the periphery of the city, had created a sense of alienation between the social classes. This segregation was visible in a marked distinction in Chalmers's parish of St John's between 'the congregation' and 'the parish'. The congregation consisted of wealthy people, who lived outside the parish but could afford the high pew-rents charged by the town council for attendance at the main Sunday services. 'The parish' were poor people, who actually lived in St John's, and attended the church, if they did at all, at special cut-price Sunday evening services.[16] Irving, who was, after all, the son of a tanner and a farmer's daughter, felt more at ease with the parish than the congregation.

Antagonism between the social classes in Britain's industrial cities was exacerbated by the economic depression and mass unemployment which followed the end of the Napoleonic Wars. In 1820, it reached a crisis point in Glasgow, with the events which came to be known, rather grandiosely, as 'the Radical War'. In February, twenty-seven members of a Glasgow radical committee were arrested on suspicion of conspiring with English radicals to plan simultaneous uprisings on both sides of the border. On 1 April, a placard appeared on the streets of Glasgow and surrounding towns, calling for an immediate national strike to be followed by a rising on 5 April. Sixty thousand workers downed tools. On 5 April, the streets of Glasgow were lined with troops. In the event, the dreaded rising consisted of scuffles between the troops and the radicals in Glasgow, where there were no casualties, and at Bonnymuir, where there were four wounded. There were forty-seven arrests; three men were executed and the rest released.[17] Irving wrote to Thomas Carlyle a few days after these events, on 15 April:

> It is very dangerous to speak one's mind here about the state of the country. I am very sorry for the poor; they are losing their religion, their domestic comfort, their pride of independence, their everything; and if timeous remedies come not soon, they will sink, I fear, into the degradation of the Irish peasantry; and if that class goes down, then along with it sinks the morality of every other class. We are at a complete stand here; a sort of military glow has taken all ranks. They can see the houses of the poor ransacked for arms without uttering an interjection of grief on the fallen greatness of those who brought in our Reformation and our civil liberty, and they will hardly suffer a sympathising word from anyone . . .[18]

We can see here how Irving clung to the ideal of a national cohesion which transcended economic class, and lamented the collapse of this cohesion which was evident in the callous indifference and fear with which some members of the propertied classes in Glasgow regarded the tribulations of the Glasgow poor. The basis for this ideal cohesion, in Irving's mind, was the shared achievement of the whole Scottish nation, but especially of the common people of Scotland, in bringing in 'our Reformation and our civil liberty'. This ideal national cohesion excluded the considerable proportion of the population of St John's parish whose ancestors had not played any part in introducing the Reformation to Scotland because they were Irish Catholic immigrants.[19] To be fair, this implied sectarian and nationalistic exclusiveness might not, at this time in Irving's life, have been consciously intended. There are hints in a couple of letters from his Glasgow days that Irving was not at that time the fanatical opponent of Roman Catholicism that he would later become. He appears, like Chalmers, to have been happy to visit the Irish Roman Catholic poor in St John's, and to have shared Chalmers's relatively tolerant attitude to their religion.[20]

Irving's conception of the Church of Scotland, and particularly its Presbyterian polity, as the creation and the patrimony of the whole Scottish nation, is again underlined in the 'Farewell Discourse' which he delivered on leaving St John's in 1822, where, in the course of a tirade against patronage, the issue on which Chalmers, a decade after Irving's death, was to lead the Disruption of the Church of Scotland, Irving apotheosized his native land as 'the only land . . . of a free plebeian church, which never pined till she began to be patronised'.[21]

But if Irving saw the Scottish Reformation and the Church of Scotland as the creation of the Scottish nation, he also believed that it was only through the Reformation that the Scots had gained true nationhood. As he put it in his first book, *Orations*, in 1823:

> Before that blessed aera [sic], [Scotland] had no arts but the art of war; no philosophy; no literature . . . and little government of law. She was torn and mangled with intestine feuds, enslaved to arbitrary or aristocratic power, in vassalage or in turbulence. Yet, no sooner did the breath of truth from the living oracles of God breathe over her, than the wilderness and the solitary place became glad, and the desert rejoiced and blossomed like the rose. The high-tempered soul

of the nation . . . did now arise for the cause of religion and liberty – for the rights of God and man.[22]

We see here, as we have seen in the letter from Glasgow above, how close was the connection between 'our Reformation and our civil liberty' in Irving's mind. For Irving, Protestantism, particularly Presbyterianism, as finally secured by the Glorious Revolution of 1688, was closely bound up with the nation's civil liberty; Roman Catholicism and Jacobitism were conducive to enslavement to 'arbitrary or aristocratic power'.

For Irving, the Scottish Reformation was not an event which had occurred in 1560, but 'more than a long century' of struggle which had only finally been successful in 1688. True to his Covenanting heritage, it is the latter part of this struggle, the 'killing times' from Bothwell Brig to the Glorious Revolution, which he focused on as the single most formative epoch in the forging of the nation. It was only from the final vindication of the Covenanters' fidelity to their Presbyterian principles, and the ousting of the Roman Catholic Stuarts in 1688, that he dated the flowering of everything that was praiseworthy in the national character:

> The pastoral vales, and upland heaths . . . now rung responsive to the glory of God, attuned from the hearts of his persecuted saints. The blood of martyrs mingled with our running brooks; their hallowed bones now moulder in peace within their silent tombs, which are dressed by the reverential hands of the pious and patriotic people. And their blood did not cry in vain to heaven for vengeance. Their persecutors were despoiled; that guilty race of kings were made vagabonds upon the earth. The church arose in her purity like a bride decked for the bridegroom; religious principles chose to reside within the troubled land; bringing moral virtues in their train, and begetting a national character for knowledge, industry, enterprise, every domestic and public virtue, which maketh her children an acceptable people in the four quarters of the earth.[23]

However, Irving was not untouched by the re-evaluation and romanticization of the Scottish past which was taking place in the first decades of the nineteenth century, of which Sir Walter Scott was the most famous proponent. In his *Historical View of the*

Church of Scotland from the Earliest Period to the Time of the Reformation, published in 1831, Irving reclaimed for the nation and the church the centuries which he had dismissed as barbarous in 1823. In this work he idealized those enigmatic monks of the Celtic Church, the Culdees, as proto-Presbyterians. Although modern scholarship dates the appearance of the Scottish Culdees to the ninth century, Irving, citing a recent translation from the Latin of the sixteenth-century Scottish historian, George Buchanan, dated it to the third century. He maintained that when St Columba arrived in the sixth century, he founded Culdee monasteries, thus consolidating a tradition of discipline and doctrine which had already existed in Scotland for three centuries.[24]

Irving in fact applied the designation Culdee to all of what we would now term the Celtic Church. He was at pains to point out that this Culdee Church had not merely differed from the Roman Catholic Church in the apparently minor matters which were contested at the Synod of Whitby, but 'in everything, that constitutes the Christian church, distinct from the synagogue of Satan'. It had rejected such 'Papal inventions' as confession and confirmation, anointing with oil at baptism, the dedication of churches to saints, prayers for the dead, works of supererogation and clerical celibacy. It had rejected justification by works, holding justification by faith alone. Above all it had rejected episcopacy.[25] The Culdees, according to Irving, had 'maintained a noble resistance' against the development of a diocesan episcopate from the tenth century onwards, and the introduction of Roman Catholic monasticism from the twelfth century on, and had only finally disappeared from the historical record in the fourteenth century.[26] Thereafter, Irving speculated, they might well have gone underground,

> to preserve in the recesses of the country, the record of a better age, and plant in the memory and traditions of Scotland that love of primitive simplicity which, at the Reformation, burst forth in its strength, like Samson out of his sleep, and shook off the bonds of darkness with which it had been bound.[27]

Thus, Irving could maintain that 'the dawnings of the Reformation . . . almost met with the last twilight of the primitive Culdee Church,' and 'that Scotland since the second [sic] century hath not wanted a primitive apostolical church, and an orthodox faith, over which the Papacy came like an eclipse that soon passed away'.[28]

Irving concluded his account of the Culdees as follows:

> To me, reflecting upon the long-lived traditions of my native land, evidenced by the poems of Ossian and the minstrelsy of the Border, and those tales which have appeared in our own day, and of which ten times more than have yet appeared, do circulate among the people of Scotland; – to me, I say, reflecting upon the traditional lore of my native land, and the reverence for antiquity which characterizes the people of the Scottish name, it is a thing beyond doubt, that the wrestlings of the Culdees against the Papacy did disseminate through Scotland that hatred of Roman superstition, and preserve that love of religious liberty, and preference of a primitive church, without pomp or ceremonies, which have distinguished and blessed us amongst the nations of Christendom.[29]

Mrs Oliphant has recorded his fondness, even as an undergraduate, for Ossian (the epic Gaelic bard supposedly translated, but largely composed by James Macpherson in the 1760s), passages from which he was given to reciting to his companions with 'sonorous elocution and vehement gesticulation',[30] a youthful predilection which probably greatly influenced his mature preaching style. It is more than likely that Irving's student reading also included Sir Walter Scott's *Minstrelsy of the Scottish Borders*, which was published in 1802, when he was ten. We can see in this passage how much his desire to push back the origins of the Church of Scotland and the Scottish nation beyond the Reformation into the mists of antiquity was of a piece with the general enthusiasm for the Scottish past and Scottish folklore which was prevalent in the era of Scott. We can also see, as we have already seen in his 'Tale of the time of the martyrs', how Irving's reading of the nation's history tended to blur the lines between folklore, fiction and historical fact.

Having served three years as an unordained assistant in Glasgow, and having failed to be called to the ministry by any congregation in Scotland, Irving was overjoyed to be called, in 1822, to the ministry of the Caledonian Chapel in Hatton

Garden, London. As a minister of the Church of Scotland in London, Irving considered his first duty to be the pastoral care of Scottish expatriates in the city. Writing to Chalmers during his first visit to Hatton Garden in December 1821, he noted that the congregation consisted 'mostly of young men'. These were probably inmates, or past pupils, of the Caledonian Asylum, an orphanage for the sons of deceased Scottish servicemen, whose trustees were the managers of the Caledonian Chapel. Irving was deeply concerned about the corrosive effects of London life on the spiritual health of these young Scotsmen: he feared that they would be

> a prey to amusement and dissipations, to which they are the more inclined that they burst upon them with the freshness of novelty, and the more incited by the vigorous health and constitution which they grow up with in the temperate region of morals from which they come.

Irving wished that he had Chalmers's force of personality to rescue his young countrymen from such dissipations, and 'make Scotsmen as much the blessing of London, as they are said to be of foreign parts'.[31]

In 1828, Irving issued, under the aegis of the Scotch Presbytery in London, *A Pastoral Letter ... Addressed to the Baptized of the Scottish Church Residing in London*. This letter offered up chauvinistic hymns of praise to the Church of Scotland and the Scottish nation, and threatened the Scotsmen and Scotswomen of his own generation, both in London and in Scotland, with the wrath of God for turning away from their glorious religious and national heritage. Irving lamented the fact that, of the 100,000 Scotsmen then living in or around London, less than 1,000 continued to worship in Church of Scotland congregations; that the Kirk had lost not the one sheep of the parable, but the ninety-nine.[32]

He complained of the tendency of members of the Scottish ruling classes, when resident in London, to go to the Church of England, and when back in Scotland, to go to the Episcopalian Church. While he honoured the Church of England as 'a true sister', he maintained that the 'defection' of the ruling classes to her and to the Episcopalian Church was a very great evil to our nation, which hath for three centuries adopted, with great suffering maintained, and is devotedly attached to the Presbyterian worship and polity. For thereby a diversity of feeling is engendered between the upper and the lower ranks in our native land, which is daily drawing them more and more asunder.

Irving complained that many of the legal patrons of the Church of Scotland were now Anglicans or Episcopalians. What is most striking about this complaint is Irving's assertion that 'the origin of [this] evil is in London'; that more and more of the Scottish ruling classes were converting to Anglicanism and Episcopalianism simply because they had been exposed to the former while residing in London. This is to ignore the fact that the majority of the Scottish nobility and gentry, even in the Lowlands, had been on the Episcopalian, Royalist side in the seventeenth century, and had retained Episcopalian and Jacobite sympathies after 1688, and even after the '45 rebellion. When, after the repeal of the Penal Laws in 1792, the ruling classes had begun to convert from the Church of Scotland to the Episcopal Church, they had not been, as Irving maintained, converting to what was miscalled by Lowland Presbyterians 'the English Church' out of 'an unworthy spirit of compliance' with English ways, but returning to the church of their fathers. As in his letter from Glasgow, Irving was here lamenting the loss of what he believed to have been a national cohesion, founded on a common religious heritage, which transcended social class; while he may have been justified in asserting that the Glasgow poor, with the exception of the Irish Roman Catholics, and the Glasgow middle classes shared such a common heritage, he was greatly in error in attempting to extend it to the Scottish nobility and gentry.[33]

Irving believed that the people of Scotland were, like the people of Israel, singled out by God to be endowed with manifold privileges and gifts. But, 'to whom much is given, of them much should be required'. Just as the people of Israel 'of all the nations were punished with the longest and sorest visitations of the wrath of God, because they . . . trampled underfoot their singular privileges', so the people of Scotland would incur 'a double portion of wrath and retribution' if they did not repent of their great national sin of abuse of, and ingratitude for, the gifts and privileges which God had given them.[34]

Perhaps the most notable of these gifts was the Scottish spirit of enterprise. Scottish merchants and tradesmen in London were universally admired and envied for their success and prosperity. Irving attributed this success to the qualities which they derived from their religious heritage, but accused them of having abandoned that heritage, and perverted their God-given gifts, in the pursuit of worldly success:

> The knowledge and fear of God – in which all our people . . . far beyond any [other] people, are brought up from their youth . . . doth naturally work in us, from childhood, a spirit of freedom from outward fears, and a habit of acting for ourselves from self-conviction, which is little known to the people of other lands . . . From [the] self-searching and self-determining character of the Scottish Church, cometh that intrepidity of adventure, that single handed boldness, self-armed fearlessness, and unexampled success, for which our countrymen are famous in all regions of the earth . . . This distinguishing characteristic of the children of our Church, Satan . . . hath separated from religion, the parent which gave it birth, and made it to be regarded as a characteristic of the nation, in which it may boast itself against other nations . . . Being thus perverted in the soul, this excellent spirit of adventure degenerates into a low and grovelling pursuit of earthly objects, an earnest plodding after wealth, a mean and degrading request for place and preferment.[35]

The other great national gift which had been bestowed upon the Scottish people by God through the Church of Scotland, and, according to Irving, sorely abused and perverted by them to ungodly ends, was the gift of the intellect. Irving believed that

> the intellectual strength of the Scottish people, and their capacity of firmly grasping abstract and spiritual truth, which is thought to pertain only to the learned in other lands, is the offspring of the Church . . . [and] that the intellect of our land grew and flourished by the preaching of the word.[36]

But this intellect was perverted in the course of the Scottish Enlightenment to the service of infidelity. Irving, who was to a great degree a child of the Scottish Enlightenment and a graduate of Edinburgh University, attacked both for destroying the nation's faith:

> [The] cause of this proneness of our countrymen to infidelity . . . is the infidel character with which the most famous of our Scottish philosophers, and economists, and men of science and literature, have been impressed for almost a century, and which hath obtained a seat and habitation of a long time in the most famous university and capital city of our nation . . . O! how the intellect of Scotland is proving her bane![37]

Perhaps the most visible assertion ever of the presence of the Church of Scotland in London was the building of the Scotch National Church in Regent Square. This magnificent twin-towered Gothic church, with a frontage which was modelled on that of York Minster, and accommodation for over 1,400 worshippers, was the largest and most impressive building ever to be occupied by a Church of Scotland congregation in London. It was built by the congregation of the Caledonian Chapel on the strength of Irving's phenomenal success as a preacher.[38] Irving wrote on 5 November 1822, a few months after his arrival in London, 'Thank God, [my success] seems now beyond a doubt. The Church overflows every day, and they already begin to talk of [building] a right good Kirk, worthy of our mother and our native country.'[39]

Irving's vision of the new church as a focus for Scottish religious and national identity, and an assertion of Scottish national pride in London, is apparent from the sermon which he preached on the day on which the foundation stone was laid, 1 July 1824:

> We are about to establish another church for setting forth the doctrine, and discipline, and government, and worship of the Church of Scotland; dear to many of us from the remembrance which distance doth but awaken with fresh tenderness, and strengthen, like the songs of Zion, in the land of the stranger.[40]

Irving maintained that for a Scotsman to lose either his national or religious identity in England was an act of betrayal and ingratitude.

> That man would be the most ungrateful of men, who, having been born and bred up in the privileges of Scotland, should not hold his country dear; and still more ungrateful would that man be, who, having been trained up in the sound faith and simple customs of the Scottish people, should slight the mother of his soul, or ever . . . surrender himself to the care of another.[41]

The new church was to be 'for a sign to our nation, and for the gathering together of the scattered people of our nation'. Irving confessed his 'shame that our nation, whose industry in this metropolis hath been so blessed of God, and who dwell in palaces, and have got . . . much riches' had not yet built a church in London commensurate with their success there. He hoped that other Church of Scotland congregations would follow the example of his congregation in building imposing new churches, and 'that this may be the beginning of an era in the history of our church in this metropolis, when she shall take a character as an established church, and profit by all the service which she hath done for the sake of the Lord and her country'.[42]

Irving's concern that the Church of Scotland in England should maintain her status, which was not technically recognized,[43] as an Established, rather than a Dissenting Church, implied cordial recognition of the validity of the Established Church of England. In the *Pastoral Letter* he wrote:

> We put you upon your guard against the spirit of enmity towards all established churches which is poured out upon the Dissenters in these parts. And, because we believe the Church of England to be a true church, and a bulwark of the Reformation, we exhort you to dwell in these her borders, in all good neighbourhood and brotherly love towards her.[44]

Irving regarded the Established Church of England as the church to which members of the English nation should belong, in the same way as the Church of Scotland was for the Scottish. His conception of national and religious identity as inseparable, whether as English Anglican, or Scottish Presbyterian, or British Protestant, lay behind his consistent and fervent championship of the principle of establishment.

Irving's belief that Protestantism was of the essence of British national identity was greatly reinforced by his conversion in 1825, to pre-millennialism. He believed that the French Revolution and the Napoleonic Wars had been predicted as 'the great day of . . . the wrath of the Lamb' in the sixth chapter of Revelation. This, he believed, was a period of judgement on the Roman Catholic nations of Continental Europe. Protestant Britain was exempt from these judgements, because its inhabitants represented the only 'true worshippers, and faithful servants of God and the Lamb, in the midst of the general defection of the earth unto the mother of harlots'. Protestant Britain was represented by the twelve tribes of Israel which were sealed against the wrath of the Lamb in the seventh chapter of Revelation.[45]

Irving regarded Bonaparte as the scourge of God, an instrument which God had used to visit his righteous judgement on the papacy and on the Roman Catholic nations, prior to destroying him for his own infidelity. The atheistic 'infidelity' of the French Revolution and the 'apostasy' of Roman Catholicism were morally equivalent enemies of 'the pure religion of Christ'; the conflict between them was 'Satan in one form, fighting against Satan in another form'.[46] The fact that during the quarter century of the Napoleonic Wars, Britain was practically the only European country not to be invaded by the French was clear evidence that she had been preserved by God on account of her pure Protestant religion. Having used the infidel beast, Bonaparte, to chastize the Roman Catholic nations, God had used his own British Protestant nation, and its great hero, Wellington, to destroy Bonaparte. With reference to the two successive occupations of France by the allies in 1814 and 1815, which he believed to have been predicted in Revelation by the fifth vial, which was 'poured out upon the seat of the beast', Irving wrote:

> Now, though it be not written in the text, it is diligently to be noted by what nation chiefly the Lord wrought this work of recompense upon the infidel scourge of the Papacy. By the Protestant nation, – that nation which was sealed before the day of wrath began, even the BRITISH nation, which the infidel beast had raged against, and striven with infernal zeal to overcome; but could not, because the

everlasting arms were around her. By our arms and our captain of war, as by another Joshua, did the Lord discomfit the infidel power, through long years of warfare in the Peninsula of Spain. [original typography][47]

Irving's conception of Britain as the Protestant nation, chosen by God to be the scourge of infidelity and papacy, meant that he was passionately opposed to those measures which threatened to dilute the nation's Protestant identity and to open the floodgates to religious pluralism and disestablishment. He regarded both the Repeal of the Test and Corporation Acts in 1828 and Catholic Emancipation in 1829 as acts of national apostasy. In *A Letter to the King on The Repeal of the Test and Corporation Laws as it effects Our Christian Monarchy*, which he published as the Bill was being debated in Parliament in 1828, Irving outlined his theocratic vision of the British Constitution and the British nation. It was, he wrote,

> the constitutional doctrine of the kingdom of England, and the kingdom of Scotland, as cleared from Papal errors at the Reformation, confirmed at the Revolution, and unchangeably fixed at the Union . . . that [the King] governs under Christ, and for Christ, as do also all the authorities under your Majesty.[48]

The British nation, by rejecting the papal error 'of putting the king under the church, instead of putting him under Christ the head of the Church', had taken 'the highest post of honour upon the earth, the post of maintaining the royal priesthood of Christ, against the royal priesthood of the Bishop of Rome', and shown itself to be 'a nation united for God, against nations confederate for idolatry and man-worship'. Addressing George IV directly, Irving reminded him of what God had enabled him and his father George III to do, as the heads 'of the great Protesting nation of the earth'. When 'another monstrous form of power', that of democracy, 'which is power derived from the people and not from Christ', had raised its ugly head at the French Revolution, 'your Majesty's father, of beloved memory, was stirred up by God, mightily to withstand this invention of the Devil'. To George IV himself, as Prince Regent, 'did God reserve it, to subvert the great infidel supremacy over Europe, and to restrain the person of the great infidel king', Napoleon Bonaparte. George IV had also been enabled of God to 'lay prostrate . . . the chief cities of Mahomet, of Bramah, and of Budh, the three principal superstitions of the east'.[49]

Given the high honours which God had reserved for the British monarchy and the British nation, it was surely incumbent upon George IV, as 'a Christian King, to repress, by all the means which Christ hath permitted, those who set at nought his supreme authority in Church and State, in heaven and in earth'.[50] It was for this purpose that the Test and Corporation Acts had been instituted, to oblige everyone who would hold any office in the British state to take 'the oath of allegiance unto Christ – the only one which he hath authorised, [which] is the eating, by faith of his flesh, and the drinking of his blood, in the Holy Sacrament'.[51] If Britain should manifest such gross ingratitude to God, should so forget the particular favour which God had bestowed upon her in delivering her from Napoleon, as to countenance the repeal of 'those laws, which we possess, as the transmitted piety . . . of our fathers',[52] then she would suffer for her ingratitude even as did Israel:

> For as Sennacherib shook his hand over Jerusalem, but was not permitted to cast a stone into it, so the mighty Infidel Prince, now no more . . . did long and bitterly rage against us, but at length fell, crushed by our men of war; which deliverance of God, if we forget, and open the high places of the kingdom unto unprofessing and unbelieving men, and even unto infidels, then, as surely as Nebuchadnezzar was raised up in Sennacherib's room, to lay Jerusalem on heaps, and carry her people unto Babylon, so surely shall God raise up a scourge for Britain, to do that of which it will be a pain even to hear the report.[53]

An even greater act of national apostasy, in Irving's view, was the Catholic Emancipation Act of 1829. In an article which he published in *The Morning Watch* in March 1829, the month before the Bill was passed, Irving defined the question which lay before Parliament as 'whether we shall remain an Anti-catholic and Protestant kingdom, or whether we shall take the seed of the serpent again into our councils and administration'. For Irving, toleration of Roman Catholicism amounted to a betrayal, a denial of the Reformation,

> for we know well, from every document and from every relic of the Reformers, that it was the distinct, unqualified, and incessant preaching of the Pope as Antichrist, and of Rome as Babylon, and of the papal system as the great whore of Babylon, which wrought that mighty tide of holy wrath and indignation.

If the Roman Catholic Church was not 'that apostacy, that Babylon, from which the saints are called to come out', then 'the Protestant Reformation is no better, is no other, than a great consummate act of schism'.[54]

The political purpose of Catholic Emancipation was the assimilation of Roman Catholic Ireland into the United Kingdom following the Union of 1800, as Presbyterian Scotland had been assimilated into Great Britain following the Union of 1707. While Irving could accept that, because of their separate ecclesiastical histories, Scotsmen should be Presbyterians, and Englishmen should be Anglicans, he could not accept the proposition that Irishmen should be Roman Catholics. He attributed what he perceived to be the savagery and misery of the Irish, compared to the civilization and prosperity of the English and the Scottish, directly to their Roman Catholicism.

In a sermon which he gave for the London Hibernian Society in 1826, Irving graphically described the backward state of the Irish peasantry:

> with famine at their door and epidemic disease ever ready to hatch ... their irascible passions bringing forth crimes such as were rarely heard of ... murders, not of solitary individuals, but of whole companies; abductions of women for marriage, like so many New Holland savages; their superstitious observances at the mouths of wells and other places, more like South Africans than any others.[55]

This moral degradation was due entirely to their Roman Catholicism, which, because it was a sensual, rather than, like Protestantism, a spiritual religion, encouraged its adherents to indulge the evil propensities of the sensual man. Also, because

Roman Catholicism was polytheistic, insofar as it encouraged worship of the Virgin Mary and the saints, it drew upon the Irish peasantry the divine opprobrium which God had visited upon the polytheistic enemies of Israel in the Old Testament.[56]

In support of his contention that Roman Catholicism was the root cause of the misery of the Irish, Irving compared Ireland with Scotland:

> Scotland hath been oppressed far beyond Ireland; twice the seat of civil war . . . her nobility, in a great measure, non-residents . . . her soil more scanty; her polish more rude. And yet she has been kept from disorder, and though greatly opposed, has not failed to maintain the dignity of her character.

In the north of Ireland, Irving pointed out, although it had 'no advantages of outward condition' over the south, 'the cruelties and atrocities of the South are rarely heard of' because of the presence of 'a large body of Presbyterian Dissenters, who have maintained good doctrine, and wholesome discipline'. Even in Glasgow, Irving claimed, he had been able to distinguish the houses of Irish Roman Catholic immigrants, by their 'general squalidness and misery'. '*All this gives us shrewd reason to suspect that* THE ROOT OF THE EVIL IS IN THEIR RELIGIOUS SYSTEM.' [original typography][57]

Given the evil effect of Roman Catholicism on the Irish peasantry, Irving was appalled that the British government was considering not only Catholic Emancipation, but the payment of stipends to Catholic priests, and the institution of state-supported non-denominational parochial schools throughout Ireland, in which Catholic priests as well as Protestant ministers would be allowed to give religious instruction.[58] Irving was particularly scandalized by this last proposal:

> Is it possible that the **British** government, which has seen the judgements of God upon idolatry for the last thirty years, should agree that Catholics should be brought up as such, and maintained at the public cost! Make all your parliament Catholics; let your general and admirals be Catholics; but for God's sake do not command the children of *five millions of people* to be made Catholics! O Son of

God! Thou who saidst, 'Suffer little children to come unto me, and forbid them not,' prevent such a crime from being perpetrated by the lawgivers of the land in which we breathe! [original typography][59]

To introduce such measures would be 'to make no difference between the sensual worship of idolatry, and the true spiritual worship of the living God'. The remedy for Ireland's sufferings was not to tolerate Roman Catholicism, 'but to attack the evil at once . . . and to drive it out', through a vigorous programme of preaching, dissemination of the scriptures and the education of Irish children in the Word of God. Only by undertaking this great philanthropic mission could the people of Britain prove that 'we are yet a Protestant nation', 'a chosen generation, a peculiar people'.[60]

Edward Irving was at the extreme end of the spectrum of Scottish Presbyterian and British Protestant chauvinism, and would have been regarded, even by many of his contemporaries, as a ferocious bigot. However, the notions which he so forcibly expressed, that Presbyterianism was an essential component of Scottish national identity and that Protestantism was an essential component of British national identity, were widely accepted by a great many Scottish Presbyterians and British Protestants well into the twentieth century, and may well be cherished in the breasts of a few hardy souls to this very day. Like all such exclusive notions of national identity, they depend upon a partial reading of history and demography, and a wilful ignorance of those historical and demographical facts that tend to invalidate them. As we have seen, for Irving himself the myth of the nation's struggle for the national Kirk, as it was celebrated in folklore and fiction, was at least as important as the historical facts.

For membership of one particular religious group to be really co-extensive with membership of one particular nation, it would be necessary for that religious group to have been so dominant in that nation for such a long time that it had successfully converted or extirpated every remnant of every other religious group. This was never the case in Scotland. Despite the best efforts of the Hanoverian government after the '45 rebellion, Scottish Episcopalianism and Scottish Roman Catholicism were never completely extirpated; the Scottish nation was never completely Presbyterian.

For a nation to be defined by a common religion, or even a common ethnicity, depends on the manifestly false notion that populations are geographically static and discrete; that everyone grows up and dies in the place in which they were born and, preferably, marries their first cousin. Irving might have been expected to have realized that this was not the case, given the number of Irish immigrants which he encountered in Glasgow, and the fact that he was a minister to a congregation of Scottish immigrants in London. It is perhaps significant that he appeared to expect the members of his congregation and their descendants to remain resolutely Scottish in perpetuity; he had no notion of the assimilation of immigrants into the host nation. Irving could not admit that the Scottish nation could include Scottish Episcopalians and Scottish Roman Catholics; one shudders to think of how he would have reacted to the Scottish nation of the present day, which includes Scottish Muslims, Scottish Sikhs and Scottish Buddhists.

To end on a positive note, I would suggest that Irving's notion of an integrated national and religious identity is alien to the vast majority of the Scottish nation today. Despite the persistence of a few colourful but insignificant archaisms, such as the Act of Settlement, which, of course, only affects another colourful but insignificant archaism, the monarchy; despite the quaint, atavistic decision, in 1999, to have the new Scottish Parliament, the Parliament of the whole Scottish nation, 'Kirked', but not churched, mosqued, templed or synagogued, I think it is safe to say that the Scottish nation no longer defines itself in terms of religious allegiance, but includes all of the people living in Scotland, regardless of colour, culture or creed.

Notes

[1] Mrs Oliphant, *The Life of Edward Irving*, I (London, 1862), pp. 150–61.

[2] J. Fleming, *The Life and Writings of the Rev. Edward Irving* (London, 1823), p. 29.

[3] Edward Irving, *Babylon and Infidelity Foredoomed of God. A*

Discourse on the Prophecies of Daniel and the Apocalypse which relate to these latter times, and until the Second Advent (2nd edn., Glasgow, 1828), pp. v, 141–2, 268.

4 Oliphant, *Life of Edward Irving*, II, pp. 231–301.
5 Ibid., pp. 319–50.
6 Sir Leslie Stephen in *Cornhill Magazine*, quoted in CD-ROM issued by Scottish National Galleries to accompany the exhibition 'O Caledonia! Sir Walter Scott and the Creation of Scotland' at the Scottish National Portrait Gallery, Edinburgh, 7 May to 17 October 1999.
7 T. C. Smout, *A History of the Scottish People, 1560–1830* (London, 1969), pp. 261–310.
8 Ibid., pp. 366–71.
9 Ibid., pp. 451–83.
10 Edward Irving, *The Coming of Messiah in Glory and Majesty: by Juan Josafat Ben-Ezra, a Converted Jew: Translated from the Spanish, with a Preliminary Discourse, By the Rev. Edward Irving, A.M.*, I (London, 1827), p. cxciii.
11 Oliphant, *Life of Edward Irving*, I, p. 19.
12 Edward Irving, 'A tale of the times of the martyrs', reprinted in William Jones, *Biographical Sketch of the Rev. Edward Irving A.M.* (London, 1835), pp. 216–28.
13 For the fate of James Guthrie's head, see John Howie, *The Scots Worthies (Revised by W. H. Carslaw)* (Edinburgh, 1870), p. 267; Hew Scott, *Fasti Ecclesiae Scoticanae*, IV (Edinburgh, 1923), pp. 319, 321. The old woman who told Irving the tale identified herself as the daughter of the minister at Irongray, and the wife of the minister at Kirkmahoe (Jones, *Biographical Sketch*, pp. 227–8), and so can be identified as Mary Lawson in Scott, *Fasti Ecclesiae Scoticanae*, II, pp. 288, 283. As Scott's article on her father, James Guthrie, records that he graduated MA at Edinburgh University on 28 June 1690, it is at least possible that he began his divinity course at Edinburgh in that year. For the real William Guthrie, see Robert Wodrow, *The History of the Sufferings of the Church of Scotland*, I (Glasgow, 1828), pp. 109, 406–9, 427; Howie, *The Scots Worthies*, pp. 320–35. For evidence which strongly suggests that Edward Irving was an enthusiastic reader of Howie's *Scots Worthies*, in which the true stories of James Guthrie's head and the real William Guthrie appear, see John. C. Johnston, *Treasury of the Scottish Covenant* (Edinburgh, 1887), p. 639.
14 Oliphant, *Life of Edward Irving*, I, pp. 18–21.
15 Thomas Carlyle, *Reminiscences*, I (London, 1881), pp. 81–2.
16 Stewart J. Brown, *Thomas Chalmers and the Godly Commonwealth in Scotland* (Oxford, 1982), pp. 116–44.

17 Smout, *A History of the Scottish People*, pp. 418–19.
18 Letter from Edward Irving to Thomas Carlyle, 15 April 1820, National Library of Scotland, Edinburgh (NLS), MS.1764. fos. 175–6.
19 Brown, *Thomas Chalmers*, p. 112; Andrew Gibb, *Glasgow: The Making of a City* (London, 1983), p. 106.
20 On 14 June 1822 Irving alludes jocosely to the manner in which 'our worthy Irish parishioners' address the latter as '*your ravrence*', Edward Irving to Thomas Chalmers, 14 June 1822, New College Library, Edinburgh, Thomas Chalmers Papers (TCP), CHA 4.21.3; on 24 July 1820 in a letter to Carlyle from Dublin, Irving disapproves of the religion of Irish Protestants as consisting largely of 'the hatred of Catholics', Edward Irving to Thomas Carlyle, 24 July 1820, NLS, MS.1764. fos. 183–4. For Chalmers's attitude to the Irish Roman Catholics, see Brown, *Thomas Chalmers*, pp. 112–13.
21 Edward Irving, *Farewell Discourse (on 2 Cor. xiii.11) to the Congregation and Parish of St John's, Glasgow* (Glasgow, 1822), pp. 15–16.
22 Idem, *For the Oracles of God, four Orations: For Judgement to Come, an Argument in nine parts* (London, 1823), p. 237.
23 Ibid., p. 238.
24 John T. McNeill, *The Celtic Churches: A History AD 200 to 1200* (Chicago, 1974), p. 208; Edward Irving, *The Confessions of Faith and the Books of Discipline of the Church of Scotland, of date Anterior to the Westminster Confession: To which are prefixed a Historical View of the Church of Scotland from the earliest period to the time of the Reformation, and a Historical Preface, with Remarks* (London, 1831), pp. xx–xxi; Irving's citation of Buchanan is from James Aikman, *The History of Scotland, translated from the Latin of George Buchanan*, I (Glasgow, 1827), pp. 199–200.
25 Irving, *The Confessions of Faith*, pp. lxxv–lxxvi, lii.
26 Ibid., p. lxxx.
27 Ibid., p. lxxix.
28 Ibid., pp. lxxxi, xvii.
29 Ibid., pp. lxxx–lxxxi.
30 Oliphant, *Life of Edward Irving*, I, p. 31.
31 Edward Irving to Thomas Chalmers, 24 December 1821, TCP, CHA 4.18.6.
32 Idem, *A Pastoral Letter, from the Scottish Presbytery in London, Addressed to the Baptized of the Scottish Church Residing in London . . . and in the Southern Parts of the Island* (London, 1828), pp. 6–7.
33 Ibid., pp. 8–10; John Clive, 'The social background of the Scottish Renaissance', in N. T. Philipson and Rosalind Mitchison, *Scotland*

in the Age of Improvement (Edinburgh, 1970), pp. 225–44; William Ferguson, *Scotland: 1689 to the Present* (Edinburgh, 1967), p. 232. In 1830, William Chambers claimed that, although the Episcopalian Church contained only 55,000 out of an adult population of 2,000,000, this included 'about a half of the landed proprietors, and a vast proportion of the educated and upper classes'. William Chambers, *The Book of Scotland* (Edinburgh, 1830), pp. 473, 466.

34 Irving, *A Pastoral Letter*, pp. 20–2.
35 Ibid., pp. 28–9.
36 Ibid., pp. 17–18.
37 Ibid., p. 36.
38 John Hair, *Regent Square: Eighty Years of a London Congregation* (London, 1898), pp. 45–7, 50, 53–4, 349.
39 Oliphant, *Life of Edward Irving*, I, p. 157.
40 Edward Irving, *Thirty Sermons, by Edward Irving, preached during the first three years of his residence in London* [recorded in shorthand by T. Oxford] (London, 1835), p. 121.
41 Ibid., p. 125.
42 Ibid., p. 124.
43 George G. Cameron, *The Scots Kirk in London* (Oxford, 1979), pp. 256–7, 71–2, 247–8.
44 Irving, *A Pastoral Letter*, p. 41.
45 Idem, *Babylon*, p. 169.
46 Ibid., pp. 179–82, 250.
47 Ibid., pp. 185–8.
48 Idem, *A Letter to the King on the Repeal of the Test and Corporation Laws, as it affects our Christian Monarchy* (London, 1828), p. 11.
49 Ibid., pp. 13–14.
50 Ibid., p. 6.
51 Ibid., pp. 8–9.
52 Ibid., p. 17.
53 Ibid., pp. 14–15.
54 Idem, 'On the doctrine and manifestation and character of the apostasy in the Christian Church', *The Morning Watch*, I/1 (March 1829), 102, 100.
55 Idem, Sermon 'For the Benefit of the London Hibernian Society', reproduced in *The Pulpit*, VI/160 (11 May 1826), 225.
56 Ibid., pp. 227–9.
57 Ibid., p. 226.
58 Ibid., pp. 232–3. Sir Francis Burdett's Roman Catholic Relief Bill was carried in the House of Commons with a majority of 22 on 10

May 1825, but defeated in the Lords with a majority of 48 on 17 May 1825. Many supporters and opponents of this Bill assumed that government stipends for Irish Catholic priests were a necessary concomitant to Catholic Emancipation. Lord Gower's resolution to this effect was carried in the House of Commons in 1825 with a majority of 43. *Hansard's Parliamentary Debates, New Series*, vol. XII (1825), cols. 785, 811–12, 838, 1247, 1251, 1114, 1148; vol. XIII (1825), cols. 27–8, 66, 76–7, 81–2, 104–5, 110, 120, 122, 308–35, 558–62, 766. The recommendation that Catholic priests should be allowed to give religious instruction in non-denominational parochial schools was made in the *First Report of the Commissioners on Education in Ireland*, 30 May 1825 (British Sessional Papers, House of Commons, 1825 (400) xii/1), p. 97.

[59] Irving, Sermon 'For the Benefit of the London Hibernian Society', p. 236.

[60] Ibid., pp. 232–7.

~ 13 ~
The Formation of a British Identity within Scottish Catholicism, 1830–1914

BERNARD ASPINWALL

In 1850 several hundred Glasgow Catholics gathered at Carstairs House, the home of the renowned wealthy convert, Robert Monteith, to enjoy a picnic in his magnificent grounds with bands and dancing round the maypole beneath the Union Jack. A similar excursion took place at Murthly Castle, the home of Sir William Drummond Stewart, the remarkable traveller in the American West. Some 2,500 Catholics, well dressed and sober, with bands, choir, sodalities, confraternities and clergy travelled from Dundee.[1] Such occasions passed off without incident, with temperance, music and good fellowship in a disciplined body: they hardly matched the popular perception, then and since, of unkempt, squalid bog-trotters in drunken fête. Unity, discipline, mutual concern and respect prevailed under the flag. It was an appropriate gathering to celebrate the British character of Scottish Catholicism.

The son of a phenomenally wealthy entrepreneur, Monteith lived in the reputedly first neo-Gothic mansion in Scotland. He was a director of the Caledonian Railway Company which in 1846 completed the first direct link between London, Glasgow and Edinburgh via Carstairs Junction, the station at the end of his driveway. That year, 1846, under the close personal influence of John Henry Newman, he became a Catholic, was baptized at Oscott by the Passionist the Revd Ignatius Spencer (convert son of Lord Spencer and brother of Lord Althorp, Chancellor of the Exchequer), and began to import ten tons of statues into Lanarkshire.[2]

Like Spencer, Ambrose Phillips de Lisle and Kenelm Digby, Monteith was a Trinity College, Cambridge man: there tradition and new wealth met. At Carstairs, he had welcomed his Cambridge friends, his cousin, James A. Stothert, antiquarian, barrister, poet and later priest; Richard Monckton-Milnes, Lord Houghton, and Alfred Tennyson. Although they might visit in future, other guests were likely to include Cardinals Wiseman, Newman and Manning, Georgiana Fullerton, Coventry Patmore or Spencer, who died on the driveway in 1864. Wilhelmina Mellish, Monteith's wife, came from landed and consular official background, deeply steeped in the German Romanticism of Weimar: the Monteiths reputedly introduced the Christmas crib into Scotland. Conversion, cultivation, concern for social amelioration and even condescension united to bring Scottish Highlander and Irish migrants together in an urban, industrial church. Catholicism in Scotland was being incorporated economically, culturally and spiritually into a British identity. Ultramontanism and Britishness went hand in providential hand.

A few years earlier, in 1848, Monteith had played a leading role in establishing the St Margaret Association to raise and distribute funds to poor parishes, to pay for seminary education and schools and unite the various classes in one cohesive Catholic body.[3] In 1851 at the height of the Ecclesiastical Titles issue, Monteith was prominent in the Catholic Defence Association in Dublin. In the 1860s, he used quiet influence in the appointment of Charles Eyre to the troubled Western District. Beset by conflict between old Scottish Highland resistance to change and zealous Irish nationalism, by divisions between Scottish and Irish clergy, between apprehensive quiet laity and more assertive ultramontanes, Monteith welcomed the Englishman to his post. Within a decade the Scottish hierarchy was restored and Monteith and his friends presented a landau to Eyre. Conservatives with a social conscience, Monteith and his son resisted Irish nationalism, home rule or any threat to the hierarchical order. In that stance they joined significant Catholics north and south of the border: the Norfolks, Lothians, Butes, Lovats, Hunter Blairs, Constable Maxwells and others.

Scottish clergy educated abroad usually shared similar notions for quite different reasons.[4] The reasons are pastoral and strategic. Religion was viewed as the cement of the social order rather than the sustenance of a pilgrim church. A conservative

Vatican endorsed charity within the existing order and resistance to revolutionary change. It felt the British Empire had providentially spread the faith throughout the English-speaking world: to North America, South Africa, Australia and New Zealand or in missionary opportunities within the colonies.[5] Rome might embarrass Protestant capitalism and encourage the working faithful by social criticism, but it recognized the greater good of Empire.

British Catholics knew their parliamentary strength relied on Irish representation. Their social and political weakness determined attitudes. Before 1914 Scotland had, briefly, one Catholic MP. In the event of home rule, Catholics, a mere 4 per cent of the population without any parliamentary voice, would be defenceless. Fear of enfranchised Protestant masses seemed justified: at Cumnock in 1878 a huge international Orange rally called for the repeal of Catholic Emancipation.[6] The Catholic élite for their part feared for their (Irish) property. The duke of Norfolk, Lord Lovat, president of the Inverness Liberal Association, convert David Hunter-Blair and sons of converts, Edwin Phillips de Lisle MP and Joseph Monteith opposed any concessions. Catholic Unionism continued highly visible to 1914.[7]

Within Scotland, several other factors operated. While anti-Catholics – or some modern historians – might support the identification of Catholicism in Scotland with the Irish population, it was, in fact, far more rooted and diverse.[8] The history of modern Highland Catholic experience remains to be written. As early as 1848 there was a German Catholic Association in Glasgow and by 1890 several thousand Lithuanians and Italians as well as Polish, Spanish, English and American-born faithful.[9] Its composition was constantly shifting. Economic booms and busts, and better opportunities elsewhere, encouraged mobility. Many left, only to return. Clergy in the early nineteenth century often moved to America: even later some clergy proved restive under a restored hierarchy. It was what I have previously called 'the revolving door society', with groups settling, acquiring capital, skills and education and moving on within Britain or out to the English-speaking Empire.

That British character was hardly new. Mr Bagnall, a Staffordshire Catholic, had his business destroyed by rioters amid the first parliamentary attempts at Catholic relief. Scottish Catholics had served on the British Catholic Committee. Sir John Joseph Dillon had tried to win relief through his influence in the General Assembly of the Church of Scotland: only Bishop John Milner and his Irish friends thwarted him. From Preston, the heartland of Catholic recusancy, Catholics had underwritten the early days of the Glasgow mission. The British Catholic Institute with Scottish members produced popular defence tracts throughout the 1830s. The (British) Catholic Poor Schools Committee consistently gave disproportionately generous grants to Scottish educational endeavours through the mid-nineteenth century. In 1836 Daniel O'Connell's tour won liberal Scottish support, although his Repeal campaign proved less attractive to Scottish Catholic clergy: Bishop Scott of the Western District was concerned at his disruptive influence over Irish priests and laity in Scotland. He forced out several zealous supporters of Repeal, most significantly the Revd Hugh Quigley, the clerical novelist who was forced to leave for America. Respectable conservative Unionists were preferable to that of the unruly radical masses: they were less likely to endorse vulgar provincial bigotry.[10]

The advent of the English Archbishop Charles Eyre, whose father was a count of the Holy Roman Empire and a railway director, strengthened that shift. With three brothers, a Stonyhurst Jesuit, a secular priest and a considerable Irish and Mayfair landowner, he and his policies embodied the drive to Britishness. At odds with his Jesuit brother, he ruthlessly disciplined archdiocesan clergy with regular visitations, spiritual and financial oversight, mass-produced Pugin churches and numerous parochial organizations. Dissent faded. Catholic education massively expanded: in the Glasgow archdiocese between 1878 and 1908 the number of schools more than doubled and pupils more than quadrupled.[11] A patron of Celtic Football Club with Michael Davitt, he united his flock. A centralizer, he established an archdiocesan seminary, promoted the League of the Cross in every parish, encouraged the St Vincent de Paul Society (SVP) and the Scottish Society for the Prevention of Cruelty to Children. His public role was recognized in the first Catholic honorary degree since the Reformation by the University of Glasgow. Bureaucratic routine, some Irish clergy claimed, preceded more spiritual concerns. More accurately, they realized he had emasculated their 'Irishness' to pastoral advantage and built a British identity.

As in Presbyterianism, property and popular interests clashed. Traditional Highland deference merged more into the social Romanticism of converts than the democratic nationalism of Irish migrants who railed at Protestantism and social privilege. In time that balance shifted toward social democracy. The élite, Jesuits and conservative Scottish clergy, then moved to contain social criticism from the Revd Patrick Lavelle, the Land League or enfranchised masses, through the Catholic Institute, the Catholic Social Guild and the Back to the Land movement. Until then a poor, ill-educated and ill-trained laity depended upon clerical leadership, élite generosity and their own limited efforts within British society. Unity served all interests: fragmentation none.

Initial Scottish Catholic efforts to serve or to contain Irish masses floundered. Ultramontanism worked to Scottish clerical advantage by reducing unruly newcomers to obedience under clerical leadership. Irish clergy served in large numbers but were never a majority of priests in Scotland. Equally, apart from the brief, unfortunate coadjutor vicar-apostolic, James Lynch, from 1866 to 1869, no Irish-born bishop was appointed until 1985. Fear of Protestant reaction, misgivings about image, education and even commitment to Scotland rather than to Irish exiles, fostered resistance to Irish ecclesiastical advancement in Scotland. They remained infantrymen or at best NCOs in the church militant.[12]

Somewhat dazed by the Famine, shocked by the shift from rural to industrial village and Protestant hostility, Irish immigrants developed a tragic vision. They proved receptive to a Catholic revivalist message: repentance, submission and solidarity. The faith was often their only possession. Reinterpreted by preachers from religious orders, it became an eternal life insurance policy with profits here below: sobriety, thrift and industry would empower the disfranchised poor to improve their lot. Like American Catholics they were sceptical:

> having witnessed so many experiments tried on poor credulous humanity by new doctors who turn out to have been quacks . . .

inclined to suspect and distrust all those crudely conceived political changes which disturb the peace of communities and nations, without improving their lot.[13]

Parish revivalist missioners used that mentality to inculcate discipline into their charges. Problems were attributed to mixed marriages, drunkenness and lack of education. But their successes were containment of Ribbonism and Fenianism.

Alternative, 'loyal' organizations were encouraged and developed. Conservative influences, Fr Mathew's parochial temperance organizations and later League of the Cross, were welcome, whatever the impact of the slogan, 'Ireland sober, Ireland free'.[14] Temperance reinforced clerical leadership and helped the slow integration of the needy within a larger society. Property ownership begot the vote, communal defence and stability: modest wealth, passage to America or lands of opportunity. Steady income increased collections, built Catholic infrastructure and kept the faithful from proselytizers and from the poorhouse.

Dean Richard O'Brien's Catholic Young Men's Society desired 'No politics . . . no object within our premises, within our organisation unless to make men good and by goodness make them happy.'[15] Spread through Scotland from 1854 its sobriety, thrift, harmony, education and recreation removed the impressionable from revolutionary or divisive political influences. The SVP and CYMS proved excellent church fund-raisers: they attracted more generous contributions than political bodies.[16]

Lay–clerical relations had remarkable chemistry. Respect grew, as witnessed by numerous presentations of gold watches, purses or even horses to priests.[17] At St Peter's, Aberdeen, even the poorest gave 5 shillings each towards St Patrick's altar: Irish identity was subsumed within local ultramontane pride.[18] To that extent ultramontane British identity fulfilled a need: loyalty to one was loyalty to all. By 1914, 567 clergy served 424 churches, 254 missions and 214 schools, with 546,000 faithful: one priest to every 963 Catholics.[19] It had worked. In a poor church burdened by immense debts, stability was vital in planning new, more elaborate churches, expanded Catholic education, enlarging Blairs or building new diocesan seminaries after 1878. To that process religious orders made a substantial contribution.

To return to Monteith. He exemplified the élite and converts who encouraged and strengthened British identity. They largely drew their social, political and religious influence from the status quo. Old Catholic tradition, the Constable Maxwells, Lovats and others in Highland and Banffshire heartlands had kept faith through penal times. The number of English-educated converts of substance boosted self-confidence: they brought prestige, patronage and substantial benefactions to hard-pressed clergy. The duchesses of Buccleuch and Hamilton, the Lothians, J. Hope-Johnstone, Monteith, William Douglas Dick, Lord, later the Revd, Archibald Douglas and others were to provide land, churches, schools or subsidize religious orders. The duchess of Leeds gave around £10,000 to the Jesuits and £300 annually for seminary education.[20] Hope-Scott built the Goldie church at Moidart.[21] The marquess of Bute gave munificently: churches by William Burges at St Ninian's, Cumnock, reputedly the first church lit by electricity, Santa Sophia, Galston, at Aberfeldy and sites at Whithorn and Troon, sustained local schools and gave generously to the Jesuit school. He reintroduced Premonstratensians into Scotland, founded a boys' farm colony and greatly encouraged church music. He bequeathed £20,000 each to the churches at Oban and Whithorn, and a further £2,000 if Blairs seminary were transferred to St Andrew's University.[22] A Tory, he nurtured strong Scottish sympathies: he and the church served the land in which they dwelt.

Other denominations did provide clergy: convert Aberdeen Presbyterian, Alexander Munro (1820–90), influential priestly opponent of Irish nationalism, and fellow Aberdonian and Quaker, George Wilson, became priest of Elgin and canon of Aberdeen. But the Oxford Movement brought over Episcopal clergy. The most significant was the Revd William Humphrey, chaplain to Bishop Forbes of Brechin, received by Cardinal Manning in 1868. He became a Jesuit controversialist. Oxford graduates, William Douglas Dick, lord-lieutenant of Forfarshire, Charles Trotter of Woodhill, lord-lieutenant of Perthshire, the Revd Thomas W. Hunter, rector of Callander, and the Revd George Angus, all converted, the latter becoming chaplain at St Andrew's; Arthur J. P. Urquhart of Oxford, and of landed family in Westmeath and Aberdeen, and Norfolk curate, William Wall of Cambridge, convert, joined the Benedictines at Fort Augustus. The Revd T. C. Robertson, chaplain to the duke of Buccleuch, the Revd W. C. A. McLaurin, dean of Moray and Ross, his wife and family, John Steuart of Ballechin and his wife, the Revd R. M. Stewart, late parish minister of Galashiels and his son from Balliol followed. The tutor to the sons of the marquess of Bute, Samuel Sproston, was a convert curate and Cambridge graduate, as was Canon Robert Campbell, chaplain to the Episcopal bishop of Aberdeen.[23] But more significantly for our purposes, several Oxford and Cambridge converts served as priests in Scotland.

One of the most influential was the Roxburgh-born Revd Robert Belaney. After Cambridge, he was ordained an Anglican priest. Serving in Ireland, he took a keen interest in Irish hardship and oppression. After conversion and ordination in Glasgow, 1852, he was largely responsible for the Jesuits returning to Scotland.[24] An outsider, he attributed the dire condition of Catholicism to timid Scottish clergy:

> Here as a body, the Church is nothing while numerically it is a quarter of this great city. The want of clergy and churches lies at the root of all our endeavours, blighting them as they are put forward and nothing will ever be done I feel certain until the religious orders are welcomed and enlisted in the great and difficult work to be done. Heretofore, I am told, there has been a dissimulation on the part of the clergy to have religious orders established in Scotland. I do not believe this feeling is of much prevalence now.[25]

He was right: Scottish caution dissuaded religious in fear of ultramontane steel, heavier debts and a changed world. Religious orders, ultramontane and disciplined, injected Britishness, not Scottishness or Irishness. Their regular missions incorporated shifting, shiftless masses into the local parish. They made a stabilized community in a common cause: in mutual help, deference to the priest and marked bounds of acceptable behaviour.

Even so, Jesuits irritated many clergy and Irish.[26] But Jesuits had long known 'the hereditary dislike' of seculars and that continued.[27] They had lamented the decline of educated Scottish Catholics.[28] Seculars failed to educate leaders. Even Jesuit property had fallen under the Scottish vicars-apostolic but they returned with powerful patrons like J. R. Hope-Scott and the American-born duchess of Leeds.[29]

In 1858 Bishop James Gillis of Edinburgh was ambivalent. After several false starts, three prominent lay converts, Monteith, Campbell of Skerrington and Hope-Scott, acquired property but, financially strapped, Gillis refused to allow any appeal for funds.[30] Prepared to secure premises in the New Town for 'a middle class school', he demanded a church 'void of all expensive ornament'.[31] The school never came to fruition. Not for the first time Gillis's enthusiasm outran his resources.

His successors proved less hospitable. Although Jesuits built up regular communicants, schools and outposts, Bishop John Strain and later Archbishop MacDonald proved persistent irritants. Strain objected to Dalkeith Jesuit 'incursions' and emphasized their tenant status, much to the chagrin of the Hope-Scott and Lothian families, who heavily underwrote their extensive Border missions. Given his lack of priests and their proven incompetence, his behaviour seems pure power play. Eventually the Jesuits left in 1902 and 1944.[32]

Lord Lovat offered Fort Augustus to Jesuits in 1869 while the duchess of Leeds offered Dornie. Both were refused. Dornie was, as the Revd J. H. Corry observed after a horrendous trip, 'like building a cathedral at Juan Fernandez for Robinson Crusoe and his man Friday and asking us to serve it'.[33] Under pressure from Hope-Scott who wanted to do something for the Scots after helping the Irish in Scotland, the Jesuits did take a small summer mission at his developing resort of Oban.[34] A scheme for a school and chapel in Aberdeen foundered.[35] Jesuits felt their manpower to be more effective in industrial centres.

As suggested earlier, bishops were cool. After some discussions with two Jesuit priests, Belaney and the Revd Peter Forbes, a renowned Highland priest, bought a site for a Glasgow church and school. Bishop Murdoch opposed the move. In his absence, Bishop Smith, his coadjutor, if welcoming, denied Belaney's authority to make an offer.[36] Outraged by Belaney's 'unwarrantible [sic] liberty', by Forbes's approaches to the Jesuit Irish Province, and by pressure from Robert Campbell of Skerrington (an Episcopalian convert) for a Jesuit school, Bishop Murdoch offered a poor parish, St Joseph's.[37] Once this was agreed, Murdoch, apprehensive about his displaced Irish priest, the Revd J. Danaher, and his parishioners, urged the Jesuits to come in three weeks: 'That horrid cry of nativity is ever the greatest cry of religion whenever the Irish are out of their country.'[38] Danaher (1821–86), a rare pastor among local Irish priests, allegedly mobilized resistance among his flock.[39] A public meeting condemned 'wanton aggression on this parish' and 'anti-Irish prejudice'.[40] That anger was understandable in the light of local bigotry, antipathy of many Scottish clergy and bitter Famine experience.

In the event, former Anglican priest, the Revd T. B. Parkinson, SJ (1819–1904), a graduate of Queens' College, Cambridge, won the congregation in a successful mission.[41] Raising funds was more problematic as Monteith could not help.[42] At the same time, Bishop Smith repeatedly showed his disdain. Their motives in re-entering Scotland were, he said, to strengthen claims to an inheritance. Jesuit intervention in a dispute for the Sisters of Mercy against Franciscans further incensed Smith.[43] Even worse, Jesuits allegedly encouraged a Franciscan nun with her inheritance to found a convent in a Jesuit mission at Exeter, Plymouth diocese, under the brother of the Revd R. Vaughan, SJ, previously involved in the Scottish negotiations.

Progress was slow. Parkinson struggled to develop St Aloysius's school. An early advocate of Catholic social mission he soon lost two priests through typhus. Three years later he was busy lecturing on education in Glasgow to promote the infant school.[44] The dispiriting nature of the mission was clear. He found few Catholic primary schools. One was a room 27 by 20 feet with 170 boys and girls. Less than half the Catholic children were enrolled in school while less than two-thirds of those enrolled were in regular attendance.

The church underwent an organizational revolution in the nineteenth century. The expanded vicariates and the later restoration of the hierarchy are the best known. But the increase in *Romanitas* was far greater than in England. Religious orders, schools and missions spread rapidly; faced with fewer older Catholic customs and practices than in England, by 1880, devotions, sermon and benediction had almost totally replaced vespers in the few places where they existed. The expanding railways further reinforced that mentality by speeding up the deployment of British religious as missioners, preachers at openings of churches and other celebrations. More important for our purposes was the comprehensive organization of laity through voluntary bodies which gave corporate identity, self-esteem and fulfilment.[45] Parochial organizations, like the SVP for times of need, the parish library and school for education, concerts and soirées for entertainment, various devotional bodies encouraged loyalty to Rome, to the area and to the British state.[46] Popular Catholic literature, novels and *The Lamp*, further inoculated members against 'alien' threats. A round of parish activities limited time for angst or other endeavours, political or vicious. Repositories, booksellers and, later, the Scottish Catholic Truth Society, advanced these ideas. After several failures, the *Glasgow Observer* began in 1885. Strongly sympathetic to Irish aspirations, its sporting and social concerns were important features. The CYMS in Glasgow 1890, for example, demanded better wages, health and working conditions, while 'leakage' increased concern for education, social ethics and activism.[47] Irish dreams continued but gradually permanent settlement altered priorities.

Scottish sentiment emerged. The convert James Grant (1822–87) drafted the only Scottish nationalist agenda in the nineteenth century: his son served as priest at Hammersmith.[48] The Tory marquess of Bute encouraged cultural renewal through his *Scottish Review* (1882–1900). He unveiled the Wallace Monument at Stirling while Ruari Erskine of Marr later revived the *Scottish Review* and the Gaelic *Guth na Bliadna*.[49] A Catholic Caledonian Association flourished, especially in Jesuit St Joseph's, Glasgow. Tensions between Irish and Scottish Catholics surfaced. But pastoral concerns prevailed over nationalism.

Two other forces, however, proved even stronger: ultramontanism and social justice. Scottish-born advocate of lay trusteeism, the lawyer James Fraser Gordon, WS (1817–61), was a founder member of the Edinburgh SVP, the only successful national body for the defence of Catholic interests.[50] Its steady spread and fund-raising efforts proved more influential than nationalist efforts.[51] The Caledonian Association greatly relieved the starving Irish.[52] The Dundee-born Revd Joseph Keating, SJ, explored the social issue and Jesuits Dominic Plater and Leo O'Hare developed the influential Catholic Social Guild. Archbishop John Maguire and John Wheatley helped integration into larger British society.[53]

The Revd Reginald Middleton, SJ, a conservative social reformer, was a product of Beaumont, Downside and Ampleforth and a Berkeley Square home. He had begun a Catholic Social Reform organization 'to combat anti-religious socialism'.[54] To inculcate the ideas of *Rerum Novarum* and Continental Catholicism into the locality, he lectured every fortnight for two years. His friend, the Swiss-born Revd Joseph Egger, SJ, supported Cowcaddens Social Reform Association and with Bro Shields, SJ, founded the Apostleship of the Sea.[55] Middleton's Glasgow Catholic Institute, supported by Professor J. S. Phillimore, had 530 members and six social study libraries. Numerous luminaries addressed their meetings.[56] For Middleton, Labour, *the* party of the future, 'should be leavened by Catholic principles'.[57] Jesuits were already lamenting leakage, declining Mass attendance especially among poorer people.[58] The future of the church was with the toiling laity.

The *Month* rallied support. Not all Catholics were convinced. To the outraged Stuart Coats, an ultra-conservative convert of the Scottish textile family, the Jesuits had lost their way. They even reviewed socialist books favourably: the order was no longer a dependable bastion of conservatism.[59] The Jesuits pushed their spiritual and social ideas through the retreat movement. The Revd Dominic Plater, SJ, saw advantages in uniting all kinds and conditions in godly renewal and social harmony. Considerable manpower and resources were sunk in the enterprise. In November 1914, sixty alumni of St Aloysius's attended a retreat.[60] A year later a retreat house was established under the Revd R. Middleton, first at Rochsoles, the Gerard family property, and more successfully at Craighead. By 1920, 900 attended and by 1937 over 2,000. A restrained, informed demand for social justice ensued.[61]

The Marists, largely French or Irish, ran St Mungo's Glasgow school of advanced studies with a practical bent. They taught in several infant schools like St Andrew's, where they regularly marched 600 boys to Sunday Mass.[62] They, the Franciscans and Sisters of Mercy, recruited from Ireland, were helped by many local professed and pupil-teachers. Later orders of nuns included many French and English sisters. They were hard-pressed: the Sisters of Mercy were crippled by heavy debts while Franciscan nuns at St Alphonsus's confronted 700 girls and 600 in St Andrew's Sunday school. The Christian Brothers significantly were not brought to Scotland even after 1872. Irish teachers or textbooks proved short-lived.[63] Even Gaelic, Irish and Scottish, was eroded.

Teachers were recruited and formally trained in England until 1894: many with a vocation invariably came from heartlands of Catholic recusancy in north-western England. Women trained at Liverpool under the Sisters of Notre Dame to 1894 or under the Faithful Companions of Jesus at St Leonard's, 1858–63. Men trained mainly at Hammersmith College.[64] The Catholic Poor Schools Committee continued its generosity to Scotland. In 1874, for example, Scotland received 47 per cent of grants.[65] As Scots took greater responsibility, some 1,400 women trained at Dowanhill before 1914. Teaching and motherhood were the two feminine vocations.

But schools were part of the *British* experience. At Stirling in 1859, the Revd Paul McLachlan, a pamphleteering priest, held a soirée in support of St Francis Xavier schools with the national flags of England, Ireland and Scotland given equal prominence and the national anthem played by a recently formed congregational band.[66] The sense of community was reinforced by novel, open-air processions at Dalbeth or a lavish High Mass which drew more than a thousand to Hamilton.[67] The parish soirée was a device to promote common (British) identity, loyalty and raise school funds.[68] Leo XIII gave added force to that argument in his 1898 encyclical to the bishops of Scotland. He demanded educational excellence for a harmonious, patriotic Catholic body.[69]

The Jesuits faced serious problems on their arrival. The first Jesuit priest, the Revd P. Thomson, found himself alone among some 10,000 abjectly poor Catholics at St Joseph's, Glasgow.[70] The congregation suffered from chronic instability, constantly moving from place to place and job to job. As the Revd Robert

Whitty, SJ, observed, migrants from the north of Ireland assimilated more readily than those from elsewhere. Even with an Epsicopalian convert gentry base and youthful alienation from Presbyterianism, Catholicism was making little impression in Scotland.[71]

The Jesuits reinforced the British dimension within Scottish Catholicism. By 1860 six priests and two scholastics were in Scotland. Spat upon and jeered, they continued their enterprise. In the wake of the Phoenix Park murders, the Revd James F. Splaine, SJ, organized a meeting of Irish to express their horror at the outrage.[72] Jesuits did not confront the existing order; they sought to transform it.[73] As Gerard Manley Hopkins said, the Irish poor were not all the dirtiest, but knowing moral virtue and cleanliness was not the same as practising them.[74] In 1888, twenty-one priests, two scholastics and three brothers were active: their influence expanded with their numbers.

Of the Jesuits who served in Scotland more than ninety came from northern England, overwhelmingly from Lancashire.[75] In the early days and much of the nineteenth and early twentieth centuries they were drawn from substantial backgrounds, often converts and highly educated by any standard both before and subsequently within the Society. After the papal acceptance of the right of Catholic students to attend the ancient universities, the Society quickly committed its members to degrees at Oxford University (1894). They came well trained and formed in a British mould.

By 1970, twenty-two churches of 446 Scottish parishes were named after Jesuit saints or the Sacred Heart, a very Jesuit devotion. Even more significantly, none dated from before 1846 while more than two-thirds were opened between 1846 and 1878, the period of initial settlement and consolidation under ultramontane influence prior to the restoration of the Scottish hierarchy.[76] Their priests were self-confidently British, ultramontane and conservative. They startled bishops by wearing the Roman collar in public and their intelligent magazine balanced the extremes of the *Dublin Review* and the *Rambler*. The *Month* was born and subsequently flourished under the Lanarkshire-born Revd John Gerard.[77] They found Irish clergy so ill-educated and 'valde benigini' that young men neglected their faith.[78]

Their higher school was part of their drive for amelioration and incorporation. In support of Archbishop Eyre's League of the Cross campaign, they established temperance organizations in their two Glasgow parishes. By 1900 their new hall for the League of the Cross and the Boys' Guild had accommodation for 900 and they ministered every summer to the Industrial School boys' tent camp on Cumbrae. They indirectly contributed to Catholic home nursing. Miss White, superintendent of the Glasgow Sick and Nursing Poor Association, dismissed on her conversion to Catholicism, was recommended by Jesuits to Lady Bute. The result was the foundation of St Elizabeth House for home and district nursing. A Catholic nursing home began in three houses and a flat. With an operating theatre and room for twenty patients, it boasted nine district nurses with thirty other nurses for in-patients who were mainly non-Catholic.[79]

Sometimes Catholic demonstrations proved counter-productive. A procession of the Blessed Sacrament through crowds around Sacred Heart church in 1899 was followed by another to the convent of Mercy in 1901. It was, significantly, the work of a rare Irish-born Jesuit in Scotland, the temperance advocate, the Revd Mathew Power, SJ, (1857–1926), whose brother was an Irish Nationalist MP. He began open-air preaching to 5,000 at Galashiels. From 1903 to 1905, he held open-air services for over 1,000 in Edinburgh's Grassmarket and in Lothian Road. One address was provocatively entitled 'Last illness and death of the Church of Scotland: A retrospect of work done at the General Assembly 1903'. Pressure from his provincial, the archbishop and the police ended his outdoor harangues and he subsequently became a military chaplain.[80] Confrontation was not an English Jesuit trait. Dialogue was preferable and far more effective.[81]

A combination of rescue and protection, outreach and better relations with other denominations, was more common. In 1889, the Sacred Heart SVP society with the support of the Sisters of Mercy opened a Catholic Home for Working Boys to protect youths at risk from intemperate parents, vice and proselytism. The committee included Lord Ralph Kerr, president, Campbell of Skerrington, vice-president, and Frederick J. Smith, a dedicated SVP member for over forty years.[82] By 1891, twenty-four boys were in care and as the premises were formally licensed they were able to receive another seven on licence from the United Industrial School as good relations developed between the two bodies. Residents, often from Smyllum Orphanage or St Joseph's Industrial School, enjoyed free admission to Hibernian Football Club. Four years later forty-five boys were resident and its reputation attracted Cardinal Logue in 1899 and the Revd Dominic Plater, SJ, the social apostle, in 1912. By 1915 over 1,000 had been aided. Some were doing well in South Africa or the United States. More pertinent to our purposes, such enterprises fostered service and duty to higher (British) ideals. In the first year of the Great War, 180 former residents enlisted, three were prisoners of war and seven were killed. One former resident, Patrick Campbell, killed at Gallipoli, had previously sent £40 to aid the home. The home continued until the Second World War.[83] That reflected the emergence of a more affluent, confident and assertive body.

Jesuit support for pilgrimages to Iona was marked. In 1897 the Jesuits shared in the great summer pilgrimage to mark the 1300th anniversary of St Columba. The Church of Scotland left the temporary roof in place and allowed Catholics free use of the facilities. At the High Mass, a redoubtable Gaelic-speaking Jesuit well-known in Nova Scotia and among Gaels in the Glasgow Caledonian Society, the Revd Archibald Campbell, preached 'a forceful and fluent' sermon punctuated by occasional pinches of snuff![84]

On the occasion of Queen Victoria's Jubilee, 1897, the rector of St Aloysius's delightedly reported his Irish congregation standing for the national anthem rather than leaving.[85] With strict obedience and discipline the Jesuits projected those values onto the community at large. They wished to produce quintessential English gentlemen but gradually they sought to develop leadership as priests, doctors and lawyers in serving faith and community. University education was essential.[86] In creating a right public attitude, like their patron, J. R. Hope-Scott, they would be defending the best British social and political traditions.[87] In particular Jesuits proved attractive to Scottish Episcopalian converts.[88] The convert Lothians, for example, fought a lengthy dogged fight against secular clergy in their parishes. In 1885, on laying the foundation stone for the new St Aloysius's school buildings, the marquess of Bute observed that he shared a platform with four convert Jesuit priests.[89]

In the imperial mould, Augustus Henry Law, son of an Anglican priest, the younger son of Lord Ellenborough, served in the Royal Navy all over the world before becoming a Catholic and entering the Jesuits. As a scholastic he spent three years in a garret at Charlotte Street school, Glasgow. Immensely popular for his catechizing, drilling and football, he established a library and began dramatic productions before leaving to die a horrific death on the Zambezi mission.[90] Oxford convert the Revd Gerard Manley Hopkins served briefly in Glasgow and Oban. Others included the Revds George Tickell, John Wynne and J. McLeod: Wynne gave £6,000 to the Edinburgh mission while McLeod wrote a new Scottish catechism.[91]

Others later perished gloriously in serving the cause of Christianity and the British Empire. Henry Schomberg-Kerr, a member of the Lothian family network, had served as a naval officer and introduced strict discipline among his young charges at St Aloysius's, Glasgow: his regime of drill and marching seems to pre-date the work of William Smith and the Boys' Brigade by a number of years. He subsequently spent years on the South African mission.[92] The Revd John Gerard, SJ, son of a wealthy Airdrie convert, later provincial and editor of the *Month*, endorsed that imperial mission. In St Joseph's Glasgow, he said their purpose was 'to send out God-fearing and self-restraining men to elevate savage races'.[93]

In this respect, the most colourful Scottish-born Jesuit was the Revd Charles Gordon (1831–1911). His chequered career began as an improving Highland landlord. In 1867 he recruited some sixty Irish volunteers to fight in defence of the Papal States. After being seriously wounded in battle, he returned and entered the Jesuits in 1869. He served in South Africa then in 1879 he returned as superior in Glasgow, built the new college and attracted scholarship funds from the marquess of Bute who laid the foundation stone in 1883 and formally opened the new school buildings in 1885. Archbishop Eyre blessed them. Gordon subsequently became vicar-apostolic of Jamaica, 1889–1908.[94]

The most influential were the Revds Edward Bacon and Eric Hanson. Bacon, a former lay Anglican missionary in London docks, schoolmaster in British Guiana and Lisbon seminarian, finally entered the Jesuits in 1867. A friend of Hopkins he spent forty-four years serving the Glasgow poor.[95] A graduate of Christ Church, Oxford, Hanson became a Catholic and then taught at Downside under Dom Aidan Gasquet before entering the Society in 1888.[96]

Jesuits enjoyed widespread influence. Even before their formal return to Scotland, they frequently directed priestly retreats. Through their influence over the religious orders of women, the sisters of the Sacred Heart and those of Notre Dame, their notions permeated many schools from 1882 and 1894 respectively. St Aloysius's College, Glasgow, produced more than 400 secular and fifty-five Jesuit priests: only fifteen of the Jesuits served in Scotland. Only seventeen Irish as against sixteen European Jesuits served in Scotland.[97]

They were influential through the Jesuit-inspired Apostleship of Prayer which rapidly grew from a solitary Scottish group in 1866 to 138 on the eve of the Great War: Glasgow (1866) had fifty-eight, Edinburgh (1869) thirty, and Galloway (1873) twenty-four, Aberdeen sixteen, Argyll and the Isles ten.[98] However patronizing and conservative these organizations might appear to critics, they gave a structure of faith and hope to a mobile population, beset by innumerable personal crises, here and in the hereafter. In demand as confessors and preachers, the Jesuits attracted masses to their churches.

As in earlier days the Jesuits offered an alternative community: their lavishly decorated churches with aural and visual images, choirs, sermons and non-liturgical devotions provided defence against threatening cultural hosts.[99] They often gave lecture series for non-Catholics. In Glasgow, addresses on 'The evidences of Christianity' were 'the talk of the town'.[100] In 1878, in Scotland they heard 81,887 confessions. By 1887 the number was just under 100,000, or approaching a quarter of the total Catholic population.[101]

From the earliest days they preached throughout Scotland as supply priests, at clerical retreats and as missioners.[102] The idea of Gerard Manley Hopkins preaching

> to put plainly to a Highland congregation of MacDonalds,

MacIntoshes, MacKillops and the rest what I am not putting so plainly to the rest of the world, 'That Nature is a Herculean Fire and the comfort of the Resurrection' at Fort William is worthy of contemplation.[103]

In 1860 one of their first missions at Saltcoats was a startling success. They heard 478 confessions, reclaimed 460 and nineteen converts. Even more striking they reclaimed 100–50 Ribbonmen and effectively destroyed the Great Ribbon Lodge.[104] In 1864 at Dundee, six Jesuits heard 6,000 confessions and reclaimed 200 in a two-week mission. They allegedly were so busy they had no time for converts.[105] In 1883 two Glasgow parish missions produced astonishingly high male responses with 4,266 male confessions against 2,346 women, and 3,265 male Easter duties against 2,053 for women.[106] When Glasgow like other British cities began simultaneous missions to all parishes Jesuits were to the fore.[107] Six years later Jesuits ran their most successful Glasgow missions. Three parishes proved astonishingly responsive to their call.

Jesuit Missions, Glasgow 1894

Parish	Number of priests	Population	Confessions	Easter duties
St Joseph	5	11,000	4,763 (43%)	5,235 (48%)
St Aloysius	7	5,400	3,750 (69%)	1,617 (54%)
St Mary	4	14,000	7,795 (56%)	7,561 (54%)
Total	14	30,400	1,630 (54%)	4,443 (48%)
Proportion	1	1,900	1,019	903

Source: Archives, English Province, Farm Street, London.

Later forays were well attended. During a Glasgow city mission in 1910, for example, St Aloysius's was packed: 'all passages, steps, altar, floors were occupied while many could not obtain admission at all'.[108] Before the Great War, St Aloysius's was invariably packed for Sunday sermons: 'so much so that it gives rise to jealousy among certain of the secular clergy'.[109] School sodalities, pilgrimages, social study programmes extended Jesuit influence. The mass-circulation Jesuit *Messenger of the Sacred Heart* periodical provided further influence. Although their church architecture in Edinburgh and Glasgow was redolent of Italy, unlike the prevailing neo-Gothic, their outlook permeated the church.[110]

Their example inspired service: some to enter the Jesuits or to serve in the Empire. Many more entered the secular priesthood within Scotland. As early as 1886 a pupil from St Aloysius's school reputedly went up to Oxford. In 1902, for example, seven boys went up to Glasgow University and three went to the Jesuit noviceship.[111] By 1903, the school had 200 pupils but to Hanson's chagrin, many left school early, without qualifications for the universities or professions, to remain within the west of Scotland.[112] Many others migrated to North America or parts of the Empire. Even so, A. J. Cronin went on to become a renowned novelist of the Scottish Catholic experience.[113] Hanson confronted his charges with unpalatable truths.

The church was on the move. The community was changing slowly but surely. If Irish identity still remained a sustaining force of Catholic loyalty, Hanson clearly marked a considerable advance on the simple ethnic loyalties of an earlier generation. They and their children had carried the baleful legacy of the Famine. That mentality is well captured by the redoubtable Irish Dominican preacher, the Revd Thomas Burke, who enthralled audiences on both sides of the Atlantic:

> if you want to know what is faith and what truth is, all you have to do is to go out into any school in Glasgow where there are Irish children. (Applause) Go into the schools attached to the church of my friend, Fr Noonan; go into the schools of St Mary's and St Andrews and a well grown Irish boy – or go and sit down beside him and he will tell you every iota (and) tittle of the truth that Patrick taught. (Applause) . . . The Catholic faith made the Irish people a nation, as they are today in everything into the highest and the best and the purest definition of nationalism.[114]

Under Hanson the school was transformed. A vigorous champion of his school, he rejected the excuses for failure and low ambition in the local community. 'The chief difficulty is to persuade the pupils and their parents of the utility of universities.'[115] In a lecture to the Scottish Catholic Truth Society,

Hanson uncompromisingly reiterated his disgust at Catholic apologies for failure:

> Is there, I would ask, any place in the British dominions where you would find so vast a number of Catholics with so few among them possessed of means or position or influence, or any sort of distinctive pre-eminence, as you find in this great city and in its neighbourhood? Here within a small radius we have a trifling number of 200,000 Catholics. Include the whole Archdiocese and the number is 320,000. It is one of the great industrial centres of the world. How many Catholic employers of labour have we? Where are the master engineers or shipbuilders who are Catholics? How many Catholics among our merchant princes? Or among the larger shopkeepers? It is a University city. Among the 2,500 students at Gilmorehill could we find a dozen Catholics? Dr. Sophie Bryant recently published figures. In Ireland she found that among Episcopalians 1 in 600 is attending University; among Catholics, 1 in 5,000. If that is startling what should we say of the archdiocese of Glasgow? If you find 16 Catholics in the University that gives an incredible figure of 1 in 200,000 receiving a University education! Is there one reading for a degree in Arts? Is there one who has secured an open bursary there? Leaving one religious order aside is there a single schoolmaster who possesses a University degree? There may be one I don't know him. How many can you find?[116]

And, not pulling any punches, he continued;

> You will be near the mark if you admit the absence of Catholic apprentices is due not to poverty, not to the machination of Jews and Freemasons, nor to the bigotry of Protestants but to the deplorable fact that only a small proportion of our boys and young men are apprenticed to skilled trades and few thus apprenticed have little ambition to rise high in their profession or knowledge how to do it.[117]

Within three years, one of his pupils, Joseph Scanlan, was first in the Glasgow University Bursary competition and perceptions of the school, Jesuits and Catholics began to adjust.[118] The quality and success of the school was unassailable from 1900. Regular appearances of the marquess of Bute on ceremonial occasions or Lord Ralph Kerr at the 1905 school prize-giving provided useful publicity. In 1904 the staunchly Protestant Sir

John Ure Primrose was the first lord provost to present the prizes.[119] All-round success in academic, moral and sporting areas put the school in the public eye. It achieved remarkable results in certificate examinations.[120] Continued achievements in the Glasgow University Bursary were matched on the football field. In 1911 the soccer team topped all other secondary schools.[121] Catholics had put down British roots. They were here to succeed, not to lament past failure.

Demand for places rapidly grew. In the early days the school had struggled to recruit pupils. Fr Bacon and his fellows had resorted to house-to-house visits through the west of Scotland to recruit, but now pupils came from as far afield as Edinburgh and remote parts of Ayrshire. By 1912, 100 pupils from twenty-five schools sat entrance scholarship examinations and the following year ninety-seven pupils from thirty schools entered.[122]

Bacon instituted the sodality, a very useful body in cultivating spiritual and social cohesion. By 1907 some 270 pupils were members. Those addressing them included the Revd Bernard Vaughan, SJ, and activities included support for foreign missions in the British Empire, social study, pilgrimages to places of Catholic interest.[123] Refining his social reform ideas in Glasgow, the Revd Charles Plater addressed the sodality in 1919, significantly as the Gordon Highlanders occupied the school in response to Red Clydeside. He then spoke to 600 at St Mungo's, 200 at Notre Dame Training College and Springburn Irish Labour Party. A college certificate in Catholic social study was established in the wake of his zeal.[124] Catholic salvation, missionary zeal and self-fulfilment coincided within a superior British cultural ideal.[125] Darkest Cowcaddens was excellent training for darkest Africa – and vice versa.

The Revd Charles Karslake, SJ (1839–1915), came of a solid legal background. His father had been solicitor to the duke of Kent and two of his brothers became MPs; Sir John Burgess Karslake (1821–76) served as Attorney-General under Disraeli, 1867–8 and 1874, while Edward Kent Karslake (d. 1892) firmly defended the Established Church and favoured fair representation 'not only of property, but of education and such other qualifications as raise a man in the social scale'.[126] Frederick Karslake was an early advocate of the cause of the Revd John

Ogilvie, SJ[127] After serving on the English mission, the Revd George Constable Maxwell, SJ, brother of Lord Herries, the Dumfriesshire laird, served his latter days in Dalkeith. The first Puseyite convert priest to serve in Scotland, the Revd John Xavier Biden, SJ, spent 1859–61 in Glasgow and fellow Oxford-educated convert, the Swiss-born Revd Edward de Wattelville, SJ (1818–69), died from typhus in Glasgow.[128] Another amazing character, the Revd Bartholomew C. Dawson, SJ (1864–1937), boasting of his royal lineage and an Oxford accent, lasted only a year in St Joseph's, Glasgow. He used to wear Cardinal Manning's frock coat, cloak and skull cap (which he had owned from his days as a Bayswater oblate) as he walked through the Cowcaddens! Devoted to the sick, poor and 'blacks', his unfortunate affectations made him something of a liability: even in Guiana 'his Oxford accent, intense piety and the same class complexes remained unchanged'.[129]

The Benedictines at Fort Augustus came of a similar considerable background. Of well-heeled, established families they added stability by their rule, their outlook and their influence through their retreats for laity and their boarding school. The Conservative and convert the Revd Oswald Hunter Blair entered the monastery and eventually became its superior. Of substantial landed background, he had generously aided churches and schools in Kirkoswald, Newton Stewart and Wigtown.[130] Charles R. Scott Murray, the convert husband of Amelia, eldest daughter of the fourteenth Lord Lovat, and Mgr Thomas Capel were instrumental in the conversion of the marquess of Bute to Rome.[131]

The Redemptorist foundation at Kinnoull proved an asset to the local community. It did not confront but served the area. Religious women who worked in close association with clergy came of considerable background. Their superior was the Hon. Elizabeth Langdale, a relative of leading Catholic families including the Constable Maxwells. Her convent was supported by the Monteith, Herries, Lovat and Kerr families.[132] At its opening, Archbishop William Smith-Sligo of Inzievar, son of a landed and mine-owning family, rejoiced at local friendly religious relations. The huge convent and school on Corbelly Hill, Dumfries, was established by the dowager Lady Herries.[133] Such folk were hardly disturbers of British peace.[134]

To return to my main argument: after several invitations from leading laity, the Jesuits arrived at the invitation of a convert priest, much to the annoyance of the Scottish episcopacy.[135] Their Glasgow school survived. Two remarkable convert priests, the Revd Fr Bacon and the Revd Eric Hanson, aided by the marquess of Bute and others, built up the numbers of pupils, quality and reputation of the school. By 1907 two Jesuits gave lectures at the University of Glasgow. Hanson wanted to get away from rote learning, secular and religious: he wanted intelligent, questioning adults in faith.[136] He had missionary priests address pupils, held debates, promoted social study and the boy scouts. Mind and body were integrated in Christian service.[137] Their purpose was, as the convert Revd Edward Purbrick, SJ, Jesuit Provincial, said,

> to make our young men Catholic English gentlemen – *strangers to no culture which bestowed on their fellow countrymen.* We wish to enable them to compete in the professions; in the public careers, *in society with the best educated scholars in the kingdom.* We wish to relieve them from their progressive paralysing sense of inferiority, to add to the supernatural virtues of true practical Catholics which fit them for heaven, the natural virtues both intellectual and moral which far from being necessarily prejudicial to the supernatural virtues . . . are essential to fit them for the world.[138]

A sense of personal sin and communal responsibility was deeply ingrained in the faithful. Priests and bishops turned those sentiments to advantage in building churches, chapels, schools and other institutions. The sheer volume of churches built in the nineteenth century by a poor community is staggering: they were part of a Catholic ethos, pride in group achievement. In that respect they were a blast against the prevailing Protestant individualism. At the same time, encouraged by their clergy, the poor developed a strong sense of self-help. That might be savings banks like that established in Dundee in 1839 by the renowned catechism priest, the Revd Stephen Keenan (1804–62); building societies, like that begun by the Revd Peter Forbes at St Mary's Glasgow; Bishop James Gillis's Holy Guild of St Joseph in Edinburgh in the 1830s, or the lay St Vincent de Paul Society (SVP) which arrived in Edinburgh in 1846 and in Glasgow two years later. Such endeavours promoted community formation and mutual help, encouraged loyalty to the faith, curtailed Protestant proselytism and prevented desperate men from resorting to violent, radical causes.[139]

The strains within Scottish Catholicism were increasingly apparent from 1880. Democracy and dignity challenged property. The church remained sympathetic to small-scale familial levels of production against *laissez-faire* liberals.[140] In Ireland the emergence of Parnell, Davitt and the Land League coincided with the withering criticism of Henry George on his tour: 'this is the most damnable government that exists outside Russia'.[141] Some Irish and English bishops sympathized with these concerns. Hostility came from the substantial landed elements like the duke of Norfolk, Lord Lovat and other fellow travellers like Coventry Patmore.[142]

Equally, relations between seculars and Jesuits were often strained. In the wake of the Vatican Council, bishops sought to extend their powers and curb religious like local popes. In England, the Jesuits fought a prolonged battle in 1874–5 with Bishop Vaughan over opening a school in Salford.[143] The archbishop of Edinburgh also discouraged a school in his city: 'the Bishops will not be satisfied until they get everything into their hands'.[144] They feared their creeping control: 'it was preposterous to look to the secular clergy alone'.[145] The church should use those with 'a special vocation, a special preparation and special opportunities'.[146]

In Glasgow Archbishop Eyre pursued a similar course. Although somewhat hostile in his early days, he had however considered a seminary associated with St Aloysius's before establishing Partickhill. His personality, his drive to a regimented church under the restored canon law, his financial concerns and family clashes led to difficulties. His brother, the Revd W. H. Eyre, SJ, of Stonyhurst contested their father's £400,000 will. It proved a flashpoint culminating in an 1883 court case which irreparably damaged relations with the order. Whatever the Jesuit success, Archbishop Eyre proved 'vir difficilis et indoles peculiaris'.[147]

Eyre questioned imaginative Jesuit ministry to Gaelic speakers within St Joseph's through a chapel, St Columbanus, within the existing parish. The Revd Archibald Campbell, SJ, began a Catholic Caledonian Society, Gaelic lectures, campaigns to protect young women and against drink. He knew Gaeldom through lectures, missions and retreats: at Benbecula, Arishaig, Ardkenneth, Eriskay and the West Highlands, 1894–1912. In 1907 he spent five months among recent migrants in Nova Scotia. In Barra he found faithful living less in the style of Pugin and Michelangelo, more in 'the Lobengula style'.[148] In Arishaig he was appalled at the return of a Conservative, Colonel MacDonald, brother of the archbishop of Edinburgh. He defeated a Presbyterian minister supported by a Stonyhurst-educated landlord who previously 'evicted more crofters than any Protestant landlord' but was now a firm Land Leaguer.[149]

Eyre subsequently claimed the college was 'not up to the wants of the day', praised the rival Marists at St Aloysius's prize days and demanded religious inspection under seculars.[150] Although the provincial was satisfied with Scotland overall, in spite of admitting less talented or less able teachers, that unfriendly attitude persisted.[151] More than twenty years later, Bishop Mackintosh, coadjutor in Glasgow, appeared impossible, unfriendly and ill-humoured. He did not even speak at prize days, still less praise the pupils. But the Revd Eric Hanson believed attitudes in Edinburgh were even worse, implying that Scottish bishops had less zealous activism. Only Jesuits showed interest in higher education students.[152] Jesuits were unusual in their specialist pastoral care. They established a centre for Italian migrants. Although based in Edinburgh, the Revd Felix Rota with the Revd Joachim Mosca of Naples served 5,000 Italians in Glasgow, providing special Masses, confessions and even Carl Rosa Opera performances.[153] Two Lithuanian and a Lithuanian-speaking German Jesuits served Lithuanians at Dalkeith, and during 1914–18 Belgian Jesuit Edward Legros (1961–38) served fellow refugees.[154]

Several events suggest the completion of the British identity process. Pupils of the Jesuit school were increasingly upwardly mobile – professionals whose loyalty was to their faith, family and fulfilment. The Jesuits and others inculcated a critical, practical sense of self-help, self-restraint, future fulfilment on earth and in heaven. Sir Denis Brogan's father, for example, was a founder member of the Glasgow Irish Gaelic League. His son became an outstanding Jesuit pupil, renowned academic and a regular columnist in the *Spectator*. His brother, Colm, was a renowned journalist and apologist for the right.[155] It was a long way from Donegal.

Success from within rather than revolutionary confrontation was a result of a British Catholic identity. Active participation with Irish revolutionaries in 1848, 1866, the 1880s or beyond was infinitesimal. Their concern was social justice: life, liberty and happiness under God. Catholic patriotism was unquestionable. At St Joseph's, Glasgow, for example 300 men and a sixth of Fr Bacon's boys club died on active service in 1914–18.[156] In so far as there was an Irish identity, it mobilized loyalty to the parish, in hymns like 'Hail Glorious St Patrick', in Celtic Football Club or social justice within a constitutional British Catholic framework. Insofar as there was a Scottish identity, it lay in remembrance of Scottish Catholic tradition, in the martyrdom of John Ogilvie, SJ, and a fair deal. These folk memories merged with other European heritages within an ultramontane, Jesuit framework to achieve unity, harmonize class and ethnic tensions under a British parliamentary democracy. In disciplined cohesion, educated faithful made reasonable demands for social improvement. British Catholicism was here to stay.

Notes

1. See Bernard Aspinwall, 'The Scottish dimension: Robert Monteith and the origins of modern Catholic social thought', *Downside Review*, XCVII (1979), 46–68; idem, 'David Urquhart, Robert Monteith and the Catholic Church: a search for justice and peace', *Innes Review*, XXXI (1980), 57–70. Also *The Tablet* (9 July 1853; 13 September 1862); and an excursion to Fleurs Castle, *The Tablet* (25 August 1861). Monteith's son kept up the custom for St Aloysius's Glasgow outings. Similar outings took place to Lochgilphead, Hamilton Palace and Edinburgh, *Glasgow Free Press* (17 August 1861; 20 July 1863).
2. See Aspinwall, 'The Scottish dimension'; idem, 'David Urquhart, Robert Monteith and the Catholic Church'. Monteith and his Russophobe friend, David Urqhuart, employed Karl Marx on their

paper, *The Free Press*. For Stothert, see *The Tablet* (6 March 1847, 15 December 1849). See also Stothert's *A Short Series of Lectures on the Parochial and Collegiate Antiquities of Edinburgh* (Edinburgh, 1845); *Lectures on the Religious Antiquities of Edinburgh* (Edinburgh, 1846); and *Sonnets* (Edinburgh, 1856). He also contributed occasionally to the *Rambler* and *Liverpool Catholic Institute Magazine*.

3   Aspinwall, 'The Scottish dimension'; idem, 'Before Manning: some aspects of British social concern before 1865', *New Blackfriars*, LXI (1980), 113–27.

4   Opposition to Irish demands on social, property and ethnic grounds. See Bernard Aspinwall, 'Towards an English Catholic social conscience, 1829–1920', *Recusant History*, XXV (2000), 106–19.

5   Cf. J. F. Broderick, *The Holy See and the Irish Movement for the Repeal of the Union with England, 1829–1847* (Rome, 1951); M. Buschkuhl, *Great Britain and the Holy See, 1746–1870* (Dublin, 1982).

6   *Kilmarnock Standard* (20 July 1878). *The Presbyterian Record* (6 April 1885), 223 claimed H. E. H. Jerningham, a convert, sat for a Scottish constituency: 'Berwick on Tweed'. Also see A. Langdale, *The Tablet* (1 May 1880) and CYMS Conference Dumfries, 13 August 1881. *The Tablet* (26 June 1868) claimed that the SVP was the only national Catholic voice in Scotland.

7   See *The Tablet* (2 April 1887). Monteith claimed home rule was 'treasonable and wicked' and that in 1882 his father wrote against clerical failure to denounce vicious crime. Also ibid. (30 April 1887; 16 February, 30 March 1889); obituary of Lord Lovat, ibid. (10 September, 10 December 1887; 11 July 1914). E. de Lisle, *Pastoral Politics* (London, 1885).

8   Cf. Compton MacKenzie, *Catholicism and Scotland* (London, 1936), p. 183.

9   For example *The Tablet* (4 January 1862) for the Glasgow German Catholic Reunion with German-language lecture and books.

10 For example ibid. (22 June, 5 October, 27 July, 7 December 1844) among many reports; for collections in London for Kilmarnock, see ibid. (31 March 1849); for Perth priest collecting in England, see *Catholic Magazine* (April 1841). See Bernard Aspinwall, 'Was O'Connell necessary? Sir John Joseph Dillon, Scotland and the Movement for Catholic Emanicipation', in D. M. Loades (ed.), *The End of Strife: Death, Reconciliation and Expressions of Christian Spirituality* (Edinburgh, 1984), pp. 114–36; W. J. O'Neill Daunt, *A Life Spent for Ireland* (1896: Dublin reprinted, 1972), p. 72. Menzies

of Pitfodels, a massive patron of the Church, opposed O'Connell on Repeal then relented.

11   See Reports of Religious Examinations 1888–89, 1908–9 and 1918–19, Glasgow Archdiocesan Archives (GAA). Eyre significantly had attended the opening of Pugin's Cheadle chapel, *The Tablet* (5 September 1846).

12   For list, see James Darragh, *The Catholic Hierarchy of Scotland* (Glasgow, 1986).

13   Archbishop John Hughes of New York quoted in David J. O'Brien, *Public Catholicism* (New York, 1996), p. 64.

14   For example, *Catholic Magazine* (August 1840). See Colm Kerrigan, *Father Mathew and the Irish Temperance Movement, 1838–1849* (Cork, 1992); Elizabeth Malcolm, *Ireland Sober, Ireland Free: Drink and Temperance in Nineteenth Century Ireland* (Dublin, 1986); the Revd R. Belaney and the Revd J. Thomson, SJ, addressed a large temperance rally in the Pollok estate, *Glasgow Free Press* (13 July 1861).

15   See *The Tablet* (12 January 1858). See Scottish CYMS entertainments, lectures, devotions, savings banks, in ibid. (10, 17 February, 21 July, 22 December 1855; 19 January, 2 February, 8 March 1856; 12 January 1858; 29 March, 28 June 1862). Thomas Earnshaw Bradley, editor of *The Lamp* helped on his tours. Ibid. (10 February 1855) at Paisley.

16   For example, ibid. (3, 24 November 1855).

17   For typical Scottish presentations, see *Catholic Magazine*, August 1841; *The Tablet* (9 October 1847; 12 January 1849; 16 February, 18 May, 19 October 1850; 31 January 1852; 18 September 1858; 16 July, 24 September 1859; 7 April 1860; 27 April 1861); *Glasgow Free Press* (6 April 1861).

18   *The Tablet* (22 September 1860; 30 November 1861).

19   *Scottish Catholic Directory* (SCD) (1914).

20   Provincial, 2 April 1860; 1 February 1864; Jesuit Archives, Generalate, Rome (JAR), v.5.xxii.7.

21   *The Tablet* (18 October 1862).

22   Bishop W. Turner letter, 3 December 1903, 27/42 Scots College Archives, Rome (SCAR). See O. Hunter Blair, *John Patrick: The Third Marquess of Bute* (London, 1922).

23   These individuals are mostly readily listed in W. Gordon Gorman, *Converts to Rome* (London, 1899). Also 'Conversions to Romanism', *Presbyterian Review*, VI (April 1885), 201–25. William Simple, late regent in Glasgow, Hugh Rosse and Andrew Young, later regents in Aberdeen, are also listed in *The Tablet* (24 January 1846); Dr Alexander MacDonald, Aberdeen (26 January 1850).

24 Revd J. Belaney to Provincial, 27 November 1857, S/2 10, Jesuit Archives, Farm Street, London (ASJL). He was pro-Irish and ferociously pro-temperance, *Glasgow Free Press* (29 November 1862).
25 MSS record, Revd R. Vaughan, quoting letter of Revd R. Belaney, November 1857, ASJL.
26 See Revd J. Johnson, 27 May 1859, JAR v.4.iii.35.
27 Quotation from Revd C. Plowden to Jesuit General, 15 December 1819, JAR. See also his letters 20 January 1818, 13, 20 February 1819, 8 January, 27 January, 8 May 1820, JAR 1011/1, fo. 111, and 12 June 1820, 1012 12.i.2; Revd W. Strickland to Revd George Maxwell, n.d. November 1801, SCAE 33/4; Revd C. Plowden, 15 December 1819, Rome, JAR 1011, fo. 111; Revd G. Pepper to Revd C. Maxwell, 21 January, 21 June 1802; 20 January 1803, JAR 33/7; Revd M. Stone to Revd C. Maxwell, 4 April 1810; JAR 33/17; Revd C. Plowden, 20 January 1818; 29 December 1817, JAR 1011/11; Bishop J. Cameron to Revd J. Lingard, 15 October 1819, quoted in Joan Connell, *The Roman Catholic Church in England, 1780–1850* (Philadelphia, 1984), p. 149; Bernard Ward, *The Eve of Catholic Emancipation*, 3 vols. (London, 1912), esp. III, pp. 19–56; Malcolm Hay, *Failure in the Far East: How and Why the Break between the Western World and China Began* (London, 1956), p. 176.
28 Revd W. Strickland to Revd George Maxwell, n.d. November 1801, Scottish Catholic Archives, Edinburgh, 33/4; Revd J. Pepper to Revd C. Maxwell, 18, 27 March 1803, SCA, 33/12. See also *Letters and Notices*, CLXXIII (October 1908), 516.
29 Revd A. Weld called Hope-Scott the greatest benefactor of the Church in Britain, 3 March 1877, JAR, Beckx Miscellanea 4 ii 93. Also Robert Ornsby, *Memoirs of J. R. Hope-Scott*, II (London, 1894), p. 194. Ironically, the Jesuits have educated 29 Scottish bishops since 1827.
30 MSS records, Revd R. Vaughan, 18 January 1859, ASJL; J. R. Hope-Scott, *Scotsman* (22 October 1861). A. V. Smith of Inzievar presented an organ in 1867.
31 See the mass of correspondence, 1862–97, in JAR and London; The Mission of Galashiels, *Letters and Notices*, CLXII (July 1908), 145–52; CLIII (October 1903), 217–32; The Dalkeith Mission, *Letters and Notices*, CCXX (1920), 23–6; CLIII (October 1903), 219.
32 Letter 18 August 1862, ASJL. Also Extract Minutes, JAR, 1018.ii.4; Obituary Revd R. Whitty, SJ (1817–95), *Letters and Notices* (January 1896); duchess of Leeds, 2 April 1860, 1 February 1864, JAR v.5.xxii.5-x-56; Revd R. Whitty, 28 July 1862, JAR v.5.xxii-7; Revd J. H. Corry, 19 August 1862, and Revd R. Belaney, 7 February 1860, ASJL.

33. Quoted in Revd A. Weld, SJ, to Provincial, 12 August 1878; J. R. Hope-Scott, 12 March 1878; Revd Collins, 13 February, n.d. and 30 July 1875; Revd H. S. Kerr, 22 February, 26 March, 10 May 1878, ASJL.
34. Revd W. Law, SJ, 18 October 1894, and Revd E. Whyte, SJ, 27 August, 12 September 1895, ASJL. Although the Redemptorist bishop favoured them, his clergy opposed.
35. Ibid.
36. Bishop A. Smith to Provincial, 5 November 1857, SJA, London; Record, Revd R. Vaughan, SJ, quoting letter from Revd R. Belaney, November 1857, and replies of Bishop A. Smith, 5, 17 December 1857.
37. Bishop J. Murdoch, 17 August, 9 October, 14 December 1858, SJAL, and MSS Record, Revd R. Vaughan, September, November, 15 December 1857; 9, 15 December 1858, SJAL.
38. Quote from Bishop J. Murdoch, 2 April 1859, also Bishop Smith to Provincial, 9 January, 6 January 1859; Bishop J. Murdoch, 10, 28 February 1859, SJAL.
39. Bishop Smith to Provincial, 6 March 1859, SJAL.
40. Ibid. However, Dahner enjoyed good relations with the Jesuits to his death in 1886. *Letters and Notices*, CXXII (January 1896), 399–405. See Bernard Aspinwall, 'Scots and Irish clergy ministering to immigrants, 1830–1878', *Innes Review*, XLVII (1996), 69–80. The Irish were willing to use ultramontanism to contain Scottish dominance and uplift themselves.
41. Revd T. B. Parkinson, 9 June 1859, ASJL; *Letters and Notices*, CLXXVI (January 1909), 97–100.
42. R. Monteith, 1 April 1859; Colonel Gerard, 22 September 1859, ASJL. Interestingly in 1908 one Patrick Docherty, a workhouse inmate for three years, left the Jesuits £1,000, including £300 for St Aloysius's. Revd W. J. Crofton, 23 January 1908, ASJL.
43. Bishop Smith to Revd J. H. Corry, 15 July 1860; an undated copy of another letter *c*.1860; 13 February 1860, ASJL.
44. *The Tablet* (10 May 1862).
45. My view on Scotland differs from Mary Heimann, *Catholic Devotion in Victorian England* (Oxford, 1995). See James Britten, 'Catholic clubs', *Month*, LV (1885), 181–96.
46. *The Tablet* (3 March 1855) claims 500 Children of Mary, St Mary's Glasgow.
47. Ibid. (12 July, 9 August 1890). Also 'The leakage of the Catholic Church in England', *Month*, LIX (1887), 176–89; 'How to stop the leakage', *Month*, LXXXIX (1895), 106–16; James Britten, 'The loss of our boys', *Month*, LIX (1887), pp. 457–87, esp. p. 466.

48 *The Tablet* (7 May 1887).
49 See ibid. (9 July 1887). Bute believed that home rule would regenerate Scotland. See ibid. (19 October 1889). Also James Britten, 'The loss of our boys', and *The Tablet* (9 April 1887) on Bishop Cameron, Antigonish and the Irish.
50 Obituary, *The Tablet* (11 May 1861). Before the Law Society of Scotland began in 1948, Edinburgh lawyers subscribed to the Signet Library and were known as Writers to the Signet (WS).
51 Ibid. (24 February, 3 March, 21 July 1855; 16 July 1858; 26 March 1858).
52 Ibid. (28 February 1880; 9 December 1882). Also Glasgow archdiocesan collection, 17 March 1883.
53 See C. C. Martindale, *Charles Dominic Plater, S.J.* (London, 1912), *passim*.
54 Revd R. R. Middleton, SJ, to General, 26 December 1912; 10 July 1911, JAR 20.11.24.
55 Revd W. Crofton, SJ, to Provincial, 6 June 1910, ASJL. Egger obituary, *Letters and Notices*, CLXXXII (January 1911), 60–70; *Letters and Notices*, CCXC (October 1938), 140–41; *Glasgow Herald* (1908) and (1910) mentions the Cowcaddens organization a number of times; P. F. Anson, *Harbour Head* (London, 1944), pp. 102–7.
56 Revd Crofton, 10 July 1911; 17 March 1914; 16 March 1915, JAR 20.11.24 J.
57 Revd R. Middleton, SJ, 26 December 1912, JAR 20.11.24.
58 Revd W. MacMahon, SJ, 2 January, 7 October 1914, 20.ii.38, 46; 6 April 1915, 20.ii.46, JAR.
59 S. Coats, 18 August 1913, JAR 20.6.4. William P. Larkin, a former Aloysian, returned from the USA on a visit as Chief Director of the Knights of Columbus. MSS St Aloysius College Diary, June 1919, and Colm Brogan in *College Magazine* (June 1919), 13.
60 MSS School Diary, November 1914.
61 Revd E. Hanson, 4 April 1913, JAR 20.ii.3; Revd R. Middleton, 3 October 1913, JAR 20.ii.35; Revd R. Ritchie to Revd R. Middleton, 7 February 1914. Revd R. Middleton, 17 November 1920; 12 September 1922; ASJL; *Catholic Social Yearbook* (1928), a volume devoted to the retreat movement. *Letters and Notices*, CCLXXII (January 1934), 181–3; CCLXXIV (October 1934), 275–6 and every issue to 1938. See Martindale, *Plater*, pp. 117, 139.
62 SCD 1862, St Andrew's. The neglected social justice aspect of British Catholic revival appears in Bishop J. Gillis's Holy Guild of St Joseph, for example *The Tablet* (27 February, 18 September 1847) talking of his ideas concerning the provision of cheap housing and

refuges, and the Revd George Porter, SJ, 'The wants of Catholicism in Scotland', *Glasgow Free Press* (12 September 1863), union in one nation, diligence, temperance, better housing and real homes. SCD 1862. *The Tablet* (16 August 1862, 26 August 1854) notes thirty-one nuns and sixteen novices at Charlotte Street, Glasgow.

63 St Andrew's Glasgow school logbook, 25 March 1868; St Mungo's logbook, 16 May 1864; St Mary's logbook, 22 May 1870. St John's logbook, 14 February and May 1868, noted the arrival and departure of Mr John McAleer, a National School of Ireland teacher. Strathclyde Archives, Glasgow.

64 See Bernard Aspinwall, 'Catholic teachers for Scotland: the Liverpool connection', *Innes Review*, XLV (1994), 47–70. W. J. Battersby, 'Educational work of the religious orders of women, 1850–1950', in A. Beck (ed.), *English Catholics, 1850–1950* (London, 1950), pp. 337–54. However, Barry M. Coldrey, *Faith and Fatherland: The Christian Brothers and the Development of Irish Nationalism, 1838–1921* (Dublin, 1988), esp. pp. 223–5, argues that superiors were attached to the status quo.

65 *Annual Report* (1874), p. 2.

66 *The Tablet* (11 February 1859).

67 Ibid. (8 July, 9 December 1854) St Alphonsus's, Glasgow; (12 June, 8 July 1858).

68 For example, at Perth and St John's, Glasgow, *The Tablet* (11 January 1862) and Stirling, *The Tablet* (13 December 1862).

69 Copy, 25 July 1898, SCAR 27.

70 Letter to General, 3 August 1861, JAP Rome v.5.xxii.2.

71 Revd R. Whitty, 12 April 1862, v.5.xxii.4, JAR. *Census of Great Britain 1851: Religious Worship and Education Scotland Report and Tables* (1854) suggests the size of the problem with thirty-two Catholic day and 60 Sunday schools with 3,509 (61 per cent) and 10,954 (84 per cent) of those enrolled in attendance.

72 *Letters and Notices*, CLXXVI (July 1909), 170–7; *Letters and Notices*, CXLVI (January 1902), 352. On their British mentality see the ex-Jesuit E. Boyd Barrett, *The Jesuit Enigma* (London, 1928), pp. 100, 183, 218, 222–3, 316–17, 322, 326.

73 Cf. A. Lynn Martin, *The Jesuit Mind: The Mentality of an Elite in Early Modern France* (Ithaca, NY, 1988), pp. 206–7, 232.

74 G. M. Hopkins to R. Bridges, 3 February 1886; *The Letters of G. M. Hopkins to Robert Bridges*, ed. C. C. Abbott, 2 vols. (London, 1935), I, p. 299.

75 Figures from obituaries in *Letters and Notices* to 1995. Also see Maurice Taylor, *The Scots College, Valladolid* (Valladolid, 1971), p. 216, for Jesuit retreats and Mark Dilworth, 'Religious orders in

Scotland', in D. McRoberts (ed.), *Modern Scottish Catholicism, 1878–1978* (Glasgow, 1979), pp. 92–109.

76 Figures based on Catalogues of the English Province 1860 onwards; the *British Province* (1995) and an analysis of statistics in the *Scottish Catholic Directory* (1970).

77 Revd Alban Christie, SJ, 5 December 1853 and Revd R. Whitty, Dalkeith, 28 July 1862, JAR v.5.xxii.7.

78 Revd B. Lee to General, 19 October 1862, JAR v.5.xxii.8. The same letter acknowledged £50 from Monteith.

79 *Scottish Catholic Directory* (1878–1901) and *Letters and Notices*, CXXXVII (1899), 258–60.

80 *Edinburgh Catholic Herald* (16 June 1899); *Letters and Notices*, CXXXVI (July 1899), 173–7; CXLIV (July 1901), 199–203; CLII (July 1903), 211; CLVIII (January 1904), 54; CLXXXV (October 1911), 258–60.

81 For Jesuits addressing Glasgow students, see Revd W. Crofton, SJ, 28 October 1907, JAR 20.ii.8.

82 *Lauriston Magazine* (December 1905), 11. They were building on the earlier work of Mother Mary Francis Bell of the Poor Clares. The daughter of an Edinburgh stockbroker, she dealt with some 200 children from 1884 to her retirement in 1899.

83 *Annual Reports* (1891–1939) and *Edinburgh Evening News* (22 August 1939).

84 *Letters and Notices*, CXXVIII (July 1897), 199. On the resurgent interest in pilgrimage see Victor Turner and Edith L. B. Turner, *Image and Pilgrimage in Western Culture* (New York, 1978); Mary Lee Nolan and Sidney Nolan, *Christian Pilgrimage in Modern Western Europe* (Chapel Hill, NC, 1989).

85 *Letter and Notices*, CXXVIII (1897), 201. Also D. O. Hunter Blair, *A New Medley of Memories* (London, 1922), p. 73 and note for two similar incidents.

86 See Revd W. Petre, *Remarks on the Present Condition of Catholic Liberal Education* (London, 1877), esp. p. 19; Petre, *The Position and Prospects of Catholic Liberal Education* (London, 1878), pp. 11–18, 32–4; Petre, 'Large or small schools', *Dublin Review*, 31 NS (October 1878), 279–318.

87 Quoted in Ornsby, *Memoirs of James Robert Hope-Scott*, II, p. 194.

88 Revd R. Whitty, SJ, 12 April 1862, JAR Ang 5.xxii.4; 28 July 1862, JAR 5.xxxii.7. Also see J. H. Newman quoted in J. C. H. Aveling, *The Jesuits* (London, 1981), p. 308.

89 *Glasgow Herald* (1885) clipping in St Aloysius's College Collection.

90 *A Memoir of the Life and Death of Rev Augustus H. Law, S.J.*, 2

vols. (London, 1882); Ellis Schreiber, *The Life of Augustus Henry Law* (London, 1893); Anon., *Augustus Law, S.J., Notes in Remembrance* (London 1886) ignores his Glasgow days and puts him 'briefly' in Edinburgh; *A. H. Law: Sailor and Jesuit* (London, 1893), a CTS pamphlet places him in Blackpool and Dalkeith.

91 Revds J. Wynne and J. MacLeod, obituaries in ASJL.
92 Mrs Maxwell Scott, *Henry Schomberg-Kerr: Sailor and Jesuit* (London, 1901), pp. 135–9.
93 *Letters and Notices*, CXXXVIII (January 1900), 327; Foley, *Records*. For background, see John Springhall, *Youth and Empire: British Youth Movements, 1883–1940* (London, 1977); Springhall, *Sure and Steadfast: A History of the Boys' Brigade, 1883–1983* (Glasgow, 1983), pp. 36–93; John McKenzie, 'Popular imperialism and the military', pp. 1–24; McKenzie, 'Heroic myths of Empire', pp. 109–38, in McKenzie, *Popular Imperialism and the Military, 1850–1950* (Manchester, 1992); also McKenzie, *Propaganda and Empire: The Manipulation of British Public Opinion, 1880–1960* (Manchester, 1984).
94 *Letters and Notices*, CLXXXVI (January 1912), 353–4; *St Aloysius's College Magazine* (June 1930), pp. 165–6.
95 See *Glasgow Observer*, obituary clipping and MSS St Aloysius's Diary, 18 September 1920; 11 December 1922. He preserved Hopkins's manuscripts.
96 *Letters and Notices*, CCLXXVI (1935), 156–60.
97 Figures compiled from Jesuit returns and obituaries. JAR.
98 See JAR 1019.vi.16.
99 Cf. Anne J. Cruz and Mary Elizabeth Perry, *Culture and Control in Counter Reformation Spain* (Minneapolis, 1992), esp. pp. 1–24.
100 MSS School Diary, 13 February, 6 March 1887. Another followed in 1888, Diary, 8 January 1888.
101 Figures from the annual returns, Jesuit archives, London.
102 For example, at Kilmarnock, 27 June 1886; Abbotsford, 24 December 1886; Helensburgh, 24 April 1889; at Falkland, 24 April 1889. College MSS Diary.
103 See his letter from Fort William, 18 August 1888, *The Letters of G. M. Hopkins to Robert Bridges*, ed. Abbott, p. 279.
104 Saltcoats Mission, 17 September 1860, SJAL.
105 Revd R. Whitty to General, 25 April 1864, JAP R, v.5.xxii.11.
106 *Letters and Notices*, LXXVI (April 1883), 112. Also see LXXXI (July 1884), 171–5 and LXXXV (July 1885), 217–18.
107 *Mission Diary* (7 October 1888); *Glasgow Observer* (October 1888); *Letters and Notices*, XCVII (December 1888), 197.
108 Revd W. Crofton to General, 23 April 1910, JAR 20.ii.14. Also Revd

W. Lawson to General, 28 April 1896, JAR 10118.iii.18.
109 Revd W. Crofton to General, 23 April 1910, JAR 20.ii.14.
110 An exception in Glasgow was the Sacred Heart, Bridgeton, built by a former Jesuit pupil, Canon Michael Hughes (1858–1921). He championed the poor, and brought Eric Gill and prominent Dominicans and others to his parish. See Bernard Aspinwall, 'Broadfield revisited: some Scottish Catholic responses to wealth, 1918–1940', *The Church and Wealth: Studies in Church History*, XXIV (1987), 393–406.
111 Report to the Provincial, 1902, ASJL. I have been unable to confirm the Oxford claim about a Mr Boyd.
112 *Glasgow Herald* (24 December 1903).
113 College Sodality MSS Minute Book, 1871–91, contains lists of members and often details of their subsequent careers. Cronin was admitted in 1912.
114 Revd Thomas Burke, *The Faith of the Irish People and What Preserved it: A Lecture in City Hall, Monday, 26 October 1874*, printed for the Bridgeton SVP (Glasgow, 1874), pp. 9–10. See also J. S. McCorry, *A Panegyric of St Patrick* (Edinburgh, 1851); Revd P. Lavelle, *Glasgow Free Press* (4 October 1862) for similar views.
115 Clipping from *Catholic Times* (n.d. October 1909), in College Clippings Book. Also *Glasgow Herald* (22, 25 October 1909); *Letters and Notices*, CLI (April 1903), 125.
116 Quoted Church of Scotland, *St Andrew* (4 January 1906), clipping in the College Collection.
117 Ibid.
118 See letters from W. Menzies, Chief Inspector of Schools, 14 October 1909; Revd Alban Goodier, SJ, 13 October 1909; Revd R. Sykes, SJ, Provincial, 13 October 1909, College Clippings Book.
119 *Glasgow Herald* (24 December 1904).
120 Report 1920–1, ASJL claimed 82% success compared with the Glasgow High School 63%, Hillhead 62%, Bellahouston 54%.
121 Revd W. Crofton, SJ, to General Rome, 10 April 1912, JAR 20.ii.18.
122 *Glasgow Observer* (29 June 1912; 29 June 1913).
123 St Aloysius's MSS Sodality Minutes, 1 October 1913; *Glasgow Observer* (26 April 1913).
124 Sodality and College MSS Collection, 24 March, 12 May, 9 June 1916; St Aloysius's MSS College Diary, January 1919; *College Magazine* (June 1919), 26; (December 1919), 19; Martindale, *Plater*, pp. 138–9, 266.
125 For example, Revd John Conway (1853–1915); Revd P. Conway to Mr Towry Law, 27 February, July 1883, *Woodstock Letters*, XLV (1915), 242–7; *St Aloysius's Magazine* (December 1920), 24–5.

126 Quoted in *Who's Who of British Members of Parliament*, I, pp. 1832–85, ed. M. Stenton (Hassocks, 1976), p. 216.
127 'An authentic account of the imprisonment and martyrdom of Fr John Ogilvie SJ', *Dublin Review*, 30 NS (January 1878), 240; Revd D. Conway in *Month* (January and February 1878). Both coincided with the restoration of the Scottish hierarchy.
128 Foley, *Records*, VIII, pp. 822–3.
129 *Letters and Notices*, CCLXXXVII, p. 193.
130 See Bernard Aspinwall, 'The making of the modern diocese of Galloway', in R. McCluskey (ed.), *The See of Ninian: A History of the Diocese of Whithorn and the Diocese of Galloway in Modern Times* (Ayr, 1997), pp. 83–187.
131 See D. O. Hunter-Blair, *John Patrick: The Third Marquess of Bute*.
132 *The Tablet* (12 July 1890).
133 Ibid. (17 July 1890). Similarly St Margaret's, Edinburgh, boasted four nuns, two English and two Presbyterian converts, when Elizabeth Mary, daughter of Charles Langdale entered. Ibid. (16 January 1847).
134 *Report Conventual and Monastic Institutions* (1870), CCCLXIII, pp. 1680, 1735, 1818.
135 Monteith made offers of property in 1851, 1856, 1859, the Hope-Scott and Lovats in 1850s. See JAR v.4.f. xviii Revd J. Etheridge, 2 September, 21 December 1851; Revd J. Johnson, 1, 19 May 1856; 24 January 1858 and v.4.iii.34.
136 For example, leaflet of the Secondary Education Association of Scotland, 2 December 1911. Also *Glasgow Herald* (18, 29 May 1915); *College Magazine* (December 1922), 18; (December 1924), 32.
137 Handbill for visit of the Revd John Atkinson, SJ, Trichnopoly, India. Questions were to be in French. College Sodality Notebook, 25 October 1912, debate on home rule; St Aloysius's Social Guild typescript n.d. but c.1914–18; *Star* (9 December 1910).
138 Quoted in Revd William Petre, *The Problem of Catholic Liberal Education* (London, 1871), p. 3. Mary F. Cusack, 'The Nun of Kenmare', *The Black Pope: A History of the Jesuits* (London, 1896), pp. 161, 176, 177 used Petre's pamphlet to show Jesuit practical and intellectual limitations. Rupert Wilkinson, *The Prefects: British Leadership and the Public School Tradition* (Oxford, 1964), p. 221, grants Jesuit success in creating an élite but stresses their lack of imagination.
139 *Orthodox Journal* (7 September 1839). See Bernard Aspinwall, 'The formation of the Catholic community in the west of Scotland', *Innes Review*, XXXIII (1982), 44–57.

140 See, for example, A. J. Coale and Susan Cotts Watkins, *The Decline of Fertility in Europe: The Revised Proceedings of a Conference on the Princeton European Fertility Project* (Princeton, 1986), pp. 271–3. Also see correspondence from the Revds Henry Murphy, Thomas Keane and others in Aspinwall, 'The making of the modern diocese of Galloway'.

141 Quoted in E. P. Lawrence, *Henry George in the British Isles* (East Lansing, 1957), pp. 15, 40.

142 See Christopher Hollis, *The Mind of Chesterton* (Coral Gables, 1970), p. 172, on Norfolk's presentation of the sword to Sir Edward Carson at Blenheim. See Coventry Patmore, *Courage in Politics and Other Essays* (London, 1921), p. 16.

143 *The Jesuit Claim to Found a College of the Order in Manchester in Opposition to the Ordinary* (1875) and *The Bishop of Salford's Reply: Uncanonical Opening of Jesuit College: Summary of the Whole Case* (1875), copies in SCHA, Edinburgh. Also J. G. Snead-Cox, *Life of Cardinal Vaughan*, 2 vols. (London, 1910), I, pp. 270–304, 320–57.

144 Revd A. Weld to General, 9 March 1876, JAR.

145 Quoting H. J. Coleridge, 'Dangers to the Church in England and France', *Month* (October 1878), 129–42, 135–6; Coleridge, 'The Tractarian and Ritualist views of the episcopate', *Month* (September 1878), 1–13. Revd A. Weld to General, 18 May 1876 and 9 March 1881, JAR 4.ii.102 and 1014 Ang 14.

146 *Month* (October, 1878), 136. Also see *The Tablet* (14 September, 5 October, 5 November 1878) and Revd Pubrick to General, 19 May 1881, JAR, 1014.iii.3.

147 See Revd J. Clayton, SJ, 19 March 1893, JAR v.6.ii.45 and his letters 19 February 1893, 26 July 1895, JAR v.6.ii.43; Revd W. H. Eyre to Archbishop C. Eyre, 21 January, 3 March, 13 July, 1881 and Archbishop C. Eyre to Revd W. H. Eyre 20 September 1881; B. Parker letters 24 July, 3 August; D. MacDonald, 25 September 1883, GAA 1P-E24; T. Eyre to Lord Arundell, 30 April 1884, JAR v.6.iv.2; *Glasgow Herald* (8 August 1883); *St James Gazette* (28 July 1883); *The Tablet* (28 July, 11, 25 August 1883).

148 'Mission to Benbecula', *Letters and Notices*, CXXII (January 1896), 333–8.

149 'Mission at Barra', *Letters and Notices*, CVI (July 1894), 478–80. A St Columbanus Society existed in Glasgow in 1857; *Glasgow Free Press* (12 January 1861).

150 Points for Consideration, St Aloysius's to Provincial, 7 June 1888; August 1888, ASJL; Revd E. Whyte to General, 12 November 1891, JAR v.7.iv.3.

151 27 December 1890 and 10 December 1891, JAP 6.ii.13 and 25 and De Statu Rerum in Angliam Monumentum, JAP, Ang 17, iii.104.
152 Revd E. Hanson, SJ, 4 January 1913; undated 1913, JAR 20.ii.29 and 34. Also Revd A. Campbell, SJ, July 1912, JAR 20.ii.22; Revd M. MacMahon, SJ, 3 July 1913, JAR 20.ii.3.
153 Hosts saw Italians as threats, *Glasgow Herald* on ice cream parlours (12 March; 2, 31 May; 2 October; 2, 13, 25 December 1907); violence (16 March 1914; 10 May 1913); ice cream shops, 1892, 1894, 1906 in *United Free Church Assembly Proceedings* and sex in 1912, p. 359. Revd Fr Ambruzzi, SJ, a Cambridge student visited. MSS School Diary, 2 April 1914; Revd M. MacMahon, 17 December 1917, JAR 1023, v.25; Revd F. Green, n.d. 1917, JAR v.28; St Aloysius's School Diary n.d., 23 October 1918; 7 October 1919; 26 June 1920; 10 March 1872; 2 November 1873; 6 May 1876; 7, 13, 21 November 1887; Revd J. Wright, SJ, 19 July; 7 October 1919; 23 July; n.d. September; 18 November 1918; JAR 1023.v.41. On the background, see Terri Colpi, 'The Italian community in Scotland: senza un campanile?', *Innes Review*, XLIV (1993), 153–7, esp. pp. 153–7.
154 Revd F. King, SJ, to General, 11 June 1913, JAR 19.iii.77. On the background, see K. Lunn, 'Reactions to Lithuanian and Polish immigrants in the Lanarkshire coalfield, 1880–1914', in K. Lunn (ed.), *Hosts, Immigrants and Minorities: Historical Responses to Newcomers in British Society, 1870–1914* (Folkestone, 1980), pp. 308–42. St Aloysius's MSS Diary 1910–18, and *School Magazine* (1908–18).
155 Sir Denis Brogan was a legendary academic authority on America and France. See Colm Brogan's numerous contributions to the American Bill Buckley's *National Review* to his death.
156 St Aloysius's Diary, 14 November 1918, 18 September 1920, 11 December 1922.

~ 14 ~
The Language of Heaven?: The Highland Churches, Culture Shift and the Erosion of Gaelic Identity in the Twentieth Century[1]

DONALD E. MEEK

Dùsgadh

Dùsgadh!
Abair gu bheil feum air dùsgadh anns a' chladh seo.
Tha fear san oisinn thall rinn ainm dha fhèin
leis an eòlas a bha aige air teinntean Ifrinn;
fear eile aig a robh searmoinean Spurgeon
air a theanga;
fear a thàinig dhachaigh le creud coimheach
a fhuair e air bruaichean Chluaidh,
is fear eile chaidh cho fada ri Plymouth;
tha duineachan beag briathrach fon chloich sin
a chaidh domhainn anns an t-soisgeul a-rèir Mharx –
cha do leugh e facal Gàidhlig 'na bheatha.
O, nan tigeadh soisgeulaiche
a lorgadh ceann-teagaisg air na seann chreagan seo,
anns a riasg donn,
ann a flùraichean na machrach,
nar cainnt fhìn.

Re-awakening

Re-awakening!
Indeed there's need for it in this cemetery.
There's a man in that corner who made a name for himself
by his knowledge of the fires of Hell;
another who had Spurgeon's sermons
off by heart;

> a man who brought home an outlandish creed
> he found on Clydeside,
> and another who went as far as Plymouth;
> there's a talkative mannikin beneath that stone
> who drank deep of the Gospel according to Marx –
> never read a word of Gaelic in his life.
> O, for an evangelist
> who would find a text on these ancient rocks,
> in the brown peat,
> in the flowers of the machair,
> in our own tongue.

So the contemporary Gaelic poet, Ruaraidh MacThòmais (Derick Thomson), writing of his native island of Lewis, comments wrily on the multiplicity of creeds, sacred and secular, which have been espoused by islanders during the twentieth century and are now represented in a single graveyard.[2] His point can be applied across the Highlands and across the centuries. Though 'Highland religion' is often regarded as an indigenous growth, the Scottish Highlands and Islands have imported their main expressions of the Christian faith, and these have been indigenized to a certain extent through the use of the Gaelic language. From at least the time of Columba, who came to Iona from Ireland in *c*. AD 563, the region has hosted all the principal Christian alignments of Ireland and Britain. Throughout the Middle Ages, the Highlands and Islands were Roman Catholic, though later Protestants have detected enduring traces of pagan cults. After the Reformation, the stage was set for the creation of a potent Presbyterian presence in the region, and for the displacement of Roman Catholicism. After 1690, the Established Church of Scotland became the dominant force in the heart of the Highlands, while Roman Catholicism was relegated to the eastern and western edges of the Highland mainland. Catholicism was also preserved in some of the Hebrides, notably Barra and South Uist, and the Small Isles (Rhum, Eigg, Muck, and Canna).[3] Episcopacy, which was once strong in the region in the seventeenth century, was also displaced, but survived in Perthshire, Inverness-shire, and mainland Argyllshire.[4] This remains the broad picture. In certain parts of the mainland (notably the eastern and southern edges of the Highlands, where Gaelic was weakening) and in the Inner Hebrides, smaller independent Protestant bodies, notably Congregationalists and Baptists, appeared from the end of the eighteenth century, and carried much influence in their own localities during the nineteenth century. Their emergence reflected dissatisfaction with the preaching and pastoral provision of the Established Church. Most had, however, disappeared by 1900, particularly from the mainland, but Baptist churches dating from the early nineteenth century are still to be found in the Inner Hebridean islands of Tiree, Islay, Mull and Colonsay.[5] This evidence alone would suggest that the sea-girt communities of the Highlands and Islands are apparently better able than the mainland to preserve the more conservative forms of evangelical expression.

The Presbyterian presence in the Highlands and Islands has retained its pre-eminence until the present time, but since the middle of the nineteenth century its strength has declined in numerical terms, certainly as a single cohesive force. The reduction of the power of Presbyterianism is related to a number of processes which need to be considered before we examine the ways in which the churches influenced (and, to some extent, still influence) society.

Establishing the Faith

At the outset, it is important to note that Presbyterianism was, and remains, prone to disruption and secession. The Highlands imported not only Presbyterianism, but also the various debates which have destroyed the Presbyterian consensus over the last century and a half. Indeed, some might suggest that these debates and their consequences were received, and even fomented, with particular relish in the region.[6] It is telling that an overview of the various disruptions and secessions that have occurred in Scotland provides no less than a potted history of the various denominations active in the Highlands. It is no less telling that these secessions have lasted longer in the Highlands than anywhere else in Scotland.

The tendency to disruption goes back to the Reformation itself. The Reformation can be seen as a form of disruption or secession from what was regarded by the Reformers as a corrupt church. Protestantism came to birth in protest and issued in the creation of an alternative church. It thus carried within it the seeds of disruption, and these were to be found within Presbyterianism. Secessions from the national Church of Scotland were occurring in the national context in 1733 (with the creation of the First Secession Church by Ralph and Ebenezer Erskine), but this had relatively little influence in the Highlands. This was followed in 1761 by the emergence of the Relief Church, which established only a couple of congregations in the Highlands.[7] It was only in 1843 that a significant disruption formally hit the Highlands, when the Free Church of Scotland was formed. The Free Church, which rejected patronage and parted company with the Church of Scotland on this issue, attracted massive Highland support. This was because the Highland area had been strongly influenced by evangelicalism from the beginning of the nineteenth century, and the evangelical principles of the Free Church were attractive to those who had already become evangelicals.[8]

The Free Church offered a form of evangelicalism which was rooted in purity of worship and doctrine, regulated by the Westminster Confession of Faith. The concept of a pure evangelical church, braced by subordinate standards, appealed strongly to contemporary Highlanders. Why this should have been so is not clear; it may be that a church with a strong sense of purpose and a very firm adherence to biblical authority provided stability in the midst of the significant changes which occurred in Highland society – through improvement, clearance and emigration – in the preceding seventy years. Loyalty to purity of worship and doctrine became an identifying mark of Highland Presbyterians, but it also became a fruitful source of secession.

Breaching the Peace

The peace of the Free Church was disturbed twice by the beginning of the twentieth century, first by a secession and then (paradoxically) by a union. In 1893, the Free Presbyterian Church of Scotland was created by a couple of ministers in

Highland charges who disagreed with the Free Church's position on the Westminster Confession of Faith. Through the passing of its Declaratory Act, the Free Church was seen as being disloyal to the confession, and undermining its authority. In 1900, a substantial proportion of the ministers of the Free Church – those who were broadly in support of the Declaratory Act – left it to join with the United Presbyterians, forming the United Free Church of Scotland. A remnant of the original Free Church continued as the Free Church (Continuing), and repealed the Declaratory Act, thus asserting its loyalty to the Westminster Confession. This body, which has grown to become the Free Church of Scotland, is sometimes known as 'the Wee Frees'.[9]

In 1989, the Free Presbyterian Church of Scotland was rocked by a high-profile controversy triggered by the attendance of one of its most prominent members, Lord Mackay of Clashfern, the lord chancellor, at a Roman Catholic requiem mass. This fracas brought to a head tensions which had been simmering for several years within the church, and it resulted in another secession, whose members formed the Associated Presbyterian Churches (APC).[10] These churches continue to exist in a very uneasy relationship with the Free Presbyterians, the tension being caused mainly by claims and counter-claims to manses and church buildings. The strength of the APC appears to be diminishing in the process. Liberty from the shackles of Free Presbyterian synodical jurisdiction was fundamental to the APC's position, but the quest for freedom has not stopped there; the more progressive and influential ministers and members, who were crucial to the emergence of the APC, have sought emancipation from traditional APC worship styles and have moved to other churches, sometimes within evangelical independency in a non-Gaelic context.[11]

In the mid-1990s the Free Church of Scotland also entered a period of great tension, caused partly by the clash between 'conservatives' and 'modernizers'. This struggle found its focus in another high-profile leader, Professor Donald Macleod, currently principal of the Free Church College, who was cleared by an Edinburgh sheriff of alleged sexual assault in 1996. The argument of the defence, that Macleod was the victim of a conspiracy within his own denomination, was upheld by the sheriff. This left a number of unanswered questions which are periodically given an airing by those out of sympathy with the verdict. As Macleod is perceived by some within the Free Church as its chief modernizer and liberalizer, the more conservative elements have tended to rally round the anti-Macleod banner. Opposing groups, Free Concern and the Free Church Defence Association, emerged within the church, though Free Concern had disbanded by 1997. Eventually, in January 2000, pending the disciplining of some thirty ministers, a dissenting minority group seceded and have named themselves 'The Free Church of Scotland (Continuing)'. This group is, in effect, a reconstituted version of the Free Church Defence Association.[12]

Although the various 'Macleod affairs' are regularly presented in terms of challenges to authority, conservatism and orthodoxy, they also have a deeply cultural and Gaelic dimension, if not a paradox, at their heart: Macleod hails from the conservative Free Church heartland of Lewis, but he has failed to conform fully to the ecclesiastical and cultural paradigms expected of Lewis-born leaders of the Free Church of Scotland. His most vigorous opponents have included some of the ministers of his own island, notably the Revd Angus Smith, Free Church minister of Ness until his retirement and his subsequent move to the Free Presbyterian Church. This does not mean, however, that Macleod is a complete non-conformist with no support in Lewis: in the final stages of the showdown with leaders of the Free Church Defence Association, several younger ministers with strong Lewis connections took a leading role in welcoming Macleod to communion services, and also in attacking and ejecting the 'dissidents' through the General Assembly. The support of this group was of vital significance to the termination, at least at the formal level, of a period of great unhappiness within the denomination.[13]

Of course, Lewis – sometimes dubbed 'the last stronghold of the gospel' – has never been a haven of ecclesiastical uniformity. The island has accommodated all, and nurtured several, of the foundations, fragments and fissures of Scottish Presbyterianism throughout the centuries: the Church of Scotland, the Free Church of Scotland, the Free Presbyterian Church of Scotland, the United Free Church, 'relief' congregations of the Free

Church, and most recently the Free Church (Continuing). In Lewis, as elsewhere in the Highlands, a 'cold peace' has been maintained between the various groups, while natural decay has simplified the ecclesiastical landscape, thus removing some earlier sources and symbols of strife. The United Free Church has gradually disappeared from the Highlands, partly as a result of reunion with the Church of Scotland in 1929. The other bodies remain, with some variation in their distribution. The Church of Scotland is found throughout the region; the Free Church has a following in most areas, and notably in Lewis, but it is weakest in the Inner Hebrides and Argyll; the Free Presbyterians are strong in Skye, Harris and North Uist; while the APCs are found mainly on the mainland. The Free Church (Continuing) has much support in Lewis, but its strongest and most cohesive body of support (as distinct from 'splits') appears to lie in Skye.[14]

It can be debated whether secession or disruption has strengthened or weakened Highland Presbyterianism. The Disruption of 1843 and the creation of the Free Church of Scotland undoubtedly strengthened evangelicalism in the Highlands. The Free Church provided an identity for the various evangelical forces which were at work in the region in the preceding half-century. It is probably true of every disruption or secession in the Highlands that it has provided at least a temporary new identity for a disgruntled group; the new body, reacting against the old, asserts its standards, and enjoys 'liberty' in its own terms. Supporters rally round the new flag. However, the process is likely to repeat itself, and the consequent fragmentation of the churches hardly serves to strengthen their effectiveness in the longer term. Since 1989 it has led to squabbles which have not enhanced the churches' standing in the eyes of the Scottish public, who are now deeply secularized, commonly out of sympathy with Christianity and bemused by contentious clerics. The tendency to fight over theological detail, particularly in defence of subordinate standards like the Westminster Confession, has divided resources and loyalties, sometimes within localities and even families; and it has encouraged a fair degree of strife not only within, but also between, the churches themselves, especially the more conservative churches, since each new body is anxious to claim that it is more loyal to the original intentions of the founders and closer to the 'notes' of the pure church laid down in the Bible and the Westminster Confession.[15]

Secession is, however, only one of the factors that have weakened the contemporary Highland churches. Migration has also curtailed their influence, and has diluted their Gaelic identity. Migration and emigration took people away from the Highlands, and away from the churches, during the nineteenth century. The smaller churches, notably those of Baptists and Independents, were seriously damaged by chain migration.[16] Highlanders who migrated to the Lowlands established Gaelic chapels, in Edinburgh, Glasgow and Aberdeen, and in places like Cromarty.[17] This pattern was replicated in the dominions. Over the past twenty-five years, however, the pattern has worked in the opposite direction, and the Highlands have received an incoming population, with Lowland and non-Highland cultural perspectives. The majority of such people are unlikely to be sympathetic to the churches' position on Highland life and culture, and are therefore liable to be catalysts in the reduction of the churches' power in the face of globalizing forces.

Change within Highland society has also taken place as the Highlands have been exposed progressively to the outside world. During the nineteenth century, but most noticeably in the twentieth, the nature of Highland society has altered dramatically. The old community ethos of the Highlands has all but disappeared in many parts, as the region has become a part of the wider world of British society. Incomers from areas beyond the Highlands and Islands have brought new lifestyles.[18] Television and radio have laid down new yardsticks, especially in the field of morality and social values. Highlanders need no longer look only to the churches for moral guidance. Other values are pervasive, and often more attractive to modern Highlanders. Although church-going is still important in the Highlands, it is evident that not all people in all communities agree with the views of the church. Some of the church's opponents are very capable and are prepared to have their say. A very potent factor in reducing the influence of the churches in Highland society is thus the changing nature of Highland society itself.[19]

EROSION OF GAELIC IDENTITY IN THE TWENTIETH CENTURY

Controlling the Culture

Although the main churches in the Highlands and Islands have entered the region from outside, they have nevertheless been influenced strongly by the Gaelic culture of the area. It may seem to some that the churches have existed in opposition to the culture, but the fact is that they have been able to absorb aspects of that culture, and to work with it, almost without knowing it. All came into existence at a time when Gaelic culture was strong in the region. Gaelic culture imparted to them a particular flavour, making them culturally different from the corresponding wings of the same churches in the Lowlands. It could indeed be argued that 'churches within churches' were formed, because of the distinctiveness of the Highland dimension.

To understand the place and perspectives of the main Highland churches within contemporary society, we have to consider the ways in which they have influenced Highland and Gaelic culture in the past. What have been the traditional roles of the churches in Highland and Gaelic society? Having answered that question, we may then assess how many of these roles are maintained at the present time.

First, we can say that the Protestant churches in the Highlands originally had a civilizing role in the region. Though not a direct arm of the government, they were nevertheless seen as important means of achieving the overall goals of Lowland Scottish, and later British, government in the area. The maintenance of the Protestant church in the Highlands was one of the obligations which were placed on Highland chiefs by the Statutes of Iona in 1609. There was therefore a political dimension to the role of the churches in the Highlands. The civilizing of the Highlands included the eradication of the Gaelic language, which was seen as one of the causes of barbarism in the region. In theory, the church had to acquiesce in the wider aims of government, but in practice it had to use Gaelic as a means of communication. It was therefore committed to the production of books of basic instruction, such as the Gaelic version of Knox's *Book of Common Order*, translated by John Carswell in 1567. Translations of catechisms followed from the 1630s, and the Synod of Argyll attempted (unsuccessfully) to translate the Bible into

Gaelic in the 1650s.[20] Yet, for all their pragmatic use of Gaelic, the Protestant churches in the Highlands retained a potent role as regulators of political involvement well into the nineteenth century.

Second, the Protestant churches promoted a programme of moral improvement. The eradication of habits which were deemed unhelpful to ordinary living was high on their list of priorities. Christians were to be different from the world, and the world itself required to be cleansed of its evil. Thus the churches waged a campaign against excessive consumption of alcohol and immorality. In effect, the church was a moral policeman, and inculcated its programme through the Kirk session. Parishioners who had transgressed were summoned before the Kirk session, and were fined. The churches also tried to separate people from practices, such as superstitious customs and revelries of various kinds, which were considered to be harmful to life. It has to be said, however, that during the course of the eighteenth century, the Established Church was rather lax in the preservation of these aims in the Highlands, and the relative dominance of Moderate, non-evangelical ministers led to decadence. The balance was redressed firmly when evangelicalism began to enter the Highlands powerfully from the end of the eighteenth century. Communion services, which were in effect 'holy fairs' in the late eighteenth and early nineteenth century, were transformed into sacred occasions, when preaching by popular ministers and the sharing of spiritual experience became the keynotes. The increasingly evangelical complexion of the church meant that great stress was laid on separating genuine Christians from the evils of the world; the lines of demarcation between the church and the world were firmly drawn. Sabbath-keeping was given a high priority.[21]

Third, the Protestant churches had a high commitment to education. This followed from the commitment of the reformers to the provision of schooling in the parishes. Scholars like Donald Withrington have argued that the provision of parish schools in the Highlands was probably more extensive than has been allowed by writers such as Durkacz and Withers. By the early eighteenth century the educational role of the church was being supplemented by ancillary agencies like the Society in

Scotland for Propagating Christian Knowledge (SSPCK). In the nineteenth century, the Highland educational programme, so to speak, was intensified by the arrival of the Gaelic Schools Societies, which aimed to make the people sufficiently literate in Gaelic to be able to read the Gaelic Bible. The Gaelic Bible was the main textbook of the Gaelic schools.[22] As part of its educational role, the Established Church produced books for the benefit of those who became literate in the Gaelic schools, and was able to implant political, social and moral perspectives through literature. In the first half of the nineteenth century these were uniformly pro-establishment. The Disruption of the church in 1843 tended to divide the resources and the readerships, however, and important journals were unable to find sufficient subscribers.[23] In 1872, when the Education Act was passed and education was nationalized, the role of the churches was severely curtailed. Gaelic scholarship too gradually lost ecclesiastical support. Ministers of all the major denominations had made significant contributions to collecting, editing and writing Gaelic material from at least the middle of the eighteenth century, but by the early twentieth century ministerial devotion to Gaelic studies had diminished considerably, and was the exception rather than the rule by 2000.[24] Although Departments of Celtic were established at the Universities of Edinburgh, Glasgow and Aberdeen from 1882 to provide sound academic training in Gaelic for ministerial candidates, as well as for those entering other professions, the departments contributed in the long term to the laicization of Gaelic scholarship.[25]

Fourth, the overall work of the churches in the Highlands can be summed up in one word – mission. The churches' concern with mission increased during the eighteenth century, and was intensified by the missionary drive which was inherent in evangelicalism. At the end of the eighteenth century, the Highlands had the status of a foreign mission field in the eyes of the various voluntary bodies which were set up to engage in what is called 'home mission'. In the national context, the distinctive nature of the Highlands as a mission field came to be acknowledged by the creation of special sections of the wider denominational structure. These were given a particular remit to look after the Highlands.[26]

Well into the twentieth century, the churches generally tended to preserve the view that the Highlands and Islands constituted an area which was in particular need of spiritual attention, compared with other parts of Scotland. Indeed, the Church of Scotland maintained lay 'missionaries' in the islands until at least the 1960s. Such an approach had a somewhat patronizing ring to it, but it helped to preserve Gaelic commitment. Most Church of Scotland 'missionaries' were Gaelic-speaking men. However, as the Highlands and Islands became more evidently bilingual and were penetrated increasingly by Lowland culture, the need to create and maintain special arrangements for the Highlands became less pressing, and specific Highland agencies were absorbed into the larger structures of the denominations. 'Home mission' was assumed to be a normal part of the churches' work, rather than a distinctive aspect in need of promotion by special structures.[27] At the beginning of the twenty-first century, it is debatable how far the churches are able to maintain a strong missionary role, except in the broadest terms. As financial support declines, often as a result of secessions or internal conflict, or simply through loss of members, survival rather than mission is becoming the chief concern of most churches.

To sum up these processes, then, we can say that the churches have had a powerful influence on Highland society since the seventeenth century, through their political alliances, their regulation of morals through the Kirk session, through social welfare, education and mission. Substantial changes have, however, taken place. We may now consider how far the churches have retained their power in these domains, in the face of the various attritional processes which have been at work since 1900.

Keeping Control

As far as the twentieth century is concerned, we can eliminate the churches' role in education to a very large extent. Since 1872, education has been within the remit of the local authorities and national agencies. We can also eliminate the churches' role as significant publishers of Gaelic literature. This role has been seriously affected by the loss of their educational function. They publish Gaelic books only very occasionally. Similarly, the churches have lost influence in the area of social welfare. The usual pattern nowadays is for individual denominations to maintain eventide homes for older members, but, on balance, their role in social welfare is relatively slight. Here, as in education, responsibility has passed to secular authorities, with occasional clerical or ecclesiastical input.

Where the Presbyterian churches do retain their influence to a certain extent is in the field of moral guardianship. Thus the churches are very active in inculcating moral values consistent with their understanding of the Bible. They also do their utmost to preserve Sabbath observance and, in Lewis and Harris in particular, they offer strong opposition to the possibility of Sunday sailings by Caledonian MacBrayne. Likewise, they will oppose the Sunday opening of hotels and public houses, and will go to the expense of hiring QCs to support their case. The granting and extension of licences for the sale of strong drink are often opposed by the churches. Issues of national significance are sometimes raised by the more conservative bodies, often in order to rebuke secularizing tendencies.[28]

In this respect, the Presbyterian churches still see themselves as having a duty to keep society clean. The great evangelical thrusts into the Highlands in the course of the eighteenth and nineteenth centuries cast the churches in the roles of purifiers of what was perceived to be an impure society. The fact that they adhered to the establishment principle gave them the authority to 'police' wider society, and to place restraints on people who might not be churchgoers themselves. Nowadays the churches might be described as the negative conscience of society, reacting against trends which they do not like, rather than taking positive action. Having lost their earlier roles as powerful institutions, they have not replaced them with structures which might help to reassert their principles sensitively in terms of contemporary society. No Highland church known to me has produced a blueprint for linguistic, social or political development within the region.

In political matters, the churches have, on the whole, been less than enthusiastic participants. It is probably true to say that the

Highland wings of the churches are fairly conservative in their public voice, though their ministers and members represent a varied cross-section of political opinion. It could still be claimed, nevertheless, that the churches encourage political quietism and loyalty to the establishment, including the British crown. Ministers of the various churches have served in recent years as councillors on local councils, as have priests. The first convener of the Western Isles Islands Council, the Revd Donald MacAulay, was a Church of Scotland minister. It is, however, clear that, for members of the more conservative Presbyterian bodies, public service of this kind is not without its hazards. The Free Presbyterian Church, for instance, has been uneasy with the actions of some of its ministers who have served on local councils, and at least one has been the subject of censure – a censure which was one of the factors which added to the tension which resulted in the creation of the Associated Presbyterian Churches in 1989. The difficulty is that involvement in secular affairs exposes ministers and members of the churches to contamination by the world.[29]

Contemporary Culture

When the Free Presbyterian Church of Scotland – the smallest of the main Presbyterian denominations in the Highlands – was created in 1893, the Highlands came close to having their own distinctively Highland and thoroughly Gaelic church, but, in due time, the Free Presbyterian Church extended its congregations to embrace bodies in the Lowlands and England. Most recently it has added to its number two congregations, one in Canada and the other in Texas, which came into contact with the Free Presbyterians through information placed on the Internet. The Free Presbyterians, often regarded as the most conservative of all the Presbyterian denominations in the Highlands, are obviously not averse to the use of modern technology in the search for members. According to one Free Presbyterian minister, 'The Romans built roads before the coming of Christ and their engineering marvels helped spread the word of God. So e-mail may also prove to be a wonderful way to spread the word of God around the world.'³⁰ This initial affirmation of the value of the Internet, coming from a Free Presbyterian, is particularly interesting, since one might have expected the Free Presbyterians to be extremely wary of the Internet because of its potential for distributing highly dubious material intended to corrupt, rather than to edify, the recipient.

The appreciation of the Internet as a means of communicating the gospel stood in contrast to the despairing view which the same minister took of the Gaelic language. Only a few weeks previously, he had proclaimed that, 'As far as the FP Church is concerned, Gaelic is now at an end. I say that with a heavy heart, but it's God's providence that this be so.'³¹ The difference in attitude hinges on the fact that Free Presbyterians have encountered severe difficulties in maintaining a Gaelic-speaking ministry, despite their position as the most thoroughly Gaelic of all the denominations in the Highlands and Islands. Gaelic is seen to belong to the past, and to be outmoded, in sharp contrast to the potential of the Internet.

The minister quoted above is always at pains to emphasize that he is expressing a personal view of Gaelic when he makes such statements. Other ministers are more guarded, and most prefer to stay silent on language issues, but it is by no means unlikely that this perception will be found in churches other than the Free Presbyterians. Similarly, ministers in other denominations will make pragmatic judgements on the value of such things as the Internet; not all aspects of twentieth-century culture come under suspicion, though many aspects of secular culture are rejected by the Highland churches. Much depends on whether they can or cannot be harnessed to proclaim the gospel, and that same pragmatism applies to the Gaelic language.³²

In assessing the ways in which the churches approach Gaelic, we need to bear in mind that Gaelic culture, including language, has given a distinctive shape to the Highland sectors of these churches. This means that the churches must strive to meet a range of culturally conditioned expectations, and such expectations can create tensions when they cannot be readily fulfilled. The churches have to acknowledge the simple fact that Gaelic preaching is still preferred in many parts of the islands, though less so on the mainland. Worship, to be meaningful to a considerable proportion of people in Lewis, for instance, has to be Gaelic worship. To provide Gaelic worship, Gaelic preachers are required, and the Free Presbyterians are not alone in encountering considerable difficulties in maintaining a supply of Gaelic ministers. This is not necessarily because the Almighty has turned his back on Gaelic, as an occasional Free Presbyterian minister might claim. Rather, it is because the churches have failed to develop adequate strategies for the training and placement of Gaelic ministers — a point to which I shall return. Beyond the question of the language itself, it is also evident that styles of preaching, praying and singing have been influenced by Gaelic tradition.[33]

The Gaelic cultural context in which the churches operate has been, and continues to be, a conservative one. This has helped the churches to maintain a conservative view of theology, and worship, and also of culture, though they are now inclined to reject Gaelic as a medium of communication. Even in areas where Gaelic has ceased to be used, it is often possible to recognize a Gaelic or Highland tone to the worship of the more conservative churches.[34]

The Highland churches are able to plan their own response to the culture and the challenges which it presents in their respective areas. This is evident beyond the Presbyterian bodies. The Roman Catholic Church is able to address and serve the island areas through the Diocese of Argyll and the Isles. It is noteworthy that the Catholic Church has been able to maintain a supply of Gaelic-speaking priests fairly successfully for its island charges. This may have something to do with the close sense of Gaelic identity within the diocese; but it also has to do with the way in which Roman Catholics view culture. At parish level, Catholics do not maintain the dividing line which so clearly separates sacred from secular in the evangelical wings of the Protestant churches. In the Roman Catholic context, separation from the world is achieved through monastic seclusion.

Even so, the Diocese of Argyll and the Isles was not without difficulties in the 1990s, which, in retrospect, can be seen to have been a disastrous decade for most Highland churches. These difficulties may have affected the status of Gaelic as perceived by Catholic leaders beyond the diocese. The most recent incumbent of the bishopric of Argyll and the Isles, Bishop Ian Murray, appointed in 1999, does not speak Gaelic. Murray's eventual appointment followed a three-year vacancy in the diocese, caused by the spectacular departure of Bishop Roddy Wright, who abandoned his diocese to take up residence with his future wife.[35] The dramatic and high-profile disappearance of Wright – a Gaelic speaker with family roots in South Uist – may have reduced the importance of Gaelic in the eyes of the hierarchy, who may have been concerned to find a bishop with strong pastoral gifts, irrespective of his linguistic qualifications. Bishop Murray has nevertheless given strong support to Gaelic initiatives within his diocese.[36]

The Presbyterian churches exert local power through their Presbyteries, operating within their own districts. While answerable ultimately to the Synods and General Assemblies of the churches, the Presbyteries have considerable power at ground level, so to speak. This is certainly true of the Presbyteries of the Free Church of Scotland and the Free Presbyterian Church. The Highland Presbyteries are known for their distinctiveness, and the wider Scottish denominations are often reminded forcefully of the existence, and distinctive perspectives, of their Highland parishes and Presbyteries. When theological or other controversies arise, there is a marked tendency for the Highland wings of the churches to be on the conservative side, and to be very vocal in making their views known. Perhaps it would be nearer the mark to say that the island churches are on the conservative side, while the mainland churches tend to become less and less conservative as one moves south. The current tensions within the Free Church of Scotland indicate that there are aspects of modern church life, that is to say aspects of 'church culture' in its broadest sense, which certain members and ministers of the Free Church do not wish to countenance, and on these matters there is often something of a north–south divide.

The Cultural Pyramid

How do the Presbyterian churches generally view Highland culture, and specifically Gaelic culture, at the beginning of the twenty-first century? In broad terms, their attitudes can be represented by drawing an inverted pyramid, with the larger churches at the 'broad end' showing a greater willingness to accommodate Gaelic culture, the middle-range churches showing some commitment and the smaller churches (as one approaches the narrow end of the inverted pyramid) showing no interest, or lacking the Gaelic-speaking capacity to do so. This model has ominous implications for the maintenance of Gaelic ministry within an increasingly fragmented ecclesiastical context. Although new bodies which have split from older alignments may be able to sustain some degree of Gaelic ministry in the shorter term, they are unlikely to be able to maintain it in the longer term. In Lewis, groups which have left the official Free Church already make much use of retired ministers and elders to maintain Gaelic services.[37]

There is also a possible link between the maintenance of Gaelic and the type of theology that prevails within the bodies represented in the pyramid. At the risk of some generalization, it may be said that the churches with the 'broader' theology are similarly those at the upper end of the model, and that theology tends to become narrower as the bodies become smaller. The loss of Gaelic may signal not only shrinking cultural horizons, but also a more 'committed' theology, which tends to be exclusive or more closely regulated by loyalty to a confessional position. Finding Gaelic ministers in such a context may be very difficult, particularly if such men, scarce at the best of times, are required to go through the eye of the theological needle. Furthermore, in churches which have traditionally accommodated a range of theological perspectives, it is conceivable that Gaelic may have had a 'cohering' or 'cushioning' effect which encouraged tolerance. 'Cultural cushioning' is certainly evident in the relationship between Protestants and Roman Catholics in the Highlands across the centuries; bigotry is hardly in evidence, and is publicly inarticulate, because of the shared Gaelic culture.[38] The elimination of Gaelic may thus make it more, rather than less, likely that theological tension will enter the Highlands, particularly from non-Gaelic bodies at the bottom end of the proposed pyramid, and that the tension will work its way upwards to the larger bodies in the years ahead.

Looking at some bodies individually, it is clear that, in the Church of Scotland, there is a much wider spectrum of opinion on cultural matters than one would find in the other churches. Members and adherents of the Church of Scotland would vary in their attitudes to Gaelic culture; some would be happy to attend cèilidhs and dances, and ministers might occasionally act as chairpersons at cèilidhs and concerts. It is evident that, in the twentieth century, the Church of Scotland has been the body which has given most support to the development of Gaelic culture. A number of Church of Scotland ministers have been very happy to support *An Comunn Gàidhealach*, for instance, and several have made major contributions to Gaelic scholarship. The Revd Thomas Moffat Murchison (d. 1984) edited *An Comunn Gàidhealach*'s newspaper, *An Gàidheal*, and gave prominent support to the Mod – a position unthinkable among Free Presbyterians.[39]

It is also clear that, within the Free Church of Scotland, there is a range of opinion with regard to the limits of what may be termed 'church culture', 'culture beyond the church' and overtly secular culture. Some Free Church members and adherents are inclined to draw a distinction between what happens within the actual church on the Sabbath day, or on occasions of formal worship, and what happens in a non-formal setting. On the basis of such evidence, it could be said that culture as such is not, in itself, a big issue as far as the churches are concerned. It becomes an issue only when members or adherents of churches, and especially office-bearers, cross the line of demarcation which, in the view of church leaders, separates the world from the church, or compromise worship styles as laid down by the 'regulative principle'. At that point, negative views are expressed, usually by one denomination at the expense of another, but sometimes by one Presbytery against another. At present, denominational point-scoring (or hitting out at factions within the denomination) seems to be the main aim of such sallies.[40]

Defining one's position relative to the boundary line between sacred and secular is always a challenge for those in the churches. After all, they do have to live in the real world, rather than the world of retrospective virtual reality. It is probably true to say that members and adherents adopt a fairly discerning approach to secular culture, an approach which is able to distinguish between the more dangerous threats of the secular world and relatively innocent temporal pursuits. Free Church members and adherents have been active in local history societies, *comainn eachdraidh*, and some have made, and continue to make, major contributions to the preservation of Gaelic language and culture.

How members and adherents act relative to secular culture does not necessarily reflect the institutional view, so to speak, particularly as articulated by the clergy. Though members and adherents help to maintain the Gaelic language, for example, the same cannot always be said about the institutions themselves. It is perhaps fairest to say that, with regard to Gaelic, the churches as institutions tend to emit conflicting signals so that, on balance, the institutional view of Gaelic appears to be neither supportive nor unsupportive. A kind of silent neutrality prevails, broken only by the very occasional statement for or against the language by individual ministers who are brave enough to break the silence. Generally the churches do not make any major public statements which are supportive of Gaelic. On the practical side, they do not undertake any major new initiatives on behalf of the language even within their own ranks. While it is obvious to many that the lack of Gaelic preachers in the churches could be remedied, at least partly, by courses within the denominational training colleges or the universities, the churches have not made any institutional moves to provide such courses or to support those which already exist, although they may offer bursaries to students who want to learn Gaelic. Some of the denominations have gained considerable financial benefit because of their associations with Gaelic.[41] Some, too, have funds which have been provided specifically for the training of Gaelic preachers. Nevertheless, they have few opportunities to apply these funds within their own institutions, while there is no policy of resource-sharing which would allow co-operation with secular bodies which may have the expertise to help. The churches are willing to sustain Gaelic-speaking ministers in Gaelic charges when such men are available, but they have no programme to ensure that such men will be trained adequately if or when they appear. The churches do not protest when 'Gaelic essential' charges are changed to become 'Gaelic desirable', and thus obtain a minister who cannot speak Gaelic (as has happened in Stornoway High Church of Scotland).[42]

There are, however, occasional signs that some Presbyteries are aware of the need for policies to support Gaelic. As recently as the spring of 1997, the Free Church Presbytery of Lewis produced a Gaelic policy aimed at strengthening the place of Gaelic in the bounds of the Presbytery, but it remains to be seen how this policy will be implemented.[43] Apart from the funding of Gaelic ministries where these are naturally provided, so to speak, the main denominations produce Gaelic pages or Gaelic supplements as part of their national organs. Their publishing houses have all but abandoned their earlier Gaelic interests, and publish Gaelic books only occasionally. The official Free Church of Scotland, however, has provided a range of Gaelic texts on its Website, and thus offers a very useful service (in another sense) for Gaelic readers and learners of the language. In this respect, the church's contribution is consistent with trends which will surely increase and diversify the use of the Internet as a textual resource for Gaelic and other languages in the years ahead. The Free Church, nevertheless, makes it clear that, in providing Gaelic texts, language maintenance is not its primary concern:

> Tha an eaglais air a gairm gu bhith a' craobh-sgaoileadh an t-soisgeul anns a' cheud aite, agus chan ann gu bhith a' dion canain. Ach tha meas aig daoine air a' chanain, agus tha iad a' miannachadh a bhith 'ga faicinn air a cleachdadh agus air a misneachadh.
>
> The church is called to propagate the gospel in the first place, and not to preserve a language. But people are fond of the language, and they wish to see it being used and encouraged.[44]

The Free Church is thus anxious to distance itself from Gaelic language revivalism. Beyond the Church of Scotland, the view taken by the churches of what is popularly called 'the Gaelic lobby' tends to be negative. According to one representative of the Free Church of Scotland, the Gaelic lobby has 'little or no interest in the church' (as was claimed in the *Free Church Record* in August 1996). This flies in the face of the evidence that Free Church members and adherents are among the most committed supporters of Gaelic initiatives, though perhaps the churches would not regard their own flock, however committed to language, as part of the 'Gaelic lobby'. The 'lobby' consists of the vocal activists. Presumably the Free Church suspects that hidden agendas are at work.[45] One might, however, reach the conclusion that the more conservative churches, which were once bastions of Gaelic preaching and publishing, are aware that they have lost the initiative in Gaelic language development, and are seeking ways to justify their current official non-involvement by attributing a wholly secular, if not anti-church, mind-set to the promoters of the language. The churches appear to resent the fact that Gaelic-language bodies have taken over the promotion of the language; these bodies are perceived to have commandeered Gaelic for entirely secular ends. Investment in Gaelic television is sometimes seen by the more conservative ministers as a way of opening the door to moral values of which they strongly disapprove, particularly in the one and only 'soap opera', *Machair*, which was broadcast on Gaelic television.[46] The possibility that some of the new money available for Gaelic television could be used constructively for the development of religious programming is not one which is actively pursued, beyond the screening of Gaelic services. The churches, it would seem, are not too keen to use money from secular sources to promote Christian values in wider society, even when there are many opportunities for that, and the world is crying out for a positive Christian presence. The view taken by the incoming apostolic and other groups – that the traditional churches are generally weak on mission – is probably accurate in general terms.

New Churches

As the traditional Highland churches have 'fought the good fight' on various issues, other smaller bodies have continued to come into the region. To some degree, these bodies are repeating the patterns characteristic of Baptists and Congregationalists who penetrated the Highlands and Islands in the early nineteenth century, but it must be noted that, in the case of the Baptists at least, the impetus is not based on the old-style missionary endeavour that planted the first generation of churches before 1850. Retirement, disenchantment with previous roles beyond the Highlands, job availability and a range of personal factors, have brought several 'new Baptists' to the region. Such people do not fit easily into the predominantly Presbyterian structures of their areas, and this has been a stimulus to missionary activity.

Over the last decade or so, new evangelical groups, some of them associated with wider Scottish and British networks of various kinds, have arrived in the mainland Highlands and the Inner Hebrides. Small independent churches and congregations associated with the Apostolic Fellowship are to be found in Skye, Kyle and Glenelg, and in Stornoway, Tain, Nairn and Newtonmore.[47] A small Baptist venture, unrelated to earlier Baptist work in Skye, is under way in Bracadale, and is led by a couple who are formally connected with the Baptist Union of Great Britain (rather than the Baptist Union of Scotland). A Scottish Baptist church has recently been formed in Dingwall.[48]

It is unlikely that the new groups will recruit many older Gaelic speakers, since the latter will be aware of significant cultural differences, and may be uneasy in the 'close' and informal environment which these groups encourage. Their main recruits are likely to be people, probably 'incomers' in the first instance, who, like the leaders themselves, have been unable to find a place within existing Presbyterian structures. Nevertheless, the groups will aim to evangelize their localities, in the face of what they will probably regard as 'neglect' by the Presbyterian churches and 'traditional' or 'out of date' religiosity. Their general perception of existing religious patterns will be of an old-fashioned, and largely lifeless, loyalty to outmoded practices. While some of these groups may be inclined to encourage the pentecostal gift of tongues, they are very unlikely to have any deep interest in the indigenous Gaelic tongue. Gaelic too will be regarded as a thing of the past, irrelevant to the faith. Both the size and the cultural attitudes of these groups place them firmly at the sharp (lower) end of the inverted pyramid described above.

Despite their earlier Gaelic affiliations, Baptists too would occupy a similar position in this model. The older Baptist congregations of the Inner Hebrides had lost their Gaelic preaching capacity by 1965, and had to move to English-only ministries.[49] In so doing, they have found it extremely difficult to identify and maintain forms of ministry which are well suited to the multicultural profile of present-day Highland society. In Baptist churches which have been to some extent revitalized by an incoming group (as in Mull and, more recently, Tiree), the earlier membership, which may be residually Gaelic-speaking, has found it difficult to make adjustments to new worship styles derived from Spring Harvest and other mainstream British evangelical jamborees. Guitars jangling in small island chapels, overhead projectors and more obviously participatory forms of worship, sometimes led by young men and women in casual clothes who are determined to make the congregation learn a constantly changing set of 'choruses' projected on to the wall, do not appeal to the older membership. Comparisons with earlier, more deferential worship patterns are inevitably drawn, and 'renewal' becomes a hollow term, which is often contrasted with the idealized 'revivals' which these churches had experienced in an earlier day.[50]

This reaction is not, however, peculiar to older Baptist members, nor is it restricted to churches. The mounting of local, mildly charismatic 'celebrations', such as 'Skye Alive', in the Highland areas has been greeted with a range of views, from the welcome of younger people and 'incomers' to the condemnation and dismissal of the more conservative Presbyterians. The latter are contemptuous, not only of worship styles, but also of the tendency to 'mix' the denominations and to invite controversial speakers, such as Professor Donald Macleod.[51]

Conclusion

The tensions between, and within, the various ecclesiastical bodies are more than evident in the Highlands today, and interweave to some degree with cultural change in the region. This may be an indicator, in broad terms, of the churches' difficulties in coming to terms with contemporary cultural patterns. The nature and amount of strife within the churches since the late 1980s is rooted in their desire to be faithful to the purity of the true church, in the face of globalizing tendencies and loss of adherence to spiritual yardsticks. But it also demonstrates a gradual loss of authority, which is recovered periodically through the very firm use of Presbyterian principles against 'dissidents'. To non-Presbyterians, the assertion of such principles by the more 'moderate' party may well seem heavy-handed, if not even jack-booted. At the very least, it is an incontrovertibly clear indication that the Presbyterian churches are far from healthy, and that they are struggling to control dissent engendered by the activities of high-profile members. As wider forces come into play, a certain kind of cumbersome control is being reasserted at a massive price – though, according to influential ecclesiastical leaders, it is a price worth paying for the 'peace' of the church.

As they wrestle to control their disenchanted members and maverick ministers, it is also evident that the churches are not now as active as they once were in the communities, and that they are gradually losing their links with the culture around them. The battle for purity is being waged increasingly within the churches, at the same time as the culture of the Highlands and Islands is changing in a manner which the churches cannot regulate as effectively as they once did. There may thus be a link between the development of a new Highland pluralist culture with the accompanying erosion of Gaelic, and the tendency of the churches to fragment into more conservative or more progressive realignments.

It is hard to know how long the Highland churches will be able to preserve their influence in the fields which are still within their grasp, or how long they will maintain a serious commitment to Gaelic. As we enter the twenty-first century, it is becoming evident that the churches are devoting much of their energy to maintaining the status quo in the face of diminishing (and increasingly divided) resources, rather than to promoting any new approach to evangelism and social action. For old bodies, as for new, survival is the first priority. The maintenance of the status quo is becoming harder not only because congregations are dwindling, but also because the churches do, in fact, have within them ministers and other spokespersons who are not prepared to toe the conventional line on ecclesiastical, political and other issues. This sometimes leads to internal strife which

EROSION OF GAELIC IDENTITY IN THE TWENTIETH CENTURY

grabs the headlines, produces raucous and controversial articles in the press, and increases the public perception of 'Highland Christianity' as a negative, and ultimately self-destructive, force. The broader cushion of public sympathy is thus eroded, and the gulf between the churches and secular society grows ever greater.

The fact that such self-defeating strife is created partly in an attempt to modernize the churches, and to make them more relevant to 'the world out there', is unfortunate. Modernization, which retains intact the core of the Christian faith but recognizes both the older Gaelic culture and the variety of incoming cultures, is urgently needed. In the meantime, there is a distinct possibility, indeed a probability, that the new charismatic fellowships, already established in small towns from Kyle of Lochalsh to Tain, will occupy an increasingly significant place in Highland church life as disenchantment with existing structures grows.

Given the wider challenges and issues with which they have to grapple, it is hardly surprising that the churches have little time or inclination to worry about Gaelic. Whatever the views of individuals within the churches may be with regard to Gaelic, it is evident that the churches as institutions are taking a back pew in promoting the language, at a time when their support would be most valuable. This suggests that they are indeed uncomfortable in the pluralist culture of the Highlands, that they are uneasy with the inroads being made by new activists and promoters of the language, and that they have ceased to use Gaelic (even negatively) as a shield against modernization. Despite some degree of support for Gaelic, they appear to accept, almost by default, that, as English is fast becoming the main language of the Highlands, it should be used in the churches. Maintaining a commitment to Gaelic may, for them, be only a matter of time. Their Gaelic identity, such as it is, can be jettisoned for ever. The gospel is more important than Gaelic, and the message is more important than the medium.

The consequences for Gaelic are stark. Gaelic may once have been regarded as 'the language of heaven', but it is probably safe to conclude that it is no longer considered to be the primary medium for the message of the gospel in the Highlands and Islands. The consequences for the churches may also be stark. It may be that the dominant Presbyterian bodies are winning the battle with 'dissidents', but they are gradually losing the war with cultural change and pluralism, and are bidding farewell to many loyal members who have been wounded on one or other of the front lines. Derick Thomson's poem, 'Dùsgadh', has much relevance to the contemporary Highland churches, as the region bids fair to become the graveyard of competing creeds and factions. His concluding lines, with their wistful prayer for a revival of natural paganism, may be as much a prophecy as a rebuke:

> O, nan tigeadh soisgeulaiche
> a lorgadh ceann-teagaisg air na seann chreagan seo,
> anns a riasg donn,
> ann a flùraichean na machrach,
> nar cainnt fhìn.
>
> O for an evangelist
> who would find a text on these ancient rocks,
> in the brown peat,
> in the flowers of the machair,
> in our own language.

Notes

[1] Readers should note that, because most of the events and circumstances which are described in this chapter are (at the time of writing) very recent, I am offering to some extent my own impressions and preliminary observations, which are subject to personal bias (though I should make it clear that I am not in membership of any of the churches or denominations which are discussed). I am grateful to other observers of ecclesiastical affairs in the Highlands who have helped me to clarify my thoughts; in particular, I wish to thank Fraser MacDonald, Research Fellow at the Arkleton Institute, University of Aberdeen, for several illuminating discussions and useful references.

[2] Ruaraidh MacThòmais, *Creachadh na Clàrsaich: Plundering the Harp; Cruinneachadh de Bhàrdachd 1940–1980* (Edinburgh, 1982), pp. 150–1.

[3] The main works which give an overview of the Protestant and Presbyterian churches are John MacInnes, *The Evangelical Movement in the Highlands of Scotland, 1688–1800* (Aberdeen,

1951), and Douglas Ansdell, *The People of the Great Faith: The Highland Church, 1690–1900* (Stornoway, 1998). For Roman Catholicism, see Roderick Macdonald, 'The Catholic Gaidhealtachd', *Innes Review*, XXIX (Spring 1978), 56–72; Alasdair Roberts, 'Roman Catholicism in the Highlands', in James Kirk (ed.), *The Church in the Highlands* (Edinburgh, 1999), pp. 63–88.

4 The Episcopal Church in the Highlands has been very seriously neglected by contemporary historians, but this imbalance is due to be redressed in a forthcoming book by Dr Rowan Strong, Murdoch University, Australia, which contains a chapter on 'Highland Episcopalianism'.

5 Donald E. Meek, 'Evangelical missionaries in the early nineteenth-century Highlands', *Scottish Studies*, XXVIII (1987), 1–34.

6 Douglas Ansdell, 'Disruptions and controversies in the Highland church', in Kirk (ed.), *The Church in the Highlands*, pp. 89–113.

7 Kenneth B. E. Roxburgh, *Thomas Gillespie and the Origins of the Relief Church in Eighteenth Century Scotland* (Bern, 1999).

8 Ansdell, *The People of the Great Faith*, pp. 53–5.

9 Ibid., pp. 183–211.

10 There is as yet no reliable history of the emergence of the APC grouping. Accounts such as that found in John MacLeod, *No Great Mischief if you Fall* (Edinburgh, 1993), pp. 119–34, tend to be somewhat personalized.

11 This observation is based on personal acquaintance with the members of one such group.

12 Again, we are too close to events to analyse the dynamics of this secession. The *Monthly Record of the Free Church of Scotland* and its rival *Free Church Foundations* for the period 1997–2000 carry their own interpretations in articles and editorials; see, for example, 'Around the church' and 'What was the secession about?', *Monthly Record* (March 2000), 52–6. The trial of Professor Macleod was reported extensively in Scottish newspapers in 1996. For an overview of the circumstances leading to the trial, and its subsequent impact on the churches, see Fraser MacDonald, 'Scenes of ecclesiastical theatre in the Free Church of Scotland, 1981–2000', *Northern Scotland*, XX (2000), 125–48.

13 Ironically, it was the Free Church Presbytery of Lewis that finally proscribed the Free Church Defence Association; see 'Scenes of ecclesiastical theatre', p. 142.

14 This reflects the presence in Skye of ministers such as the Revd William MacLeod, Portree, who were key figures in the FCDA, and have joined the FC(C).

[15] For some general perspectives on this tendency with some specific reference to Scotland, see Steve Bruce, 'Authority and fission: the Protestants' divisions', *British Journal of Sociology*, XXXVI/4 (1985), 592–603. See also MacDonald, 'Scenes of ecclesiastical theatre'.

[16] Donald E. Meek, '"The Fellowship of Kindred Minds": some religious aspects of kinship and emigration from the Scottish Highlands in the nineteenth century', in *Hands Across the Water: Emigration from Northern Scotland to North America*, Proceedings of the 6th Annual Conference of the Scottish Association of Family History Societies held on 22 April 1995 at the University of Aberdeen (Aberdeen, 1995), pp. 18–33. MacInnes, *The Evangelical Movement*.

[17] Ian R. MacDonald, 'The beginning of Gaelic preaching in Scotland's cities', *Northern Scotland*, IX (1989), 45–52.

[18] Angus MacLeod and Geoff Payne, '"Locals" and "Incomers": social and cultural identity in late twentieth century Coigach', in John R. Baldwin (ed.), *Peoples and Settlement in North-West Ross* (Edinburgh, 1994), pp. 391–411.

[19] Donald E. Meek, *The Scottish Highlands: The Churches and Gaelic Culture* (Geneva, 1996).

[20] For the political background, see MacInnes, *The Evangelical Movement*. For literary activity, see Donald E. Meek, 'The Reformation and Gaelic culture: perspectives on patronage, language and literature in John Carswell's translation of "The Book of Common Order"', in Kirk (ed.), *The Church in the Highlands*, pp. 37–62.

[21] MacInnes, *The Evangelical Movement*.

[22] D. Withrington, 'Education in the seventeenth century Highlands', in Loraine MacLean of Dochgarroch (ed.), *The Seventeenth Century in the Highlands* (Inverness, 1986), pp. 60–9; Victor Edward Durkacz, *The Decline of the Celtic Languages* (Edinburgh, 1983), pp. 96–153; Charles W. J. Withers, *Gaelic in Scotland, 1698–1981* (Edinburgh, 1984), pp. 161–81.

[23] The most important writer in this respect was the Revd Dr Norman MacLeod, *Caraid nan Gàidheal*: see Donald E. Meek, 'The pulpit and the pen: clergy, literacy and oral tradition in the Scottish Highlands', in Adam Fox and Daniel Woolf (eds.), *The Spoken Word: Oral Culture in Britain, 1500–1850* (Manchester, 2001).

[24] Meek, *Scottish Highlands*, pp. 54–7.

[25] William Gillies, 'A century of Gaelic scholarship', in Gillies (ed.), *Gaelic and Scotland* (Edinburgh, 1989), pp. 3–21; Meek, *Scottish Highlands*, pp. 54–7.

26 Durkacz, *The Decline of the Celtic Languages*, provides some background, but the history of 'home mission' in the Highlands by various churches remains to be written.
27 For Baptist perspectives, see Donald E. Meek, 'Baptists and Highland culture', *Baptist Quarterly*, XXXIII (1989), 155–73 (esp. pp. 169–70).
28 This is particularly evident in the case of the Free Presbyterian Church.
29 Macleod, *No Great Mischief*, p. 122, relates the suspension of the Revd Alex Murray in 1988, for calling on Father Thomas Wynn to pray at a committee meeting of the Highland Regional Council.
30 *Scotsman* (8 January 1998).
31 Peter MacAulay, 'Loosening link between Gaelic and the churches', *West Highland Free Press* (21 November 1997), 7.
32 See further Donald E. Meek, 'God and Gaelic: the Highland churches and Gaelic cultural identity', in Gordon McCoy (ed.), *Gaelic Identities: Aithne na nGael* (Belfast, 2000), pp. 28–47.
33 Gaelic patterns of intonation and rhetorical expression are currently being researched by Ms Julie Heath in the island of Lewis.
34 This is evident in such areas as the Black Isle, for example, with which I am familiar.
35 The case was covered extensively in national newspapers at the time.
36 Ailig Ó Hianlaidh, 'An t-easbaig ùr agus a' Ghàidhlig', *Scotsman* (1 March 2000), 13.
37 'Free Church split causes shortage of ministers', *Scotsman* (26 May 2000), 13. Meek, *Scottish Highlands*, provides some comment; see also Meek, 'God and Gaelic'.
38 In this respect, Gaelic Scotland differs significantly from Northern Ireland, and the importing of Scottish Gaelic is sometimes viewed (rather naïvely) as a possible solution to the political/linguistic tensions posed by the use of Irish in the province. See Meek, 'God and Gaelic', for some further exploration of the wider theme.
39 *An Comunn Gàidhealach* was founded in 1891, and, among many other contributions to the promotion of Gaelic, it has organized the National Mod annually to the present day. See Frank Thompson, *The First Hundred: Centenary History of An Comunn Gàidhealach* (Inverness, 1992). Also, Meek, *Scottish Highlands*, pp. 54–7.
40 A revealing example of this can be found in 'The Church and world (2)', *Free Presbyterian Magazine*, CII (April 1997), 124–5. The incident is used by the commentator to claim that 'the level of spirituality within the [Free] Church is far from what it ought to be'. This naturally implies that the spirituality of his own Church is 'what it ought to be'.

41 Meek, *Scottish Highlands*, provides some comment; see also Meek, 'God and Gaelic'.
42 Pàdraig MacAmhlaigh, 'Eaglais ann an staid mu chànan/Church lost for words on Gaelic policy', *Scotsman* (7 January 1998), 12.
43 Copy in writer's possession.
44 Free Church of Scotland Website.
45 See my somewhat indignant response to this claim in the *Monthly Record* (October 1996), 229.
46 This view has been expressed to me in correspondence by one minister.
47 I am very grateful to Alasdair Matheson, pastor of Skye Bible Church, Portree, Isle of Skye, for providing me (in August 1998) with an illuminating overview of these churches.
48 Information from the Highlands and Islands Strategy Group of the Baptist Union of Scotland, on which I serve as an adviser.
49 Meek, 'Baptists and Highland culture', pp. 168–9.
50 I am familar with these tensions through my knowledge of the churches concerned.
51 This approach was taken by *Free Church Foundations*, II (October 1997). For Professor Macleod's view on the contemporary Highland churches, see Donald Macleod, 'The Highland churches today', in Kirk (ed.), *The Church in the Highlands*, pp. 146–76.

Select Bibliography

General

Bradshaw, B., and Morrill, J. (eds.), *The British Problem, c.1543–1707* (London, 1996).
Bradshaw, B., and Roberts, P. (eds.), *British Consciousness and Identity: The Making of Britain, 1533–1707* (Cambridge, 1998).
Colley, L., *Britons: Forging the Nation, 1707–1837* (London, 1994).
Kidd, C., *British Identities Before Nationalism: Ethnicity and Nationhood in the Atlantic World, 1600–1800* (Cambridge, 1999).
Murdoch, A., *British History, 1660–1832: National Identity and Local Culture* (London, 1998).
Pittock, M., *Inventing and Resisting Britain: Cultural Identities in Britain and Ireland, 1685–1989* (London, 1997).

Wales

Ballard, Paul H., and Jones, D. Huw (eds.), *This Land and People* (Cardiff, 1979).
Davies, D. Hywel, *The Welsh Nationalist Party, 1925–1945: A Call to Nationhood* (Cardiff, 1983).
Davies, John, *A History of Wales* (London, 1994).
Hughes, Trystan Owain, *Winds of Change: The Roman Catholic Church and Society in Wales, 1916–1962* (Cardiff, 1999).
Jenkins, Geraint H., *Literature, Religion and Society in Wales, 1660–1730* (Cardiff, 1978).
Jenkins, Geraint H., *The Foundations of Modern Wales, 1642–1780* (Oxford, 1993).
Jenkins, Geraint H. (ed.), *The Welsh Language Before the Industrial Revolution* (Cardiff, 1997).

SELECT BIBLIOGRAPHY

Jenkins, Geraint H. (ed.), *The Welsh Language and its Social Dimensions, 1801–1911* (Cardiff, 2000).
Jones, R. Tudur, *The Desire of Nations* (Llandybïe, 1974).
Morgan, D. Densil, *The Span of the Cross: Christian Religion and Society in Wales, 1914–2000* (Cardiff, 1999).
Morgan, Derec Llwyd, *The Great Awakening in Wales*, tr. Dyfnallt Morgan (London, 1988).
Morgan, Kenneth O., *Rebirth of a Nation: Wales, 1880–1980* (Oxford and Cardiff, 1981).
Morgan, Kenneth O., *Wales in British Politics, 1868–1921* (Cardiff, 1995).
Morgan, Kenneth O., *Renewal and Reformation: Wales c.1415–1642* (Oxford, 1993).
Tudur, Geraint, *Howell Harris: From Conversion to Separation, 1735–1750* (Cardiff, 2000).
Williams, Glanmor, *Religion, Language and Nationality in Wales* (Cardiff, 1979).
Williams, Glanmor, *The Welsh and their Religion* (Cardiff, 1991).
Williams, Glyn (ed.), *Crisis of Economy and Ideology: Essays on Welsh Society, 1840–1980* (Bangor, 1983).
Williams, Gwyn A., *When Was Wales?* (London, 1985).

Scotland

Ansdell, Douglas, *The People of the Great Faith: The Highland Church, 1690–1900* (Stornoway, 1998).
Broun, D., and Clancy, T. O. (eds.), *Spes Scotorum: Hope of Scots* (Edinburgh, 1999).
Broun, D., Finlay, R. J., and Lynch, M. (eds.), *Image and Identity: The Making and Remaking of Modern Scotland through the Ages* (Edinburgh, 1998).
Brown, C. G., *Religion and Society in Scotland since 1707* (Edinburgh, 1997).
Brown, Stewart J., *Thomas Chalmers and the Godly Commonwealth in Scotland* (Oxford, 1982).
Devine, T. M., and Young, J. R. (eds.), *Eighteenth Century Scotland: New Perspectives* (Edinburgh, 1999).
Drummond, A. L., and Bulloch, J., *The Scottish Church, 1688–1843* (Edinburgh, 1973).
Ferguson, W., *The Identity of the Scottish Nation: An Historical Quest* (Edinburgh, 1998).
Gillies, W. (ed.), *Gaelic and Scotland* (Edinburgh, 1989).

SELECT BIBLIOGRAPHY

Kidd, C., *Subverting Scotland's Past: Scottish Whig Historians and the Creation of an Anglo-British Identity, 1689–1830* (Cambridge, 1993).
Kirk, J. (ed.), *The Church in the Highlands* (Edinburgh, 1999).
MacInnes, John, *The Evangelical Movement in the Highlands of Scotland, 1688–1800* (Aberdeen, 1951).
McRoberts, D. (ed.), *Modern Scottish Catholicism, 1878–1978* (Glasgow, 1979).
Meek, Donald E., *The Scottish Highlands: The Churches and Gaelic Culture* (Geneva, 1996).
Phillipson, N. T., and Mitchison, R., *Scotland and the Age of Improvement* (Edinburgh, 1970).
Roxburgh, Kenneth B. E., *Thomas Gillespie and the Origin of the Relief Church in Eighteenth Century Scotland* (Bern, 1999).
Sher, Richard B., *Church and University in the Scottish Enlightenment* (Edinburgh, 1985).
Smout, T. C., *A History of the Scottish People, 1560–1830* (London, 1969).
Walker, G., and Gallagher, T. (eds.), *Sermons and Battle Hymns: Protestant Popular Culture in Modern Scotland* (Edinburgh, 1990).

Index

A History of Modern Enthusiasm, 24
A History of Wales, 15, 31, 338
A Letter to the King, 258, 266
A Pastoral Letter, 252, 256, 265, 266
Abbé Pezron, 21, 23, 26, 34
Aberdeen, 209, 274, 275, 276, 285, 296, 314
Aberdeen, St Peter's, 273
Aberdeen, University of, 317, 333, 335
Aberfeldy, 274
Aberystwyth, 104
Act of Union (1536), 3, 20, 43, 142
Act of Union (1707), 37, 52, 191, 192, 193, 201, 202, 243, 258, 260
adherents, 74, 140
Africa, 289
Age of the Saints, 14, 139
Airdrie, 284
Albany, duke of, 177
Albert, Prince, 166, 176, 177, 180
Albert Victor, Prince, 166, 168, 169, 170, 178, 180
Allan, David, 192, 198
Althorp, Lord, 268
America, 74, 82, 97, 145, 230, 270, 271, 272, 273, 283, 287
Ampleforth, 279
An Humble Attempt, 209
Anderson, Christopher, 27
Anderson, Robert, 230, 231, 232, 240
Anglican, 3, 4, 5, 6, 8, 18, 23, 44, 45, 46, 47, 48, 51, 54, 55, 61, 62, 64, 69, 70, 76, 80, 88, 94, 95, 96, 98, 99, 100, 103, 104, 107, 112, 113, 114, 115, 116, 118, 123, 124, 125, 126, 127, 128, 129, 130, 131, 132, 133, 134, 137, 140, 141, 142, 143, 144, 149, 150, 155, 156, 158, 165, 166, 167, 168, 169, 170, 175, 177, 181, 201, 214, 242, 252, 253, 256, 260, 275, 277, 284

Anglican, Thirty-nine Articles, 87
Anglicization, 16, 29, 30, 75, 124, 133, 144, 151, 153, 156
Anglo-Saxon, 14
Angus, Revd George, 274
Annan, 243, 244
Ansdell, Douglas, 7, 8, 334, 339
anti-Semitism, 151
Apostleship of Prayer, 285
Apostleship of the Sea, 279
Apostolicae Curae, 115
Archbishop MacDonald, 276
Archbishop Tait, 97, 101, 102
Archimandrite Barnabas, 127, 136
Ardkenneth, 293
Argyll, 285
Argyll, Synod of, 315
Argyllshire, 308, 313, 322, 323
Arishaig, 293
Antediluvians, 201
Aspinwall, Bernard 9, 12, 294, 295, 299, 303, 304
Associated Presbyterian Churches, 311, 313, 320
Atlantic, 56, 203, 287
Auckland, Lord, 93
Augustine (of Canterbury), 129
Australia, 270
Ayrshire, 289

Babel, 21, 26, 28
Bacon, Revd Edward, 284, 288, 291, 294
Bala, 44, 72
Bangor, 88, 91, 93, 96, 100, 118, 127, 128, 140, 155
Bangor, Bala-Bangor Congregational College, 152
Bangor, University College of North Wales, 111, 117, 120

341

INDEX

baptism, 129, 222, 228, 232, 250
Baptists, 62, 80, 137, 140, 141, 143, 147, 152, 309, 314, 328, 329, 330, 336, 337
Baptists (general), 221, 223, 224
Baptists (Particular), 221, 222, 223, 224, 227, 228, 229, 230, 231, 234, 236
Barcadale, 329
bards, 21
Barmouth, 104, 105, 119
Barn, 156
Barra, 293, 308
Barth, Karl, 152, 162
Batchelor, John, 168
Bothwell Brig, battle of, 244, 249
Baxter, Richard, 71
Beaumont, 279
Bebb, Ambrose, 110
Begg, George, 234
Belaney, Revd J., 296, 297, 298
Belaney, Revd Robert, 275, 276
Belgium, 145
Benbecula, 293
Benedict XV, Pope, 150
Benedictines, 275, 290
Berkeley Square, 279
Best, Geoffrey, 85
Bethell, Bishop, 88, 89, 91
Bevan, Aneurin, 149
Beverley Scotch Baptist Church, 225, 228, 231, 232, 239, 241
Biden, Revd John Xavier, 290
bishops, 5, 47, 84, 85, 86, 87, 88, 89, 90, 91, 92, 93, 94, 95, 96, 99, 100, 114, 115, 127, 129, 131, 132, 142
Blackfriars, 131, 135, 137, 138
Blackpool, 302
Blaenafon, 145
Bocock, Robert, 165–6
Boers, 12
Bonaparte, Napoleon, 257, 259
Bonhoeffer, Dietrich, 156
Bonnymuir, 247
Book of Common Order, 20, 174, 315, 334
Borrow, George, 16
Boston, Thomas, 201, 207, 214
Bowles, Thomas, 86, 87, 100
Boy Scouts, 172
Boys' Brigade, 172, 284
Brad y Llyfrau Gleision (1847), 4, 29, 63, 65, 78, 92
Bradley, Ian, 123, 127, 134, 135, 136, 137, 138

Brecon, 51
Breconshire, 56
Bristol, 165, 203
Britain, 9, 193, 194, 195, 197
British, 268, 269, 271, 272, 273, 274, 275, 278, 280, 281, 283, 288, 289, 290, 293, 294, 314, 329
British Catholic Institute, 271
British Empire, 191, 270, 284, 287, 289, 302
British Guiana, 285, 290
Britons, 4, 22, 38
Brogan, Colm, 294, 299, 306
Brogan, Sir Denis, 293, 306
Brown, D., 187, 198, 199, 339
Brown, Keith, 192, 193, 198
Brown, Roger L., 5, 80, 100, 101, 102, 161
Browne, Bishop, 95, 101
Bruce, Andrew, 226
Bruce, H. A. (Lord Aberdare), 94, 95, 96, 101
Brutus of Troy, 21, 39
Bryant, Sophie, 288
Buccleuch
 duchess of, 274
 duke of, 275
Buchanan, George, 250
Buddhism, 159, 263
Bulloch, J., 192, 199, 216
Burgess, William, 274
Burgher Church, 246
Burke, Revd Thomas, 287
Burns, Robert, 244
Bute, family, 269
Bute, Lady, 282
Bute, marquess of, 164, 165, 181, 182, 183, 274, 278, 284, 288, 290, 291, 299, 304

Caerleon, 94
Caernarfon, 96, 105, 156
Caernarfonshire, 222
Caernarvon Boroughs, 143
Caledonian Asylum, 252
Caledonian MacBrayne, 319
Caledonian Mercury, 204
Caledonian Railway Company, 268
Calvin, John, 67
Calvinistic Methodists, 4, 12, 15, 17, 18, 22, 23, 24, 28, 29, 41, 42, 61, 62, 67, 69, 70, 71, 72, 73, 77, 78, 79, 113, 114, 117, 140, 141, 147, 151, 152, 155, 156

INDEX

Cambridge, 11, 84, 85, 92, 108, 268, 269, 275
    Queen's College, 277
    Trinity College, 268
Cambridgeshire, 165
Cambuslang, 202, 204, 206, 209, 210, 212, 215, 217, 218
Cameron, Bishop, 299
Cameron, Catherine, 210, 211, 219
Cameronians, 207, 216
Campbell, Alexander, 230, 231, 239, 240, 241
Campbell, Revd Archibald, 283, 293
Campbell, Duncan, 211
Campbell, Bishop James Colquhoun, 93, 94, 95, 102
Campbell, Patrick, 283
Campbell, Robert (Skerrington), 275, 276, 282
Campbell, Thomas, 230
Canada, 51, 320
Canna, 308
Canterbury, 3, 86, 88, 98, 103, 125, 128, 132, 142
Capel, Mgr Thomas, 290
capitalism, 270
Cardiff, 7, 84, 156, 164, 165, 166, 167, 169, 171, 172, 173, 174, 180, 181, 182, 183
    Cathays Park, 171, 172, 173, 184
    Pembroke Terrace Chapel, 172
    Roman Catholic diocese, 150
    St Andrew's, 171
    St David's, 171
    St John's, 168, 169, 170, 171, 172, 183
    St Mary's, 168, 171
    Wood Street Congregational Church, 171
Cardiff and Merthyr Guardian, 164, 165, 182, 183
Cardiff Times, 168, 169, 172, 183
Cardigan, 89
Carey, Bishop, 91
Carlyle, Thomas, 244, 246, 247, 264, 265
Carmarthen, 27, 53, 156
Carmarthenshire, 15
Carstairs House, 268, 269
Casswell, John, 315, 334
Cecil, Lord Hugh, 11
Celtic Christianity, 6, 123, 134
Celtic Church, 123, 124, 125, 126, 127, 129, 130, 132, 134, 250, 265
Celtic lands, 6, 139

Celtic saints, 123, 142
Celtic-speaking, 15
Celts, 26
Cennick, John, 43, 44
census (1801) 166
census (1951), 153
census (religious, 1851), 62, 63, 75, 77, 182, 300
Chalmers, Thomas, 7, 11, 72, 81, 163, 164, 165, 166, 175, 180, 181, 182, 184, 245, 246, 248, 252, 264, 265, 339
chapels, 3, 63, 64, 68, 74, 127, 133, 141, 144, 148, 154, 155, 171, 172
Charles, Thomas (Bala), 19, 23, 24, 26, 28, 38, 39, 40, 41
Charlotte, Princess, 175, 184
Charlton, John, 228
Charnock, 71
Chinese, 12
Church in Wales, *see* Anglicans
Church Lads' Brigade, 172
Church of Scotland, 8, 174, 175, 176, 179, 189, 200, 201, 202, 203, 204, 205, 207, 211, 212, 214, 215, 242, 243, 244, 246, 248, 251, 252, 253, 254, 255, 256, 271, 282, 283, 303, 308, 310, 312, 313, 318, 320, 325, 327
Church Times, 103, 104, 113, 118, 119, 122
Churches of Christ, 238
Claggett, Bishop Nicholas, 56
Clarence, duke of, *see* Albert Victor, Prince
Clement, Mary, 54, 60
Cloud of Witnesses, 189, 198
Coats, Stuart, 279
Cockermouth, 85
Coffin, Walter, 167, 168
Colonsay, 309
Columba, 308
Congregationalism, 24, 62, 73, 77, 80, 115, 140, 141, 151, 174, 309, 314, 328
Conservative Party, 89, 105, 106, 110, 150, 157, 165, 167, 169, 174, 269, 274, 278, 290, 293
Constable-Maxwell, family, 269, 274, 290
Constable-Maxwell, Revd George, 290
Copleston, Bishop Edward, 87, 91, 100
Corry, Revd J. H., 276
Court of Arches, 87
Covenanters, 2, 7, 8, 9, 186, 188, 189,

INDEX

190, 191, 192, 193, 195, 196, 197, 198, 201, 202, 203, 205, 213, 243, 244, 245, 246, 249
Cowan, John, 238, 241
Craighead, 279
Cromarty, 314
Cronin, A. J., 287, 303
Crusoe, Robinson, 276
Culdees, 243, 250, 251
Culloden Moor, 243
Cumbrae, 282
Cumnock, 270
Cumnock, St Ninian's 274
Currie, R., 74, 82
Cymmrodorion, 22, 86, 105
Cymro, Y, 128, 131, 136, 137
Cymru Fydd, 106, 107, 110, 113
Cynwyl Gaeo, 15, 17, 31

Dalbeth, 280
Dale, David, 222
Dalkeith, 276, 290, 293, 302
Danaher, Revd J., 277
Daniel, D. R., 117, 122
Daniel, Fr Ivor, 133
Daniel, J. E., 111, 152, 161
Dark Ages, 14
Davidson, Thomas, 209
Davies, D. Hywel, 110, 119, 121, 338
Davies, Sir David, 89
Davies, Ellis W., 110, 111, 112, 117, 120, 121
Davies, John (Mallwyd), 16, 32
Davies, John, 15, 31, 121, 162, 338
Davies, Lewis, 130
Davies, Pryce, 47
Davies, Bishop Richard, 38, 124
Davies, W. T. Pennar, 157, 160, 162
Davis, Thomas, 107
Davitt, Michael, 271, 292
Dawson, Revd Bartholomew C., 290
Ddraig Goch, Y, 14
de Hirsch-Davies, J. E., 126, 129, 130, 135, 136
de Wattelville, Revd Edward, 290
Denbighshire, 222
Derby, Lord, 93, 101
Descriptio Kambriae, 15
Development Board for Rural Wales, 158
Devonshire, 177
Dick, William Douglas, 274
Dickens, Charles, 66, 78
Dickie, Henry, 230

Digby, Kenelm, 268
Dillon, Sir John Joseph, 271
Dingwall, 188, 329
disestablishment, 5, 6, 48, 94, 98, 103, 104, 113, 114, 115, 116, 118, 124, 125, 126, 131, 133, 141, 143, 144, 149, 155, 258
disestablishment, Bangor scheme, 114, 115, 118
Disraeli, Benjamin, 98, 119, 166, 169, 177, 289
Disruption (1843), 7, 72, 174, 176, 186, 189, 194, 248, 313, 317
disruption (general), 309, 310, 313
Dissent, 47, 49, 88, 95, 124, 125, 140, 141, 142, 143, 148, 150, 152, 154, 157, 174, 175, 176, 256, 261
Dolgellau, 234
Dolyswydd, Radnor, 27
Dominican, 287
Donegal, 294
Dornie, 276
Douglas, Revd Archibald, 274
Dowanhill, 280
Dowlais, 145
Downside, 279
dreams, 49
Druids, 21
Drummond, A. L., 192, 199, 216
Drych y Prif Oesoedd, 23, 41
Drych yr Amseroedd, 23, 41
Dublin Review, 281
Dublin, 176, 178, 180, 269
Dumfries, 290
Dumfriesshire, 290
Duncan, Andrew, 228
Dundee, 209, 229, 233, 234, 244, 268, 279, 286, 291
Dunfermline, 204
Durkacz, V. E., 316, 335, 336
Durkheim, Emil, 166

Easter Ross, 203
Ebbw Vale, 145, 147
Ecclefechan, 246
Edinburgh Review, 244
Edinburgh, 7, 11, 163, 165, 166, 173, 175, 176, 177, 178, 179, 180, 181, 184, 186, 192, 207, 208, 209, 216, 217, 221, 224, 225, 227, 229, 231, 232, 233, 234, 235, 236, 237, 245, 268, 282, 284, 285, 289, 291, 292, 293, 294, 295, 297, 301, 302, 304, 311, 314

INDEX

Braid Hills, 204
Bristol Place Church, 227, 230, 231
  Clyde Street Scotch Baptist Church, 226
  Morningside, 174
  St Giles's, 176, 177, 178, 179
  Tabernacle Church, 226
  University of, 72, 192, 207, 255, 317
  West Kirk, 201
education, 29, 73, 157, 316, 317, 318, 319
Edward VII, 166, 171, 172, 179, 180
Edwards, Archbishop A. G., 98, 99, 128, 135, 143, 144, 149
Edwards, Revd H. T. (dean of Bangor), 96, 135, 142, 143, 150, 160, 161
Edwards, Henry, 94
Edwards, Jonathan, 203, 209, 217
Edwards, Lewis, 11, 61, 62, 72, 75, 76, 78, 81
Egger, Revd Joseph, 279
Eigg, 308
eisteddfodau, 28
Elgin, 274
Elias, John, 62, 67, 70
Elizabeth I, 124, 125
Ellenborough, Lord, 284
Ellis, Tom, 105, 106, 107, 108, 113, 114, 118, 119, 120, 121
e-mail, 320
Encyclopaedia Britannica, 3, 88
England, 3, 4, 8, 9, 11, 15, 22, 27, 44, 48, 51, 63, 64, 68, 73, 75, 88, 98, 104, 108, 109, 117, 140, 141, 146, 150, 151, 170, 172, 176, 177, 181, 201, 202, 203, 204, 221, 222, 228, 229, 243, 245, 255, 256, 277, 280, 281, 292, 295, 302
English, language, 18, 25, 26, 27, 29, 30, 42, 44, 45, 54, 65, 69, 73, 75, 76, 78, 84, 85, 86, 87, 92, 96, 98, 99, 104, 128, 149, 152, 155, 237, 243, 244, 330, 332
English, people, 12, 21, 22, 28, 48, 51, 63, 65, 66, 71, 77, 79, 88, 90, 117, 166, 168, 169, 178, 180, 191, 242, 247, 260, 270, 271, 280, 283, 291, 292, 295
Enlightenment, 8, 139, 200, 205, 244, 254, 255
Episcopalianism, 1, 2, 3, 9, 174, 201, 243, 244, 250, 253, 262, 263, 274, 275, 276, 281, 283, 308, 334

Eriskay, 293
Erskine, Ebenezer, 202, 204, 205, 207, 215, 219, 310
Erskine, John, 207, 209, 217, 219
Erskine, Ralph, 202, 204, 212, 214, 219, 310
Erskine, Ruari (Marr), 278
Established Church, 2, 3, 4, 7, 10, 45, 61, 72, 74, 100, 101, 115, 124, 141, 142, 143, 154, 166, 174, 175, 200, 202, 204, 205, 212, 256, 289, 308, 309, 316, 317
ethnicity, 2, 8, 52
Ettrick, 201
Europe, 15, 21, 89, 163, 244, 257, 294
Evangelicalism, 8, 10, 11, 18, 28, 61, 65, 67, 71, 84, 190, 191, 193, 194, 195, 197, 213, 309, 310, 311, 313, 316, 317, 319
Evans, Christmas, 65, 67, 70, 76, 78, 79, 80
Evans, Gwynfor, 156
Evans, Theophilus, 19, 23, 24, 40, 41
Everson, James, 225, 230, 231, 232, 239, 240, 241
Exeter, 277
Eyre, Archbishop Charles, 269, 271, 282, 284, 292, 293, 306
Eyre, Revd W. H. (Stonyhurst), 292

Faner, Y, 131
Ferguson, William, 187
Festival of Britain (1951), 153
filioque, 128
Finlay, Richard J., 187, 192, 198, 199, 194, 197, 199, 215, 339
First Secession Church, 310
Fisher, Archbishop Geoffrey, 132
Fisher, James, 207
Flint, 150
Forbes, Bishop (Brechin), 274
Forbes, Revd Peter, 276, 291
Fort Augustus, 275, 276, 290
Fort William, 286, 302
Foster, Emily, 104
Foster, Thomas Campbell, 63
France, 48, 50, 145, 257
Franciscans, 277, 280
Frederick, Prince of Wales, 50
Free Church Defence Association, 312, 334
Free Church of Scotland (Continuing), 310, 312, 313

345

INDEX

Free Church of Scotland, 72, 163, 164, 174, 176, 186, 188, 194, 198, 310, 311, 312, 313, 323, 324, 325, 326, 327, 328, 334, 336
Free Church of Scotland, the 'Wee Frees', 310
Free Concern, 312
Free Presbyterian Church of Scotland, 310, 312, 313, 320, 321, 322, 323, 325, 336
French Revolution, 257, 258
French, 244, 279, 280
Frere, James Hatley, 242
Frogmill, Oxfordshire, 45
Fuller, Andrew, 229, 236
Fullerton, Georgiana, 269

Gaelic Bible, 317
Gaelic
  culture, 308, 309, 310, 311, 312, 313, 314, 315, 316, 317, 318, 319, 320, 321, 322, 323, 324, 325, 326, 327, 328, 329, 330, 331, 332, 333, 334, 335, 336, 337
  language, 8, 10, 11, 12, 25, 26, 194, 196, 243, 278, 280, 283, 292, 293, 308, 315, 316, 317, 318, 319, 321, 322, 323, 324, 326, 327, 328, 329, 330, 331, 332, 336, 337
  preaching, 321, 328, 335
  worship, 321
Galashiels, 229, 238, 241, 275, 282, 297
Gallipoli, 283
Galloway, 285, 305
Galston, Santa Sophia, 274
Gasquet, Dom Aidan, 285
Geiriadur Ysgrythurol, 23
Gelligaer, 84, 86
Geneva, 206
Geoffrey of Monmouth, 21, 34
George II, 50
George III, 50, 258
George IV, 165, 258, 259
George, Henry, 292
Georgia, 56
Gerald of Wales, 15, 32, 116
Gerard, Colonel, 298
Gerard, Revd John, 281, 284
German, 293, 295
Germany, 109, 145
Gib, Adam, 213, 220
Gibbon, Edward, 112
Gibson, Mel, 2

Gilbert, A. D., 74, 82
Gillespie, Thomas, 209, 210, 213, 218, 219, 334, 340
Gillis, Bishop James (Edinburgh), 276, 299, 291
Gladstone, William Ewart, 88, 94, 95, 96, 97, 98, 99, 101, 102, 106, 166, 170, 172, 178
Glas, John, 221
Glasgow, 209, 244, 245, 246, 247, 248, 249, 251, 253, 261, 263, 265, 268, 270, 271, 275, 276, 277, 278, 282, 284, 285, 286, 289, 290, 291, 292, 296, 299, 301, 302, 303, 314
  Celtic Football Club, 271, 294
  Charlotte Street School, 284
  Cowcaddens, 289, 290, 299
  Cowcaddens, Social Reform Association, 279
  German Catholic Association, 270
  Hibernian Football Club, 283
  Irish Gaelic League, 294
  Roman Catholic Institute, 279
  Roman Catholic parishes, 286, 287, 300
  Scotch Baptists, 228, 229, 233, 234
  Sick and Nursing Poor Association, 282
  Smyllum Orphanage, 283
  St Aloysius's, 294, 298
  St Aloysius's School, 277, 279, 283, 284, 285, 287, 289, 292, 293, 299, 301, 302, 303, 304, 305
  St Alphonsus's, 280, 300
  St Andrew's, 300
  St Andrew's School, 279, 280
  St Elizabeth House, 282
  St John's, 246, 247, 248, 300
  St Joseph's, 277, 278, 280, 284, 286, 292, 294
  St Joseph's Industrial School, 283
  St Mary's, 291
  St Mungo's School, 279
  United Industrial School, 283
  University of, 81, 271, 287, 288, 289, 291, 317
Glasgow Observer, 278
Glenelg, 329
Glorious Revolution 9, 200, 249
Glyndŵr, Owain, 107, 110
Gomer, 21, 26, 35, 41
Goodwin, 71
Gordon, General Charles, 169

INDEX

Gordon, Revd Charles, 284
Gordon, James Fraser, 278
Grant, James, 278
Grieve, George, 225, 236
Griffith, W. P., 4, 11
Griffiths, Ellis, 111, 112
Griffiths, James, 147, 149
Griffiths, Revd John (Llandeilo), 96, 102
Gruffydd, W. J., 153
Gurnal, William, 71
Guthrie, James, 245, 246, 264
Guthrie, William, 245, 246, 264
Gwaed y Teulu, 152
gwerin, 4, 11, 33, 42, 96, 97
Gwynne, Marmaduke, 23

Haggate Baptist Church, 225, 226, 239
Hall, Robert, 71
Hall, Sir Benjamin, 89, 101
Hamilton, 280
Hamilton, Alexander, 245
Hamilton, duchess of, 274
Hamilton, William, 71, 72
Hammersmith, 278
Hammersmith College, 280
Hanover, 142
Hanson, Revd Eric, 284, 287, 288, 291, 293, 299, 306
Hardie, J. Keir, 147
Harris, 313, 319
Harris, Howell, 4, 17, 19, 23, 27, 30, 37, 39, 40, 43–60, 120
Harris, Joseph, 45, 56
Harris, Thomas, 56
Harvie, Christopher, 195
Hawarden, 94
Hebrew, 4, 21, 23, 26
Hebrides, 308, 309, 310, 311, 313, 329
Hegel, G. W. F., 109, 121
Henllan Amgoed, Carmarthenshire, 46
Henry II, 15
Henry VII, 22, 25
Henry VIII, 109
Herald, 196, 199
Herries, family, 290
Herries, Lady, 290
Herries, Lord, 290
Highlands, 7, 8, 9, 10, 27, 186, 189, 190, 191, 194, 195, 196, 197, 243, 269, 270, 272, 274, 276, 284, 285, 293, 308, 309, 337
Hinduism, 159
Historia Regum Britanniae, 21

Historical View of the Church of Scotland, 249–50
History of the Sufferings of the Church of Scotland, 189, 198, 199
Holborn, St Albans, 113
Holland, Robert, 22, 35, 36
Holy Guild of St Joseph, 291, 299
Holy Spirit, 18, 69, 201, 203, 212, 213, 218, 233
Honest to God, 156
Hook, Walter Farquhar, 166
Hope, Adam, 246
Hope-Johnstone, J., 274
Hope-Scott, Revd J. R., 276, 283, 297, 298, 301
Hopkins, Gerard Manley, 281, 284, 285, 300, 302
Horsley, L., 74, 82
Houghton, Lord, 269
How Green Was My Valley? 2
Howie, J., 189, 198, 264
Hughes, Revd Joshua (Llandovery), 97, 98, 99
Hughes, Trystan Owain, 6, 12, 135, 160, 161, 338
Hume, David, 244
Hunter, Revd Thomas W. (Callander), 274
Hunter-Blair, family, 301, 304
Hunter-Blair, David, 269, 270
Hunter-Blair, Revd Oswald, 290
Hynd, William, 235, 236

Iddesleigh, Lord, 177
Image and Identity, 187, 198, 199
Independent Labour Party, 147
India, 228, 236
industrialization, 140
Internet, 320, 321, 327
Inverness, 270
Inverness-shire, 308
Inverness Courier, 163
Iona, 308, 315
Ireland, 123, 163, 165, 172, 176, 180, 260, 261, 273, 280, 281, 288, 292, 295, 308
Ireland, home rule, 107, 109, 269, 270, 295
Ireland, Land League, 292
Irish, language, 25
Irish, people, 9, 12, 25, 107, 109, 151, 167, 174, 230, 247, 248, 253, 260, 261, 262, 263, 265, 269, 270, 271,

347

INDEX

272, 273, 275, 276, 277, 278, 279, 281, 282, 283, 284, 285, 287, 292, 294, 295
Irongray, 245, 264
Irvine, 203
Irving, Edward, 8, 9, 11, 51, 242, 243, 244, 245, 246, 247, 248, 249, 250, 251, 252, 253, 254, 255, 256, 257, 258, 259, 260, 261, 262, 263, 264, 265, 266, 267
Islam, 159
Islay, 309
Italian, 107, 244, 270, 293, 306
Italy, 145, 287
Iwan, Dafydd, 17, 32, 156

Jacobinism, 48, 55, 193, 201, 243, 249, 253
Jamaica, 284
James VI (I of England), 22, 36, 37
James VII (II of England), 200, 201
James, E. Wyn, 3, 4, 42, 120
James, John Angell, 71, 81
Japheth, 21, 35, 41
Jarman, A. O. H., 19
Jeffrey, Francis, 244
Jenkins, Geraint H., 18, 33, 34, 35, 38, 39, 40, 42, 83, 100, 118, 338, 339
Jenkins, R. T., 29, 41, 58
Jenkinson, Bishop, 89
Jesuits, 271, 272, 274, 275, 276, 277, 278, 279, 280, 281, 282, 283, 284, 285, 286, 287, 288, 289, 290, 291, 292, 293, 294, 296, 297, 298, 300, 301, 302, 303, 305, 306
John, E. T., 108, 110
Johnes, A. J., 89
Johns, Thomas (Llanelli), 73, 81
Jones, Revd Basil, 98
Jones, D. Gwenallt, 127, 162
Jones, Revd D. Parry, 99
Jones, David (Llangan), 69, 80
Jones, David (Panteg), 90, 96, 100, 101
Jones, Evan (Ieuan Gwynedd), 62, 63, 64, 69, 77, 78, 80
Jones, Griffith (Llanddowror), 4, 19, 24, 25, 26, 27, 29, 40, 46, 54, 55, 60
Jones, J. C., 155
Jones, J. Idwal, 236, 240
Jones, J. R., 156
Jones, John (Tal-y-sarn), 67, 70, 79
Jones, John Puleston, 65, 82
Jones, John Richard (Ramoth), 222, 225, 227, 230, 234, 237, 239, 240

Jones, Maurice, 150
Jones, R. M. (Bobi), 18, 42, 157, 162
Jones, R. Tudur, 13, 38, 39, 40, 41, 42, 59, 80, 83, 157, 160, 162, 339
Jones, Robert (Rhos-lan), 23, 28, 40, 41
Jones, Robert Ambrose (Emrys ap Iwan), 12, 13
Jones, William (Liverpool), 222, 223
Jones, William (London), 228
Joseph of Arimathea, 21
Josiah, 50
Jowett, Benjamin, 112, 121
Judaism, 46

Kaffirs, 12
Karslake, Revd Charles, 289
Karslake, Edward Kent, 289
Karslake, Frederick, 289
Keating, Revd Joseph, 279
Keenan, Revd Stephen, 291
Kent, duke of, 289
Kerr, family, 290
Kerr, Lord Ralph, 282, 288
Kidd, Colin, 192, 340
Kilmarnock, 295, 302
Kilmuir, Skye, 188
Kilsyth, 203, 206, 216, 217
Kingdom of God, 140, 147
Kinnoull, 290
Kirk of Shotts, 203
Kirkoswald, 290
Knight, Bruce, 85
Knight, Frances, 5, 135
Knox, John, 174, 203, 206, 215, 315
Knox, R. Buick, 46, 58
Kyffin, Edward, 36
Kyle, 329
Kyle of Lochalsh, 332

Labour Party, 110, 146, 147, 148, 149, 151, 157, 279, 289
Lamp, 278, 296
Lampau y Deml, 71
Lampeter, St David's College, 84, 92, 96, 97, 114, 115, 122, 150, 161
Lanarkshire, 281, 306
Lancashire, 151, 281
Langdale, Elizabeth, 290
Largs, 229, 239
Latin, 4, 21, 44, 45, 54, 55, 128, 250
Latter Day Saints, 167
Lavelle, Revd Patrick, 272
Law, Revd Augustus Henry, 284, 301, 302

348

INDEX

Lawson, Mary, 245, 264
League of the Cross, 271, 273, 282
Leeds, 166, 169, 225
Leeds, duchess of, 274, 276
Lees, James Cameron, 177, 178, 179, 184, 185
Leith, 173
Leo, XIII, Pope, 280
Lewis, 308, 312, 313, 319, 324, 327, 334, 336
Lewis, Ewart, 131
Lewis, H. D., 156
Lewis, Saunders, 14, 30, 31, 33, 34, 41, 110, 111, 112, 127, 132, 134, 136, 151, 154, 161
Lhuyd, Edward, 21, 26
Liberal Party, 82, 103, 105, 106, 107, 110, 111, 118, 146, 147, 149, 151, 167, 169, 174, 270, 292
Liddel, Andrew, 231, 240
Lincoln's Inn, 104
Lisbon, 285
Lithuanian, 270, 293, 306
Liverpool, 80, 90, 222, 280, 295
  Faithful Companions of Jesus, 280
  St Leonard's, 280
Liverpool, Lord, 242
Llandaff, 84, 85, 86, 87, 89, 91, 92, 93, 100, 140, 150, 155, 165, 167, 168, 169, 171, 172
Llandovery, 90, 155
Llandrindod Wells, 109, 117, 135
Llanelli, 147
  Capel Als, 73
Llangefni, 28
Llewelyn, Richard, 2
Lloyd, Sir J. E., 105, 106, 110, 115, 116, 118, 119, 120, 121, 122
Lloyd George, David, 105, 106, 107, 110, 113, 114, 119, 120, 121, 143, 146
Llwyd, Morgan, 23
Llwyn-llwyd Academy, 54
Llywelyn the Great, 110
Lochgilphead, 188, 294
Logie, 205, 215
Logue, Cardinal, 283
London, 22, 43, 53, 56, 86, 88, 90, 92, 104, 105, 106, 111, 117, 176, 180, 203, 243, 252, 253, 254, 255, 256, 263, 268, 284, 295, 297, 302
  Caledonian Chapel, 242, 251
  Hibernian Society, 260, 266, 267
  National Scotch Church, 242, 255

St Paul's Cathedral, 176, 178
  Tower of, 56
  Windmill Street Scotch Baptist, 228
Lord's Supper, 223, 231, 235, 236, 238, 259, 316
Lothian, family, 269, 274, 276, 283, 284
Lovat, family, 290, 304
Lovat, Lord, 269, 270, 274, 276, 290, 292, 295
Lowlands, 7, 8, 9, 10, 186, 193, 194, 195, 201, 243, 244, 253, 314, 315, 318, 320
Luther, Martin, 109
Lynch, James, 272
Lynch, M., 187, 198, 199, 339

'Mab Darogan' (Son of Prophecy), 22
Macclesfield, 92
MacAulay, Lord Donald, 320
MacCowan, R., 190, 198
McCrie, Thomas, 175, 184, 215
McCrone, David, 187, 198
McCulloch, William (Cambuslang), 202, 206, 208, 209, 210, 211, 215, 218, 219
MacDonald, Alexander, 296
MacDonald, Colonel, 293
Machynlleth, 110
Mackay of Clashfern, Lord, 311
Mackintosh, Bishop, 293
McLachlan, Revd Paul, 280
McLaurin, Revd W. C. A., 275
McLean, Archibald, 222, 224, 225, 227, 228, 229, 230, 233, 234, 235, 236, 237, 239, 240, 241
Macleod, Donald, 311, 312, 330, 334, 337
MacLeod, Finlay, 196, 197, 199
MacLeod, John, 186
McLeod, Revd J., 284
Macpherson, James, 251
MacRae, Kenneth, 185, 189, 196, 197, 198
Maguire, Archbishop John, 279
Manchester, 88, 91, 92
Manchester Guardian, 103
Manning, Cardinal, 269, 274, 290, 295
Manx, 25
Martin, Norman E., 125
martyrdom, 2, 133, 138, 244, 251
Marx, Karl, 308
mass, 279, 280, 283, 293, 311
Matthews, Revd Edward (Ewenni), 61, 62, 63, 64, 65, 66, 67, 68, 69, 73, 74, 75, 76, 77, 78, 79, 80, 81, 82, 83

INDEX

Mazzini, Joseph, 107
medieval, 139
Meek, Donald E., 3, 10, 12, 134, 334, 335, 336, 337, 340
Meirionnydd, 104, 106, 150, 222
Melbourne, Lord, 89, 90, 91, 101
Mellish, Wilhelmina, 269
Menevia, 150
Menevia Record, 131, 137
Merthyr Tydfil, 93, 145, 152
  Cyfarthfa iron works, 145
Messenger of the Sacred Heart, 286–7
Michelangelo, 293
Middle Ages, 15, 16, 21, 22, 308
Middlesbrough, 167
Middleton, Revd Reginald, 279, 299
Midleton, William, 36
Miles, Gareth, 18, 19, 33, 58
militia, 44, 50, 51, 55, 56
Milner, Bishop John, 271
Minstrelsy of the Scottish Borders, 251
Minto House, 227
Mirfield, 150
Moidart, Golden Church, 274
monarchy, 4, 44, 48, 49, 50, 51, 55, 56, 107, 320
Monckton-Milnes, Richard, 269
Moncrieff, Alexander, 207, 213
Monmouth, diocese of, 150, 155
Monmouthshire Merlin, 84, 99
Monteith, family, 290
Monteith, Joseph, 270
Monteith, Robert, 268, 269, 270, 274, 276, 277, 294, 295, 298
Month, 279, 281, 284, 298, 304
Montrose, 233, 234
Morgan, D. Densil, 3, 6, 82, 118, 160, 161, 162, 239, 240, 339
Morgan, Revd Herbert, 147
Morgan, Kenneth O., 13, 100, 104, 118, 119, 120, 121, 122, 161, 167, 182, 339
Morgan, Revd Richard Williams, 94
Morgan, Thomas, 45, 58
Morning Watch, 259
Morris, Archbishop Alfred Edwin, 131, 138, 155, 162
Morris, Ebenezer, 67
Morris, R. Hopkin, 111
Morton, Graeme, 174
Mosca, Revd Joachim, 293
Mostyn, Archbishop Francis (Cardiff), 131, 137, 150, 151

Mostyn, Sir Piers, 150
Muck, 308
Mull, 309, 330
Munro, Alexander, 274
Murchison, Revd Thomas Moffat, 325
Murdoch, Bishop J., 276, 277, 298
Murray, Bishop Ian, 323
Murthly Castle, 268
Muslims, 263
Muswell Hill, 105
myth, 4, 7, 11, 30, 187

Nairn, 329
Naples, 293
Napoleonic Wars, 243, 247, 257
National Curriculum, 159
National Health Service, 153
nationalism, English, 9
nationalism, Irish, 269, 282
nationalism, Scottish, 278
nationalism, Welsh, 5, 6, 13, 14, 19, 77, 103, 104, 105, 106, 107, 108, 109, 110, 111, 112, 113, 114, 115, 116, 117, 118, 119, 120, 121, 122, 132, 143
New Jersey, 203
New Lanark, 222
New York, 163
New Zealand, 270
Newburgh, 235
Newington, 174
Newman, John Henry, 268, 269, 301
Newport, 146
Newton Stewart, 290
Newtonmore, 329
Newtown, 105
Nicea, 128
Nicholas, Revd T. E. (Glais), 147, 148, 161
Noah, 21, 35
Nonconformist Conscience, 154
Nonconformity, 5, 6, 18, 24, 61, 62, 63, 64, 68, 69, 70, 71, 72, 73, 74, 88, 94, 97, 98, 114, 116, 117, 124, 126, 127, 128, 130, 132, 133, 140, 141, 142, 143, 144, 147, 148, 149, 152, 154, 155, 156, 157, 158, 166, 167, 169, 170, 171, 181, 183
Norfolk, duke of, 269, 270, 292, 305
North British Daily Mail, 164
North Uist, 313
Northern Ireland, 336
Nova Scotia, 293
Nuttall, Geoffrey, 49, 58, 59

INDEX

Oban, 274, 276
O'Brien, Richard, 273
O'Connell, Daniel, 163, 180, 185, 271, 295, 296
Offa's Dyke, 6, 44
Ogilvie, James, 210, 218, 219
Ogilvie, Revd John, 289-90, 294, 304
O'Hare, Leo, 279
Old Bailey, 112
'Old Mortality', 188, 189, 196, 197, 198
Old Scotch Independents, 222, 224
Oliphant, Mrs, 244, 251, 263, 264, 265, 266
Ollivant, Alfred, 84, 85, 86, 92, 93, 95, 96, 97, 102
On the Thirty-nine Articles, 45
Oscott, 268
O'Shea, Kitty, 180
Ossian, 250
Owen, David (Brutus), 69, 70, 80
Owen, John (bishop of St Davids), 98, 115
Owen, John, 71
Oxford Movement, 274
Oxford, 11, 44, 45, 95, 103, 104, 105, 108, 111, 119, 122, 274, 275, 281, 284, 287, 290, 303
  Balliol College, 104, 112, 121, 275
  Christ Church College, 285

paganism, 15
Paisley, 229, 244
Palmerston, Lord, 92, 169, 177
Pankhurst, E., 108, 120
Parkinson, Revd T. B., 277
Parnell, Charles Stewart, 180, 292
Parry, John, 72
Parry, R. Ifor, 154, 162
Partickhill, 292
Patmore, Coventry, 269, 292, 305
patronage, 202, 246, 248
Peel, Sir Robert, 89
Pembrokeshire, 53
Pencader, 15, 26, 29
Pengam, 84, 100
Pennsylvania, 56
Perth, 204, 205, 215
Perthshire, 308
Peulin (Paulinus), 15, 17
Phillimore, J. S., 279
Phillips de Lisle, Ambrose, 268
Phillips de Lisle, Edwin, 270
Phillips, J. L. (dean of Monmouth), 127

Phillips, John, 72
Phoenix Park, 281
pilgrimages, 131
Plaid Cymru, 31, 103, 110, 132, 156; *see also* Welsh Nationalist Party
Plater, Revd Charles, 289
Plater, Revd Dominic, 279, 283, 299, 303
Playfair, John, 244
Pleasance church, 235, 239
Plymouth, 308
Poland, 145
Polish, 270, 306
Pontypool, 145
Pontypridd, 146
Port Talbot, 125, 157
Porter, Revd George, 299
Power, Revd Mathew, 282
Powis, Lord, 91, 93, 101
preaching, Gaelic, 12
preaching, Welsh, 4, 61, 62, 65, 66, 68, 69, 70, 73, 74, 75, 76, 94
pre-millennialism, 242, 257
Premonstratensians, 274
Presbyterian, Irish, 261
Presbyterian, Scottish, 2, 7, 8, 9, 10, 12, 163, 164, 165, 174, 175, 176, 179, 180, 181, 189, 190, 192, 193, 196, 197, 200, 201, 213, 214, 235, 243, 244, 248, 249, 253, 260, 262, 263, 272, 274, 281, 296, 304, 308, 309, 310, 312, 319, 320, 322, 323, 329, 330, 331, 332, 333
Presbyterian Church of Wales, *see* Calvinistic Methodists
Presbytery of Relief, 209
Preston, 271
Price, J. Arthur, 5, 6, 11, 103, 104, 105, 106, 107, 108, 109, 110, 111, 112, 113, 114, 115, 116, 117, 118, 119, 120, 121, 122, 135
Primrose League, 105
Primrose, Sir John Ure, 289
Pritchard, Vicar, of Llandovery, 23
Province, 131, 132, 133, 135, 137, 138
Pryce, W. T. R., 75, 83
Pugh, Alun, 112
Pugin, A. W. N., 293
Purbrick, Revd Edward, 291
Puritan, 24, 36, 71, 154, 155
Pwllheli, 110

Quaker, 24, 274
Quigley, Revd Hugh, 271

INDEX

Rae, Lord, 209
railways, 278
Rambler, 281
Rastafarianism, 159
Re-awakening, 307, 333
Rebellion (1745), 50, 209, 243, 253, 262
Redemptorists, 290, 298
Rees, D. Ben, 68, 79, 81
Rees, D. E. (Bangor), 128
Rees, David (Llanelli), 74
Rees, Henry, 67, 71, 78, 81
Rees, Thomas, 62, 75, 77, 80, 83
Rees, Timothy, 150
Reformation, 8, 9, 20, 123, 124, 125, 133, 138, 175, 203, 209, 210, 213, 247, 248, 249, 250, 251, 256, 258, 260, 271, 308, 309, 310, 335
Reichel, Sir Harry, 111
Relief Church, 310, 312–13, 334
Renaissance, 20, 21, 151
Renan, Ernest, 187
Review, 131, 137
revival (evangelical), 3, 8, 11, 17, 18, 19, 23, 24, 29, 30, 40, 43, 48, 54, 190, 196, 197, 200, 201, 202, 203, 206, 209, 210, 211, 212, 213, 216, 217, 218
revivalism, 11, 73, 74, 82, 139, 203
Rhondda, 146, 157
Rhum, 308
Rhyl, 114
Rhymney, 146
Richard, Ebenezer, 67
Richard, Henry, 94, 117, 143
Richards, John (Bron Menai), 93
Richards, Joseph, 234
Richards, Morgan, 73
Richards, Thomas, 67, 69, 79, 81, 82
ritualism, 6, 7
Robe, James (Kilsyth), 202, 207, 209, 213, 215, 216, 217, 218, 219
Roberts, Evan, 147
Roberts, Revd R. Silyn, 147, 161
Roberts, Robert, 222
Robertson, Revd T. C., 275
Robertson, William, 192, 205, 244
Robinson, John, 156
Rochsoles, 279
Rogers, Thomas, 45
Roman Catholic Defence Association, 269
Roman Catholic Institute, 272
Roman Catholic Poor Schools Committee, 280

Roman Catholic Social Guild, 272, 279
Roman Catholic Young Men's Society, 273, 278, 296
Roman Catholic Apostolic Church, 242
Roman Catholicism, 3, 6, 9, 10, 11, 12, 16, 21, 49, 50, 55, 56, 115, 117, 123, 125, 126, 127, 128, 129, 130, 131, 132, 133, 134, 142, 150, 151, 152, 158, 163, 167, 171, 172, 174, 180, 201, 243, 248, 249, 250, 251, 253, 257, 258, 259, 260, 261, 262, 263, 265, 267, 268, 287, 288, 289, 290, 291, 292, 293, 294, 295, 296, 297, 298, 299, 300, 301, 302, 303, 304, 305, 306, 308, 311, 322, 324, 334
Caledonian Association, 278
Caledonian Society, 293
Social Reform, 279
Boys' Guild, 282
Christian Brothers, 280
Poor Schools Committee, 271
Roman Empire, 14
Romans, 21, 320
Rome, 115, 123, 124, 125, 126, 129, 130, 131, 138, 150, 270, 278, 290
Rosa, Carl, 293
Rota, Revd Felix, 293
Rowland, Daniel (Llangeitho), 23, 28, 39, 40, 43, 44, 50, 51, 53, 57, 67, 69, 79, 81
Roxburgh, 275
Roxburgh, Kenneth B. E., 8, 213, 334, 340
Royal Navy, 284
Russell, Lord John, 85, 86, 89, 91, 92, 101
Russia, 24, 292
Russian (language), 128
Rutherford, Samuel, 206, 215

Sabellianism, 233, 234, 240
Sacramental Meditations on the Sufferings and Death of Christ, 211
Sacred Heart, 281, 282, 285, 302
St Andrew's, University of, 274
St Asaph, diocese of, 91, 95, 96, 98, 99, 100, 140, 144, 214
St Bees, 96
St Beuno, 142
St Chad, 129, 136
St Columba, 250, 283
St Columbanus, 292
St Cybi, 128, 142
St David, 14, 31, 34, 124, 128, 131, 132, 139, 142

INDEX

St Davids, diocese of, 89, 90, 98, 100, 115, 116, 122, 124, 128, 135, 140
St Deiniol, 128
St Dunawd, 128
St Dyfrig, 139
St Frances Xavier, 280
St Illtud, 139
St Margaret Association, 269
St Ninians, 204
St Patrick, 273
St Seiriol, 142
St Teilo, 142
St Vincent de Paul Society, 271, 273, 278, 282, 291, 295, 303
Salesbury, William, 20, 33, 34
Salford, 292, 305
Salisbury, Thomas, 35, 36
Saltcoats, 231
Saltcoats, Great Ribbon Lodge, 286
Samothes, 21
Sankey, Lord, 125
Saturday Review, 103
Saunders, Joseph, 49
Scanlan, Joseph, 288
Schomberg-Kerr, Henry, 284, 302
Scotch Baptists, 8, 221, 222, 223, 224, 225, 226, 227, 228, 229, 230, 231, 232, 233, 234, 235, 236, 237, 238, 239, 240, 241
Scots Worthies, 189, 198, 264
Scotsman, 163, 178, 179, 182, 184, 185
Scott, Bishop, 271
Scott, Sir Walter, 89, 174, 188, 189, 198, 243, 244, 249, 251, 264
Scott, William, 237
Scott-Murray, Charles R., 290
Scottish Catholic Truth Society, 278, 287
Scottish Parliament, 1, 263
Scottish preaching, 66
Scottish Review, 278
Scottish Society for the Prevention of Cruelty to Children, 271
Scottish Society for the Propagation of Christian Knowledge, 316–17
Secession (general), 309, 310, 313, 314, 318
secession (1733), 202, 204, 205, 206, 207, 212, 213, 246
Second Vatican Council, 156
Second World War, 130, 153, 283
secular, 326
Sermon on the Mount, 147
Shaftesbury, Lord, 92

Short, Bishop, 91, 94
Shotton, 157
Shrewsbury, 104
Sikhism, 159
Sikhs, 263
Simon, Glyn, 155, 156, 161, 162
Simprin, 201
Sisters of Mercy, 277, 280, 282
Sisters of Notre Dame, 285
Skye, 190, 191, 198, 313, 329, 334, 337
Skye Alive, 330
Smith, Adam, 244
Smith, Revd Angus, 312
Smith, Bishop, 276, 277, 298
Smith, Frederick J., 282
Smith, James (Newburn, Fife), 224
Smith, William, 284
Smith-Sligo, Archbishop William (Inzievov), 290
Smout, T. C., 191, 192, 198, 218, 264, 265, 340
socialism, 147, 148, 149
Socinianism, 223, 225, 233, 237
sodalities, 268, 289, 303, 304
Solomon, 50
Solzhenitsyn, Alexander, 1
South Africa, 270, 283, 284
South Uist, 308, 323
South Wales Star, 103, 110
Spain, 145, 258
Spanish, 270
Spectator, 294
Spencer, Lord, 268
Spencer, Revd Ignatius, 268, 269
Splaine, Revd James F., 281
Sprague, William B., 163
Spring Harvest, 330
Sproston, Samuel, 275
Spurgeon, C. H., 71, 81
Staffordshire, 270
Stainer, John, 178
Steuart, John, 275
Stevenson, Ayrshire, 231
Stewarton, 203
Stirling, 204, 205, 245, 246, 278, 280, 300
Stornoway, 188, 327, 329
Stothert, James A., 269
Strain, Bishop John, 276
Stuart, Charles, 225, 236
Stuart, Charles Edward, 48
Stuart, Neil, 233, 234
Stuarts, 142, 189, 249

INDEX

Swan, Samuel, 225, 226, 239
Swansea and Brecon, diocese of, 150, 155

Tablet, 133, 135, 137, 138
Tain, 329, 332
Talbot, Brian, 8, 238
Taliesin Ben Beirdd, 14, 16, 31
Tennyson, Alfred, 269
Texas, 320
The Identity of the Scottish Nation, 187
The Men of Skye, 190, 198
The Theological Repository, 222
The Wrestlings of the Scottish Church, 189, 198
Thirwell, Bishop Connop, 90, 92, 96, 97, 101, 102
Thomas, Owen, 65, 67, 72, 75, 78, 79, 81, 83
Thomas, Revd George, 84, 85
Thomas, Revd Thomas (Caernarfon), 92
Thompson, Charles John, 169
Thompson, J., 189, 198
Thomson, Derick, 308, 333
Thomson, Revd P., 280
Thurso, Baptist Church, 226
Ticknell, Revd George, 284
Tillich, Paul, 156
Times, 63
Tiree, 309, 330
Tory, see Conservative Party
Trawsfynydd, 104
Treaty of Versailles, 145
Tredegar, 146
Trefdraeth, 86, 100
Tregynon, 94
Trevecka, 17, 27, 44, 49, 51, 54
Trinity, 233
Troon, 274
Trotter, Charles (Woodhill), 274
Tryweryn Valley, 156
Tudors, 22, 142
Tudur, Geraint, 4, 120, 339
Tyerman, Luke, 48, 58
typhus, 277, 290

ultramontanism, 9, 151, 269, 272, 273, 281
unemployment, 146
Union Jack, 9, 268
United Free Church of Scotland, 181, 306, 310, 312, 313
United Presbyterian Church, 174, 215, 310

University of Wales, 108, 111, 118
Upton, Liam, 8
Urquhart, Arthur J. P. (Oxford), 274

Valentine, Lewis, 112, 152
Vatican, 270
Vaughan, Revd Bernard, 289
Vaughan, Bishop Francis (Menevia), 131, 138
Vaughan, Bishop (Salford), later Cardinal, 292, 305
Vaughan, Dean, 98
Vaughan, Revd R., 277, 298
Victoria, Queen, 95, 166, 167, 168, 170, 171, 172, 179, 180, 283
Virgin Mary, 233, 261

Wade-Evans, Revd A.W., 128, 130, 136
Walker, Robert, 234, 235
Wall, William, 274
Wallace, William, 2
Watcyn-Williams, Revd Morgan, 152, 161
Watford (Caerphilly), 53
Waverley, 243
Website, 327, 337
Webster, Alexander, 210, 218, 219
Weimar, 269
Wellington, duke of, 166, 167, 168, 175, 257
Welsh Assembly, 1, 159
Welsh Catholic Times, 127, 131, 135, 136, 138
Welsh Development Agency, 158
Welsh Land Authority, 158
Welsh language, 4, 5, 6, 11, 12, 16, 18, 19, 20, 21, 23, 24, 25, 26, 27, 28, 29, 30, 42, 51, 54, 55, 64, 65, 66, 75, 84, 85, 86, 88, 89, 90, 91, 92, 93, 94, 95, 96, 98, 99, 104, 108, 116, 128, 132, 133, 141, 144, 149, 150, 151, 152, 153, 154, 230, 237
Welsh Language Society, 156
Welsh Nationalist Party, 6, 14, 31, 103, 110, 111, 112, 132, 151, 152; see also Plaid Cymru
Welsh Office, 156, 158
Welsh Outlook, 103, 108, 109, 110, 119, 120, 121, 122, 129, 135, 136, 137
Welsh People, 29
Welsh Piety, 24, 27, 40
Welsh saints, 124, 126, 128, 130
Wesley, Charles, 23, 43, 44, 49
Wesley, John, 27, 28, 43, 44, 47, 48, 49, 58

INDEX

Wesleyans, 62, 68, 70, 79, 140, 141
West Indies, 51
West Riding, 89, 92
West Wales Guardian, 130
West, Elizabeth, 201, 202, 214
Western Mail, 128, 130, 131, 133, 135, 136, 137, 138, 169, 170, 172, 183
Westmeath, 274
Westminster, 158, 177
Westminster Abbey, 178
Westminster confession, 310, 311, 313, 314
Westminster Hall, 49
Wheatley, John, 279
When Was Wales? 2, 32, 339
Whig, 89, 90
Whitby, Synod of, 250
White, Eryn M., 19, 59, 60
Whitefield, George, 43, 48, 49, 56, 58, 60, 202, 203, 204, 206, 209, 214, 216, 217, 219, 220
Whithorn, 274
Whitty, Revd Robert, 280–1, 297, 301, 302
Who's Who, 103
Wigtown, 290
Wil Brydydd y Coed, 69, 80
Wilberforce, Samuel, 95
Wild Wales, 16
William and Mary, 201, 245
William IV, 165
William, Thomas, 46, 58
Williams, D. J., 112
Williams, David (Caernarfon), 71
Williams, G. O., 155, 156
Williams, Glanmor, 134, 135, 138, 158, 160, 339
Williams, Gwyn A., 3, 13, 32, 339
Williams, Isaac, 114
Williams, Archdeacon John (Cardigan), 89, 91

Williams, John (Llandovery), 90
Williams, John (MP), 92
Williams, Llewelyn, 110, 111
Williams, William (dean of St Davids), 116, 130, 137
Williams, William (of Wern), 67
Williams, William (Pantycelyn), 15, 17, 18, 19, 23, 28, 29, 32, 33, 39, 41, 45, 57
Williamson, David, 201
Williamson, James, 235
Willison, John, 207, 210, 212, 214, 216, 218, 219
Wilson, George, 274
Wilson, Patrick, 221
Wilson, William, 204, 207
Winchester, 86, 95, 101
Windsor, 172, 178, 179, 180
Wiseman, Cardinal, 269
Withers, C. W. J., 316, 335
Withrington, Donald, 316, 335
Witness, 164
Wodrow, R., 189, 193, 198, 199
Wolffe, John, 7, 181, 185
Wooler, 229
Wormwood Scrubs, 112
Wrexham, 105, 222
Wright, Bishop Roddy, 323
Wynne, Revd John, 284

Y Ffydd Ddi-ffuant, 23
Yarmouth, 50, 51
York, 98
York Minster, 255
Yr Eglwys o Ddifrif, 71
Ysbryd y Cwlwm, 18

Zambezi, 284

355